Hegel's
Phenomenology of Spirit

Hegel's *Phenomenology of Spirit*

Not Missing the Trees for the Forest

Howard P. Kainz

LEXINGTON BOOKS

A division of
ROWMAN & LITTLEFIELD PUBLISHERS, INC.
Lanham • Boulder • New York • Toronto • Plymouth, UK

LEXINGTON BOOKS

A division of Rowman & Littlefield Publishers, Inc.
A wholly owned subsidary of The Rowman & Littlefield Publishing Group, Inc.
4501 Forbes Boulevard, Suite 200
Lanham, MD 20706

Estover Road
Plymouth PL6 7PY
United Kingdom

British Library Cataloguing in Publication Information Available

Library of Congress Cataloging-in-Publication Data

Kainz, Howard P.
 Hegel's Phenomenology of spirit : not missing the trees for the forest /
Howard P. Kainz.
     p. cm.
 Includes bibliographical references (p.   ).
 ISBN-13: 978-0-7391-2585-4 (cloth : alk. paper)
 ISBN-10: 0-7391-2585-0 (cloth : alk. paper)
 1. Hegel, Georg Wilhelm Friedrich, 1770-1831. Phänomenologie des Geistes. 2.
Phenomenology. I. Title. B2929.K275 2008
 193—dc22

                                                                2007049802

Printed in the United States of America

⊗™ The paper used in this publication meets the minimum requirements of American
National Standard for Information Sciences—Permanence of Paper for Printed Library
Materials, ANSI/NISO Z39.48–1992.

Contents

Preface

Numerous commentaries, including my own,[1] have been published on Hegel's *Phenomenology of Spirit* since the 1970s, and I have contributed to several review articles.[2] The general procedure, in most of the commentaries, has been to "follow Hegel's exposition," paragraph by paragraph, or section by section—sometimes even line by line. The rationale for this procedure is justified by the fact that the work as a whole consists in a tightly-knit argument—not argument in the usual sense, with theses, evidence, proof—but sequences of dialectic that one must follow as closely as in ordinary arguments, or even more closely. The supposition here, of course, is that the *Phenomenology* is a highly systematic work. (There are some who doubt this, and this position will be considered in chapter five.)

My own analyses/commentaries have adhered to this convention, but not without some distress. I have at times in studying the *Phenomenology* come across insights or applications that would merit additional comment—maybe even an entire book. For example, in the early chapters I noticed numerous apparent parallels with some works of Kierkegaard, and occasionally added some notes to that effect. However, a special type of self-control is required

---

[1]*Hegel's Phenomenology, Part I: Analysis and Commentary*, Tuscaloosa: University of Alabama Press, 1976; *Hegel's Phenomenology, Part II: The Evolution of Ethical and Religious Consciousness to the Absolute Standpoint*, Athens: Ohio University Press, 1983.

[2]"Recent Work on Hegel," by Frederick G. Weiss and Howard P. Kainz, *The American Philosophical Quarterly* July 1971, 203–22, viii, 3; "Recent Work in Hegel," with Thomas Lutzow, *The American Philosophical Quarterly*, Oct. 1979, XVI, 4, 273–85; "Recent Interpretations of Hegel's Phenomenology," in *Hegel-Studien*, April, 1981, 245–51; review article: "H.S. Harris' Commentary on Hegel's Phenomenology in the *Bulletin of the Hegel Society of Great Britain*," Dec., 2001; and review article: "Spirit," (annotated translation of chapter six of the *Phenomenology*) in the *Bulletin of the Hegel Society of Great Britain*, February, 2005.

for one who wants to comment on any philosopher: For the commentator to expatiate on items that he himself is especially interested in can detract from his main goal, which is to facilitate the understanding of the philosopher. One should resist the temptation to use the facade of a commentary and the invocation of a famous name to expatiate on insights—however significant—that are peripheral to the work being studied. Like a translator, the job of the commentator is to stand in the background, letting the approach and the ideas of the original take the limelight, rather than his own insights or impressions. John the Baptist's rhetoric of self-effacement is appropriate in this case—"he must increase, I must decrease."

But in the present book I am allowing myself some indulgence—like the strict dieter who is allowing herself a "sabbatical" with some chocolate cake. In other words, I will be focusing on some areas of special interest turning up in the *Phenomenology*, isolating them, organizing them into categories for the purposes of clarity, and striving to add just enough of Hegel's arguments to put them into context. One predecessor in this enterprise has been William Earle, who in his *Public Sorrows and Private Pleasures*[3] applied ideas from the *Phenomenology* to some of the social upheavals taking place during the 1960s. But my own intention is broader—including some social or ethical applications, but also some metaphysical insights and some reflections pertaining to the composition and makeup of the *Phenomenology* itself. My intention is to do this without producing still another commentary. Whether this can be done successfully without distorting Hegel's meaning, the reader must judge.

In the chapters that follow, I have given special attention to the following topics, focusing on the insights, highlights, patterns, and characteristics that seemed to jump out at me as I became more and more familiar with the work:

Language: The important function of *die Sprache* during the course of the dialectic—in particular, the role of language in bringing impasses to a head and leading to their resolution or *Aufhebung*.

Characters: Certain *Gestalten* that arise as distinct personality-types, with a universality that is relevant to our own era as well as to Hegel's.

Themes: Verbal snapshots of ethical or metaphysical insights or principles that come to the forefront, but are easily lost in the course of the phenomenological dialectic.

Kierkegaard: A counterpoint to the general view of Kierkegaard as the classic antipode to Hegel. Kierkegaard's "borrowings."

Hegel's own implicit editing and systematizing of his work: Using Labarrière's analysis of structural and dynamic parallels or recapitulations to show

---

[3]Bloomington: Indiana University Press, 1976.

how Hegel, without giving the overt "cues" to structure such as are found in this later system, nevertheless was consciously systematizing, and commenting, almost from a third-person standpoint, on the results of preceding dialectical developments.

The Phenomenology *and Literature*: The relevance of the *Phenomenology* to literature—with special emphasis on some unappreciated or rarely appreciated literary aspects; and the importance of these aspects for understanding the work.

"Absolute Knowledge" and the History of Modern Philosophy: Going beyond some of the vague impressions prevailing about Hegel's theory of absolute knowledge, in order to show that it is not just a dated remnant of German idealism, but makes an important contribution in the history of modern philosophy.

The Phenomenon of Language in Hegel's *Phenomenology*

As Jere O'Neill Surber notes,[1] there are three loci in which Hegel gives specific attention to the issue of language—initially in his 1803/04 *Jenaer Systementwürfe I* concerning the "Power of Speech" and in his 1805/06 *Jenaer Systementwürfe III* in the section on *Intelligenz*, during a phase in which he is still under the influence of Schelling and is considering the possibility of language as a "Subject-Object"; next in the Preface to his *Phenomenology of Spirit*, §§63–65, where Hegel discusses the difference between "speculative propositions" in philosophy and ordinary language; and finally in the *Berlin Enzyklopaedie*, in the sections on theoretical psychology, §§459–462, in which the function of language in the transition from intuition to thinking is discussed. Recent treatments of Hegel on language,[2] and the essays in Surber's anthology, either are related to these three areas, or focus on one particular issue in the corpus of the *Phenomenology*—Hegel's discussion in chapter I of language concerning "Heres" and "Nows" is frequently considered and his treatment of Conscience towards the end of chapter VI has also been analyzed.[3] But most often discussed, with reference to the *Phenomenology*, is the text mentioned above from the Preface, which was written after the book had been completed, and was meant to provide a transition to Hegel's forthcoming system of philosophy. No systematic attention has been given, however, to all the eleven major areas in the

---

[1] Jere O'Neill Surber, Ed., *Hegel and Language* (Albany: SUNY Press, 2006), 10–14.

[2] E.g. Jeffrey Read, *Real Words: Language and System in Hegel* (Toronto: University of Toronto Press, 2007).

[3] E.g., in Karen Feldman's *Binding Words: Conscience and Rhetoric in Hobbes, Hegel, and Heidegger* (Evanston, IL: Northwestern University Press, 2006); see also Jonathan Robinson's earlier study, *Duty and Hypocrisy in Hegel's* Phenomenology of Mind: *an Essay in the Real and the Ideal* (Toronto: University of Toronto Press, 1977).

body of the work where language (*die Sprache*) acts like a "middle term," allowing the phenomenological analysis to proceed further—a methodological catalyst, an internal "engine" bringing dialectical movements to their culmination. My intention is to focus on these areas.

The general importance of language in the *Phenomenology* can best be gauged by reconsidering the overall problematic of that work. Hegel begins in his Introduction with then-current (and still persistent) questions about how we can get access to the truth, especially truth about the "Absolute." Should we focus on knowledge as an "instrument," as Kant (as Hegel interpreted him) suggested, in order to decide what our instrument could do, and what kind of truths, if any, were attainable by using it? Or should we focus on knowledge as a kind of "medium," like a prism through which truth might shine through, allowing us to make our way back through the variegated rays of the spectrum in pursuit of their source? But if our starting point consists of considerations like these, we seem to be presupposing for some reason that our subjective knowledge is in some strange way sharply *divided from* objective truth; and isn't this presupposition the real source of our epistemological problems? Might this not be the cause of our incessant and inevitable inability to access the truth? In other words, Hegel sees Cartesian/Kantian dualistic notions about the separation of subject from object, and the corollary sacrosanct separation of cognition from things-in-themselves, and thought from being, as the precise obstacles which prevent our epistemological questions from ever being answered satisfactorily. Hegel's proposal is to approach all such dualisms of consciousness, and their ramifications in social and cultural consciousness, with a thoroughgoing skepticism, subjecting them to appropriate corrections or "fine-tuning" in the expectation that we will finally get beyond the ostensible dichotomies to an "absolute knowledge" in which finite concepts are no longer separate from finite objects, the "in-itself" no longer at odds with the "for-itself" of consciousness, and being and thought finally coincide. As Hegel proceeds towards this goal, subjecting all sorts of pretensions to skeptical reexamination, language at important junctures turns out to be crucial for problem-solving and phenomenological progress—as the following examples will show.

LANGUAGE VS. MEANING IN SENSE-CERTAINTY

In his analysis of Sense-Certainty,[4] Hegel discusses the common opinion that we are confronted with bare particulars, "Thises"—a particular "Now" or a

---

[4]G. W. F. Hegel, *Phänomenologie des Geistes,* (Band 9 of the "Akademie" edition, *Gesammelte Werke* [Hamburg: Felix Meiner Verlag, 1980]), edited by Wolfgang Bonsiepen and Reinhard Heede; hereafter abbreviated as *PG*. Chapter I.

particular "Here." Some philosophers, says Hegel, even point to concentration on such particulars as the bedrock of certainty, from which all progress in knowledge should begin. But Hegel challenges this claim as an unexamined nostrum, whose fallaciousness becomes apparent in our speech. "In speech we directly contradict our very own *intention*."[5] If our intention is to point out particular "Thises," i.e., particular "nows" or "heres," every time we try to do this our language corrects us. For example, I say "now it is daytime," but a little later I can say "now it is nighttime" without contradicting myself; since "now" by definition is a universal which is not to be identified with any particular time. The same applies in our use of "here" to designate some particular place; subsequently, we designate some other place, and still use the term, "here," without contradiction. We are *trying* to capture particular moments or situations, but the language we use moves us away from sensory particulars and in the direction of thought with its universal concepts. "Language . . . possesses the divine nature of directly subverting, metamorphosing, and thus hindering the verbal expression of, meaning."[6]

Thus as we try to refer to particular "Thises" a dialectical transition from particular to universal, from existent being to universalizing thought, is continually set in motion. If we subject the process of particular reference to further phenomenological examination, we find that it constantly involves a very elaborate three-tiered dialectic (§107): (1) We try to designate some "now," but (2) as soon as we have done this we realize that the now has passed, and we negate its presence; finally (3) we negate this negation and thus reinstate its nowness through the double negation. Similarly, (1) we try to designate a here, but then (2) realize that it has a left and right part which are also "heres," as well as parts above and below which are "heres," and thus disappears into a manifold of heres all around it. Thus we are impelled to negate the "hereness" of our original designation, but finally (3) negate this negation to reinstate its "hereness." And in general our language about particulars involves a circular process in which we are continually negating the particular and returning to it through a double negation which involves a continual synthesizing of moments, points, or spaces. This is the process resulting in sensory experience which, far from being locked into particulars, is willy nilly constantly engaged with universals.

---

[5]§97 Die Sprache aber ist, wie wir sehen, das Wahrhaftere; in ihr widerlegen wir selbst unmittelbar unsere *Meinung*. Paragraph references are to the numbering system first used in the A.V. Miller translation of the *Phenomenology of Spirit* (Oxford: Oxford University Press, 1977). The same paragraph numberings are used in more recent English translations, including the translation of chapter VI by Dan Shannon et al (Indianapolis, IN: Hackett, 2001) and my own bilingual edition of *Selections from the Phenomenology* (University Park: Pennsylvania State University Press, 1988), hereafter abbreviated as *PSK*. In the present book, the translations in addition to the *PSK* translations are also my own.

[6]§110 . . . dem Sprechen, welches die göttliche Natur hat, die Meinung unmittelbar zu verkehren, zu etwas anderem zu machen, und so sie gar nicht zum *Worte* kommen zu lassen. . . .

LANGUAGE EXPRESSING THE DISCREPANCY
BETWEEN INNER AND OUTER

Pseudo-sciences such as palmistry, phrenology, and physiognomy have been unmasked in our enlightened era for doing a lot of mischief. However, they are at the very least interesting attempts to understand the relationship of the inner life of humans to their outer expressions. Can language do any better than these pseudo-scientific attempts? Does it give us a more accurate depiction of what is going on within persons, and how their "inner" relates to their outer phenomenal appearances? From a sophisticated analysis of a person's language, might we not gain a privileged insight into his or her innermost self? Unfortunately, in spite of the fact that it seems to be a promising *modus operandi*, we should not expect too much from it:

> Language and work are self-externalizations in which the individual no longer retains and possesses himself, but lets what is within get completely outside himself, and surrenders it to another. Thus we could say with equal right that these externalizations express too much, or that they express too little.[7]

Language as an expression of what is within inevitably results in a dilemma: Either it functions as an external eruption of the inner, so that it is not just a limited and judicious "expression of the self" but is the whole thing, leaving no interesting dynamic between the secret and the public self; or it is a deceptive counterfeit of the self, a completely detached substitute which does not reflect what the individual self really is. The revelation of the "whole self" may indicate to the onlooker that there are no significant inner personal qualities worth knowing; or, the revelation may be a smokescreen, hiding the real self. But, that being said, language is the best we have. In spite of such ambiguities, it is the major medium by which a man actualizes and manifests himself, and is the best indicator we have of what is going on within the consciousness of a person (§315).

LAW, AS THE UNIVERSAL LANGUAGE FOR
SOCIAL CONSCIOUSNESS

The individual, in Hegel's estimation, is not just instinctively oriented towards others—a "social animal," as Aristotle put it—but in a very real sense

---

[7]§312. Sprache und Arbeit sind Äußerungen, worin das Individuum nicht mehr an ihm selbst sich behält und besitzt, sondern das Innere ganz außer sich kommen läßt und dasselbe Anderem preisgibt. Man kann darum ebensosehr sagen, daß diese Äußerungen das Innere *zu sehr*, als daß sie es *zu wenig* ausdrücken.

participates in an ongoing spiritual entity, which Hegel calls the "ethical substance." And just as the individual gives expression to his thoughts, values, and attitudes in language, so also do the individuals united in society give appropriate *universal* expression to their commonality through the language of laws:

> The universal substance with which the individual is united utters a *universal language* of its own through the customs and laws of the people; but this unchanging extant legal entity is nothing other than the expression of the selfsame particular individual himself, who appears to be set over against the law. The laws give expression to what each individual *is* and *does*. The individual looks upon the laws not as his *universal* thing like objectivization, but rather perceives himself in it, or sees it as *particularized* in his own individuality and in the individuality of each of his fellow citizens.[8]

Hegel's strong emphasis on intersubjectivity, which is apparent in spite of multiple individual dialectical vicissitudes in the *Phenomenology*, does not envision a submersion of the individual in society, but an enhancement of individuality through social relations, and the reciprocal enhancement of social structures and laws through the constant contributions of the citizenry. The language of law is the means by which we express our social/spiritual substantiality. Thus it is of the utmost importance that interconnected individuals be able to "find" themselves in the laws of modern society, although the inevitable evolution to a heightened sense of individual freedom is a formidable challenge to the "spiritual" mandate of progress towards social and political unity.

THE LANGUAGE OF FLATTERY, CREATING WHAT IT EXTOLS

In his long section on *Bildung* ("civilization," "culture"),[9] Hegel describes various antithetical relationships of social consciousness that emerged in the aftermath of the middle ages. The imagery in this section calls to mind an era of lords, knights, nobles, monarchs, courtiers, and their underlings. The overarching dialectic is the gradual development of an initial antithesis of wealth

---

[8]§351 Diese Einheit des Seins für Anderes oder des sich zum Dinge Machens und des Fürsichseins, diese allgemeine Substanz redet ihre *allgemeine Sprache* in den Sitten und Gesetzen eines Volks; aber dies seiende unwandelbare Wesen ist nichts anderes als der Ausdruck der ihr entgegengesetzt scheinenden einzelnen Individualität selbst; die Gesetze sprechen das aus, was jeder Einzelne *ist* und *tut*; das Individuum erkennt sie nicht nur als seine *allgemeine* gegenständliche Dingheit, sondern ebensosehr sich in ihr oder [sie] als *vereinzelt* in seiner eigenen Individualität und in jedem seiner Mitbürger.

[9]§§484ff.

and state power, two extremes which become imbedded in various types of consciousness in positive or negative ways. Wealth and power become intertwined in a positive, complementary way in the "noble consciousness" (*das edelmütige Bewußtsein*) and in a negative way in an antithetical type of consciousness, the "base consciousness" (*das niederträchtige Bewußtsein*), which has a discordant relationship to both wealth and power. The noble consciousness accomplishes an initial synthesis of wealth and power by means of "mute service" (*der stummen Dienst*), leading often to a sacrifice of life by nobles for the sovereign; and eventually achieves a final synthesis, in which he manages to retain and secure life, *along with* wealth and honor, through a new type of language—the "heroism of flattery" (*der Heroismus der Schmeichelei*) (§§508–512). The result is a new species of political creativity:

> This new sophisticated style of speech brings into the highlight the spiritual self-effacing [noble] "middleman" who not only reflects into himself his own [monarchical] extreme, but also reflects the extreme of universal power back into this [monarchical] self and makes this power, which initially is just *implicit*, into an *explicit existent* with the individuality of a self-consciousness. Through this process the spirit of this newly individualized power becomes an existent *unlimited monarch—unlimited*, because the language of flattery elevates the power into its unadulterated *universality*.[10]

By extolling the universal state power to the highest degree, without any reservations, the united nobles are actually able to *create* a real, concrete universal power, individualized in an absolute monarch, who can say, surrounded by coteries of adulating hangers-on, that he "as this individual is the universal power."[11] Hegel's oblique reference is to the court of Louis XIV, the monarch who famously proclaimed "I am the state," *"L'état c'est moi"*; and Hegel emphasizes that the very name of the individuality thus created is not just a symbol of power, but *is* a de facto real power. In other words, great personages can actually be created by great flatterers.

The imagery here is redolent of an unending succession of tyrants in history whose power depended solely on a tight circle of fawning and adulating yes-men, remaining "relevant" and in power by constantly stoking the ego of the great leader. Hegel's time-bound monarchical example, can with no great

---

[10]§511 Diese sprechende Reflexion des Dienstes macht die geistige, sich zersetzende Mitte aus und reflektiert nicht nur ihr eigenes Extrem in sich selbst, sondern auch das Extrem der allgemeinen Gewalt in dieses selbst zurück und macht sie, die erst *an sich* ist, *zum Fürsichsein* und zur Einzelheit des Selbstbewußtseins. Es wird hierdurch der Geist dieser Macht, ein *unumschränkter Monarch* zu sein;— *unumschränkt*: die Sprache der Schmeichelei erhebt die Macht in ihre geläuterte *Allgemeinheit*.

[11]§511: Er, dieser Einzelne, weiß umgekehrt dadurch sich, diesen Einzelnen, als die allgemeine Macht. . . .

strain be applied to other political formations, e.g. to cabinets in democratic governments, or professional PR hirelings.

If we of the twenty-first century were to look for a version more aligned with capitalistic democracies, we might substitute not only political lackeys, but publicists, "spin doctors," and (in the world of business and commerce) agents, and unscrupulous advertisers willing, if the price is right, to build up even the most worthless product and give it "name recognition." Such flatterers are able to produce political power, celebrity, name-recognition, and/or predominance in the marketplace, through their judicious and persistent praises. In a sense, the flatterer can actually *create* the greatness and recognized worth of patrons or clients who would be unrecognized and nondescript without these devoted (and often well-reimbursed) services.

THE LANGUAGE OF DISINTEGRATION, RECORDING CULTURAL CONTRADICTIONS

In Hegel's portrayal, the language of flattery, after achieving ascendancy among elite consciousnesses in culture, gradually degenerates into a baser form—the "base flattery" of the professional sycophant, prostituting himself/herself to reap the rewards of union with the powers-that-be (§514). This new state of consciousness, however, is not a merely negative development; in a dialectical rebound, it lays the groundwork for the creation of an immensely important, creative type of consciousness, found in a few elite spokespersons. The language of this consciousness is the "language of distraughtness" (*Zerrissenheit*), which rises to a comprehension of the contradictions in which it is caught up, and a comprehension of modern cultural contradictions in general (§§517ff.).

> This is *pure culture* as the absolute and universal perversion and alienation of reality and thought. What is experienced in this world, is that neither the essential *reality* of power and of wealth, nor their specific *concepts*, good and evil, nor the "noble" or "base" consciousness of good and evil, possess any truth. Rather, all these aspects are transmuted into one another, and each is the opposite of itself.[12]

The "distraught consciousness" is an intellectual juggler who not only comprehends the contradictions in new ways, but gives expression to them. The

---

[12]§521 Er ist diese absolute und allgemeine Verkehrung und Entfremdung der Wirklichkeit und des Gedankens; die reine Bildung. Was in dieser Welt erfahren wird, ist, daß weder die wirklichen Wesen der Macht und des Reichtums noch ihre bestimmten Begriffe, Gut und Schlecht, oder das Bewußtsein des Guten und Schlechten, das edelmütige und niederträchtige, Wahrheit haben; sondern alle diese Momente verkehren sich vielmehr eins im andern, und jedes ist das Gegenteil seiner selbst.

resulting distraught language is witty, insightful—the most accurate presentations of the human situation to date. Contemporary counterparts of this state of consciousness would be novelists, poets, comedians, and others who are embedded in cultural contradictions and give voice to them, often with self-deprecation, exemplifying a heightened appreciation and evaluation of their compromising circumstances. Thus they offer the "truest" expression of the realities of society and culture (§522).

The intellectuals of society can cap off and organize these tendencies. During the French Enlightenment, following Hegel's imagery, the dialectical proficiency in comprehending and fielding cultural contradictions becomes encapsulated in literary compendia—Hegel has in mind works such as Voltaire's *Dictionnaire philosophique* and Diderot's *Dictionnaire encyclopédique*:

> This [distraught] type of language comprises eclectic, immediately forgettable judgements based on trendy chit-chat—a "unified whole" only for some third consciousness. Such a "third consciousness" can distinguish itself as *pure* insight only by gathering together those scattered impressions into a universal portrayal, and making this into the "insight of all". . . . The resultant collection depicts for most people the existence of a better (or at least a more diversified) wittiness than their own, and shows that "knowing better" and "judging better" are something universal now and generally accepted.[13]

ENLIGHTENED FREEDOM AND THE REVOLUTIONARY INHIBITION OF LANGUAGE

The Enlightenment efforts to universalize the new dialectically correct language, however, is an abortive attempt at integration and sophistication. The contradictions of thought and language finally seep into the bedrock of concrete historical reality. The contradictions of culture can no longer be mediated intellectually, but reach their culmination in the real world with the absolute distraughtness of the revolutionary mentality[14] in which in final acts of desperation all meaningful "works of language" are suppressed (§588) in the interests of abstract freedom—freedom from contradictions, freedom from cultural antagonisms and countercurrents:

---

[13]§§539–540 Indem diese Sprache zerstreut, die Beurteilung eine Faselei des Augenblicks, die sich sogleich wieder vergißt, und ein Ganzes nur für ein drittes Bewußtsein ist, so kann sich dieses als *reine* Einsicht nur dadurch unterscheiden, daß es jene sich zerstreuenden Züge in ein allgemeines Bild zusammenfaßt und sie dann zu einer Einsicht Aller macht. . . . Die Sammlung zeigt den meisten einen besseren oder allen wenigstens einen vielfacheren Witz, als der ihrige ist, und das Besserwissen und Beurteilen überhaupt als etwas Allgemeines und nun allgemein Bekanntes.

[14]See Section B.III, §§582ff., "Absolute Freedom and Terror."

The process of revolutionary freedom in its culmination is consciousness' interaction with itself in such a way that it permits not even the semblance of some *object freely* standing over against it. As a consequence, this state of abstract freedom can lead to no positive accomplishments—neither universal real work nor the universal works of language, neither laws and universal institutions of *conscious* liberty, nor deeds and achievements characterized by *committed* liberty.[15]

This is a final ironical development—an attempt to escape from the inveterate contradictions in culture by resorting to an organized mandatory cult of abstract absolute freedom, standing in silent, but real, hostility to all the feared social and political contradictions that might emerge from literary works and other creative efforts. The revolutionary champion of freedom, carried away by a passion for an abstraction, shuts himself/herself off from the normal and indispensable cultural embodiments of freedom.

CONSCIENCE AS NECESSARILY EXPRESSED IN LANGUAGE

We sometimes use "conscience" as a synonym for "morality," but Hegel has a special technical meaning for conscience. He contrasts conscience with the Kantian notions of morality prevailing in his era.[16] Morality in Kant's sense, as Hegel interprets it, emphasizes the knowledge of abstract universal duties; and persons following this version of morality easily get involved in disputes as to what is the universal duty which should be implemented, who should implement it, how it is to be implemented, and so forth. These universal duties stand in contrast with "nature"—the hard realities existing both externally and internally. External realities often conflict with duties, and contribute to an individual's unhappiness rather than happiness; and internal nature, the psychic reality of natural inclinations, is constantly at odds with the moral person's intentions.

But the person of conscience, as Hegel portrays him or her, has *transcended* such conflicts. The happiness of the *conscientious* person consists in a quasi-intuitive, consistently judicious, response to external circumstances, and a connatural, habitual channeling of personal inclinations towards the accomplishment of moral objectives. Those who have attained such coordination with external and internal "nature" form a kind of ethical

---

[15]§588 Diese Bewegung ist hierdurch die Wechselwirkung des Bewußtseins mit sich selbst, worin es nichts in der Gestalt eines *freien* ihm gegenübertretenden *Gegenstandes* entläßt. Es folgt daraus, daß es zu keinem positiven Werke, weder zu allgemeinen Werken der Sprache noch der Wirklichkeit, weder zu Gesetzen und allgemeinen Einrichtungen der *bewußten*, noch zu Taten und Werken der *wollenden* Freiheit kommen kann.

[16]See chapter VI.C.c.

"church," the members of which do not look for Kantian-style justifications in terms of universal moral laws from one another, but only for evidence that each of them has acted *from conscience*. They mutually recognize one another as persons whose only criterion for right and wrong is acting "from conscience." But in order to obtain and maintain this mutual recognition, language is essential. They must *say* what their conscience tells them to do, express their deep feelings of conscientiousness (§654). By this means, they not only give utterance to their universalized individuality, but actually *create*, as well as participate in, a universalized ethical fabric of spirit, while ideally escaping from a tangle of laws. In the church of consciences, the only important requirement is that all members be willing to testify that they are acting according to conscience, and to recognize the same type of affirmations from the other members.

EXPRESSIONS OF CONSCIENCE LEADING TO MORAL RELATIVISM

The commitment to mutual recognition of expressions of conscience becomes the new "universal," replacing imperfect universals such as conventional moral laws or the universalized duties of the Kantian type. But while the ascendancy of conscience creates moral harmony and consensus on one level, on a more fundamental level it contains the seeds of disintegration. For example, one conscientious person may resort to violence to maintain his/her freedom, while another equally conscientious person may eschew violence to maintain his/her spiritual equilibrium and help maintain the fabric of social organization. Thus "what others characterize as 'violence' and 'wrong,' is implemented as the duty of asserting one's independence from others; and what the conscientious but 'violent' persons call 'cowardice,' is the duty of maintaining one's life and usefulness for one's neighbors."[17] As a result, the church of conscience begins to encounter strains and pressures:

> This universal uniformity—the language with which all mutually recognize themselves as acting conscientiously—disintegrates into the disparity of individual self-existence. Each consciousness is utterly reflected out of its erstwhile "universality"; with this development an opposition necessarily comes on the scene of individuality against other individuals and against the "universals" of these others.[18]

---

[17]§644 So erfüllt das, was andere Gewalttätigkeit und Unrecht nennen, die Pflicht, gegen andere seine Selbständigkeit zu behaupten; was sie Feigheit nennen, die Pflicht, sich das Leben und die Möglichkeit der Nützlichkeit für die Nebenmenschen zu erhalten.

[18]§659 Die Sprache, in der sich alle gegenseitig als gewissenhaft handelnd anerkennen, diese allgemeine Gleichheit zerfällt in die Ungleichheit des einzelnen Fürsichseins, jedes Bewußtsein ist aus seiner Allgemeinheit ebenso schlechthin in sich reflektiert; hierdurch tritt der Gegensatz der Einzelheit gegen die anderen Einzelnen und gegen das Allgemeine notwendig ein.

Even when the strongest commitment to recognize the sanctity of other persons' consciences prevails universally, situations will come about where I am asked to recognize expressions of conscience which diametrically contradict my own conscience. The atmosphere of tolerance, which emerges among conscientious people who want to maintain the semblance of unity amid such disparities, unfortunately is a poor substitute for the harmonious self-certainty that was the promising keynote of conscience in its state of immediacy.

NON-EXPRESSION OF CONSCIENCE LEADING TO MORAL DISINTEGRATION

Granted that the mutual expressions of conscience among conscientious persons have their drawbacks, as just described, total unwillingness to communicate matters of conscience can be even more damaging to intersubjective relationships. This becomes apparent in the extreme case that Hegel considers, in which an individual is troubled in conscience about his behavior, and confesses his delinquencies to his virtuous confidant, who prides herself on her uprightness and the beauty of her soul, and spurns these attempts at reconciliation:

> The person who acknowledges his guilt sees himself rebuffed and discerns injustice in his confidant, who disdains to permit anything from within herself to emerge into verbal existence, and simply contrasts this overture of the miscreant with the beauty of her own soul, countering the confession with the stiff neck of her own unchanging character and the inanity of her retreat into her self and her non-engagement with an other person.[19]

However, for the continued existence of the heightened ethical state of the church of consciousness, a *sine qua non* is the harmony, continuity, and mutuality of consciences. The "conscientious" person who refuses to reciprocate sincere expressions of the conscience of another isolates herself from the spiritual unity of consciousnesses, contradicting the wonted unity which characterized the church of consciences, and ends up in a state of pathological spiritual distress:

> [The incommunicative conscience], as the consciousness of this contradiction in its unreconciled immediacy, slides into derangement and dissolves into consumptive longing.[20]

---

[19]§667 Dasjenige, das sich bekannte, sieht sich zurückgestoßen und das Andere im Unrecht, welches das Heraustreten seines Innern in das Dasein der Rede verweigert und dem Bösen die Schönheit seiner Seele, dem Bekenntnisse aber den steifen Nacken des sich gleichbleibenden Charakters und die Stummheit, sich in sich zu behalten und sich nicht gegen einen anderen wegzuwerfen, entgegensetzt.

[20]§668 Die wirklichkeitslose schöne Seele . . . ist also, als Bewußtsein dieses Widerspruchs in seiner unversöhnten Unmittelbarkeit, zur Verrücktheit zerrüttet und zerfließt in sehnsüchtiger Schwindsucht.

EXPRESSIONS OF MUTUAL FORGIVENESS AND THE EMERGENCE OF ABSOLUTE SPIRIT

The resultant moral disintegration leads to a state of isolation from the inter-subjective union of ethical consciousnesses. The incommunicative, hard-hearted conscience, reduced to extreme isolation, sees itself mirrored in the isolation which it has caused in the repentant conscience, which it has judged as "evil" and thus as outside the church of consciences. This new realization drives it to renounce its intransigence, and to express its forgiveness, thus causing a reactivation of Spirit:

> The words of reconciliation are the *existent* Spirit that encounters the pure knowl-edge of itself as *universal* being in its opposite, i.e., in the pure knowledge of itself as the Absolute-existent-in-its-*individuality*—a mutual recognition that constitutes *Absolute* Spirit. . . . The "yes" of reconciliation, through which both egos desist from their antithetical *being*, is the *existence* of the ego expanding itself into a du-ality that nevertheless remains self-identical and retains its self-certainty even with its complete self-divestment in its opposite. This expanded existence is God ap-pearing in the midst of those who know themselves as pure knowledge.[21]

Hegel is here portraying a final state in which spirit, as social consciousness, has evolved through all the conflicts and vicissitudes of cultural and ethical rela-tionships and arrived at mutual forgiveness as the ultimate moral/spiritual state achievable, and has thus arrived at the vestibule of *religious transcendence*. (In the immediately following section, chapter VII, Hegel then takes this denouement as his springboard for beginning a new phenomenological analysis of the emer-gence of the experience of the divine in the evolution of religions.)

CLASSICAL LITERATURE AS GATHERING TOGETHER THE DISPERSED AND SCATTERED MOMENTS OF THE INNER ESSENTIAL WORLD AND THE WORLD OF ACTION

Subsequent movements towards the final reconciliation of Spirit with exis-tence in the world take place in the stages of Religion.[22] In the unfolding of

---

[21]§§670-671 Das Wort der Versöhnung ist der *daseiende* Geist, der das reine Wissen seiner selbst als *allgemeinen* Wesens in seinem Gegenteile, in dem reinen Wissen seiner als der absolut in sich seienden *Einzelheit* anschaut,—ein gegenseitiges Anerkennen, welches der *absolute* Geist ist. . . . Das versöhnende *Ja*, worin beide Ich von ihrem entgegengesetzten *Dasein* ablassen, ist das *Dasein* des zur Zweiheit ausgedehnten *Ichs*, das darin sich gleich bleibt und in seiner vollkommenen Entäußerung und Gegenteile die Gewißheit seiner selbst hat;—es ist der erscheinende Gott mitten unter ihnen, die sich als das reine Wissen wissen.

[22]Chapter VII.

the religious spirit, the full force of language in synthesizing the phenomeno-logical oppositions comes to be seen. In the initial stage of "Nature-Religion,"[23] the work of the religious craftsman producing external forms in homage to the divinity is deficient precisely because his work lacks language, in which alone self-consciousness can achieve adequate outer expression (§695), and which alone can give objective existence to what is inherently in-ternal (§697). But in Art-Religion,[24] the religious artist, constantly searching for more appropriate means of expressing the divine, is impelled towards ex-perimentation with language-forms, in which self-consciousness is synthe-sized with existence, individuality with universal continuity, independent selves with the community of selves, and the soul can finally exist *as* soul (§710). In the final stages of Art-Religion, with the development of the Epic and Tragedy by great poets, language comes to the fore as the perfect ele-ment, in which the inwardness is externalized to the greatest extent possible, the external stands for what is inward (§726), and the synthetic connection of self-consciousness and reality can be presented (§729).

In *epic poetry*, such as the works of Homer, the idealized deities are brought into communication and interaction with heroic individuals such as Achilles and Hector. But it is in the famous *tragedies* of playwrights like Sophocles and Aeschylus that a much more pronounced fusion of the univer-sal and ideal with the particular and the human takes place. This unity of op-posites, which Hegel characterizes as the speculative "Concept," leads the au-dience to a heightened understanding and assimilation of their fate through the words and actions of the actors, along with the chorus:

> This more advanced type of language, tragedy, coordinates more effectively the dispersed aspects of the ideal essentialities and the practical world; the divine substance, in accord with the exigencies of the Concept, steps forward in its var-ious guises, whose movements are similarly in accord with the Concept. As re-gards form, the language connected with these developments ceases to be nar-rative in style [as in the epic], since it is merging with the content, which ceases to be idealized. . . . The tragic characters exist as real human beings who take on the personages of the heroes and present these heroes in actual, not just narra-tive, language, speaking on their own.[25]

---

[23]Chapter VII.A.

[24]Chapter VII.B.

[25]§733 Diese höhere Sprache, die Tragödie, faßt also die Zerstreuung der Momente der wesentlichen und handelnden Welt näher zusammen; die Substanz des Göttlichen tritt nach der Natur des Begriffs in ihre Gestalten auseinander, und ihre Bewegung ist gleichfalls ihm gemäß. In Anse-hung der Form hört die Sprache dadurch, daß sie in den Inhalt hereintritt, auf, erzählend zu sein, wie der Inhalt, ein vorgestellter [zu sein]. . . . Das Dasein dieser Charaktere sind endlich wirkliche Men-schen, welche die Personen der Helden anlegen und diese in wirklichem, nicht erzählendem, sondern eigenem Sprechen darstellen.

But the most advanced classical literary form is *comedy*, in which consciousness not only comes to grip with the essentialities represented by the "gods," as well as fate, perceived as an absolute external force, but rises to the realization that it is *its own* fate. Thus the masks used in the performance of tragedies are no longer relevant.

> [With the emergence of comedy,] Fate—formerly an unconscious force that consisted in empty stillness and oblivion, outside the bounds of self-consciousness—is now united with self-consciousness. . . . By the very fact that the individual comic consciousness in its self-certainty exists as that which this absolute power had pretended to be, this "power" has lost the form of something *idealized*, something completely cut off from consciousness (as was the case with the content of epic poetry and with the powers and personages of tragedy). . . . [The self-consciousness attuned to comedy] is the reduction of every "universal" into its own self-certainty, which amounts to the complete loss of fear, along with the loss of substantiality on the part of every alien essentiality. This self-certainty is the well-being and continual satisfaction of consciousness—a state not to be found outside of classical comedy.[26]

At this point, the stage is set for Revealed Religion.[27] As Hegel observes (§755), the *absolute substance* has emerged in nature-religion in various forms and has reached the heights of self-consciousness, as art-religion finds expression in language; along with these developments, *self-consciousness* has objectified itself in ever more sophisticated ways, finally arriving at its identification with universal self-consciousness, as it demystifies the gods and other absolute essentialities. The final fusion of absolute substance and self-consciousness takes place in "revealed religion" with the appearance of a god-man. Hegel summarizes this fusion by means of a speculative reinterpretation of the Christian doctrine of the "virgin birth."

> With regard to this stage of Spirit, which discards the form of substance and enters into existence in the form of self-consciousness, you could say (using a reference taken from natural generation) that Spirit has an actual mother, but a merely implicit father; for *actuality* (i.e., self-consciousness) and substance (as

---

[26]§747 Hier ist also das vorher bewußtlose Schicksal, das in der leeren Ruhe und Vergessenheit besteht und von dem Selbstbewußtsein getrennt ist, mit diesem vereint. . . . Dadurch, daß das einzelne Bewußtsein in der Gewißheit seiner selbst es ist, das als diese absolute Macht sich darstellt, hat diese die Form eines *Vorgestellten*, von dem Bewußtsein überhaupt Getrennten und ihm Fremden verloren, wie . . . der Inhalt des Epos und die Mächte und Personen der Tragödie waren; . . . [Dieses selbstbewußtsein] ist die Rückkehr alles Allgemeinen in die Gewißheit seiner selbst, die hierdurch diese vollkommene Furcht-und Wesenlosigkeit alles Fremden und ein Wohlsein und Sichwohlseinlassen des Bewußtseins ist, wie sich außer dieser Komödie keines mehr findet.

[27]Chapter VII.C.

the *implicit* element) are the paired moments through whose complementary self-relinquishment, each being transformed into the other, Spirit enters into existence precisely as the unity of both.[28]

As we have seen from multiple examples cited in this chapter, Hegel considers language the unique *locus* in which a unity-in-distinction of opposites takes place—external with internal, subject with object, universal with particular. With this final speculative movement, the religious spirit finds its ultimate language form—the eternal Word finding ultimate external expression as the incarnate God-man, reconciling cosmic oppositions.

Language has thus been a prime instrument in fulfilling Hegel's goal of overcoming the dichotomies of philosophical consciousness. In the final chapter of the *Phenomenology*, "Absolute Knowledge," Hegel argues that one task still remains: Thought in religion is still encumbered with typically imaginative, pictorial representations. The cosmic reconciliations of religion need to be elevated to the conceptual level, and incorporated into philosophical science. This is the task undertaken in Hegel's 1817 *Wissenschaft der Logik*.

---

[28]§755 Es kann daher von diesem Geiste, der die Form der Substanz verlassen und in der Gestalt des Selbstbewußtseins in das Dasein tritt, gesagt werden-wenn man sich der aus der natürlichen Zeugung hergenommenen Verhältnisse bedienen will-, daß er eine *wirkliche* Mutter, aber einen *ansich*-seienden Vater hat; denn die *Wirklichkeit* oder das Selbstbewußtsein und das *Ansich* als die Substanz sind seine beiden Momente, durch deren gegenseitige Entäußerung, jedes zum anderen werdend, er als diese ihre Einheit ins Dasein tritt.

2

Character Types in the *Phenomenology*

In the first three chapters of the *Phenomenology*—on Sense-Certainty, Perception, and Understanding—Hegel engages in strict conceptual analysis. There is no focus on personages or types; Hegel's attention is on aspects of consciousness which can be amenable to differentiation, and on their movements and interrelationships. But in chapter IV, turning to Self-consciousness, Hegel begins to combine conceptual analysis with historical patterns and profiles, in order to chart the "necessary" dialectical development of individual and social consciousness.

THE MASTER CONSUMER

The first major character type emerges in chapter IV.A, on the "Independence and Dependence of Self-Consciousness: Masterdom and Slavery." Hegel begins by emphasizing the fact that there is no such thing as self-consciousness in a vacuum—consciousness-of-self and consciousness-of-others are inseparably reciprocal: "Self-Consciousness exists in-and-for-itself while (and because) it exists in-and-for-itself for-another; that is, it exists only as something recognized" (§178). The proper object for a *self*-consciousness is another self-consciousness, in which it is able to see a reflection of itself, and without which it would have only a vague desire for self-fulfillment; conversely, it would be impossible to apprehend the other as a self-consciousness without being oneself in the state of self-consciousness. This is not a "which comes first, chicken or the egg" problem, but a matter of a necessary conceptual interrelationship, as Hegel proceeds to elaborate in the immediately following paragraphs (§§179–181).

But the movement towards the conceptual ideal of intersubjective reciprocity is gradual; and this is where the "historical" segments begin to be interpolated into Hegel's phenomenology. A rather primitive stage of conscious interaction is first examined (§§186–188), in which a "life-and-death struggle" takes place, allowing consciousness (as Hegel interprets it) to get evidence of its transcendental self by showing its brave disregard of physical existence in heroic combat. But this process, resulting commonly in the killing of one self-consciousness, is overkill in the context of intersubjective development, which requires the interaction of two *living* consciousnesses. So a compromise is eventually reached, which allows both parties to continue their quest for mutual recognition.

The compromise, however, is imperfect, resulting in a lopsided, unequal type of intersubjectivity, which falls seriously short of the initial, target concept of reciprocity.

> There is established a pure Self Consciousness and a Consciousness which is not established purely for-itself but for-another; that is, the latter is established as existent Consciousness, or Consciousness in the configuration of thinghood. . . . They exist as two opposed configurations of consciousness, one of which configurations is the independent consciousness, for which the essential thing is existence-for-self, the other of which is the dependent consciousness, for which the essential thing is its life, or existence-for-another. The former is the Master; the latter, the Slave.[1]

It is noteworthy that one party in this interaction is referred to as a "self-consciousness," while the other is designated a "consciousness." These are technical terms in Hegel's usage, "consciousness" being a relationship to an object in some way external to the ego, "self-consciousness" involving self-knowledge and self-possession. More precisely, in the context of this chapter which has to deal specifically with self-consciousness, the slave is defined as a quasi-self-consciousness which encounters itself not directly, but indirectly, in and through its objective reflection in the determinations of the master; and in fulfillment of its overall immersion in objectivity, it deals with the hard resistance of objectivity in such a way as to free the master from such laborious

---

[1] §189 Die Auflösung jener einfachen Einheit ist das Resultat der ersten Erfahrung; es ist durch sie ein reines Selbstbewußtseyn, und ein Bewußtseyn gesetzt, welches nicht rein für sich, sondern für ein anderes, das heißt, als seyendes Bewußtseyn oder Bewußtseyn in der Gestalt der Dingheit ist. . . . Sind sie als zwey entgegengesetzte Gestalten des Bewußtseyns; die eine das selbständige, welchem das Fürsichseyn, die andere das unselbständige, dem das Leben oder das Seyn für ein anderes, das Wesen ist; jenes ist der Herr, diß der Knecht.

encounters. In a bizarre sense, this arrangement is to the advantage of both parties: the slave, in the aftermath of the "life and death struggle" maintains his life, while the master maintains freedom and independence without having to deal with the nitty-gritty that is usually involved in maintaining this state.

For Karl Marx, as a student of Hegel, this analysis was a godsend for exposing the misanthropic and oppressive mechanisms of capitalism. The worker under capitalistic relations is relegated to slavishly producing commodities, which he has little chance to consume for himself or his family. The capitalist, on the other hand, comes as close as possible to realizing the ideal, albeit perverse, state of pure consumption—a life spent simply enjoying the fruits of the labor performed by others.

But Hegel's analysis goes beyond the political or economic reverberations. The "master" in Hegel's portrayal is any type of consciousness which manages to attain, through various stratagems, the pure enjoyment of his/her subjectivity, along with something like absolute freedom from objectivity, with all of its resistance, hardness, and unpredictability. A major problematic, appearing throughout Hegel's *Phenomenology*, is the existence of unassimilated otherness, and the continuing efforts of consciousness, self-consciousness, and Spirit to overcome this obstacle, and finally—if such a thing be possible—arrive at a state where all otherness has been superseded (*aufgehoben*). The historical slave-master offers us just one paradigmatic example of the type of consciousness that manages, through various astute stratagems, to keep otherness at bay—in this case by interposing an object-like and object-oriented consciousness between itself and otherness. The result, if such efforts are successful, should be pure enjoyment, pure consumption, pure satisfaction, without any of the usual preliminaries (as with the hypothetical "pleasure machine" that analytic philosophers like to inject into discussions of mind-body issues).

The downside of this quest is that pleasure and action, like subject and object, do not easily admit of any artificial separation. The master self-consciousness, enjoying the fruits of the slave's actions without acting himself, becomes acutely conscious of the fact that he is not *doing* what the slave is doing. His satisfaction is an abstraction, completely separate from the actions that might naturally bring it about.

In Marx's reconstruction, Monsieur Capitalist ultimately arrives at the stage where he is a pure consumer—even having relegated much of the administrative nitty-gritty to higher-level lackeys who help to keep the labor force in line. He would be happy to remain in this privileged state, but is shaken therefrom, according to Marx's dialectical-materialistic analysis, by the growing power of the international labor force. The working proletariat eventually unite to establish their own hegemony, and to make sure that the new mandate "to each according to his needs, from each according to his ability," prevails. Private property monopolizing the means of production is outlawed, and capitalistic drones are dethroned.

In Hegel's version, on the other hand, it is not the massing of material forces that brings about the change, but a revolution in consciousness. The consummate consumer, the master-consciousness, completely dependent on others for his sense of freedom, discovers that he has achieved a counterfeit freedom, disconnected from the activity which should bring it about. He loses the satisfaction and sense of self-worth that he had, becoming fully aware of his abject dependence on the servile consciousness. The latter, in contrast, arrives at self-consciousness, self-esteem, and a sense of creative freedom indirectly, through the "back door," so to speak, by his hard work on objectivity, which he has been forced to form and refashion.

Real-life instances of the reversal of "independent consciousness" perspective that Hegel has in mind might be the scion born to wealth, who wakes up one day with the consciousness of being a "pure consumer" who has never done anything productive, or earned what he has; or the drug addict, trying to attain an intensity of pleasure, and continually acting to induce the experience; but eventually realizing that the consumption of substances is an action incommensurate with the experience artificially produced, a counterfeit pleasure. An example of reversal for the "dependent consciousness" might be the so-called "invulnerable" children, who thrive in spite of miserable environmental conditions, hardship and abuse, overcoming obstacles, and emerging in adulthood with characteristics of extraordinary resourcefulness and creativity.

THE UNHAPPY CONSCIOUSNESS

In the section closely following the discussion of the master-slave dialectic, Hegel moves from *inter*subjectivity to *intra*subjectivity, from the problematic of attaining unity with other self-consciousnesses to the problematic of attaining inner unity with oneself. The initial situation that he begins with is a kind of spiritual schizophrenia, acutely lacking any sense of unity, but longing for it.

> The "Unhappy Consciousness" is the consciousness of self as a merely contradictory dual-being, . . . the gazing of one Self-Consciousness into another Self-Consciousness; the Unhappy Consciousness itself is both of these Self-Consciousnesses; and the unity of both is also its essence. But it is not yet this essence (the unity of both) for-itself.[2]

[2]§§206–207 Das unglückliche Bewußtseyn ist das Bewußtseyn seiner als des gedoppelten nur widersprechenden Wesens, . . . das Schauen eines Selbstbewußtseyns in ein anderes, und es selbst ist beyde, und die Einheit beyder ist ihm auch das Wesen, aber es für sich ist sich noch nicht dieses Wesen selbst, noch nicht die Einheit beyder.

One can think of analogous situations approximating to this state. Schizophrenia and dual-personality syndromes are examples of psychopathological conditions involving a split in consciousness, from which the patient in search of a cure desires to be released. The "dark night of the soul" is described by Christian spiritual writers as a state in which the soul, having lost all sense of a divine presence, needs to proceed through a stage of life with pure faith. And William James famously differentiates the "once-born" religious person, who travels serene and unruffled by doubts through life, from the "twice-born" person:

> In the religion of the twice-born, the world is a double-storied mystery. Peace cannot be reached by the simple addition of pluses and elimination of minuses from life. Natural good is not simply insufficient in amount and transient, there lurks a falsity in its very being. Cancelled as it all is by death if not by earlier enemies, it gives no final balance, and can never be the thing intended for our lasting worship. It keeps us from our real good, rather; and renunciation and despair of it are our first step in the direction of the truth. There are two lives, the natural and the spiritual, and we must lose the one before we can participate in the other.[3]

Hegel's description of the experience is similar to James'—a dissatisfaction with finitude, leading consciousness to reach out for infinitude; a disappointment with changeability and contingency, instigating a quest for the unchangeable and necessary. Hegel includes many types of religious imagery in his description, without ever applying the concepts specifically to one religion. Traditional applications of the initial abstract stage by commentators have been to Judaism, emphasizing a monotheism incompatible with images but nevertheless seeking some determinate configuration of the divine; the later, more concrete stages have been interpreted in terms of medieval Christianity, having the advantage of a more "configured" divinity in the person of the God-man, but nevertheless lacking unity with the divinity, which it strives to attain through a variety of ineffective stratagems—monkish asceticism, religious superstitions and "sacramentals," subjection to mediating confessors, and so forth. In general, the "unhappy consciousness" in Hegel's construal is anyone whose religion involves withdrawal from the world and reality, accompanied by servile fear and/or by morbid self-denial.

Hegel's antidote to the religious aspects of this predicament is well-known—the Lutheran model sharply contrasted with what Hegel considered to be the essentially alienated aspects of traditional Catholicism. In Lutheranism, the split between religious and secular life disappeared; instead of strange and vain

---

[3]*The Varieties of Religious Experience*, Lecture VIII, "The Divided Self, and the Process of its Unification," init.

attempts to overcome the body and finitude through celibacy, penances, and other forms of mortification, the emphasis in Lutheranism (particularly German Lutheranism, as Hegel interpreted it) was the proper Christian use of material things, and devotion to family and community.

In the view of Karl Löwith, Eric Voegelin, and other critics, Hegel collapses the distance between the divine and the human, the religious and the secular, so completely that there is nothing left for religious transcendence—resulting in the "death of God," and the "secularization hypothesis," which firmly supersedes outmoded religious notions with present mundane reality. But this is an extreme view, portraying Hegel not only as a secularist, but as at least a covert atheist. Hegel was not trying to abolish transcendence, but to bring it into closer connection with the immanence of individual and social consciousness.

THE DISILLUSIONED HEDONIST

In section V.B, entitled "The Actualization of Rational Self-Consciousness through Itself," Hegel begins a series of analyses of the way that consciousness strives to bring about unity between itself and otherness through various pursuits. The first analysis is concerned with erotic relationships, and Hegel sets the theme by citing some verses, with some ellipses and modifications, from the early 1790 version of Goethe's *Faust* that was available to him.

> Consciousness scorns understanding and science,
> The incomparable human gifts;
> It gives itself over to the Devil,
> And must end up in ruin.[4]

Self-consciousness, at this stage in Hegel's analysis, has attained to a certain degree of sophistication. It is explicitly oriented to intersubjective fulfillment, and no longer satisfied with one-sided relationships oriented to an object-consciousness, as in the master-slave dialectic. It reaches out to form a union with otherness in its most advanced form, i.e. in the form of another self-consciousness. But its initial endeavors, as is usual on the phenomenological path, are on the level of immediacy. It should be kept in mind that "reason" for Hegel is a technical term which means the search for the unity of thought and being, self and other. The "rational" self-consciousness at this stage seeks through an erotic relationship with another self-consciousness to

---

[4]§360 Es verachtet Verstand und Wissenschaft, des Menschen allerhöchste Gaben-es hat dem Teufel sich ergeben und muß zugrunde gehn.

disarm unassimilated otherness, finally attaining the experience of unity with otherness, and indeed with otherness in one of its highest, personalized forms.

But the reality turns out to be far removed from this idealization.

If the ordinary, run-of-the-mill seducer would wax philosophical, he would realize that in his amorous pursuits he is merely trying to throw off his isolated individuality and connect with universality by enjoying the reflection of himself in another. But the semblance of freedom and spontaneity connected with these essentially transitory experiences vanishes as he realizes that he is being impelled by brute necessity, by fate in the form of infatuations which are the work of nature, by the earthly spirit which essentially falls short of the true intersubjectivity of Spirit. If Spirit was truly at work, it would be characterized not by necessity, but by self-conscious freedom, allowing an individual to assimilate and coordinate with otherness in a permanent, self-determined way, while recognizing and enhancing the freedom of the other.

THE MORAL SENTIMENTALIST

The moral sentimentalist[5] is impelled by an absolute trust in reason. Reason, in the Hegelian sense, involves the certainty about the unity of the self and its world; and, at the present stage, implies that the individual will be able to find himself in relationship to other subjectivities, and not meet up with unassimilable otherness. But what he immediately encounters, as he examines the intersubjective context, are long-standing social, cultural, and political traditions, which have endured because they have fostered order and unity in the past. These traditions have been fostered and protected almost unquestioningly by political and religious leaders from time immemorial. But the moral sentimentalist views them as oppressive, contradicting the laws that he feels to be part of his essential being.

A new necessity emerges—not just the necessity of finding oneself in an other, in such a way that the other is just conducive to one's own fulfillment, but the necessity of finding one's inner laws recognized and implemented in the wider intersubjective realms. The "law of one's heart" should be, and must be, it seems, the law of the land, in a rational society characterized by the unity of the individual and the universal. But as this highly esteemed law of the heart is *expressed* and enthusiastically promulgated it becomes something objective, severed from the subjectivity that gave rise to it; and it quickly becomes evident that it does not necessarily resonate with the law of *other* hearts.

---

[5]See Sect. V.B.b., §§367ff.

Initially, the moral sentimentalist's ideal—that the one important thing is to express and implement your deepest, personally felt, laws—fosters a climate of tolerance: the individual champions the position that the laws of *all* hearts must be expressed, and waits patiently for this to happen. But as this stand evolves into mere patronization, and as inevitably some of the laws of other hearts come into direct contradiction with one's own heart, a kind of madness ensues. The moral sentimentalist succumbs to a "frenzy of self-conceit," stubbornly refusing to believe that his universal is not the universal for everyone. The problem, of course, is that the "universal" was *his* universal, a nostrum, not *the* true universal embedded in all.

THE KNIGHT OF VIRTUE

The "Knight of Virtue"[6] seems to be a type of consciousness patterned after the knightly adventures described in Miguel Cervantes' novel, *Don Quixote*. Cervantes' protagonist, Don Quixote de la Mancha, is an idealistic elderly gentleman, enraptured with postmedieval nostalgia for the glorious days past, for the chivalrous way of life, which he imagines as rising above all the private interests and trivial undertakings surrounding him in the real world. Under the strain of his disappointment and depression about the state of the world, he flips into a quasi-dementia, dons knightly armor and regalia, convinces a farm laborer, Sancho Panza, to be his squire, and rides out with Sancho to conquer evils, rescue damsels in distress, and, in general, reassert nobility and goodness in the world. The individual things and persons he encounters are far removed from the ideals he harbors. He lashes out at them, tilting at windmills and engaging imaginary ogres in combat—behavior that, once noticed by the public, needs to be whitewashed, and sometimes concealed, by friends or well-wishers. Finally the don wakes up from his state of dementia and before dying is able to find goodness in mundane reality and the individuals around him.

Hegel's account follows a somewhat similar pattern. He describes the self-imposed mission of the Knight of Virtue as someone whose "victory" consists in

> The production of distinctions which are non-distinctions, pompous rhetoric about the oppression of mankind and what is best for it, about sacrificing for the Good and the misuse of talents. Such idealizations and purposes devolve as

---

[6]See Section V.B.C., §§386ff.

empty words, which edify the heart and leave the rational faculty empty, a buildup which builds nothing.[7]

Hegel has in mind a moralistic visionary disturbed, almost to the state of madness, at the apparent lack of goodness in the "course of the world," and the apparently self-serving actions of the bulk of mankind. But the Knight of Virtue, not falling into the mistake of the moral sentimentalist (just described), will champion not *his individual* universal, but *the* universal, the unadulterated general good for all. In this way, he aspires to unite his individuality with the universal, becoming a true "universal individual." And thus with impassioned rhetoric he focuses on arbitrary contingencies and acts of individuality as evil, and tries to promote commitment to a pure universal goodness, which sadly seems to be lacking everywhere. In the aftermath of his vain struggles, however, he finally becomes aware of the ironical truth that any *real* goodness that is to raise its head must emerge in the seeming contingencies and self-seeking actions of the "course of the world."

PRESTIGIOUS V. DISREPUTABLE CONSCIOUSNESS-TYPES

As mentioned in chapter 1,[8] Hegel's phenomenological analysis of *Bildung* (Culture/Civilization)[9] focuses on the endemic polarizations and antitheses for which there have been numerous precedents in European culture. The two "constants," or pivotal principles which engender the dialectical relationships, are wealth (*Reichtum*) and state power (*Staatsmacht*). The atmosphere he has in mind is hard to pin down to specific dates or times. References are made to feudalism, manorial lords and vassals, as well as to absolute monarchies, 18th century courtly manners, and emerging capitalistic economic relations. One might conclude that Hegel is taking European post-medieval, Renaissance, and Enlightenment developments as paradigmatic patterns of social and cultural antitheses; and Hegel intends to mediate and synthesize such antitheses in the final sections of his long chapter on Spirit.

As the initial antitheses between wealth and state power develop in this section, two types of consciousness emerge, based on two types of "judgment." Both state power and wealth are construed in immediacy as "good," but they are

---

[7]([Der Weltlauf] siegt aber nicht über etwas Reales, sondern über) das Erschaffen von Unterschieden, welche keine sind, über diese pomphaften Reden vom Besten der Menschheit und der Unterdrückung derselben, von der Aufopferung fürs Gute und dem Mißbrauche der Gaben;—solcherlei ideale Wesen und Zwecke sinken als leere Worte zusammen, welche das Herz erheben und die Vernunft leer lassen, erbauen, aber nichts aufbauen.

[8]See p. 6.

[9]See Section VI.B.I.a., §§500ff.

converted and perverted, with the help of their proponents, into their opposites and into the opposite of good. The proponents are the prestigious/ noble (*edelmütige*) consciousness and the disreputable/base (*niederträchtige*) consciousness—two extremes between which there are conceivably many gradations. The extremes result from two dialectically opposite types of judgment: the prestigious consciousness exemplifies the judgment of identity between wealth and power; he is one in whom state power and wealth converge, and are preeminently mutually conducive, wealth to power, and power to wealth:

> [The noble consciousness] contemplates its correspondence with public authority, and the fact that it simply has in it its own *being* and actualization, and it remains in service to this authority with real compliance as well as sensitive attention. Likewise, with regard to wealth, it sees that wealth provides for it a consciousness of its other essential aspect, its *independent existence*; hence it even views wealth as *an essential factor* in its relationship, and recognizes him who provides its enjoyment as a benefactor to whom it is indebted.[10]

The opposite type, the disreputable consciousness, is characterized by a negative judgment about both wealth and state power. It is consciously alienated from both factors, becoming a low-life in society, subsisting outside the acceptable parameters of culture:

> It views the authoritative power as a chain and a suppression of *independence*, and thus hates the ruler, submits subversively, and stands ever ready to agitate. In the wealth through which it gains some enjoyment of independence, it also considers only its lack of correspondence with the stability of *being*. Since by means of wealth it arrives merely at awareness of its singularity and of transitory enjoyments, it loves it, but despises it; and with the evanescence of enjoyment—that which is intrinsically evanescent—it sees even its relationship to wealth as vanished.[11]

As the further unfolding of culture takes place in the section, a dialectical transformation of these two opposite types takes place. Prestige is transformed into disrepute, and vice versa, while wealth and power undergo parallel trans-

---

[10]In der öffentlichen Macht betrachtet es das mit ihm Gleiche, daß es in ihr sein *einfaches Wesen* und dessen Betätigung hat und im Dienste des wirklichen Gehorsams wie der inneren Achtung gegen es steht. Ebenso in dem Reichtume, daß er ihm das Bewußtsein seiner anderen wesentlichen Seite, des *Fürsichseins*, verschafft; daher es ihn ebenfalls als *Wesen* in Beziehung auf sich betrachtet und denjenigen, von welchem es genießt, als Wohltäter anerkennt und sich zum Danke verpflichtet hält.

[11]In der Herrschergewalt also eine Fessel und Unterdrückung des *Fürsichseins* sieht und daher den Herrscher haßt, nur mit Heimtücke gehorcht und immer auf dem Sprunge zum Aufruhr steht,—im Reichtum, durch den es zum Genusse seines Fürsichseins gelangt, ebenso nur die Ungleichheit, nämlich mit dem bleibenden *Wesen* betrachtet; indem es durch ihn nur zum Bewußtsein der Einzelheit und des vergänglichen Genusses kommt, ihn liebt, aber verachtet, und mit dem Verschwinden des Genusses, des an sich Verschwindenden, auch sein Verhältnis zu dem Reichen für verschwunden ansieht.

formations. Just as in the master-slave relationship, discussed above, a mutual transformation takes place: the prestigious consciousness, capitalizing to the extreme on its prestige, becomes disreputable, while the disreputable consciousness, becoming fully conscious of, and able to articulate, the content and sources of its disreputability, edges towards a dialectically significant type of prestige.

THE REVOLUTIONARY

The context in which revolutionary consciousness emerges in Hegel's analysis[12] is a new stage of Spirit. For Hegel in the early nineteenth century, the most obvious then-current exemplification of a spiritual *novus ordo* was, of course, the French Revolution, which Hegel saw as emerging inevitably and irresistibly from antecedent events in the French Enlightenment.

The French Enlightenment, in Hegel's interpretation, was the work of Spirit in the aftermath of feudalism and the Renaissance. The great contribution of the Enlightenment to the advance of Spirit was the universal elevation of the power of subjectivity, through the work of the *lumières* and the ferment of their ideas at all levels of society. Initial manifestations of the new spirit included reactions against ingrained traditions, and against the despots and priests who were perceived as the perpetuators and guardians of these traditions. The theism of Christendom was metamorphosed into deism, with an impersonal God presiding over the necessary mechanistic developments in the world, such that all major *innovative* shifts in direction would have to be instigated not by a deity, but by self-consciousnesses. A final exemplification of the power of subjectivity to disregard all conventional and traditional objective values was the "philosophy of utility," which began to dictate and even create the values to be assigned to objects and actions.

The grounds for revolutionary consciousness were supplied as the philosophy of utility was pushed to its logical extreme, systematically denuding the objective world of any *intrinsic* worth; only subjectivity was of value, and whatever things in the world were considered to be "useful" to subjectivity. As subjectivities thus became emancipated from all deference to objects, they took on the characteristic of "universal will"—the unanimity patterned after the *volonté général* of Rousseau's political philosophy, leading to a theoretical overcoming of all differences and divisions among the populace. Such ideas created a heady spiritual atmosphere, capturing imaginations and

---

[12]See Section VI.B.III., §§582ff.

conveying the experience of universal emancipation, the participation of one and all in "absolute freedom."

As the aspiration for absolute freedom advanced, and the revolution which had taken place in thought became a *real* revolution, all institutions and traditional political structures were seen as a threat to the newly emerging universal ideal of freedom. The great negative power of freedom became manifest as its champions began to tear down putative establishments of the status quo. All vestiges of social structures and institutions and class stratifications had to give way. But in order for such a massive abolition to take place in the real world through real action, an individual, hopefully charismatic, had to come on the scene to put it into effect. And thus the conditions became ripe for the emergence of the archetypal revolutionary—one who presents himself as the actual embodiment of the spirit of absolute freedom, and one who is accepted by the masses as the mover and shaker who will bring their *volonté général* into effect.

But unfortunately, *absolute* will by definition can never be realized in *any* individual. The sharp contrast between the universal subjective ideal and the individual who entrusts himself with its implementation becomes soon apparent. And this discrepancy between the individual revolutionary and the universally held ideal of absolute freedom is not capable of compromise or mediation. Other, very different would-be implementers of universal freedom are in necessary conflict with the existing revolutionary in power. Against the counter-currents, he works feverishly to reinstate the universal, by destroying all semblances of particular objectivity. And the processes of destruction and disestablishment which he implements eventually reach a critical point, at which nothing is left to destroy except the hard intransigence of atomic free individuals who entertain different ideals about the attainment of universal freedom.

> [The reigning champions of universal freedom turn to] the negation of the individual-as-existent-in-the-universal. Hence the single and unique "task" and "deed" of universal liberty is death—and more specifically a death which has no inner dimension and fulfillment, since what is negated is just the unfulfilled atomistic point of the absolutely free self. The death in question is thus the coldest, drabbest death, without any more significance than the slicing of a head of cabbage or a gulp of water.[13]

The images of terror and the guillotine hovering over the revolutionary enterprise lead to a belated and fruitless attempt at mediating the divisions, and

---

[13]§590 . . . die Negation des Einzelnen als Seyenden in dem Allgemeinen. Das einzige Werk und That der allgemeinen Freyheit ist daher der Tod, und zwar ein Tod, der keinen inneren Umfang und Erfüllung hat, denn was negirt wird, ist der unerfüllte Punkt des absolutfreyen Selbsts; er ist also der kälteste, platteste Tod, ohne mehr Bedeutung, als das Durchbauen eines Kohlhaupts oder ein Schluck Wassers.

moderating the massive destruction taking place in the real world. A government by a revolutionary council is established. But this "government" by the revolutionary regime is easily recognized as being just another faction.

> It is only the *victorious* faction that is called "the government," and the necessity for its overthrow lies simply in the fact that it is a faction; and the fact that it *is* the government *makes* it *ipso facto* into a faction and hence "guilty." If the universal will can point to an actual deed of the government as a crime perpetuated upon itself, the government in its turn can find nothing definite and publicly observable by reference to which it might establish the guilt of the universal will aligned against it; since, when you come down to it, the only thing opposing itself to the actual universality of the government is the mere will, or "intention," which lacks actuality. Thus, "to be suspect" comes to count for the same thing as "to be guilty," and the official reaction against this other "actuality" that resides in the simple interiority of intention, consists in the tedious extermination of the existing suspect-self, from whom at this juncture there is really nothing left to take away except his existence itself.[14]

When it becomes unmistakably clear that no individual revolutionary and no faction can embody the universal will, the revolution and the regime promoting the revolution fall by the wayside. No longer suppressed, natural divisions and groupings and classes gradually begin to emerge once more and take their place in the real world.

As has been noted above, Hegel uses historical images of the French Revolution, the revolutionary "Committees," the Jacobins, and the guillotine in his phenomenology of absolutized freedom. But his analysis transcends any historical imbeddedness. Karl Marx, a "Young Hegelian" who may never have read the section on "Absolute Freedom and Terror" in the *Phenomenology*, in his 1843 *Critique of Hegel's Philosophy of Right* was championing freedom when he declared that "all forms of the state have democracy for their truth, and for that reason are false to the extent that they are not democracy." Subsequently he began to absolutize an uncompromising vision of universal emancipation. His *Communist Manifesto* was a clarion call for overturning all social structures falling short of the "scientific socialism" that he

---

[14]§591 Die *siegende* Faktion nur heißt Regierung, und eben darin, daß sie Faktion ist, liegt unmittelbar die Notwendigkeit ihres Untergangs; und daß sie Regierung ist, dies macht sie umgekehrt zur Faktion und schuldig. Wenn der allgemeine Wille sich an ihr wirkliches Handeln als an das Verbrechen hält, das sie gegen ihn begeht, so hat sie dagegen nichts Bestimmtes und Äußeres, wodurch die Schuld des ihr entgegengesetzten Willens sich darstellte; denn ihr als dem *wirklichen* allgemeinen Willen steht nur der unwirkliche reine Wille, die *Absicht*, gegenüber. *Verdächtigwerden* tritt daher an die Stelle oder hat die Bedeutung und Wirkung des *Schuldigseins*, und die äußerliche Reaktion gegen diese Wirklichkeit, die in dem einfachen Innern der Absicht liegt, besteht in dem trockenen Vertilgen dieses seienden Selbsts, an dem nichts sonst wegzunehmen ist als nur sein Sein selbst.

identified with "democracy." Where these Marxist ideals have been implemented, the result has been innumerable violent deaths of resistant "atomic
individuals" up to the present. The problem, of course, is with any ideal of
freedom which requires absolute destruction of all established systems. The
fury of destruction so consumes the liberators that only their more moderate
successors are in a position to rebuild viable and stable structures.

THE BEAUTIFUL SOUL

The "Beautiful Soul" *(die schöne Seele)* is a theme from German romanticism
which receives considerable attention at the very end of Hegel's long chapter
VI[15] on the "forms of the world." It constitutes the culmination of the final
sections on morality and conscience, and provides the final *Gestalt* in the historical unfolding of Spirit, as interpreted by Hegel.

The *Gestalt* of the Beautiful Soul has been variously interpreted. Novalis'
Heinrich von Ofterdingen, Jacobi's *Woldemar*, Schlegel's *Lucinde*, Schiller's
essay, "On Grace and Dignity," Hölderlin's *Hyperion*, as well as Schleierma-
cher's *Addresses* and Fichte's *Wissenschaftslehre* have all been mentioned as
literary sources upon which Hegel is drawing. I have suggested in my *Hegel's
Phenomenology, Part II*, that the deaconess in the subsection entitled "The
Beautiful Soul" in Goethe's novel, *Wilhelm Meister's Apprenticeship* was in
the forefront of Hegel's thinking as he discussed this *Gestalt*. Hegel himself
in his *Lectures on Aesthetics* refers to Jacobi's *Woldemar* and the character,
Werther, in Goethe's *Die Leiden des jungen Werthers* as fictional portrayals
of the sentiments of a "Beautiful Soul," and in one of his book reviews points
to the author, Novalis himself, as an exemplification of the Beautiful Soul.
Needless to say, the Beautiful Soul is a composite figure, which Hegel
thought applicable to real people as well as to fictional types.

As a type of consciousness, the Beautiful Soul appears in the context of late
eighteenth-century reaction against *Moralität*, i.e., the Kantian moral theory,
perceived as a strange, anti-sentimental formulation of an ethics of pure duty.
Johann Gotlieb Fichte and others had tried to repair this perceived Kantian
damage by extolling conscience *(Gewissen)* as an ethical type of consciousness bringing deeply-held subjective feelings into play in the pursuit of a
moral life and the making of ethical decisions. As discussed above,[16] the important thing, with the focus on conscience, was not the mechanical following of rules or laws, but the serene examination of one's moral convictions

---

[15]See VI.C.c, §§658ff.
[16]See p. 10.

and the expression of these convictions in word and deed. But the problem that emerged, as Hegel analyzed the phenomenon, was that expressions of conscience only generated disparity and conflict when, as often happens, the conscientious persons to whom it was expressed were not like-minded.

But conscientiousness was still of the essence, although threatened now by verbal or behavioral expressions of conscience which will often instigate interpersonal conflict and contradictions. The strategy adopted by the Beautiful Soul then comes on the scene as a means for maintaining the peace and serenity of a good conscience while resolutely avoiding the disturbances that easily emerge from conscientious expressions. The strategy, namely, is a retreat into oneself, probably accompanied by a physical or geographical retreat, as evidenced, for example, by the deaconess in Goethe's above-mentioned segment on "The Beautiful Soul," who retires to a domestic sanctuary carefully chosen for freedom from worldly entanglements or encounters with evil. In other words, the solution is an intentionally sheltered life.

One is reminded of a question raised by Thomas Aquinas, during the emergence of medieval religious orders: namely, whether a sinner could withdraw from secular life and join a religious order. Those who objected to this maintained that the sinner should become practiced in basic morality before taking such a step. Aquinas responded that sinners who withdrew from the world to enter a religious order were simply acting prudently, judging that they could best save their soul by intentionally shutting out worldly temptations.[17]

Hegel would not agree. In the German Lutheran tradition he saw all forms of monastic flight from the world as exemplifications of the alienations in religion caused under Roman Catholicism. A truly moral or religious person should be wholly engaged with the world, bringing his/her convictions of conscience into the "light of day," being willing to stand up to the risks of encounters with evil. The truncated morality of the Beautiful Soul becomes apparent in Hegel's analysis in a subsequent and inevitable encounter with its counterpart, the Acting Conscience. The latter is someone who rolls up his sleeves, tries to bring his moral ideals into existence in the world, and in the process "gets his hands dirty" with mistakes or compromises, thus taking on the aspect of "evil," as seen with the eyes of the Beautiful Soul. Initial encounters with such "movers and shakers" in the world simply increase the resolve of the Beautiful Soul to refrain from all external expressions; and the result is a spiritual disintegration, caused by the intense and unnatural retreat into self.

But the arrival at this extreme of self-centeredness lays the dialectical groundwork for a new state of Spirit superseding such intersubjective alienations. For

[17]*Summa theologiae* II–II, q. 189, a.1.

the Beautiful Soul and the Acting Conscience at this final stage are paradigmatic opposites who sum up all the major oppositions in the ethical world — on the one hand hypocritical self-justifying righteous consciousnesses who maintain their lofty status by sheltering themselves from reality, and, on the other hand, confessed sinners, never quite able to live up to their ethical ideals, but recognizing the disparity and giving expression to it. In Hegel's portrayal, the confession of the Acting Conscience is what breaks down the hardened self-righteousness of the Beautiful Soul. What Hegel is presenting for us is the classic situation of the saint ultimately seeing his/her identity with the sinner and vice versa, the ivory-tower idealist with the activist in the street, the theoretician with the ones who "make things happen." The reconciliation of these two antithetical types of consciousness is an event of the utmost importance; it is a "closing of the circuit" for Spirit as a whole. Their interconnection through mutual understanding and mutual forgiveness is the necessary and sufficient condition for the unleashing of Spirit as the unity of opposites in the social world.

3

Phenomenological Themes

Hegel throughout the *Phenomenology* is attempting to bring out, in various ways, and with increasing levels of sophistication, the Concept—with a capital "C"—in other words, the unity-in-distinction of subject and object, the in-itself and the for-itself, consciousness and self-consciousness, self and otherness. This is the Hegelian counterpart to the Idea (with a capital "I")—the important technical term which was elaborated during Hegel's earlier collaboration with Schelling. Both Hegel's and Schelling's efforts were in the line of successive attempts by post-Kantian German idealists to overcome the glaring dichotomies between subjective and objective aspects that they discerned in Kant's philosophy (i.e., between phenomenon and noumenon, duty and inclinations, God and the world). But in the midst of Hegel's concerted attempts to bring out the Concept, he also touches on some extraordinary concepts (with a small "c")—insights which are worth dwelling on in their own right, but in the context of Hegel's systematic analysis had to function as multiple stepping-stones to Absolute Knowledge (the final instantiation of the Concept). These insights have some common features—they focus on oppositions, standoffs, or discrepancies which function as catalysts in the advance of consciousness and spirit. In what follows, I would like to isolate and bring out some of these insightful themes for closer examination, comment, and some relevant applications:

HERACLITEAN FLUX

In his *Science of Logic*, Hegel extolls the ancient Greek philosopher, Heraclitus, contrasting him favorably with his predecessor, Parmenides, and others who failed to appreciate the flux of reality:

It was the Eleatics, and especially Parmenides, who first . . . proposed the simple thought of pure Being as the Absolute and as the sole truth: "Only Being exists, and Nothingness does not exist at all. . . ." The profound thinker, Heraclitus, against such a simple and one-sided abstraction, proposed the more advanced integral concept of Becoming, and said "Being is hardly more than nothingness," or else " Everything is flowing"—i.e., Everything is Becoming.[1]

And it is with the Heraclitean flux of concepts in mind that Hegel, in the Preface to his *Phenomenology*, §71, extolls Plato's *Parmenides*, the extraordinary post-Parmenidean dialogue in which ideas are constantly transformed under examination into multiple and opposite meanings, as the "greatest literary achievement of ancient dialectic."

The *Phenomenology* as a whole is indeed Heraclitean, with ideas constantly changing before the reader's eyes, so to speak. Eric Voegelin, the political philosopher, complained that Hegel, in his philosophy of history, used "sorcery" in transforming the historical facts.[2] In the *Phenomenology*, what may seem like sorcery is considered by Hegel to be the proper task of the professional phenomenologist, applying a thoroughgoing skepticism to all claimants to epistemological certainty, and leading them into Heraclitean transformations not anticipated by the claimants. Hegel's ultimate goal is to end the dialectic at some impregnable claim of certainty which can withstand even the most skeptical sallies, and vindicate its nature as truth. Whether he actually accomplishes this goal with "Absolute Knowledge" at the end of the *Phenomenology* is still a matter for incessant debate by critics. But on the way to this goal, there is no dispute that Hericlitean developments take place: particular "Heres" and "Nows" are changed into universals, Master and Slave consciousnesses are transformed into one another, Mind becomes Thing and vice versa, the Noble consciousness of European civilization is transformed into a base consciousness, the triumph of freedom in the Enlightenment becomes the springboard to terror and totalitarianism, and the attempt to establish a purely rational morality leads to religion and the Christian ideal of mutual forgiveness.

I think the best example of the intensive Heraclitean transformation of ideas in the *Phenomenology* is to be found in the third part of chapter VII on Religion, subtitled "Revealed Religion," where Hegel discusses the *Genesis*

---

[1]*Wissenschaft der Logik,* Erster Teil, Erstes Buch, Erster Abschnitt, Erstes Kapitel, Anmerkung 1: Den einfachen Gedanken des reinen Seins haben die Eleaten zuerst, vorzüglich Parmenides als das Absolute und als einzige Wahrheit . . . ausgesprochen: nur das Sein ist, und das Nichts ist gar nicht. . . . Der tiefsinnige Heraklit hob gegen jene einfache und einseitige Abstraktion den höheren totalen Begriff des Werdens hervor und sagte: das Sein ist sowenig als das Nichts, oder auch: Alles fließt, das heißt: Alles ist Werden.

[2]Voegelin, *Collected Works*, Vol. 12, Baton Rouge: Louisiana State University Press, 1990, §II, 221–222.

story of creation, and the initial confusion of good and evil when these notions, as interpreted by Christians, are represented by the imagination. The imagination portrays the initial "Fall" and emphasizes the subsequent redemption of humans from sin by a God-man, who brings about the reconciliation of the good God with sinful humans. Seen eventually from the perspective of Spirit, this "atonement" brings about a final metamorphosis—a transformation of evil into good. But to speak in this way is to encounter an initial contradiction that must be resolved:

> To say [in regard to the atonement] that evil is identified with goodness, is equivalent to denying that evil is evil or that good is good, but rather both are nullified—evil being understood as self-seeking existence-for-self and good as selfless simplicity.[3]

In other words: Yes, in the story of the redemption of man after the Fall, there is a "fusion" of good and evil, so to speak. But, having defined evil as existence-for-self and good as simplicity, we cannot speak of this fusion as a simple identification of good and evil. This type of labeling would, in effect, make "good" and "evil" into meaningless distinctions.

> But if both ideas are interpreted conceptually, their unity becomes clear right away; for that "self-seeking existence-for-self" is the simplicity of knowledge, and the "selfless simplicity" is just as much pure self-seeking existence-for-self.[4]

In other words, if we examine the *concept* of evil as "self-seeking existence-for-self" subsisting separately from the divine simplicity, we see that this *fürsichsein* is simple consciousness or knowledge, and thus *good*; similarly, a conceptual analysis of divine "selfless simplicity" reveals it to be self-existent and self-seeking, which gives it the character of *evil*.

One could argue further that the concept of evil as a separation of human self-consciousness from the simplicity of the divine, is the simplicity of *knowledge*, and thus good; and also that the concept of good as the simplicity of the divine Being is a self-existent and *self-seeking* otherness, and thus evil.

> But just as it must be said that conceptually good and evil, insofar as [as we have just shown] they are not good and evil, are the *same* thing; so also it must be said that they are not the same thing, but are absolutely *different*, since that simple

---

[3]§780 Indem das Böse dasselbe ist, was das Gute, ist eben das Böse nicht Böses noch das Gute Gutes, sondern beide sind vielmehr aufgehoben, das Böse überhaupt das insichseiende Fürsichsein und das Gute das selbstlose Einfache.

[4]§780 Indem so beide nach ihrem Begriffe ausgesprochen werden, erhellt zugleich ihre Einheit; denn das insichseiende Fürsichsein ist das einfache Wissen; und das selbstlose Einfache ist ebenso das reine in sich seiende Fürsichsein.

existence-for-self, and also that pure knowledge are intrinsically, and in the same way, pure negativity, i.e. absolute difference.[5]

The emphasis here is on good and evil as conceptual abstractions. Abstract good and abstract evil can, as we have just seen, be changed into each other through conceptual analysis, resulting in their identification; this "identification," however, achieved through pure conceptual negativity, also constitutes an absolute difference. That is, existence-for-self is not only identity with self but difference *from* self, and pure knowledge is an identity-in-*distinction* from that which is known. The upshot of these considerations is that an apparent impasse develops, which will lead us to a more dynamic understanding of good and evil:

> Both of these [opposing] statements complete the whole: the claim and assurance of the first statement must with insurmountable resistance confront the insistence on the second statement. Insofar as both statements are right, they both are wrong; their wrongness consists in taking abstract formulations like "the same" and "not the same," like "identity" and "nonidentity" for something stable and true and real and resting in them.[6]

At this point, aside from the wordplay, a conceptual dialectical movement catches our attention. Good and evil, and their oscillating identity and nonidentity begin to be seen in the context of their necessary interrelationship. This sets the stage for the emergence of Hegel's reformulation of their interrelationship from the perspective of *Spirit*, which supersedes static pictorial representations of good or evil.

> The truth is found in neither the one nor the other, but rather in the interactive movement, where the simple identity is abstract identity and thus absolute difference, and the difference in-itself, differentiated from itself, is thus self-identity.[7]

From the standpoint of the ordinary concepts of the understanding, "identity" is something separate from "difference," and vice versa. But identifica-

---

[5]§780 Sosehr daher gesagt werden muß, daß nach diesem ihrem Begriffe das Gute und Böse, d. h. insofern sie nicht das Gute und das Böse sind, *dasselbe* seien, ebensosehr muß also gesagt werden, daß sie nicht dasselbe, sondern schlechthin *verschieden* sind, denn das einfache Fürsichsein oder auch das reine Wissen sind gleicher Weise die reine Negativität oder der absolute Unterschied an ihnen selbst.

[6]§780 Erst diese beiden Sätze vollenden das Ganze, und dem Behaupten und Versichern des ersten muß mit unüberwindlicher Hartnäckigkeit das Festhalten an dem anderen gegenübertreten; indem beide gleich recht haben, haben beide gleich unrecht, und ihr Unrecht besteht darin, solche abstrakte Formen, wie *dasselbe* und *nicht dasselbe*, die *Identität* und die *Nichtidentität*, für etwas Wahres, Festes, Wirkliches zu nehmen und auf ihnen zu beruhen.

[7]§780 Nicht das eine oder das andere hat Wahrheit, sondern eben ihre Bewegung, daß das einfache Dasselbe die Abstraktion und damit der absolute Unterschied, dieser aber, als Unterschied an sich, von sich selbst unterschieden, also die Sichselbstgleichheit ist.

tion of the simplicity and self-existence which took place in regard to good and evil has to be seen in conjunction with the differentiations of good and evil which were already implicit in their identification. This insight thus prepares the way for an understanding of Spirit, which transcends abstract notions like the Fall into evil, and the restoration of goodness by the Atonement, and which prepares the way (in Hegel's analysis) for the consummate stage of religion—the emergence of the Christian community in which mutual forgiveness overcomes the abstractions of good and evil, and the reconciliation of sinners with the divine goodness takes place implicitly.

INTERSUBJECTIVITY

Many modern and contemporary philosophers—Husserl, Habermas, Heidegger, and others—have been intensely concerned with the "problem of intersubjectivity," and some of them look to Hegel's *Phenomenology* as an important source of principles showing the rational basis for the relationship between consciousnesses. But, as Vittorio Hösle observes, there seems to be little awareness of the fact that the *Phenomenology* as a *whole* can be understood as a treatise, and a masterful treatise, on intersubjectivity. Hösle laments the fact that the contribution of the *Phenomenology* to this problematic has not been fully appreciated in Germany,[8] and finds one of the closest approximations to Hegel's approach not in continental philosophers or the Frankfurt school, but in the American Hegelian, Josiah Royce, who in his final works developed the idea of a "community of interpretation" as the fullest expression of the spiritual world.[9]

The foundation for Hegel's notion of intersubjectivity is found at the end of the first three chapters of the *Phenomenology*, dealing with the three major stages of "Consciousness"—Sense-Certainty, Perception, and Understanding. "Consciousness" in Hegel's technical terminology is object-oriented, always a consciousness *of* something outside of consciousness. Hegel's third chapter on Understanding reaches its culmination with a final moment in which the understanding turns back on *itself*, thus setting the stage for chapter IV on Self-Consciousness.

In §§179–182 of chapter IV, dealing with the concept of "recognition" (*Anerkennung*), Hegel lays the groundwork for the multiple expansions of intersubjectivity which will take place during the course of his "science of the experience of consciousness." *Self*-consciousness, just like consciousness, must

---

[8]Vittorio Hösle, *Hegels System: der Idealismus der Subjektivität und das Problem der Intersubjecktivität* (Hamburg: Felix Meiner Verlag, 1988), 385.

[9]*Hegels System*, 384.

have an *object*; but nothing below the level of consciousness can be a suitable object for a self-consciousness. In other words, a self is intrinsically and necessarily ordered to another self as its proper object and its primary source of satisfaction. And just as one would never have an idea of his/her physical body without some kind of mirroring reflection, so also, for self-understanding, a self needs to see itself reflected in an other self, as in a mirror. Thus the self *finds* itself in another. But this discovery of the self through otherness implies the existence of otherness in the self—an unstable situation which leads the self to the final movements: The self proceeds to "restore" the otherness which it had assimilated from the other self to that self, and in this process is enabled to return to itself renewed, but now mediated by its "other." A corollary of this process is that independent existence is relegated to the other self, simultaneously as self-consciousness attains its own independence. To sum up the moments of the intersubjective process: Pure self-consciousness is a mere abstraction, taken out of its natural and necessary context of relation to other selves.

As Hösle notes,[10] in the course of dialectical developments in the *Phenomenology* multiple instances of uneven and disfunctional intersubjective relationships emerge—the Master/Slave relationship, the dilemma of workers in what Hegel calls the "spiritual animal kingdom" who experience alienation from that which they accomplish, the alienation of wealthy patrons from their clients in the era of royalty and hangers-on, the disintegration of atomic free self-consciousnesses under the rubric of political revolution, and so forth. But in the interstices of these uneven situations, four major, and progressively more sophisticated, stages of intersubjectivity also emerge—(1) *Sittlichkeit*, which Hegel defines as "nothing other than the absolute spiritual *unity* of being of individuals in their independent *actuality*,"[11] (2) the mutual forgiveness of good and evil consciences, which amounts to the "*existence* of egos expanded into duality—an existence that still remains self-identical, and in its complete renunciation and its opposite possesses its self-certainty";[12] also, (3) for the Christian community, in the aftermath of the death of the God-man, "death becomes transformed into a 'universalization of Spirit,' insofar as Spirit abides within the community, dies there daily, and rises daily from death again";[13] and finally, (4) in Hegel's adumbration of "absolute knowledge," through the philosophy of history and the history of philosophy, "the

---

[10]*Hegels System*, 383.

[11]§349 "Sittlichkeit . . . ist nichts anderes als in der selbständigen *Wirklichkeit* der Individuen die absolute geistige *Einheit* ihres Wesens."

[12]§671 Das versöhnende Ja . . . ist das Dasein des zur Zweiheit ausgedehnten Ichs, das darin sich gleich bleibt und in seiner vollkommenen Entäußerung und Gegenteile die Gewißheit seiner selbst hat. . . .

[13]§784 Der Tod wird von dem, was er unmittelbar bedeutet, von dem Nichtsein dieses Einzelnen verklärt zur Allgemeinheit des Geistes, der in seiner Gemeine lebt, in ihr täglich stirbt und aufersteht.

realm of spirits . . . constitutes a series of successions, wherein one detaches itself from another and each spirit takes over the rule of the world from its predecessors."[14] This final stage of global philosophical "recollection" (*Erinnerung*) of spirits is, of course, a grand vision that most philosophers of intersubjectivity would not contemplate. It stands as Hegel's idealistic "logical conclusion" to the evolution of Spirit.

RATIONAL REALITY

Hegel's famous assertion, towards the beginning of his political philosophy, that "the rational is the real" has provoked numerous criticisms. It has been taken as a prime example of the strangeness of so-called "idealist" philosophers, who rank thoughts over things and ideas over facts; it has become an Hegelian stereotype, supposedly summing up the dangers of an a priori approach to philosophizing. Most importantly, "the rational is the real" has been portrayed as offensive to common sense. For we all know, don't we? that reality is often irrational, and what is rational can be seriously unrealistic.

In order to understand what Hegel meant by the rationality of reality, we have to understand how he defined his task as a philosopher. He shared the motivation of Fichte, Schelling, and other contemporaries, about repairing the damage that they perceived in the Kantian philosophy. In particular, Hegel objected to the fact that in Kant's *Critique of Pure Reason* "reason" is depicted as a faculty which can be manipulated as a tool to get at the truth,[15] "reality" is construed in terms of things like "real dollars,"[16] and concluded that such notions of rationality and reality are superficial, unphilosophical, irrational, and unrealistic. Hegel's own approach hinges on his interpretation of reason (*Vernunft*), not as a repository of categories to be imprinted on the external appearances of "things in themselves," but as an aspect of consciousness powerfully uniting subjectivity with objectivity in all of its manifold interactions—to the effect that "brute" unassimilated facts as well as lofty unrealizable ideas are, in proportion to their unassimilability or their unrealizability, just to that degree "unreal" or "irrational."

The Introduction to Hegel's *Phenomenology* (§§73–74) portrays strange dualistic notions of cognition—existing in some rarified sphere, standing over

---

[14]§808 Das Geisterreich, das auf diese Weise sich in dem Dasein bildet, macht eine Aufeinanderfolge aus, worin einer den anderen ablöste und jeder das Reich der Welt von dem vorhergehenden übernahm.

[15]See Kant's *Critique of Pure Reason,* Preface to the Second Edition, Bxviii–xxiii.

[16]*CPR* A599=B627.

against "true reality"—as a major hurdle in philosophy, and as the main problematic that he wishes to deal with in the work that follows. He follows systematically in the first four chapters through various claimants to valid cognition, showing the lack of satisfactory coordination between subjectivity and objectivity in each of the claimants. Finally, in the fifth chapter, he arrives at the concept of Reason, which he defines (§233) as "consciousness's certainty of being all reality. . . ." And he goes on to explain that *Being*, or the in-itself, exists only insofar as it exists for-consciousness, and . . . what is for-consciousness also exists in-itself." This is the seminal principle, the rational reality in which there is no unknowable Kantian "thing-in-itself." Hegel then proceeds to critically examine this principle of Reason as it applies in the relationship of mind to brain, of workers to their products, of moralists to the world, and so forth. The final epitome of "rational reality" that he concludes with is described in §420 as the absolute *Sache selbst*—somewhat similar in notion to (and equally untranslatable as) Heidegger's *Dasein*. Heidegger's English translators do not try to translate the German, but *Dasein*, which etymologically means "being there" in Heidegger's usage connotes the centrality of human existence, combining subjectivity and objectivity. In German, the ordinary word for "thing" is *Ding*, but *Sache* can mean "thing" in a much wider sense than *Ding*. Hegel defines *die Sache selbst* in the first paragraph of the Introduction to the *Phenomenology* as "the real cognition of the truly existent" (*das wirkliche Erkennen dessen was in Wahrheit ist*). This "rational reality" is epitomized in a human individual who is fully reconciled with the universal. We might characterize him/her as a "universal individual." The "task" of the universal individual, as we see in the following sections of the *Phenomenology* is to implement his/her unity-in-distinction with nature, society, the polity—a task whose completion is finally depicted (in chapters VII and VIII) as accomplished with the help of art, religion, and philosophy. In other words, in Hegel's usage, "reality" is worthy of the name only insofar as it evinces this unification with rationality, and a "rationality" that is at odds with reality is a pure abstraction. Hegel is obviously not concerned here with "realities" like dollar bills, or "rationalities" like Kantian categories. He is focusing primarily on thought-things, evincing the creative interplay of thought with reality—formed by universal individuals, and likewise instrumental in *forming* universal individuals.

INVALIDITY OF KANT'S CATEGORICAL IMPERATIVE

When Hegel discusses modern concepts of morality, in the *Phenomenology*, as well as in other works, he often focuses on Kant's *Fundamental Principles of a Metaphysic of Morals* and *Critique of Practical Reason*, which in Hegel's time (as well as in ours) have been accepted as major theoretical break-throughs, offering a certain and strictly logical "scientific" guide to the solution of moral problems. In the final subsection of the chapter on Reason, entitled "Reason as Testing Laws,"[17] Hegel launches into a critique of Kant's "Categorical Imperative"[18] as a methodology for moral decision-making. According to Kant, one can determine the morality or immorality of his personal "maxim" (intention to do something or behave in a certain way) by a subjective "test": one should simply attempt to universalize this maxim, and decide whether he would be willing to have it applied universally. Kant gives a number of case studies, e.g. the person who wants to borrow money without being obliged to pay it back; this person asks himself whether he would like to universalize this for everyone, even for those who would borrow from him, and of course ends in self-contradiction. Hegel portrays this as the application of the "law of self-contradiction" to morality, and he objects that this "test" only works on a superficial level, but self-destructs when we descend to the details. He gives a number of test cases of his own, but one of the most interesting is with regard to communism and capitalism. (Karl Marx makes references to Hegel's *Phenomenology* in his 1844 Manuscripts and other writings, but shows no familiarity with this section.) Hegel argues that under communism the distribution of goods according to *need* would contradict the basic goal of human equality, since individuals obviously have different needs; but *equal* distribution, ignoring differential needs, would contradict the goal of giving a fair share to everyone. Similarly, under a system of private property, the notion of having *fixed* property contradicts the essentially ephemeral characteristic of all property; the exclusiveness of the "mine" contradicts the essential unity of my ego with all other egos; and the "for me" aspect of property contradicts the "for-another" characteristic of all objects (§§430–431). Hegel's point, of course, is not to show the immorality of either communism or private property, but to show that anyone can justify or invalidate any "maxim" by using some artful sophistry. Hegel's solution? The fact that we try to determine the laws which should govern our dealings with others indicates we are already in a dysfunctional relationship with these others; so forget about trying to prove moral laws which *ought* to be, and focus on the ethical laws which already exist and encompass us as a spiritual atmosphere. Hegel, quoting Sophocles' *Antigone*[19] bids us to focus on the overarching, unwritten central law of rational human existence which "'is not for

---

[17]V.C.c., §§429ff.

[18]See the Abbott translation of the *Fundamental Principles of the Metaphysic of Morals* (Indianapolis, IN: Library of Liberal Arts, 1949), 38ff.

[19]Verses 456, 457.

now or yesterday, but is always there, living on, emanating from—no one knows where." He proceeds to clarify what he means by this primordial "law," which is conditioned and facilitated by a heightened sense of unity between individual and society, in the immediately following chapter on Spirit, beginning with a discussion of "ethicality" (*Sittlichkeit*).

NATURAL LAW

In chapter VI, "Spirit," Hegel advises us that we are making a major transition from previous chapters—no longer concerned specifically with the "forms of consciousness," but focusing now on the "forms of a world."[20] The world view that Hegel begins with is reminiscent of ancient Greek civilization, as romanticized and idealized by Hegel and his contemporaries. References are made to Greek tragedies and comedies, to the gods and Greek notions of the afterlife in Hades, but especially to the all-pervasive atmosphere of "ethicality" (*Sittlichkeit*) which Hegel portrays as a kind of social consciousness characterized by a "one for all, all for one" mentality. But in the midst of the generally harmonious existence of this era, "ethical action"[21] comes to the fore and threatens to disrupt the peace and serenity of the commonweal. The main agents of the ethical action—real or fictionalized individuals like Antigone, Creon, Oedipus, Orestes, Agammemnon, immortalized in the Greek tragedies—do not fall under the rubric of "morality" as understood by moderns. They are operating at the behest of much greater, cosmic powers. There are, in fact, just two powers, intrinsically antithetical and fighting for supremacy. On the one hand, human law (comparable to what we would call "civil law" or "constitutional law") is directed by political leaders towards the "universal ends" of peace, stability, and order; on the other hand, divine law (not what the Judeo-Christian tradition would call "divine commands," but rather comparable to "natural law" in the Western tradition) is directed towards protecting the rights of individuals and families, and even justifying the performance of duties under a "higher law" which may conflict with human laws.

The natural laws that Hegel touches on include laws against incest and patricide, as exemplified by the tragedy of Oedipus, familial obligations as exemplified by Antigone, promise-keeping as exemplified by the tragic political ambitions of the brothers Eteocles and Polynices, and laws against adultery and murder as exemplified by Orestes and Agammemnon. One might also include

---

[20]§441 "Gestalten einer Welt."
[21]See §§446ff.

the natural rights of women to overthrow oppressive male domination, as depicted in Hegel's oblique references to Aristophanes' comedy, *Lysistrata*.[22]

Over against the "divine" natural law, as a kind of historical constant, Hegel portrays the sometimes unscrupulous, and sometimes well-meaning, agents of "human law" in its various manifestations. They expend energetic efforts in maintaining public order, or preventing civil unrest, or perpetuating their own power, or strengthening the power of the state against perceived enemies. It is predictable and inevitable that they will now and then encounter opposition from proponents of the natural law—individuals like Polynices, who insisted that his younger brother, who was de facto ruler, transfer to him the kingship, as promised; like Antigone, who refused to refrain from the traditional obligatory religious burial rites for her brother; or like the Greek women depicted in *Lysistrata* who engaged in a domestic adaptation of "civil disobedience" against politically powerful husbands who insisted on continuing with the second Peloponnesian war.

Religious duties, fraternal and kinship duties, male and female reciprocal rights and duties in our own era, offer us instantiations of natural law which have changed somewhat in content, but inevitably come into conflict with political agendas and civil laws. In Hegel's portrayal, utilizing historical figures and patterns, this conflict led to the dissolution of the harmonious polity that he was analyzing. Optimistically, we may hope that this does not have to be a dialectically necessitated aftermath.

VICTORY BY SOCIAL OSMOSIS

Hegel in a section of chapter VI entitled "The Struggle of the Enlightenment with Superstition," describes the battle of the Enlightenment with Christian faith, and the eventual victory of the Enlightenment. The imagery that Hegel draws upon is of Voltaire, Diderot, and other *philosophes* of the French Enlightenment, the worldwide spread of the *Dictionnaire encyclopédique*, the weakening influence of royalty and clergy, and the frustrating attempt of simple believers to hold on to their faith unperturbed. The victory that takes place, as Hegel describes it, is not by force or argument, but by an almost unnoticeable universal change of atmosphere in which one reigning "idol" simply supplants another:

> Now the Enlightenment, as an invisible and subtle spirit, slinks through the honorable segments little by little, and soon has essentially achieved control of all the innards and organs of the unsuspecting idol. And then, "*on one*

---

[22]§475.

fine morning it gives the idols of its contemporaries a shove with the elbows, and crash! bam! the idol is lying on the floor." On *one fine morning*, whose noon is not bloody, as long as the infection has pervaded all the organs of spiritual/cultural life; then only memory still preserves the dead form of the previous stage of spirit, like a history that, somehow or other, has run its course. The new serpent of divine wisdom which is elevated for worship has thus, when you come down to it, merely painlessly shed its wrinkled old skin.[23]

The "new serpent of divine wisdom" held up for worship, in Hegel's analysis of the then-modern state of culture, is the Enlightenment. But there is a certain universality in the patterns he describes: Rather than a forceful and ugly confrontation between the new and the old, a gradual systematic profusion of the tokens and symbols of the new may bring about a seachange in the cultural landscape. In twentieth-century experience one thinks of the worldwide victory of Microsoft Windows over arguably better computer operating systems, simply by massive incentives to manufacturers and dealers to include Microsoft software; presumably even the prosecutors and judges involved in the antitrust suits against Microsoft were using the Windows operating system and Microsoft software in making up official documents for the trial! On the level of cultural values, one finds a similar example of social osmosis in the aftermath of the Kinseyean notions of sexuality. The publication of *Sexual Behavior of the Human Male* or *The Kinsey Report* in 1948, in spite of defective scientific methodology (excessive use of prostitutes, homosexuals, pedophiles, and sadists) and statistical inaccuracies, sold 185,000 copies in 1948, and began to change the way that people considered "normality" in sex. New norms bolstered the sexual revolution of the 1960s. Expressions from the 1950s like "dating" or "going steady" or "premarital sex" now sound quaint and outmoded, having given way completely to expressions like "being in a relationship" and "having a partner."

THE CHURCH OF CONSCIENCES

Hegel in the final parts of his section on "Morality,"[24] incorporates numerous ideas from Fichte's ethical writings, which are hardly discussed now,

---

[23]§545 Nun ein unsichtbarer und unbemerkter Geist, durchschleicht sie die edlen Teile durch und durch und hat sich bald aller Eingeweide und Glieder des bewußtlosen Götzen gründlich bemächtigt, und "*an einem schönen Morgen* gibt sie mit dem Ellbogen dem Kameraden einen Schub, und Bautz! Baradautz! der Götze liegt am Boden"—An *einem schönen Morgen*, dessen Mittag nicht blutig ist, wenn die Ansteckung alle Organe des geistigen Lebens durchdrungen hat; nur das Gedächtnis bewahrt dann noch als eine, man weiß nicht wie, vergangene Geschichte die tote Weise der vorigen Gestalt des Geistes auf; und die neue, für die Anbetung erhöhte Schlange der Weisheit hat auf diese Weise nur eine welke Haut schmerzlos abgestreift.
[24]Chapter VI.C, §§596 ff.

but were held in high regard by Hegel and idealist contemporaries who were searching for alternatives to Kantian moral theory. Fichte in one place makes a pointed comparison between a convergence of consciences and a church:

> The reciprocity amongst all rational beings for the purpose of producing common practical convictions, is called a *Church*, an ethical commonwealth. . . . All, necessarily, as sure as their destination is dear to them, are desirous to infuse their convictions into all others, and the union of all for this purpose is called the Church.[25]

Fichte in these passages is obviously trying to capture the essential nature of the social binding which takes place, for example, in a Christian congregation, and show that it has a much wider prevalence and applicability than in religion. The fundamental unifying factor, Fichte theorizes, is the powerful impetus of conscience, which leads individuals to seek out other like-minded "conscientious" persons to "convert" them and/or to join with them in spreading the "gospel" that has been revealed to them. Religious persons who may feel similar missionary impulses simply belong to a subset of the much larger category of ethically motivated "churches."

Hegel in the above-mentioned sections of the *Phenomenology* discusses the emergence of "Conscience"—a stage of consciousness which, like the Fichtean approach, does not characterize morality in the Kantian manner as a type of rational behavior combating and rising above all "natural inclinations," but rather emphasizes cultivation of a positive relationship of morality to deep-seated and inherently moral feelings. As this takes place in society, individuals begin to judge others, not by adherence to abstract notions of duty, but rather simply by their adherence to conscience. The conscientious way to justify oneself is not "I have fulfilled such-and-such a duty," but "this is what my conscience dictates." And such conscientious persons inevitably begin to join and collaborate with like-minded persons of conscience:

> Conscience, in the majesty of its elevation above definite law and all content of duty, puts forth its precious content in the form of its own knowing and willing; conscience is the moral genius, that knows the inner voice of its immediate knowledge to be a divine voice. . . . This solitary worship is simultaneously essentially *communal* worship, and the pure inner *self-knowledge* and sensitivity rises to the level of *consciousness* [about the community of consciences]: Conscience's

---

[25]Johann Gottlieb Fichte, *The Science of Ethics*, Kroger trans. (London: Kegan Paul, 1907), 248, 254.

self-intuition is *objective* existence for it, and this element of objectivity is the external expression of its knowing and willing as something *universal*.[26]

Conscientiousness, as Hegel portrays it, is an intensely subjective experience which also has an intersubjective "objective" aspect—the immediate empathetic sharing among those with like-minded consciences. (Hegel, in speaking of conscience rising to the "level of consciousness" is using "consciousness" in a technical sense, as necessarily oriented outward to some object, unlike *self*-consciousness.) The mutually empowering groupings of consciences envisioned by Hegel never need to refer to duties or laws; the only valid justification they require is the simple appeal to conscience. Contemporary twenty-first-century like-minded coteries that fit the Hegelian pattern might include committed pro-life and pro-choice groups, pro- and anti-gay marriage factions, and so forth. "Believing" members of such groups point to their advocacy as a matter of conscience, and stand together quasi-religiously in their positions, following the "divine voice" which they hear individually.

But unfortunately, Hegel notes, adherence to conscience inevitably and ironically leads to clashes of conscience:

> If [a "disreputable" person] compromises himself regarding his consciousness of duty, claiming that what his opponent claims to be evil, and absolutely incommensurable with the universal, is really a deed according to his inner law and conscience—in this one-sided assurance of identity with conscience there remains his non-identity with the other, who of course does not believe or recognize this "assurance."[27]

Hegel offers an arguably optimistic solution to this impasse: in the final paragraphs of the section on the "Beautiful Soul," as discussed above,[28] the persons who have diametrical differences in conscience end up admitting their inadequacies—their failure to get beyond merely abstract notions of right, or the fact that they acted without sufficient consideration of universals—and in mutual understanding and forgiveness bring about a new

---

[26]§§655, 656 Das Gewissen also in der Majestät seiner Erhabenheit über das bestimmte Gesetz und jeden Inhalt der Pflicht legt den beliebigen Inhalt in sein Wissen und Wollen; es ist die moralische Genialität, welche die innere Stimme ihres unmittelbaren Wissens als göttliche Stimme weiß. . . . Dieser einsame Gottesdienst ist zugleich wesentlich der Gottesdienst einer *Gemeinde*, und das reine innere sich selbst *Wissen* und Vernehmen geht zum Momente des *Bewußtseins* fort. Die Anschauung seiner ist sein *gegenständliches* Dasein, und dies gegenständliche Element ist das Aussprechen seines Wissens und Wollens als eines *Allgemeinen*. . . .

[27]§662 Wenn jenes sich gegen das Bewußtsein der Pflicht verleugnet und, was dieses für Schlechtigkeit, für absolute Ungleichheit mit dem Allgemeinen aussagt, als ein Handeln nach dem inneren Gesetze und Gewissen behauptet, so bleibt in dieser einseitigen Versicherung der Gleichheit seine Ungleichheit mit dem Anderen, da ja dieses sie nicht glaubt und nicht anerkennt.

[28]See p. 30.

potentiating of spirit, bringing about the presence of the divine in the midst of humanity. Hegel, no doubt fully cognizant that such world-changing reconciliations are anomalies in any era, ends the long chapter VI on "Spirit" on this idealistic note, and proceeds to chapter VII on "Religion."

THE FULFILLMENT OF RELIGION IN PHILOSOPHY

In Hegel's early religious writings, posthumously published, he gives indications that he is looking to religion for the final reconciliation of the dialectical oppositions that result from philosophical reflection.[29] But by the time he published the *Phenomenology* his position had undergone a complete reversal: it is rather philosophy that brings about the *final* reconciliation of oppositions remaining in religion. Religion indeed, especially the Christian religion, brings about important architectonic reconciliations between God and the world, good and evil, finite and infinite, divine and human. But the syntheses thus achieved are imbedded in the world of Spirit as imaginative representations—notions of Creation and the Fall, the redemption and atonement, the passion and resurrection of the God-man, and the emergence of the Christian community. These rich imaginative representations, institutionalized in doctrines and dogmas, supply the necessary and sufficient raw material for the emergence of a final *philosophical* reconciliation, in which the stage is set for overcoming the still-remaining opposition of religious "picture-thinking" to the philosophically-appropriate conceptual level:

> The content of religion expresses earlier in time than Science what Spirit is; but only [philosophical] Science is Spirit's true knowledge of itself.[30]

Religion cannot constitute the final state of Spirit's self-knowledge because of the very limitations of the types of representations and modes of expression which it must utilize:

> The religious community, insofar as it is in the first instance the substance of Absolute Spirit, is the unrefined consciousness which has the more barbarous and more difficult existence-here-and-now, the deeper its inner spirit is; and the deeper this inner spirit is, the harder is the job that its inarticulate self has with its essence—that content of its own consciousness which is foreign to it.[31]

---

[29]See GWF Hegel, *Early Theological Writings*, T.M. Knox trans. (Philadelphia: University of Pennsylvania Press, 1971), 312–13.

[30]§802 . . . Der Inhalt der Religion spricht . . . früher in der Zeit, als die Wissenschaft, es aus, was der Geist ist, aber diese ist allein sein wahres Wissen von ihm selbst.

[31]§803 Die religiöse Gemeine, insofern sie zuerst die Substanz des absoluten Geistes ist, ist das rohe Bewußtseyn, das ein um so barbarischeres und härteres Daseyn hat, je tiefer sein innerer Geist ist, und seyn dumpfes Selbst eine um so härtere Arbeit mit seinem Wesen, dem ihm fremden Inhalte seines Bewußtseyns.

It is only philosophy, which deals with concepts, and, most importantly, with the Concept of the unity-in-distinction of Being and Thought, that can bring about the final intelligible reconciliation between the distinctions and oppositions that are only partly reconciled as an inchoate "essence" in religious thinking.

Hegel's works, published and unpublished, from the time of the publication of the *Phenomenology* onward, offer us continual evidence that he consistently adhered to this philosophical ideal, taking religious truths as the springboard to systematic/scientific philosophical analysis. The clearest example of this tendency is found in his lectures on the philosophy of history. In the beginning of these lectures, Hegel delivers a trenchant criticism of theologians. He cites the scriptural injunction that we should "*know*, love and serve God," and then goes on to observe that

> In recent times Philosophy has been obliged to defend the domain of religion against the attacks of several theological systems. In the Christian religion God has revealed Himself—that is, he has given us to understand what He is; so that He is no longer a concealed or secret existence. And this possibility of knowing Him, thus afforded us, renders such knowledge a duty. God wishes no narrow-hearted souls or empty heads for his children; but those whose spirit is of itself indeed, poor, but rich in the knowledge of Him; and who regard this knowledge of God as the only valuable possession. That development of the thinking spirit, which has resulted from the revelation of the Divine Being as its original basis, must ultimately advance to the *intellectual* comprehension of what was presented, in the first instance, to *feeling* and *imagination*.[32]

Hegel then proceeds to apply this general optimism about the powers of human knowledge to the Christian doctrine of Divine Providence; he intends to do what the theologians have left undone—namely, show through rational analysis just *how* the workings of history have been providential:

> The time must eventually come for understanding that rich product of active Reason, which the History of the World offers to us. It was for awhile the fashion to profess admiration for the wisdom of God, as displayed in animals, plants, and isolated occurrences. But, if it be allowed that Providence manifests itself in such objects and forms of existence, why not also in Universal History? . . . Our mode of treating the subject is . . . a Theodicaea—a justification of the ways of God—which Leibnitz attempted metaphysically, in his method, i.e. in indefinite abstract categories—so that the ill that is found in the World may be comprehended, and the thinking Spirit reconciled with the fact of the existence of

---

[32]G.W.F. Hegel, *The Philosophy of History*, Sibree trans. (New York: Dover, 1956), 15.

evil. Indeed, nowhere is such a harmonizing view more pressingly demanded than in Universal History. . . .[33]

The same systematic "methodology" of raising religious truths to their higher conceptual level is found in Hegel's other works. The *Phenomenology* itself is described as a conceptual recapitulation of the crucifixion of the Mystical Body of Christ, the "Golgotha of Absolute Spirit";[34] Hegel describes his *Logic* as the conceptualization of the "life of God before the creation of the world,"[35] and (reflecting his lifelong interest in developing the earthly implications of the Christian doctrine of the "kingdom of God") he describes the political sections of his *Philosophy of Right* as "the march of God through the world."[36]

Theologian Karl Barth characterizes Hegel as the "Protestant Aquinas," in view of his systematic philosophical reconsideration of key Christian doctrines.[37] This is true to a certain extent. Hegel, like Thomas Aquinas, had a firm confidence in the compatibility between reason and the truths of faith, and the ability of faith to serve as a foundation for progress in reason. But for Aquinas and medieval scholastics in general, philosophy was the "handmaid" of theology, clarifying its meanings and implications. For Hegel, as has been indicated above, the relationship between theology and philosophy was reversed, theology being the handmaid encompassing the revealed *Vorstellungen* of the major accomplishments of Spirit. It is these *Vorstellungen* that supply "grist for the mill" of systematic speculative philosophy.

---

[33]*Philosophy of History*, 15.

[34]§808, ". . . die Schädelstätte des absoluten Geistes. . . ."

[35]G. W. F. Hegel, *Wissenschaft der Logik* I, in *Werke in zwanzig Bänden* (Frankfurt am Main: Suhrkamp Verlag, 1969 [hereafter referred to as *Werke*]), Vol 5, 44.

[36]G. W. F. Hegel, *Grundlinien der Philosophie des Rechts*, *Werke*, Vol. 5, §259, Addition, 403.

[37]See Barth's *Protestant Thought: From Rousseau to Ritschl*, Brian Cozzens, trans. (New York: Simon & Schuster, 1969), 268, 280.

4

Kierkegaard and the *Phenomenology*

In a previous book,[1] I discussed the manifold ways in which Karl Marx attempted to utilize Hegelian methodology, reinterpreting or reapplying Hegelian concepts in his political-economic theorizing. Marx drew heavily upon Hegel's *Logic*, *Philosophy of Right*, and *Phenomenology of Spirit*, usually in an implicit manner, but sometimes with explicit reference to Hegel, whose influence loomed pervasively over 19th century philosophical and political thought in a unique fashion. Marx in one work even offers us a paragraph-by-paragraph analysis, critique, and reinterpretation of the political sections of Hegel's *Philosophy of Right*.[2] And Mark Meaney recently published extensive and detailed evidence concerning the possibility that Marx modeled his *Grundrisse*, section-by-section, on Hegel's *Science of Logic*.[3] Marx's use of Hegel in writing *Capital* is not just a matter of speculation or circumstantial evidence. In his Postface to the Second Edition of *Capital*, Marx explicitly acknowledges his indebtedness to Hegel:

> When I was working at the first volume of *Capital* . . . , I openly avowed myself the pupil of that mighty thinker, and even, here and there in the chapter on the theory of value, coquetted with the mode of expression peculiar to him. The mystification which the dialectic suffers in Hegel's hands by no means prevents him from being the first to present its general forms of motion in a comprehensive and conscious manner.[4]

[1]*Paradox, Dialectic and System: a Contemporary Reconstruction of the Hegelian Problematic* (University Park, PA: Pennsylvania State University Press, 1988), 66–74.

[2]See Marx's *Critique of Hegel's "Philosophy of Right,"* O'Malley and Jolin trans. (Cambridge: Cambridge University Press, 1970).

[3]See *Capital as Organic Unity : the Role of Hegel's* Science of Logic *in Marx's* Grundrisse (Dordrecht: Kluwer, 2002).

[4]*Capital,* Fowkes trans. (New York: Vintage Books, 1977), 102.

Søren Kierkegaard was also a prominent nineteenth century disciple of Hegel, but owned up to Hegelian influences on his thinking only very belatedly, and with considerable nuance and qualifications:

> I feel what for me at times is an enigmatical respect for Hegel; I have learned much from him, and I know very well that I can still learn much more from him when I return to him again. The only thing I give myself credit for is sound natural capacities and a certain honesty which is armed with a sharp eye for the comical. I have lived and perhaps am uncommonly tried in the *casibus* of life; in the confidence that an open road for thought might be found there, I have resorted to philosophical books and among them Hegel's. But right here he leaves me in the lurch. His philosophical knowledge, his amazing learning, the insight of his genius, and everything else good that can be said of a philosopher I am willing to acknowledge as any disciple.—Yet, no, not acknowledge—that is too distinguished an expression—willing to admire, willing to learn from him. But, nevertheless, it is no less true that someone who is really tested in life, who in his need resorts to thought, will find Hegel comical despite all his greatness.[5]

Kierkegaard's acquaintance with Hegel is much harder than Marx's to pin down. With Marx, we have notebooks summarizing various writings of Hegel, especially the *Logic*.[6] I have not been able to find any such notes on primary Hegelian sources penned by Kierkegaard. Much of Kierkegaard's knowledge of Hegel seems to have been derived from secondary sources.

Jon Stewart traces most of the Hegelian influences on Kierkegaard through Danish works in theology and philosophy, particularly the works of J. L. Heiberg and H. L. Martensen, in which Hegel's influence predominated. Stewart observes: "overt and frequent discussions of Hegel's philosophy" are to be found in *Concept of Irony, Fear and Trembling, Concept of Anxiety, Prefaces, Concluding Unscientific Postscript, Book on Adler*. In addition, he categorizes as "Implicitly concerned with similar issues treated by Hegel," or as using Hegelian methodology or language, the following works: *Papers of One Still Living, Either/Or, Johannes Climacus, or De omnibus dubitandum est, Repetition, Philosophical Fragments, Sickness unto Death*.[7]

But almost all of Kierkegaard's *explicit* references to Hegel are criticisms. His complaints are often about the allegedly impersonal systematic excesses of Hegel's logic. But he also had other quibbles. Hegel, accord-

---

[5]*Søren Kierkegaard's Journals and Papers,* edited and translated by Howard V. Hong and Edna H. Hong, Assisted by Gregor Malantschuk (Bloomington and London: Indiana University Press, 1970), Volume 2, number 1608, 221.

[6]See Joseph O'Malley, "Marx's Precis of Hegel's Doctrine on Being in the Minor Logic." *International Review of Social History*, Vol. XXII (1977), Part 3, 423–31.

[7]*Kierkegaard's Relations to Hegel Reconsidered* (Cambridge: Cambridge University Press, 2003), 35.

ing to Kierkegaard, did not appreciate faith as an "immediacy," and, in fact, wanted to "mediate" everything; favored the universal over the individual, and the external over the internal; had no ethics, to speak of; tried to do away with all transcendence; and misunderstood the nature of concreteness.

Kierkegaard scarcely ever refers explicitly to Hegel's *Phenomenology.* The only exception I can think of is his section on "The Unhappiest Man" in Volume One of *Either/Or*, which I will discuss below. Nevertheless, there seem to be a number of parallels or reinterpretations, where Kierkegaard does not say, in effect, "now Hegel had it wrong, here's how it should have been put," or "here's the way things really are, though misunderstood by Hegel"—but where there is weighty circumstantial evidence that he has passages from Hegel's *Phenomenology* in mind. As Stewart indicates, these cases appear mostly in Kierkegaard's early "aesthetic" writings—*Either/Or, Repetition, Fear and Trembling, The Concept of Anxiety, The Sickness unto Death*, and *The Stages on Life's Way*—works where he is speaking through pseudonyms. In what follows, I will discuss the Kierkegaardian positions in which the influence of Hegel's *Phenomenology* seems most likely.

BORROWINGS

Speech as oriented exclusively towards universality:

There are a couple of cases in which Kierkegaard simply takes over important ideas in Hegel's *Phenomenology*. In Hegel's treatment of Sense-Certainty, as mentioned in chapter 1, Hegel emphasizes the difficulty or even impossibility of understanding particulars or "Thises." He challenges the reader to refer by speech to some particular "This" in speech or writing, and demonstrates that language cannot handle particulars, but can only express universals. Similarly Kierkegaard emphasizes the necessary connection of language with the universal in order to explain why Abraham, under the unique immediate impetus of faith, is, and must be, silent in carrying out God's command to sacrifice Isaac:

> Abraham cannot be mediated, and the same thing can be expressed also by saying that he cannot talk. So soon as I talk I express the universal, and if I do not do so, no one can understand me.[8]

---

[8]*Fear and Trembling*, Walter Lowrie trans. (Princeton, NJ: Princeton University Press, 1974), 70.

The Biblical Abraham, an individual chosen to undergo a paradigmatic test of faith, can offer no rationale, no justification for what he is doing. He is enveloped in a paradox which is outside the parameters of universal ethical rules.

Stoical withdrawal into self:

Hegel in chapter IV of the *Phenomenology* analyzes Stoicism as a philosophical attempt to arrive at freedom from external contingencies, by focusing purely on abstract conceptual determinations, using the power of thought to gain control over particulars.[9] Kierkegaard in similar fashion describes the initial stage of the ethical "choice of oneself" as a stoical movement:

> The first form which the choice [of oneself] takes is complete isolation. . . . [The individual's] action has no relation to any surrounding world, for he has reduced this to naught and exists only for himself. The life view here revealed . . . found expression in Greece in the effort of the single individual to develop himself into a paragon of virtue. . . . He withdrew from the activities of life . . . to act . . . in himself. . . . The fault lay in the fact that this individual had chosen himself altogether abstractly.[10]

Hegel's analysis of Stoicism is epistemologically oriented—focusing on the way that the Stoic deals with reality, in a sense disarming a reality which seems alien, and bringing it under control by the power of thought. Hegel's treatment follows immediately on the Master-Slave dialectic in the *Phenomenology*, and Hegel mentions that Stoicism functions as a state which finally overcomes the Master-Slave impasse. Thus there are also ethical implications, and Kierkegaard brings these out explicitly. What Hegel and Kierkegaard have in common regarding the Stoic mindset is a critique of excessive abstractness. The Stoic in Hegel's portrayal tries, but is ultimately unsuccessful, in controlling messy empirical realities, and passes into a stage of skepticism. The Stoic in Kierkegaard's interpretation is deficient insofar as he makes a merely abstract "choice of self." This is the beginning of the ethical "choice," but only the beginning. One enters into the ethical stage only if and when he passes from this abstract beginning to the choice of oneself in all concreteness and in the context of the real empirical circumstances of his life. Thus Kierkegaard envisions the possibility of a more sanguine aftermath to an individual's "stoical" phase.

---

[9]See my *Hegel's Phenomenology, Part I: Analysis and Commentary* (Athens: Ohio University Press, 1988), 91–93.

[10]*Either/Or* II, Lowrie trans. (Garden City, NY: Doubleday Anchor, 1959), 244–245.

AN INTERESTING PARALLEL

I can think of one case in which, although Kierkegaard is probably not borrowing from Hegel, and very likely was not familiar with the passages in question, nevertheless develops, like Hegel, the idea of "giving birth to one's own father" in the religious/spiritual order. Hegel arrives at this paradoxical concept towards the end of his discussion of the emergence of the [Christian] religious community after the death on the Cross of the God-man:

> Just as the individual God-man had a self-existent [*ansichseienden*] Father, and only a "real" mother; so in converse manner the universal man-God, i.e., the religious community, has its own action and knowledge as its "father," but for a "mother" has *eternal love*; a love which it only *feels*, but does not [yet] encounter as an actualized immediate *object* of its consciousness.[11]

Kierkegaard, discussing the transition of the individual Christian to faith, offers the following observation:

> In the world of spirit . . . an eternal divine order prevails. . . . He who will not work does not get the bread. . . . Here it is of no use to have Abraham for one's father, nor to have seventeen ancestors—he who will not work . . . gives birth to wind, but he who is willing to work gives birth to his own father.[12]

In Hegel's analysis, the religious community through the power of the Spirit after Jesus' death is able to generate itself as the ultimate religious *Gestalt*; awaiting its final objectification as eternal love eventually becomes explicit in it. For Kierkegaard, each individual must beget himself spiritually in such a way as to pave the way for the divine operations that will lead him to make the "leap of faith."

REINTERPRETATIONS

1. The *Three Stages*:

According to Mark Taylor,[13] Kierkegaard's threefold division of the aesthetic, ethical, and religious stages of life is modeled on Hegel's division

---

[11]See my *Hegel's Phenomenology, Part II: the Evolution of Ethical and Religious Consciousness to the Dialectical Standpoint* (Athens: Ohio University Press, 1983, 170.

[12]*Fear and Trembling*, 70.13. See *Journeys to Selfhood* (Berkeley: University of California Press, 1980), 230–231.

[13]See *Journeys to Selfhood* (Berkeley: University of California Press, 1980), 230–231.

of the *Phenomenology of Spirit* into natural consciousness (chapter I–V), Ethical Consciousness (chapter VI), and Religious Consciousness (chapter VII). I think it is unlikely that Kierkegaard had this in mind. Hegel's *Phenomenology as a whole* is concerned with the development of "natural consciousness" eventually to the standpoint of "Absolute Knowledge," and Hegel does not characterize chapters I–V specifically as the phenomenology of "natural consciousness." Chapter VI is indeed concerned with the "big picture" of "Spirit," evolving from ethnical solidarity (*Sittlichkeit*) through morality to religion. But Hegel's chapter VII on Religion is to a great extent connected with aesthetics under the rubric of "Art Religion," as well as natural consciousness under the rubric of "Nature Religion," and so would seem to be relevant just as much to Kierkegaard's "aesthetic stage" as to his "religious stage." I think it is more likely that Kierkegaard had in mind the basic triad that keeps reappearing in more and more sophisticated forms throughout the *Phenomenology*—the triad of immediacy or the "in-itself," reflectivity or the "for-itself," and sublation or supersession, i.e., the "in-and-for itself." Kierkegaard's alternative triad, however, lacking "mediation" and "synthesis," was meant as an antidote to Hegelianism: involving no necessary dialectical movements from one stage to the other, but spiritual transitions earmarked with freedom, from aesthetic immediacy, to (nonmediated) ethical reflectiveness, and finally to religious transcendence.

2. Determinate Negation:

Hegel, in discussing his methodology in the *Phenomenology*, focuses on the principle of "determinate negation" as the springboard which leads consciousness from one stage to a dialectically higher stage.[14] Hegel's supposition is that, as one examines the various claims of knowledge, he will eventually arrive at shortcomings or deficiencies, which will supply the impetus to search for more satisfactory claims, obviating the former limitations. Kierkegaard in his essay on "The Rotation Method" in *Either/Or*, claims to apply a similar principle to the committed aesthete's problem of "how to avoid boredom."[15] Kierkegaard's adaptation of "determinate negation" is the principle that boredom itself supplies the necessary and sufficient springboard to maximizing aesthetic experiences. "This principle," says Kierkegaard, "possesses the quality of being in the highest degree

---

[14]See the Introduction to the *Phenomenology*, §79.
[15]See *Either/Or*, Vol I, 234ff.

repellent. . . . Whoever has this principle back of him cannot but receive an infinite impetus forward, to help him make new discoveries."[16] In this essay, Kierkegaard then begins to enumerate the potential species of boredom that have to be avoided, and the specially productive (repulsive) types of boredom that can lead the dedicated aesthete to proper variegations of pleasurable experiences.

3. Faith:

Hegel, in section VI.B.II.a on "The Struggle of Enlightenment with Superstition," makes a sharp contrast between the position of religious believers and the proponents of the French Enlightenment, who oppose them and are winning the victory over faith. He writes, "Faith is Spirit itself, which gives its own testimony about itself, just as forcefully in the inwardness of the individual consciousness as through the universal presence of the Faith of the whole religious community in this Spirit."[17] Kierkegaard *almost* seems to be adopting this Hegelian position when he observes: "By faith I understand here what Hegel somewhere in his way correctly calls the inner certainty that anticipates infinity.[18] *Almost*, but not quite. Although both Kierkegaard and Hegel view faith as founded in the inner testimony of spirit, two important differences of emphasis remain: For Kierkegaard, the focus is exclusively on the individual, whereas for Hegel, faith is an aspect of Spirit emerging not only in the individual but communally, as a counterpoise to the communal expansion of dialectically proficient Reason; in other words, the two thinkers interpret the parameters of "inwardness" differently.[19] Also, it goes without saying that Hegel's final subsumption of faith and religion under "Absolute Knowledge" at the conclusion of the *Phenomenology* is out of the question for Kierkegaard.[20]

---

[16]*Either/Or*, 234.

[17]*Phenomenology* §554.

[18]*The Concept of Anxiety: a Simple Psychologically Orienting Deliberation on the Dogmatic Issue of Hereditary Sin*, Reidar Thomte trans. (Princeton, NJ: Princeton University Press, 1980), 157.

[19]See *Fear and Trembling*, 79, where Kierkegaard criticizes Hegel for not realizing that the inwardness of faith is higher than externality. Hegel speaks of the "inwardness" of the religious community, but Kierkegaard characterizes this pejoratively as "Christendom"—a form of externality.

[20]It is interesting that Hegel himself, in his early religious writings, would agree with Kierkegaard that religion "trumps" philosophical knowledge. But by the time of the writing of the *Phenomenology* Hegel's position underwent a reversal: "Absolute knowledge" reaches its zenith in raising the imaginative "picture-thinking" of religion to the philosophical/conceptual level. See earlier discussion, pp. 47–49.

4. The "Task":

Hegel in chapter V.C.a. on "The Spiritual/Animal Realm and Disenchantment: or Rational Reality [*die Sache selbst*],"[21] describes the movements of individuality to find fulfillment in the accomplishment of its tasks (*Werke*), but eventually, through an educative process which involves much misapprehension or deceit, finds that its task in life does not have to do with some external realization:

> An individuality proceeds to accomplish something; it seems in this way to have brought something into realization; it acts, becomes, in its action, for-another, and all this seems to it to have to do with reality. . . . [But] the "rational reality" that emerges ceases to be related as a "predicate" and to be characterized as a lifeless abstract universality; rather, it is substance, completely permeated by the individuality; and it is the subject in which individuality is just as much itself, or *this* particular individual, as it is *all* individuals.[22]

In other words, the true "task" of the acting consciousness is to activate its own universal individuality.

Kierkegaard through the voice of "Judge William" makes a statement about the task which bears a superficial resemblance to Hegel's assessment:

> He who lives aesthetically is the accidental man; he believes himself to be the perfect man by reason of the fact that he is the only man. . . . He who lives ethically has himself as his task. His self in its immediacy is accidentally determined, and the task is to work up together the accidental and the universal. . . . To be the one man . . . in such a way that he is also the universal man is the true art of living.[23]

But while the idea of combining individuality and universality is found in both cases, Kierkegaard's approach differs markedly. While Hegel locates the

---

[21]The rendition of *die Sache selbst* in the *Phenomenology* has traditionally posed a problem for translators. In the 1970 Hegel Symposium at Marquette University, almost the entire "Round-Table Discussion on Problems of Translating Hegel" (see *The Legacy of Hegel*, J. O'Malley et al, eds. [The Hague: Nijoff, 1973]) focused on possible solutions to this problem. A literal translation, e.g., "the fact of the matter," does not bring out the technical meaning of the term in this chapter, which is meant to contrast with the Kantian notion of *Ding* ("thing"). I am following a cue from Hegel himself, who in the first sentence of his Introduction to the *Phenomenology* characterizes *die Sache selbst* as *das wirkliche Erkennen dessen, was in Wahrheit ist*, "the real cognition of the truly existent," which implies reality conformed to reason. See also my discussion of this term in *PSK*, xiv–xv, 2n.

[22]*Phenomenology*, §§417–418: Eine Individualität geht also, etwas auszuführen; sie scheint damit etwas *zur Sache* gemacht zu haben; sie handelt, wird darin für andere, und es scheint ihr um die *Wirklichkeit* zu tun zu sein. . . . Die Sache selbst verliert dadurch das Verhältnis des Prädikats und die Bestimmtheit lebloser abstrakter Allgemeinheit, sie ist vielmehr die von der Individualität durchdrungene Substanz, das Subjekt, worin die Individualität ebenso als sie selbst oder als *diese* wie als *alle* Individuen ist.

[23]*Either/Or* II, 260–261.

fundamental human task in individual coordination with the universal social "substance," for Kierkegaard, the attainment of "universality" is the job strictly relegated to the individual—"becoming oneself," i.e., each single individual realizing his/her own *ideal* self.

5. The Unhappy Consciousness:

The only *explicit* reference in Kierkegaard's "aesthetic" writings to Hegel's *Phenomenology* is found in his essay, "The Unhappiest Man."[24] But Kierkegaard's wording of this reference is somewhat puzzling. Kierkegaard says, "in each of Hegel's systematic writings there is a section in which he treats of the unhappy consciousness."[25] This is puzzling, because the *Phenomenology* is not generally considered one of Hegel's "systematic" writings, but rather an introduction to his later System, finally embodied in his *Science of Logic* and *Encyclopedia of the Philosophical Sciences.* There are however, contemporary interpreters who consider the *Phenomenology* a part of Hegel's system, in the sense that it is a "system of consciousness, or the system as reflected in consciousness;[26] and Hegel himself in the 1817 *Science of Logic,* Part I, Book I, refers to his earlier *Phenomenology* as "the science of the experience of consciousness."[27] Possibly Kierkegaard meant something similar. But the additional implication that there are other "systematic writings," in which the "unhappy consciousness" reappears also is puzzling. In any case, Kierkegaard's essay clearly has the "Unhappy Consciousness" of Hegel's *Phenomenology* in its purview.

In the *Phenomenology,* the "Unhappy Consciousness," as described in chapter 2, is a type of consciousness that emerges in the aftermath of stoicism and skepticism, and is characterized by a kind of spiritual schizophrenia—an empirical consciousness rooted in contingency and changeability, but projecting an aspect of itself as a separate transcendent unchangeable and universal self. Kierkegaard describes a similar quasi-schizophrenic psyche:

> The unhappy person is one who has his ideal, the content of his life, the fullness of his consciousness, the essence of his being, in some manner outside of himself. He is always absent, never present to himself. But it is evident that it is pos-

---

[24]See *Either/Or* I, 179ff.

[25]*Either/Or,* 181.

[26]See, for example, Denise Souche-Dagues, *Le cercle hégélien* (Paris: Presses Universitaires de France, 1986), 17.

[27]See Part I, Book I: "Die Phänomenologie des Geistes [ist] die Wissenschaft des Bewußtseins. . . . Die Logik hat insofern die Wissenschaft des erscheinenden Geistes zu ihrer Voraussetzung, welche die Notwendigkeit und damit den Beweis der Wahrheit des Standpunkts, der das reine Wissen ist, wie dessen Vermittlung überhaupt enthält und aufzeigt."

sible to be absent from one's self either in the past or in the future. This, then, at
once circumscribes the entire territory of the unhappy consciousness. For this
rigid limitation we are grateful to Hegel.[28]

But Kierkegaard, not completely constrained by such a rigid limitation, proceeds to expand the concept in ways Hegel would not have thought of. Offering us a largely psychological reinterpretation of an "unhappy consciousness," Kierkegaard continues: There are two ways a person could be absent
from his present self: either by living in the past, or in the future. Though
these two types are indeed unhappy, even unhappier would be the man who
lives in a future which is constantly denied him, i.e., who is continually being frustrated in his hopes; or the man who lives in a past which was never
permitted to be his, e.g., the man who had no childhood, and in later life turns
back on himself looking for memories of his childhood. But there can be no
doubt but that the unhappiest man of all is one who is frustrated by memories
in his hopes *and* by hopes in his memories; i.e., who finds that his hopes still
consist of things he had already done, or failed to do, in the past—and which
cannot be relived; and who finds that his memories consist of dreams of the
future which he has had in the past, mere anticipations of thought which
ought to be hoped for rather than remembered. Such a man as this, concludes
Kierkegaard, is the one whose life is death. But Kierkegaard then ends with
the enigmatic question: who shall not say that the death of such a person is
life, and his unhappiness the greatest of happiness?

6. Transformation of a Servile Consciousness:

Towards the beginning of Chapter IV in the *Phenomenology*, Hegel describes
a primitive form of intersubjective relationship, the "Lord/Bondsman" dialectic. In Hegel's formulation, this is essentially a dysfunctional relationship
in which one party, the *self*-consciousness, achieves freedom and recognition
at the expense of the other party, an objective type of consciousness, which
has been historically bested in battle, traded its freedom for survival, and sac-
rificed personal recognition for a kind of vicarious recognition by projecting
its implicit freedom on the Lord and Master. This extremely uneven relationship arrives at a denouement when the slave, driven by fear of the master to
shield the master from needing to work on the objective world, ultimately arrives at the stage of *absolute* anxiety, a fear of fear, a negation of the negation, which amounts to a positive state of self-consciousness and emancipation from servile consciousness.[29] In Kierkegaard's version, the individual in

---

[28]*Either/Or*, 181.
[29]*Phenomenology*, §194. See earlier discussion, p. 20.

bondage to sin, and existing in a state of anxiety as he confronts his sinless Lord, finally reaches a depth of absolute anxiety which can help supply the springboard for making the leap of faith. Kierkegaard explains:

> By faith I understand . . . what Hegel somewhere in his way correctly calls the inner certainty that anticipates infinity. When the discoveries of possibility are honestly administered, possibility will discover all the finitudes, but it will idealize them in the form of infinity and in anxiety overwhelm the individual until he again overcomes them in the anticipation of faith. . . . Anxiety enters into his soul and searches out everything and anxiously torments everything finite and petty out of him, and then it leads him where he wants to go. . . . The individual through anxiety is educated unto faith. . . .[30]

7. The "outer" as expression of the "inner":

Hegel in chapter V of the *Phenomenology* examines Reason (*Vernunft*), the technical meaning for which (in Hegel's philosophy) is the coordination and union of subject and object, thought and being. The first long segment of this chapter, entitled "Observation," is often overlooked by Hegel scholars, since it contains some outdated scientific ideas, but on the whole it leads up inexorably to a perennial problem in philosophy—the relationship of mind to brain. Hegel arrives at the mind-brain problematic gradually by systematically considering all the putative connections between the "inner" and the "outer"—in inorganic nature, plants and animals, and finally in humans. He concludes that if we want to see an outer which is a true expression of the inner in humans, we have to go beyond analysis of the brain and other physical aspects of humans, and concentrate on their activities. Then he proceeds to examine various human activities, and finds smaller and smaller discrepancies between the inner intentions and the outer manifestations, until he arrives at the universal "task" (mentioned above).

Kierkegaard in the beginning of *Either/Or* likewise starts with a search for coordination between the inner and the outer. Kierkegaard's pseudonym, "Victor Eremita," explains that he had often doubted the philosophical maxim that the exterior corresponds with the interior and vice versa, and looked for evidence to support his doubts. "Victor Eremita" narrates that he came by accident on some manuscripts consisting of letters from a magistrate named William and aesthetical writings from a young man. In reading and editing these manuscripts he was quite struck by the way in which they seemed to confirm his doubts about a certain lack of correspondence evident in both of

---

[30]*The Concept of Anxiety*, 157, 159.

these persons: some discrepancy in B (William), whose exterior expression seems to be too commonplace in comparison with his spiritual depth; but a much greater discrepancy in A (the sensuous young man), in whom a serious disconnect between interior and exterior is seen.[31] Kierkegaard's ethical exploration towards the end of the second volume of *Either/Or* proceeds ultimately to expound on the question about what might be the most successful consonance between inner and outer, and what the fully integrated ethical person might be like.

8. Sensuality as a result of Christianity:

As mentioned in chapter 2, Hegel, in the section entitled "The Unhappy Consciousness" in chapter IV of the *Phenomenology*, offers a phenomenological analysis of the attempts of a consciousness, overwhelmed by its sense of contingency and changeableness, to project its own dimly-perceived, implicit unity upon "the Unchangeable." This section is replete with religious imagery, and has led interpreters to suggest multiple references to Judaism, Christianity, the Trinity, and so forth. In the middle of Hegel's analysis, following imagery of the fruitless quest of Crusaders to find fulfillment in the reconquest of the burial site of the God-man (the "Holy Sepulcher"), Hegel proceeds into imagery of medieval Catholicism—monks entering into sequestered religious life and trying to attain unity with the Absolute through devotional rituals and acts of self-mortification. Hegel then describes how their attempts to mortify their flesh through various means leads to the diametrical opposite:

> Consciousness in its animal functions is aware of itself as "this real individual consciousness". . . . It is in these functions that the Fiend reveals himself in his own distinctive form. But this Fiend generates himself in his very subjugation. Thus consciousness, establishing this Fiend solidly within itself, abides constantly by his side rather than being liberated from him, and envisions itself as constantly polluted.[32]

In Hegel's view, this experience of sensual pollution brings consciousness to a dialectical extreme which forces it to look for mediation and, as the

---

[31]See *Either/Or*, Preface.

[32]*Phenomenology*, §225: Seiner als *dieses wirklichen Einzelnen*, ist das Bewußtseyn sich in den thierischen Functionen bewußt. . . . Sie es sind, in welchen sich der Feind in seiner eigenthümlichen Gestalt zeigt. . . . Indem aber dieser Feind in seiner Niederlage sich erzeugt, das Bewußtseyn, da es sich ihn fixirt, vielmehr statt frey davon zu werden, immer dabey verweilt, und sich immer verunreinigt erblickt.

monastic imagery wanes in the background, eventually gives it the impetus towards the next "stage" of consciousness, i.e., Reason.

Kierkegaard's essay, "The Immediate Stages of the Erotic, or the Musical Erotic: Insignificant Introduction,"[33] functions almost as an application of this Hegelian insight. Kierkegaard observes that "sensuous genius" before Christianity was not a separate entity determined as yet as such by spirit—but only psychically determined, in a harmonious and comely manner. After Christianity, however, when spirit had been manifested in the world, the opposite pole of spirit—namely, sensuality—was at the same instance spiritually determined into a true *entity*, as the opposite of spirit. In this sense it is true to say that "Christianity brought sensuality into the world." Kierkegaard observes that this erotic force, unleashed by Christianity itself is illustrated, for example, by the constant impulsiveness and carefree lack of reflection of Don Juan in Mozart's opera, *Don Giovanni*.

9. The Knight of Faith:

Hegel's "Knight of Virtue," discussed in chapter 2 of the present book, is a type of consciousness enamored of universal ideals, and willing to promote these ideals even to the extreme of moralism. Kierkegaard, in his book *Fear and Trembling*, interprets Hegel's Knight of Virtue as just one more Hegelian defense of universality, but does not fully appreciate the irony in Hegel's analysis—the fact that the Knight of Virtue ends up as a somewhat comical character, promoting an idealism that is "out of bounds" for the real *Weltlauf*. Hegel's analysis is moving forward, in its own way, to the concept of true individuality, a "universal individuality" to which the Knight of Virtue's strivings were just admirable but unsuccessful approximations.

Kierkegaard counterposes to Hegel's Knight of Virtue his own protagonist, the "Knight of Faith," typified by the biblical Abraham, a religious hero who achieves a religiously-determined individuality completely outside the parameters of the Hegelian system. The Knight of Faith, embedded in a one-to-one relationship with God, cannot be encompassed by any of the generalities of ethics or philosophical categories. He typifies not only the essence of the religious stage in Kierkegaard's philosophy, but the highest pinnacle of individuality. One might even say that this is the special case showing the convergence of individuality and religious faith. And the highly individualized Knight of Faith, in Kierkegaard's portrayal, is an image of absolute seriousness—far removed from the "comical" aspects of Hegel's Knight of Virtue.

---

[33]*Either/Or* I.

The parallels listed above do not constitute any "smoking gun" indicating that Kierkegaard, perhaps like Karl Marx in writing the *Grundrisse*,[34] had the pages of Hegel's work lying open in front of him, as a convenient reference, as he went ahead with his own writings. But they seem to offer some provocative "circumstantial evidence" that Kierkegaard, perhaps unconsciously but probably intentionally, did have many of the best-known Hegelian images in view, as foils to be contested and bested, in the early stages of his own writing. The passage cited from *Journals and Papers* toward the beginning of this chapter is just about the only place where Kierkegaard acknowledges a familiarity with Hegel's thought, and the fact that he was impressed with the scope of Hegel's system. This admission seems grudging, in comparison with Marx's admission, also cited, that he was actually influenced by Hegel in his ideas and styles of presentation. The parallels I have pointed out seem to indicate a lack of consciousness on Kierkegaard's part of the extent of his Hegelian rootedness, or a lack of "full disclosure"—especially in view of the frequent criticisms of Hegel and Hegelians, for which he is most often noted.

---

[34]Mark Meaney, in his book mentioned above, leads us to conjecture that such an open book may have been the reality in Marx's case.

5

Hegel's Unsystematic Systematization

HAERING'S THESIS

Disputes about the unity of structure of the *Phenomenology* have continued unabated for many decades. For someone reading the *Phenomenology* and perusing the middle and later parts of the book for the first time, the book may seem to lack organization—unexpected expansions of concepts that may go on for several pages, overt or covert historical or literary allusions that do not seem immediately relevant. After some further reading, one might conclude that this early work of Hegel's is an example of broad erudition, but lacks the highly systematic approach that typifies Hegel's later works—for example, the *Encyclopedia Logic*, which proceeds through the major divisions of Being, Essence, and Concept, each division having subdivisions, each subdivision having further subdivisions, and so forth.

Theodore Haering developed this initial impression of lack of systematicity in Hegel into an interpretative position known as "Haering's thesis," first propounded at a Hegel Congress in 1933, and repeated in subsequent works and addresses.[1] According to Haering, Hegel, as indicated in the Introduction to the *Phenomenology*, planned by means of this work to provide an entry into philosophical science, but also *completed* this objective in the first two large sections (A. Consciousness and B. Self-Consciousness), and in the first few pages of the third section (C. Reason). But the *Phenomenology* proceeds

---

[1]See *Die Entstehungsgeschichte der Phänomenologie des Geistes* in *Verhandlungen des 3. Hegel-knogresses*, B. Wigersma, ed. (Tübingen, 1934), 118–138, and *Hegel, sein Wollen und sein Werk: eine chronologische Entwicklungsgeschichte der Gedanken und der Sprache Hegels* (Stuttgart: Scientia Verlag Aalen, 1963), 479ff.

much further beyond those first pages of section C. According to Haering, Hegel decided to add hundreds of pages which went seriously beyond his initial intentions, and in fact, if we judge from the internal evidence of these later additions, seems to have lost control over the work. The wide influence of Haering's thesis during the 20th century may help explain the fact that into the 1960s most Hegelian scholarship focused on Hegel's *Science of Logic* and other later works, while the comparatively few analyses and commentaries on the *Phenomenology* generally concentrated on the first sections, in which the organization of the work is more readily apparent.

DISCERNMENTS OF UNITY

The definitive refutation of Haering's thesis came from Otto Pöggeler, who in a 1961 article concluded that "there is no evidence that permits us to corroborate the assertion that the *Phenomenology* originally should have progressed only to the chapter on Reason."[2] Pöggeler surmised that Haering had arrived erroneously at his thesis by examining a later summary of the *Phenomenology* that Hegel had written for high school students, and also a subsection on "Phenomenology" that appeared in his later *Encyclopedia of Philosophical Sciences*, and concluding that the shortened form in these later works indicated a tacit admission that the earlier work had gone too far. Pöggeler allows that Hegel — like many authors — may not have adhered rigidly to his initial intentions as regards approach, contents to be included, and so forth; but concludes that there is strong evidence, internal and external, that Hegel originally intended the work to include all the ensuing subsections of the long Chapter V on Reason, as well as chapters VI, VII, and VIII on Spirit, Religion, and Absolute Knowledge.

   In several of my own books on Hegel, I have offered a detailed analysis of the organization of the *Phenomenology* showing a strict adherence to systematic structure from beginning to end. In my first commentary on the *Phenomenology* I offered two methods for interpreting the structure: The first is in terms of the various levels of the relationship between the in-itself and the for-itself, leading even to extremely complex developments such as the in-and-for-itself, in-itself, for-itself, and so forth;[3] the second method tabulates the progression of self-bounded and other-bounded subject-object interac-

---

[2] See "Zur Deutung der Phänomenologie des Geistes," originally appearing in *Hegel-Studien* I, 284, reprinted as Chapter 4 in *Hegel's Idee einer Phänomenologie des Geistes* (Freiburg: Verlag Karl Alber, 1973), 205.
[3] See *Hegel's Phenomenology, Part I: Analysis and Commentary* (Athens: Ohio University Press, 1988), 164–165.

tions from beginning to end.[4] And in a later book I have demonstrated how the *Phenomenology*, like Hegel's later system, can best be described as a "circle of circles"—a system of ever-widening circles culminating in a return to the starting point.[5] But admittedly, such an explanatory approach concentrates simply on the *formal* aspects of the phenomenological structures, and does not capture the idea of a self-moving conceptual content progressing necessarily in its various stages through a process of determinate negation (§87). Hegel himself in the Preface to the *Phenomenology* eschews abstract methods which strive to capture form without content (§§49–50), and holds that the proper form of organization in philosophical science has to rely on the "self-moving soul of implemented content,"[6] moving through a process in which "the simple, self-comprehending totality itself emerges out of the richness in which its reflection seemed to be lost."[7]

H. S. Harris in *Hegel's Ladder* laments that the fact that the *Phenomenology* is a logical science from beginning to end has not been understood. He observes, "hardly anyone thinks that the project [of making the *Phenomenology* a logical science] has been carried out. This is the received view that I want to challenge."[8] He mentions Kenneth Westphal as one of the few exceptions, although Westphal strangely lumps together Otto Pöggeler with Theodor Haering as asserting an abrupt and illogical break in the *Phenomenology* after Chapter V (Westphal, like Robert Solomon, cites as confirmation the article, mentioned above, in which Pöggeler *refutes* "Haering's thesis").[9] I would consider myself an exception to the "hardly anyone" assertion, but also Claus-Artur Scheier,[10] Jon Stewart,[11] and Pierre-Jean Labarrière,[12] all of whom are considered inadequate by Harris in defending the scientific aspect. Why is Labarrière's magisterial commentary considered inadequate? Because it "sets up the goal of interpreting the *Phenomenology* from within, and 'as it lies.'" What Harris considers more relevant than Labarrière's enterprise is a "free-ranging commentary *ab externo*" (I, xii). And this phrase accurately

---

[4]See *Hegel's Phenomenology, Part I*, 165–167.

[5]See *GWF Hegel: the Philosophical System* (Athens: Ohio University Press, 1996), 24–26.

[6]§53 ". . . die sich selbst bewegende Seele des erfüllten Inhalts."

[7]§53 "Dadurch emergiert das einfache sich übersehende Ganze selbst aus dem Reichtume, worin seine Reflexion verloren schien."

[8]*Hegel's Ladder I: The Pilgrimage of Reason* (Indianapolis, IN: Hackett, 1997), Introduction, xii.

[9]See Kenneth Westphal, *Hegel's Epistemological Realism* (Dordrecht: Kluwer, 1989), p. 269n.

[10]*Analytischer Kommentar zu Hegels Phänomenologie des Geistes* (Freiburg: Alber, 1980).

[11]See "The Architectonic of Hegel's *Phenomenology of Spirit*," in Jon Stewart, ed., *The* Phenomenology of Spirit *Reader* (Albany, NY: SUNY, 1998)." Stewart, basing his argument on the changes that Hegel made before publication, offers convincing evidence that the work was systematic and structured throughout.

[12]*Structures et mouvement dialectique dans la Phénoménologie de l'Esprit de Hegel* (Paris: Aubier, 1968).

describes Harris' own main contribution. Harris' paragraph-by-paragraph commentary on the *Phenomenology* charts every conceivable cultural, literary, historical, and philosophical current that might throw light on the words, concepts and arguments Hegel utilizes.

If, however, the basic structures of a highly organized work are not understood, knowing the external influences will not help much. More germane and enlightening and closer to Hegel's intentions, I believe, would be an approach "from within" which charts the stages in the self-movement of the conceptual content in such a way that the coordination of form *and* content is continually highlighted. Since the *Phenomenology*, unlike Hegel's later publications, is relatively lacking in editorial devices such as subtitles and numbering schemas, this is an especially difficult task which requires close attention to the text and context. I think the analysis which best approximates this goal is to be found in Pierre-Jean Labarrière's *Structures et mouvement dialectique*.

HEGEL'S INTERMITTENT RECAPITULATIONS: LABARRIÈRE'S ANALYSIS

Labarrière takes into account the above-mentioned debate about Haering's thesis, sides with Pöggeler regarding Haering's lack of substantiating evidence, but also suggests that Jean Hyppolite may be correct in surmising that Hegel was forced by the internal exigencies of his analysis to proceed beyond his initial expectations. Nevertheless, he concludes that "the work, even according to a somewhat cursory perusal, possesses a sufficient unity to supply the basis for a systematic study of its unitary structures."[13] In order to achieve this goal, Labarrière conducts an exhaustive analysis of Hegel's own frequent recapitulations, summaries, and comparisons. In a very real sense, he allows Hegel himself, as if compensating for the lack of internal organizational cues, to chart the development of both form and content in the *Phenomenology*. If, as has often been noted by commentators, Hegel makes a distinction between the perspective of 1) the consciousness which is being subjected to analysis in the *Phenomenology* and 2) the "we," the phenomenologists observing and tabulating the movements of this consciousness, we might observe that Hegel's frequent retrospective comments add a third viewpoint—3) the perspective of Hegel himself, offering a detailed *Grundriß*, unsystematically and almost as an afterthought, commenting, through frequent recapitulations, on the overall structures of the work, for the benefit of any incompletely initiated phenomenologists. And one finds that many of

---

[13]*Structures et mouvement dialectique*, 27.

Hegel's recapitulations or "parallels" are not just summaries; rather, ideas are added, or at least made more explicit than they were before.

Labarrière distinguishes three different types of recapitulations:

(1) *Les faux parallels*: He enumerates over a hundred of these "false parallels" —"false" because they are linear rather than circular, and do not capture the circular dialectical structure or movement that takes place. These consist of remarks like "as was mentioned earlier . . . ," "as we have seen . . . ," and so forth. He compares these references about "linear development" to the canvas of a painting,[14] which is simply the background upon which all the interesting features are imprinted. But these linear observations are of little interest for someone who is searching for a key to the essential organization of the work.

(2) *Les parallélismes de structures*: These are recapitulations that help to capture the "static circularity," the overall *form* of a new development and its similarities to some preceding formations; they show the way that various stages repeat at a higher level the threads that appeared in earlier stages. Labarrière compares them to the composition of a painting[15]—the way that the various parts depicted complement one another or stand in mutual contrast. They consist of two types: (a) *Les textes courts* are brief recapitulations which indicate how a previously analyzed dialectical relationship is now being repeated at a higher and more complex level. For example, in chapter V on Reason, §231, Hegel compares the unification of particular and universal, taking place in that chapter, with the preceding unification of particular and universal that took place in chapter IV, when the emergence of a "mediator" remedied the alienation of the "unhappy consciousness." (b) *Les grands textes architecturaux* are architectonic recapitulations that Hegel includes at the beginning of major sections, showing in considerable detail how the structures just beginning to be discussed are analogous to structures already considered at a lower level. For example, in chapter V, Reason, at the beginning of the section on the development of practical reason (chapter V.B., "The Self-Actualization of Rational Self-Consciousness," §348ff.), Hegel compares the stages of development which took place in the preceding section (chapter V.A) on theoretical reason to the stages of chapters I, II, and III (Sense-certainty, Perception, and Understanding); and then he puts the reader on notice that the stages that will now be considered will be more advanced versions of stages already discussed in chapter IV (Master/Slave dialectic, Stoicism, etc.).

(3) *Les parallélismes de mouvements*: Hegel, always insistent that form and *content* have to be examined together, devotes a large number of his recapitulations to pointing out "dynamic circularity," i.e., the parallelism of dialectical

---

[14]*Structures et mouvement dialectique*, 62.
[15]*Ibid.*

movements or interactions taking place at a lower and a higher level. Labarrière, continuing with his analogy of a painting, compares these recapitulations to the features that give "life" to a painting[16]—the color and style of the depictions, and the "chemistry" appearing to take place among the figures depicted. These recapitulations fall into three types: (a) *Les "jauges" intérieures*, internal gauges of movements, showing how a movement already analyzed is revived once more at the center of a new situation: for example, in §178 Hegel reminds us of the interaction between particular and universal that took place in the emergence of the "infinite" concept in Understanding, and indicates that this interaction is now (at the outset of the Master/Slave relationship) going to be taking place between two consciousnesses. (b) *Les contrepoints*, explanations of the way that subjective developments in Spirit and selfhood have been connected with objective developments in the world: for example, in §202, Hegel indicates how the stages of Stoicism and Skepticism, which are the next developments to be discussed, are related to the dialectic of Master and Slave, already discussed; (c) *La parenté de niveau de deux mouvements*, comparisons of two dialectical movements existing on different levels—in which Hegel either presents an earlier transition as the model or rationale for a transition that is now to take place, or shows the similarity between an earlier sequential development and a later sequence of developments: for example, in chapter VI, §480, discussing the emergence of the legal person and property rights, Hegel compares the earlier transition, from Stoicism to Skepticism and the alienated Unhappy Consciousness, to the present transition from the legal person to the alienation of his rights in a sovereign.

Labarrière charts altogether 223 parallels/recapitulations made by Hegel throughout the *Phenomenology*, including numerous "false parallels." I will outline below some of the major structural and dynamic recapitulations that Labarrière highlights; and this outline will be followed with a brief overview of the global development of the *Phenomenology*, as gleaned precisely from Hegel's own comments, especially the comments towards the final parts of the book, which tend to encompass large organizational purviews. For convenience of reference, I will include the A. V. Miller paragraph numbering (although the references are not specifically to the Miller translation); I will utilize Hegel's chapter numbering from chapter II, since there are no major recapitulations in chapter I, to chapter VIII, rather than the "A, B, C, AA, BB, and so forth." numbering that Hegel later added to his Table of Contents[17]; and I will continue to add Labarriere's numbering of the parallels (from #1–#223) summarized and categorized in Appendices I and II,[18] at the end of his book.

---

[16]*Structures et mouvement dialectique*, 62.

[17]Jon Stewart, in the article cited above, shows how this added numbering can help the reader to discern the structure of the work. But Stewart's approach, while complementary to Labarrière's, pursues a different line of argument.

[18]*Structures et mouvement dialectique*, 273ff.

HEGEL'S MAJOR RECAPITULATIONS

Table 5.1. Hegel's Major Recapitulations

II. Perception	*Reappearance of Heres and Nows.* §111, #13: The structural relationship between the Heres and the Nows in Sense-Certainty (chapter I) now reappear and are subsumed into the greater universality and necessity of Perception.
	Renewed movement from realism to idealism. §117, #15: The movement from the realism of the object to the idealism of the ego that took place in Sense Certainty (§100), reappears now in Perception.
III. Force and Understanding	*Self-conscious life as the ultimate unity-in-distinction.* §161, #36: Through the process of examining positive and negative electricity, distance, velocity, the force of attraction, etc., and showing the unity-in-distinction of opposites in these cases, the Understanding finally arrives at the concept of the unity-in-distinction of life in self-consciousness, i.e. at the Concept of Infinity.
	The "second law" of the Understanding as the converse of the "first law." §156, #34–35: The "first law" discovered by the Understanding transforms unequals into equality, while the "second law" finally arrived at by the Understanding is the law of pure dialectical change, in which equality breaks up into inequality.
IV. The Truth and Certitude of Self-Consciousness	*New meaning of "subject" and "object" in self-conscious Life.* §166, #37: In the stages of Sense-Certainty, Perception, and Understanding, the alternate unifications and distinctions of concept and being, certainty and truth, subject and object were treated; now, at the stage of Self-consciousness, the unity-in-distinction between subject and object, and so forth, becomes transparent. The new "subject, is "desire," patently in unity with its object; the new "object," is "life," patently identical with the ego.
IV.A. Independence and Dependence of Self-Consciousness: Domination and Servitude	*The dialectic of Forces sublimated into the Master-Slave dialectic.* §178,#42: The distinction and reuniting that characterized the Infinite Concept in the final stage of Understanding now takes place between two self-consciousnesses. §184, #44: More specifically, the immediate relationship of mutual recognition between two self-consciousnesses is a more sophisticated version of the way that Force bifurcated into the two extremes of Force for-itself and Force for-another, in Understanding.
IV.B. Freedom of Self-Consciousness: Stoicism, Skepticism, and the Unhappy Consciousness	*Stoicism as sublimation/interiorization.* §197, #47: The unequal Master/Slave relationship is sublimated into an "infinite" relationship in the Stoic consciousness/concept.
	Remnants of Master/Slave relationship in Skepticism. §202, #50 Stoicism brings the independence of the Master over the Slave to its conclusion in the realm of thought; and

(continued)

Table 5.1.   (*continued*)

	Skepticism likewise brings to a logical conclusion the negation of determinacy on the part of the Slave. §202, #51: In Skepticism, the negativity and negation-of-negation that characterized the Infinite Concept in Understanding is now concentrated in an individual Self-consciousness. §206, #53 The duplication of consciousness that formerly existed between master and slave now arises within the skeptical self-consciousness.
V. The Certitude and Truth of Reason	*Reason as the transcendence of the alienations of Self-Consciousness.* §231, #59: The "mediating consciousness" (§227) that allowed the Unhappy Consciousness to finally overcome the split between the particular and the universal now brings about the unification of particular and universal that characterizes the stage of Reason. §233, #61: The transcendence of otherness that took place progressively in previous stages (Sense-Certainty, Perception, and so forth, up to and including the Unhappy Consciousness), reaches its culmination as Reason finally overcomes otherness.
	Kantian-type idealism comparable to Skepticism. §238, #62: Just as Skepticism thrived by negatively relating concepts to empirical reality, abstract idealism thrives by claiming a pseudo-positive but actually negative relationship between the [Kantian] unity of apperception and the thing-in-itself.
V.A. Reason in the Stage of Observation	*New relationship to otherness in Observing Reason.* §240, #63: In Sense-Certainty and Perception, Consciousness repeatedly encountered otherness; but Observing Reason actively searches prima facie otherness for the traces of itself which it is certain are there.
V.A.a. Reason Observing Organic Nature	*New meaning of "law" as applied to organisms.* §§279–282, #69: While the laws considered by the Understanding relate universal and particular determinations, the "law" of organisms takes this process of "relating" as its object, and this object (the *relating* of inner to outer) is the only "determination" of this "law."
V.B. The Realization of Rational Self-Consciousness through Itself	*The stages of Rational Observation as comparable to the stages of Consciousness; the stages of Rational Self-Realization as comparable to the stages of Self-Consciousness.* §348, #88: The three stages of Rational Observation that are considered in chapter V.A (observation of nature, self-consciousness relating to external reality, and the body-mind relationship) correspond to the earlier stages of Consciousness—Sense-Certainty, Perception, and Understanding (chapters I-III). The two stages that now follow—Self-realization (chapter V.B) and Individualization [die Sache selbst] (chapter V.C)— correspond to the earlier two stages of Self-Consciousness— "Dependence and Independence of Self-consciousness" (chapter IV.A) and "Freedom of Self-Consciousness" (chapter

	IV.B). §349, #89: The processes of Self-realization and Individualization that take place in the stage of Reason will have as their result a final unification of individuals with the Ethical Substance in which they are rooted, through association with the laws and customs of the community, society and nation.
V. C. Individuality which is Real in and for Itself	*Final overcoming of being-thought disparities in the self-as-"category."* §§394f, #98: Disparities between thought and existence arose in Rational Observation (V.A) and in Self-Actualization (V.B). But in the present stage (V.C) individuality finds the union of self and reality (i.e., the "category") within itself.
V.C.a. The Spiritual/ Animal Realm and Disenchantment: Rational Reality	*The examination of Rational Reality focusing on* Sache *rather than* Ding. §410, #100: The Thing (Ding) whose transitions in sensation and perception took place as an object of Consciousness, has now become the Rational Reality (Sache) which will undergo similar transitions as object of self-conscious Reason.
V.C.b. Law-Making Reason	*Immediacy of laws comparable to immediacy in Sense-Certainty.* §423, #102: Just as Sense-Certainty began with the being that is immediately given by the senses, the present analysis of the spiritual/animal realm begins with an inspection of the laws of the existing [social] "masses" in their immediacy.
VI. Spirit	***Major Architectonic Correspondence.*** §438, #107: Reason (Chapter V) in the stage of Observation (V.A) finds itself in-itself; in the stage of Self-actualization (V.B) it creates itself for-itself; and finally as Rational Reality (V.C) it constitutes the beginning of spiritual reality in-and-for-itself, aware of the unity of itself with the world.
VI.A.a. The Ethical World	*Bifurcation of Spirit comparable to bifurcation in Perception.* §446, #108: Just as Perception, incorporating multiple sense properties was bifurcated into universal and particular aspects, so also Spirit-as-consciousness here coordinates multiple ethical aspects and bifurcates into two laws, one (the divine law) championing particularity, the other (human law) championing universality.
VI.A.b. Ethical Action	*Individuality initially not in opposition to the Ethical Substance.* §467, #114: The individuality embedded in the Ethical Substance no longer confronts an objectivity which stands in opposition like the "things" of Consciousness, or the recalcitrant "world" facing the Knight of Virtue; but rather is in harmony with the Substance even if coming into conflict with other individualities.
VI.A.c. The Condition of Right or Legality	*Abstract legal "person" comparable to abstract Stoic self-consciousness.* §480, #120: Just as the abstract determinations of Stoicism became prey to reality and

(*continued*)

Table 5.1.   (*continued*)

	degenerated into Skepticism, so also the abstract property-based rights in this early stage of the rule of law degenerates at the mercy of the overbearing sovereign power. §483, #121: And just as Stoicism developed through Skepticism into an Unhappy Consciousness alienated from the "Unchangeable," so also the abstract legal person here develops into a state of alienation from the state power which constitutes its Self-consciousness. §751, #206: In the final analysis, the abstract legal "person" of the Condition of Right or Legality is as unreal as the Stoic consciousness which degenerated into Skepticism and finally into the Unhappy Consciousness.
VI.B. Spirit in a Condition of Estrangement: Culture	*Dialectic of power and wealth in Culture leading to conceptual/linguistic dialectics.* §502, #130: The initial estrangement in Culture was between the ideas of good and bad on one side, and state power and wealth on the other, and the external relation of these two sides is "judgement"; this "judgement" now becomes the middle term, showing how the noble and base consciousnesses bring about an internal amalgamation of good and bad in their relationship to state power and wealth. §520, #139: All the various contradictions appearing in the stage of Culture are perfectly comprehended and expressed in "the language of distraughtness."
VI.B.b. Faith and Insight	*The Faith/Insight division comparable to earlier Divine Law/Human Law division.* §486, #123: Just as the division of the Ethical Substance into Divine Law and Human Law, and the division of the individual in that world into conscious and unconscious aspects, were finally unified as the "fate" of the abstract person—so also, the initial division of Insight from Faith in Culture will be dissolved in the "universal" "insightful" self of the Enlightenment.
	Earlier stages foreshadowing Faith. §527, #141: The contradictions of Insight give rise to the consciousness of pure thought, i.e. Faith, as a counterbalance. If we examine the phenomenological development of pure thought as object, we see that it has appeared previously: in Stoicism (§198) it was alienated from actuality; at the stage of the Knight of Virtue (§386), it was an unrealized state of reality; and in lawgiving and law-testing (§419ff.), it became universalized as laws. But in Faith, it appears as reality.
	Major Architectonic Correspondence. §528, #143: Religious Faith, in contrast with the "Insight" of the Enlightenment (chapter VI.B.b), is a substantial and determinate opposition to the contradictions of reality; thus it differs from the vague

yearning of the insubstantial Unhappy Consciousness (chapter IV.B, §§207ff.), and from the "belief" in the "shades" of the underworld, rooted in family traditions rather than some transcendent "beyond" (chapter VI.A.a, §451).

VI.B.II.a. The Enlightenment: Combat of the Lumières with Superstition

VI.B.II.b. The Truth of the Lumières

Insight as the acme of negativity. §541, #150: The various negative forms of consciousness we have previously considered, e.g., Skepticism, are inferior in comparison to the consummate negativity which characterizes the stage of Insight.

The philosophy of utility as a convergence of the interests of Faith and Insight. §581, #155: The world of Culture, with all its variegated negativity, and the world of Faith, emphasizing positive universality, coincide in the "philosophy of utility." For the useful object is positive being-in-itself and also other-oriented, i.e., being-for-consciousness.

VI.B.III. Absolute Freedom and Terror

The transition to Morality from revolutionary conflict, comparable to the transition to Faith and Insight from the conflicts of Culture. §595, #159: Just as the contradictory realities of Culture were superseded by entry into the intellectual conflict between Faith and Insight—so also, Spirit, in the form of Absolute Freedom and Terror passes out of its contradictory realities to enter the *thought-realm* of Morality.

VI.C. The Self-Certainty of Spirit: Morality

Legal focus on objects is transformed in moral focus on certainty of duty. §596, #160: The self with abstract rights that emerged as the legal person, in the wake of the ethical substance (§477) was oriented to an object outside itself. Through the estrangements of Culture and the Enlightenment it has now gone beyond legality to morality, a state in which its "object" is now nothing external, but its own certainty.

Morality sharing immediate aspects of Ethical Substance and mediated aspects of Culture. §597, 161: The moral consciousness possesses characteristics of the immediacy of the Ethical Substance (§§439ff.), insofar as it takes its duty as all reality; but it also possesses characteristics of the mediations of Culture (§§489ff.), insofar as it involves an alienated relationship to nature.

VI.C.c. Conscience, the "Beautiful Soul," Evil and the Forgiveness of Evil

Conscience comparable to other forms of selfhood, resulting from different forms of the world. §633, #166: The development of the notion of the self has taken place along with the development of the forms of the world. Just as the development of the world of the Ethical Substance culminated in the abstract legal person, and the world of Culture culminated in the Absolute Freedom of universal will, the world of Morality has culminated in the stage of Conscience.

(continued)

Table 5.1. (*continued*)

	Conscience as the final concreteness of die Sache selbst. §641, #171: In the chapter on Reason, the coordination of reason and reality emerged initially in *die Sache selbst* as an abstract predicate. At the outset of the chapter on Spirit, it became something substantial; in Culture, it gained an external existence, and it became self-knowing essentiality in Morality. But in Conscience it finally becomes subject.
	In Conscience, the dialectic of the Unhappy Consciousness is finally internalized. §658, #175: The conscience of the "Beautiful Soul," situated in a higher stage of Spirit, transforms the former restless oscillations in Chapter IV, between the Unhappy Consciousness and being, into a purely subjective oscillation between the conscientious self and real existence.
VII. Religion	***Major architectonic correspondence.*** §§473ff, #179: The previous stages included some precursors of Religion—the Unhappy Consciousness §§207ff), the belief in the "shades" of the underworld (§451), the belief in heaven, in the attitude of Faith (§528), and the supposition of a "provident Legislator" (§626) in the stage of Morality. All these precursors had an historical element, and had to do with Spirit-as-consciousness. But Religion is the *Self*-consciousness of Spirit, which has progressed in non-historical fashion from abstract to concrete forms, as will now be described.
VII.A.a. The Being of Light	*Light-Religion as a sublimation of both Sense-Certainty and the Master-Slave relationship.* §686, #180: Light-Religion, with light as an object of worship, combines two stages previously considered—Sense-Certainty as applied to a generalized object, and the servile attitude found in the Master-Slave relationship.
VII.A.b. Plant and Animal Worship	*Transition from light-worship to worship of plants and animals comparable to transition from Sense-Certainty to Perception.* §687, #181: Just as the indeterminacy of Sense-Certainty was superseded in the sensory universality of Perception, with its multiple properties, so also the abstractness of light-worship is superseded by the more definite self-like worship of plants and animals.
VII.A.c. The Religious Artisan	*The stage of religious artisanry comparable to initial stages of Understanding.* §692, #182: The formation of pyramids, obelisks, and so forth is comparable to the initial abstract stages of Understanding, still needing to be imbued with the life of Spirit.
VII.B. Art-Religion	*Art-Religion as synthesizing nature and selfhood.* §700, 184: Art-religion, going beyond the merely negative relationship to the self in the ancient [Zoroastrian] nature-religion and the religions organized into [selfless] caste-systems, is a

	positive synthesis of self and nature, embedded historically in the free nation [of the Greeks], which first manifested this positive synthesis.
VII.B.c. The Spiritual Work of Art	*Literary productions of art-religion reflecting developments in [ancient Greek] culture.* §736, #199: The oppositions which we discerned in the Ethical Substance (chapter VI.A)—between divine law and human law, male and female, consciousness and unconsciousness—are fully represented in the epics, tragedies, and comedies of art-religion (chapter VII.B). §749, #203: The displacement of the gods and the triumph of the self as absolute being in Comedy (§§744ff.) is the counterpart of the production of an inflated self as absolute being in the [Rome-patterned] stage of legality (§§481ff.).
	Classical comedy reflecting the triumph of individuality in the stage of the Ethical Substance. §745, #200: Classical comedy manifests the fact that the individual Self-consciousness is the "fate" of the gods. The division of the Ethical Substance into natural and ethical aspects is manifested in the results: Natural aspects like religious offerings of natural substances, as well as ethical aspects like government by the Demos and the family, are submitted to the critical consciousness of comedy. §747, #201: With the ascendancy of Comedy, absolute power is no longer ascribed to statues of the gods, or to representations of the gods in Epics, Tragedies, and so forth, but is appropriated by the individual self-consciousness.
VII.C. Revealed Religion	*The moments leading to the Incarnation compared to the stages of Consciousness.* §762, #213 The synthesizing of the particular with the universal in the absolute individual (Christ) takes place in a process comparable to the movement from sense-certainty through Perception to Understanding.
VIII. Absolute Knowledge	***Major Architectonic Correspondence.*** §788ff, #223: Spirit-as-consciousness (the entire chapter VI) developed in three stages which are more sophisticated versions of earlier stages which took place in Consciousness (chapters I-III) and in Reason (chapter V.A): 1). Spirit as Ethical Substance (VI.A), like Sense-Certainty and Rational Observation, emphasizes an objectivity in which subjectivity is still latent; 2) in Spirit as Culture (VI.B), utilitarianism (§560), as the attempt to make an initial conjunction between the in-itself and the for-itself reflects a similar attempt at the end of Perception (§123), and in the final stages of Individualizing Reason (§438); and 3) Spirit as Morality retraces at a higher level the synthesis of consciousness and self-consciousness at the culmination of Understanding (§164) and the emergence of the absolute Sache selbst (§420) at the culmination of Reason.

(continued)

Table 5.1. (*continued*)

While the development of Spirit as Consciousness (all of Chapter VI) was a gradual movement towards subjectivity, Spirit as *self*-consciousness (Religion, chapter VII) has proceeded in the opposite direction—towards the *objectivity* of an organized religious community.
The two reconciliations—of Consciousness with Self-consciousness in Spirit, and of Self-consciousness with Consciousness in Religion—are finally brought together in a second-order reconciliation (§802): Absolute Knowledge, giving the conceptual structure and form of Spirit to the pictorial content of religion achieves thought/being unity.

THE FINAL EMERGING ORGANIZATIONAL PATTERNS

Collapsing all these multiple recapitulations by Hegel, and especially his final recapitulations, into a summary view, what we find is a basically triadic schema for the work, in terms of the overall progression from the in-itself of Spirit, to its for-itself and in-and-for-itself states. Each segment of this overarching triad is further divided recursively into sub-triads. Spirit in-itself or Objective Spirit (i.e., all of chapter VI) as a whole is the result of the movement from the Ethical Substance through Culture to Morality; but the Ethical Substance itself is the result of the movement from Rational Observation through Individualization to the final stages of *die Sache selbst*; and the latter is the result of the movement from Consciousness through Self-Consciousness to Reason. Spirit for-itself (Religion), on the other hand, is the result of a separate evolution of self-consciousness from natural religion through art-religion to revealed religion. Spirit in-and-for-itself (Absolute Knowledge) then is enabled to give the "content" finally attained in Religion the conceptual "form" of heightened self-consciousness which was finally attained by Objective Spirit (in Chapter VI).

The fact that Hegel constructed his "system of consciousness" in such a triadic fashion will come as no surprise to one who is familiar with the tightly woven triads and sub-triads of Hegel's later *Encyclopedia of the Philosophical Sciences*, although the concatenations are harder to discern in the *Phenomenology*, and have needed expositions such as Labarrière's. Hegel's announcement in the Preface that the "absolute method" of "trip-licity" (§50), rediscovered by Kant, but misused by some of Hegel's con-

Table 5.2.

	1. Spirit-as-consciousness, i.e. Spirit in-itself	2. Spirit-as-self-consciousness (Religion), i.e. Spirit for-itself	3. Absolute Knowledge, i.e. Spirit in-and-for-itself
In-itself	Consciousness (Sections I-III), Rational Observation (V.A.), Ethical Substance (VI.A.a.)	Natural Religion (VII.A.)	Attainment of self-conscious Morality by Spirit-as-consciousness (VI.C.c.)
For-itself	Self-consciousness (IV), Rational Individualization (V.B.), Culture (VI.B.)	Art Religion (VII.B.)	Attainment of communal consciousness by Religion (VII.C. §787)
In and for-itself	Reason, die Sache selbst (V.C.), Morality (VI.C.)	Revealed Religion (VII.C.)	Synthesis of these two attainments in Absolute Knowledge (VIII §803ff.)

temporaries,[19] "has now been restored to its 'absolute significance,'" gives ample forewarning to the careful reader concerning the genre of "scientific" organization he or she will be encountering in the *Phenomenology of Spirit*. Some commentators on the *Phenomenology* have misconstrued this reference to "misuse of triplicity" as indicating Hegel's complete abandonment of triads, not just the "thesis, antithesis, synthesis" terminology of Fichte.[20] Presumably this interpretation is meant to make Hegel's approach more palatable to modern readers. But philosophy, as Hegel himself observed, is a product of its time,[21] and in his own attempt to perfect the method revived by Kant but not utilized to full advantage by Fichte and Schelling, offers us an outstanding example of this belief in philosophical synchronicity. One must let Hegel be Hegel.

---

[19]Bonsiepen in his edition of the *Phenomenology* (Hamburg: Felix Meiner, 1988), comments, 571, that Hegel has in mind Fichte, Schelling, and various students of Schelling.

[20]See for example Donald Verene, *Hegel's Recollection* (Albany, NY: SUNY, 1985), 19: "In the preface to the *Phenomenology* (Miller, 50), one of only two places where Hegel speaks of triadic thought or *Triplizität*, he identifies it with the abstract formalism of Kantian thinking."

[21]See Hegel's *Philosophy of Right*, Knox trans. (New York: Oxford University Press, 1967), 11: "Every individual is a child of his time; so philosophy too is its own time apprehended in thoughts. It is just as absurd to fancy that a philosophy can transcend its contemporary world as it is to fancy that an individual can overleap his own age. . . ."

6

The *Phenomenology* and Literature

The title, "the *Phenomenology* and literature" has several possible connotations. It can refer to literary works actually incorporated in Hegel's *Phenomenology*, or the development of a philosophy of literature in and by the *Phenomenology*, or finally, the *Phenomenology* as literature—its literary aspects. In what follows, I will expand on these three aspects, but especially on the third, which is probably the least obvious and the most controversial.

LITERATURE INCORPORATED IN THE *PHENOMENOLOGY*

If a contemporary philosophical work were to intentionally weave into its arguments characters and scenes from *The Brothers Karamazov*, *Moby Dick*, *The Grapes of Wrath*, *Ulysses,* and Kafka's *The Trial*, we would have something analogous to what Hegel does in the *Phenomenology*. Occasionally philosophers do engage in a philosophical/literary critique of works of literature—e.g., Jean-Paul Sartre's disquisitions on the writings of Gustave Flaubert and Frantz Fanon; but to consciously employ fictional narratives, without explicit reference to their authors, as a means of analyzing the development of consciousness and culture, is a unique characteristic of Hegel's *Phenomenology*. Mention has already been made above concerning Hegel's use of Cervantes' *Don Quixote* in his analysis of the "Knight of Virtue"[1] and his universalization of Sophocles' character, Antigone, in his discussion of the conflict between human and divine law.[2] Besides Antigone, numerous figures

---

[1] See earlier discussion, p. 24.
[2] See earlier discussion, p. 42.

from Greek tragedy, and comedy as well, are interpolated into Hegel's discussion of "Ethical Action." As mentioned above,[3] Goethe's early 1790 version of *Faust* is also employed, and paraphrased in some detail by Hegel in §360. The Norton Critical Edition of *Faust* includes the first two paragraphs of Hegel's chapter on "Pleasure and Necessity," and points out the parallel between the *Phenomenology* and Goethe's 1790 *Faust: a Fragment*: Hegel provides "a kind of paraphrase through abstraction, whereby the situation of Faust, as represented dramatically by Goethe in the *Fragment*, is translated into the conceptual dynamics of the developing Spirit which constitutes the argument of Hegel's *Phenomenology*."[4]

The most obvious and explicit incorporation of literature (but still, without reference to the author or book) is Hegel's use of Diderot's *Rameau's Nephew* in the chapter on "Culture" (§522ff.), with more precise quotations than in the case of *Faust*.

I would add that more implicit, but still detectable, inclusions of literature by Hegel are found in the chapter on "Understanding" (§97ff), where Hegel's discussion of the second-order "inverted world" of laws emerging with first-order laws is reminiscent of Ludwig Tieck's play, *Die verkehrte Welt* (1799), in which a play takes place within a play; and, as mentioned in chapter 2,[5] Hegel's discussion of the "Beautiful Soul," which parallels the developments in the subsection on "The Beautiful Soul" in Goethe's novel, *Wilhelm Meister's Apprenticeship*.

How did the use of these figures from literature advance Hegel's phenomenological enterprise? In almost all cases Hegel is referring to a character in literature as a universal *type*, or, more precisely, as a type whose universalization dovetails with the procession of phenomenological *Gestalten* covered in the *Phenomenology*. The Faust configurations appear immediately after the long sections on theoretical Reason (chapter V.A), which supply the springboard for the move to practical Reason and intersubjectivity (chapter V.B); and Faust stands for a consciousness-type leaving the grey world of theory and looking to erotic experience for liveliness and an escape from solitariness. As the progress in intersubjectivity advances, Don Quixote stands for the paradigmatic idealistic moralist, trying to remake the world around him without taking account of where the world wants to go and what it wants to do. In chapter VI, charting the development of social consciousness, Sophocles' Antigone is the universal figure of someone caught in a contradiction between civil laws and unwritten moral norms which require unconditional

---

[3]See earlier discussion, p. 22.
[4]Johann Wolfgang von Goethe, *Faust*, Arndt trans. (New York: W.W. Norton & Co., 1976), 439n.
[5]See p. 30.

commitment; Diderot's "Rameau's nephew" is the quintessential dialectician mediating all the contradictions in his environment and in himself, thus paving the way for the mediations of the Enlightenment; and Goethe's "Beautiful Soul" is the perennial paragon of virtue who can manage to maintain self-righteous purity only by closing off real-life encounters with the real world and thus avoiding grappling with tough decisions.

THE *PHENOMENOLOGY* DEVELOPING A PHILOSOPHY OF LITERATURE

In Hegel's later system, art and religion are considered in the context of Part III of the *Encyclopedia of Philosophical Sciences*, the "Philosophy of Spirit," just after the sections on political philosophy. Art and religion are there treated as two progressive forms of "Absolute Spirit." Absolute Spirit exists in-itself in art, for-itself in religion, and receives its ultimate expression (in-and-for-itself) in philosophy.

One must have an understanding of Hegel's technical usage of the term, "absolute," in order to appreciate these categories. Being "absolute" for Hegel involved overcoming dichotomies of subject and object, being and thought, especially of the Cartesian and Kantian variety. Art is "absolute" in this sense insofar as a true object of art, far from being just an "object," is something preeminently subjective; in fact, art at its best manifests a fusion of the objective and subjective in such a way that the two erstwhile poles are no longer distinguishable; the "absolute" result is a subject-object. In religion, similarly, the imaginative representations of divine beings and their relationships are not just subjective creations but objective cosmic realities. But while art is oriented towards the synthesis of being and thought in sensuous content, religion's synthesis is through mental representations. Having made these fundamental distinctions, Hegel goes into great detail, especially in his *Lectures on Aesthetics* and *Lectures on the Philosophy of Religion,* into further subdivisions. Art is subdivided, largely in relationship to historical periods (pre-Hellenic, Hellenic, post-Hellenic), into symbolic, classical, and romantic, depending on the relative predominance or equipoise of subjective or objective factors.

In the *Phenomenology* no such detailed distinctions of stages of art are made, and the development of art is considered intertwined with the development of religion. There are occasional references to historical periods, but no noteworthy attempt to link art-forms with specific stages of history.

The progress of both art and religion in chapter VII of the *Phenomenology* traces a gradual but inexorable movement from the "abstract" to the "concrete." In Hegel's technical terminology (utilized also by Kierkegaard in discussions of art), the "abstract" is that in which there is only an inchoate and incomplete fusion of being with thought. Thus the work of artisans exemplified in ancient Egyptian and Eastern Indian religions is discussed at the outset, in the section on "Nature Religion," and the characteristic of the artwork in those eras is the initial and imperfect attempt to capture and reflect the numinous in external religious objects. Much more successful fusions of the numinous and the external take place in the second stage, "Art Religion," a section in which most of the imagery is redolent of Greece in the Golden Age, and most of the examples are Hellenic. The progression that takes place in the substages of Art-Religion is from abstract art creations, such as the statues of the gods and the architecture of the temples housing the gods, to subjective development in rituals and hymnody and festivals, to a final optimal concretion of being and thought in the great epics of poets like Homer and Hesiod, and the tragedies or comedies of dramatists like Aeschylus, Sophocles, and Aristophanes.

Thus the philosophy of art that is discerned in Hegel's *Phenomenology* consists in the emphasis on "concreteness" in the Hegelian sense—*works of language,* i.e., existent realities imbedded in a culture, and preeminently creations of thought. Short of a bona fide religious manifestation of Absolute Spirit, the features of the divine are easiest to discern in such great spiritual creations. The greatness of such literary works consists in presenting great truths and values, which both form and are formed by the culture in which they arise. Thus works of literature can approximate almost to the level of philosophy, which, in Hegel's estimation, simply presents truths and values in a more explicit and conceptual form. Going beyond the qualities that a literary critic would focus on, Hegel's phenomenological analysis of literature emphasizes something that is not usually present in the language of literary criticism—the fact that there is a fusion of being and thought in literature; that this fusion admits of numerous degrees as well as multiple styles; and that literature is comparable to religion in providing access to the "absolute."

THE *PHENOMENOLOGY* AS LITERATURE

With a few exceptions, philosophical works have received "bad press" regarding their literary value. Plato's *Dialogues* and some works of Nietzsche and Kierkegaard are recognized as worthy inclusions in literary anthologies; but strictly philosophical works, including great classics, medieval and modern systems, and contemporary works in phenomenology and analytic or linguistic philosophy, cannot generally be classified as "works of literature" without inviting criticisms regarding a serious "category mistake."

Hegel in particular has been burdened down with the stereotype of a turgid, vague, pedantic, and verbose philosophical systematizer—almost a prototype of the genre—although questions have even been raised, and discussed in chapter 5, as to whether his *Phenomenology* is systematic at all. And even sympathetic Hegel scholars have expressed doubts as to what genre of philosophy the *Phenomenology* belongs to. Walter Kaufmann, for instance, complains,

> "What is the man talking about? *Whom* does ne have in mind?" . . . The obscurity and whole manner of the text are such that these questions are almost bound to replace the question of whether what Hegel says is right.[6]

On the contrary, I would argue, and have maintained in previous books, that the obscurities of Hegel are much exaggerated, and that many difficulties are ironed out, once the reader understands what Hegel is trying to accomplish in the aftermath of Kant's "transcendental turn," and also understands the special technical meanings Hegel attaches to words which usually have different connotations in philosophy—such as "reason," "concept," "abstract," "individual," and "spirit."[7] Looking for a solution to the question raised by Walter Kaufmann, Helmut Rehder suggests that there is an *inward* form in some of Hegel's works, as well as in works of other authors, that cannot easily be categorized according to the conventional genres. Thus we should recognize that what "happens" in Hegel's *Phenomenology* is that

> Constituent components of . . . rhythm, sound, pitch, configuration, structure . . . have been bent to serve the purpose of a singular, designing intellect.[8]

Rehder, taking into account Hegel's fascination with Goethe's *Faust* as well as Goethe's idea that what Hegel was attempting could best be accomplished by the symbolism of poetry, points to the "Classical Walpurgis Night" in Part II of *Faust* as the closest approximation to a literary "genre" for the *Phenomenology*, once allowance has been made for the difference between poetical and philosophical forms:

> If it were nothing else, this Walpurgis Night might be considered a phenomenology of emerging language, embracing the whole scale of expression from

---

[6]*Hegel: Reinterpretation, Texts and Commentary* (London: Weidenfeld and Nicholson, 1966), p. 141.
[7]See the Glossary appended to my 1976 *Hegel's Phenomenology, Part One* and the initial Notes on the Translation and General Introduction in my 1994 translation of the *Selections*.
[8]See *A Hegel Symposium*, D.C. Travis ed. (Austin, TX: University of Texas Press, 1962), 120.

primitive sounds to the most intricate forms of speech and chant. . . . The Classical Walpurgis Night deals with the problem of the materialization of energy; it is a *Phänomenologie des Geistes* in poetic form.[9]

What Rehder is saying is that the evolution of language from primitive to more sophisticated forms in *Faust* finds a philosophical counterpart in the evolution of primitive consciousness in the *Phenomenology* to self-consciousness, intersubjectivity, social consciousness, and so forth.

H. S. Harris in a 1993 essay[10] continues the inquiry about the "literary form" of the *Phenomenology*, and points to some precedents in Fichte, Schelling, and others. He doesn't think Rehder's notion that the *Phenomenology* has a completely distinctive "inward form" is adequate. According to Harris we have to take clues from three metaphors in the Preface—the plant that blooms and flowers, the ladder, and the "path"—especially the latter. The ladder is Jacob's ladder which goes up into the ethereal (but not heavenly or transcendent) sphere of ideas, and returns to earth. The path is a this-worldly resumption of the "way of the cross" leading in Enlightenment fashion, not to heavenly salvation but to Science. And in Harris' estimation, the literary form of the *Phenomenology* is not completely unique but is shared with Dante's *Divine Comedy*—the stages of consciousness being substituted in Hegel's portrayal for the successive spheres of spiritual existence explored by Dante.

Hegel as Story-Teller:

I would suggest that the literary form of the *Phenomenology* is very much like a story. On the whole, with the exception of philosophers who specialize in the history of philosophy, and thus are historians in a sense, philosophers are not essentially involved in telling stories. They are interested in problem-solving, the analysis of concepts, the principles and foundations of reality, and/or theories about values. There are some exceptions in the Western philosophical tradition, if we allow that "story" or "narrative" has a much wider extension than novels, plays, ballads, and so forth. One could argue that Thales, Anaximander, Empedocles, and other pre-Socratics were telling stories about the origin of the universe. Plato's *Dialogues* are certainly stories interwoven with conceptual analysis. And other major philosophers—for example, Cicero, Abelard, Berkeley, and Hume—when they wrote philosophical dialogues, were involved in storytelling from the nature of the medium. Likewise Augustine and Vico, in theorizing about the emergence of civilization, or Bergson and Teilhard de Chardin, in the-

---

[9]*A Hegel Symposium*, 133, 137.
[10]Cf. H. S. Harris, "Hegel's Image of Phenomenology," in Robert Stern, Ed., *G. W. F. Hegel: Critical Assessments*, (New York: Routledge, 1993), Vol. 3, 65ff.

orizing about the evolution of life, were storytellers. And it goes without saying that some of the "aesthetic" works of Kierkegaard, such as *Either/Or*, as well as the various existentialist plays of Sartre and Camus, crossed over the line separating philosophy from fiction.

Most of Hegel's works are structured like stories. Most obviously, this can be asserted of his *Philosophy of History* lectures, which examine the gradual emergence of freedom from ancient to modern times, as well as his *History of Philosophy* lectures, which trace the emergence of the "thought/being" problematic from the time of Parmenides to the modern era. But his later system also falls into this category. For Hegel characterizes his *Logic* as the story of God before the creation of the world,[11] his *Philosophy of Nature* as an account of Nature coming forth as the son of God, abiding in otherness;[12] Nature as the unfolding of the immediate existence of God (not God's existence as Spirit)[13] with physical space serving as the (Newton-inspired) "sensorium of God."[14] Hegel's *Philosophy of Nature* is the story of the gradual concretization of the Absolute Idea, starting with abstract space and time, and ending with elements, forces, and life:

> Matter, although rightfully considered the essence of multiplicity and disparateness, rises gradually towards unity through gravity, light, sentient being, and finally soul.[15]

The third major section of the system, the *Philosophy of Spirit*, starts with the emergence of consciousness in living things, and proceeds to chart the consequent development of individuality, and social and political consciousness.

Hegel's 1807 *Phenomenology* likewise has a storied structure. The first part of the *Phenomenology* is the story of the development of consciousness from the abstract functions of sensation, perception, and concept-formation, then to self-consciousness and other-consciousness, and finally to more and more sophisticated forms of reason, and the relationship of reason to the world, to the self, and to the interconnection between the self and the world. The second part is the story of the development of the various forms of spirit in the world from the abstract harmony of self and nature in the Greek polis, to the breakup of this harmony in Roman civilization and modern culture and the Enlightenment, and

---

[11]Hegel's *Science of Logic*, A.V. Miller trans. (Oxford University Press, 1969), 50: "Logic . . . is the exposition of God as he is in his eternal essence before the creation of nature and a finite mind."

[12]*Philosophy of Nature*, A.V. Miller trans. (Oxford University Press, 1970), §247, *Zusatz*.

[13]*Philosophy of Nature*, §376, *Zusatz*.

[14]*Philosophy of Nature*, §261, *Zusatz*.

[15]§389, *Zusatz*. This should not be understood in the sense of biological evolution, which Hegel rejects (§§249, Zusatz, 339, Zusatz), but in terms of the evolution of the Absolute implicit in the Idea of nature, and evolving into life and spirit.

finally to the restoration of harmony with the development of ethical conscientiousness and religious reconciliation. chapter VII then narrates the separate but concomitant story of the development of the idea of religion from an abstract unity of being and thought in Zoroastrianism, to a more concrete unity in Greek art and literature, to the final unification in the Christian story of the Incarnation and the atonement of the Christian community. Chapter VII finally presents the story's climax, describing the way the development of consciousness and spirit and the development of religion have converged in German idealism, leading to "absolute knowledge."

As in many classical novels, there are conflicts and setbacks, successes and ironical developments, flashbacks and subplots. The experience of reading the *Phenomenology* can be compared to the reading of complex novels like *War and Peace*, or *Moby Dick*—classics which take time and effort, mitigating their popularity. But this novel-like format also contributes to its uniqueness as a philosophical work, and helps to explain "what is going on" to those who encounter the *Phenomenology* for the first time.

Literary Devices Utilized by Hegel

Irony:

Without a doubt, irony is the main reappearing rhetorical device utilized by Hegel in the *Phenomenology*. Perhaps "utilized" is too strong a word, since irony was probably an accidental result rather than an intentionally calculated effect. Sometimes Hegel indicates that a word is meant ironically. Just as anglophone writers will sometimes use quotation marks to indicate that they are speaking ironically (e.g., "We all know that Mr. Smith's 'prudence' is of the highest caliber"), so also Hegel, who did not have this convention at his disposal, used italics in a similar fashion. For example, in §76 Hegel italicizes *Versicherung*, "assurance," to indicate that the "assurances" of those who claim, without any credibility, to be proponents of true philosophical science should not be taken very seriously. But the main ironical developments emerge as rather unexpected conclusions from the dialectic movement from "certainty" to "truth" which pervades all parts of the work. This process automatically and almost methodically yields numerous situations which can be characterized as truly ironic. Some of the major ironic developments include the following:

> *Realist being transformed willy-nilly into idealist*: In the first chapter, natural consciousness, starting out naturally with a naively realistic approach to knowledge, assumes that the greatest certainty can always be

attained from particular sense data. But after reexamining its basic experiences with place and time ("here" and "now"), it concludes that it is using "here" as a universal which can be applied to any place, and "now" as a universal which is applied to any segment of time. Thus, it becomes converted, hardly realizing what has taken place, to a Kantian-style idealist (§100), pointing to the ego, applying the universals, "Here" and "Now," as the source of true sensory data concerning place and time.

Master and slave changing roles: The type of consciousness that goes beyond mere relationships to objectivity and attains self-consciousness and freedom becomes, in primitive historical developments, the "master," who maintains his mastery over the objective world with the help of an object-type consciousness, the slave, who deals with the hard realities and prepares them for assimilation by the master. But the slave, working to the utmost out of "fear of the lord," eventually attains (§193) to a level of creativity and freedom which the formerly independent master, having become completely dependent on the slave, has forfeited.

Consciousness besting the Absolute: The Unhappy Consciousness, situated in contingency and changeability, but striving strenuously to overcome its sense of alienation from the Unchangeable, begins to intensify its acts of thanksgiving in order to cement its union with the universal source. But as these protestations of gratitude continue without satisfying its yearning, it arrives at the point where it realizes it is doing *more* than the Unchangeable (§222), so that the unevenness of their relationship is reversed.

The pathfinder in theoretical reason being converted from theory to practice: "Reason" in Hegel's construal is the coadaptation of being and thought, self and world. Consciousness at the initial stages of reason begins on the theoretical level, by researching the possibility that external realities in the inorganic, organic, and psychophysical world conform to rationally constructed laws and ideals. This endeavor constantly fails, and reaches the state of utter futility when the issue of the relationship of brain to mind is considered by phrenologists, who try to make predictions of what mind and personality will be like, by examining formations of the skull and brain. The consequent realization of the absurdity and futility of trying to establish the rationality of the world by such theories, leads to a contrary renewed effort (§§347ff.) to focus on the practical order: possibly the conformity of being to thought can best be established by examining not what consciousness *finds* in the world, but by what it *creates* and accomplishes.

Womankind and irony: In his discussion of the emergence the socio-political "ethical substance," Hegel discusses the way that the elaborate controls and power strategies of the male leaders are overturned by women, oriented towards the preservation of individuality and life, and "marching to a different drummer," so to speak. Hegel speaks here of womankind as the "everlasting irony of the polity" (§475).

Transformation of the moralist into a pragmatist: As rational consciousness proceeds to look for conformity between thought and being, it turns to moral ideals, the application of which seem to show promise as a key mode in which being and thought are united, and in which the ideal and the real converge. But the moral idealist ("knight of virtue"), who had hoped to verify the incorporation of moral ideals in the world, finds to his chagrin (§389) that the "way the world runs" (*Weltlauf*) follows its own distinct laws or processes, and can only be influenced by someone who understands and adapts to these processes, rather than imposing lofty ideals on them.

Nobility metamorphosing into sycophancy: Towards the beginning of the major subsection of Spirit, "Culture," Hegel introduces a type of consciousness styled as the "noble" consciousness, and redolent of the ideals of nobility integral to monarchical or aristocratic systems. The noble consciousness is defined (§500) as a type of consciousness which has a positive relationship both to state power and to wealth, and thus is typically a wealthy person who uses wealth properly in accord with the demands of his individuality, and shows nonsubservient fidelity to the state sovereign. But this erstwhile harmonious personality eventually and inevitably begins to experience a restless oscillation between the demands of patriotism and the pursuit of wealth, leading the noble consciousness to become "ignoble" (§519), and ending up as "distraught" or "disrupted" (§521), a pitiable individual groveling after means of subsistence by "paying court" to the powers that be.

The enlightened lumière *transformed into revolutionary terrorist*: The distraught consciousness, just described, is also a case study in dialectic, and his expertise in dialectical juggling of wealth and power becomes sublimated in an "insightful" type of consciousness able to master all contradictions in a new stage of Enlightenment, in which the power of the will over all reality is manifested. This power of will eventually becomes potentiated into the power imposed by particular self-styled exponents of the "universal" will; these particular wills, however, originally proudly claiming to be aligned with the universal, are inherently unable to express the universal, but can express only the particular (§588); and are doomed to obliteration at the behest of the next "universal" faction, if and when they happen to be intransigent or unassimilable (§590).

Paradox:

The term, "paradox," is often used in a wide sense to signify a statement or tenet that is contrary to the opinion or expectation of many. But in the strict sense it connotes something that sounds false and even contradictory, but is true. Numerous examples of paradox in this sense are found in literature and religion;[16] but paradox is found less frequently in philosophy. In a previous book I have documented the prevalence of paradoxes and oxymorons in Hegel's later system,[17] and I have argued that paradox, as the literary expression of the "conjunction of opposites," is the natural result of the employment of a dialectical methodology in Hegel's system, which claims to proceed from a privileged standpoint which has obviated the being-thought dichotomy. In the *Phenomenology*, which Hegel described as his "voyage of discovery," this standpoint is only attained "empirically" at the end of the work, in the chapter on "Absolute Knowledge." But the Preface to the *Phenomenology*, written after the body of that work, presupposes this standpoint and the philosophical conjunction of conventional oppositions, and offers us numerous examples of the paradoxical implications of this newly attained standpoint. Traditional concepts in philosophy now undergo major changes in connotations as Hegel reformulates their "Idea":

Substance is "simple negativity, and thus a splitting up of the simple," and a doubling that is "non diverse, and even the opposite of ordinary diversification" (§18). (This reformulation sums up Hegel's quest in the *Phenomenology* to overcome the abstract notion of substance as a simple unity, and show that "substance is subject," incorporating the inherent diversity germane to subjectivity.)

God's form, conventionally distinguished in Hegel's philosophical milieu from His essence, "is as essential as His essence" (§19) . Thus Hegel reformulates the traditional metaphysical thesis that in God there is no distinction between essence and existence.

The Absolute, traditionally portrayed as the origin of all things, is a result rather than a beginning (§20). Thus Hegel emphasizes the teleological rather than the essentialist aspect of the Absolute.

The ego, because of the simple/complex nature of self-consciousness, is defined as unmediated mediation (§20).

---

[16]See my 2006 Aquinas Lecture, *Five Metaphysical Paradoxes* (Milwaukee: Marquette University Press, 2006), 53–55.

[17]See *GWF Hegel* (New York: Macmillan/Twayne, 1996), Chapter IV.4.

The "unmoved mover"—in contrast to the traditional and Aristotelian notion of a "first cause"—is purposefulness, whose "beginning" is the end,
and whose "reality" is its concept (§22). Thus metaphysicians searching
for ultimate explanations of reality would do well to look to teleology
rather than "efficient causality" or etiology.

Our refutation of false theses requires us to bring them to their full development so that they can be properly understood; and our exposition of
principles requires us to assume a negative attitude to them, rather than
an attitude of advocacy (§24).

Familiar truths, or "received opinions," are unfamiliar and crying out for
criticism, simply because of their familiarity (§31).

Spirit, far from being any kind of fixed entity in itself, is the process of becoming other to itself (§36).

Self-identity or self-likeness, whether existing in objects or living things or
concepts, is self-differentiation, since only that which is distinct can be
compared and determined to be identical (§54); and the properly scientific philosophical standpoint is to capture pure self-likeness in self-
differentiation (§54).

The "concrete" existence of something is its logical existence, i.e., the concept which it incorporates; and its true "form" is the development of its
content (§56).

Determinate negations are never pure negations, but yield a positive content, supplying the motive power for further conceptual development in
philosophy (§59).

Metaphor:

Like "paradox," "metaphor" has a definite meaning—a word or phrase
that is used to stand for something different but analogous—but is sometimes used in a wider sense. For example, in the assertion that "the serpent
is a symbol of evil," "serpent" can be said to be a "metaphor" for something else. Donald Phillip Verene contends that the *Gestalten* of the
Phenomenology—the Master-Slave dialectic, the Unhappy Consciousness,
and so forth—are "metaphors." *Gestalten* are not metaphors, strictly
speaking; but possibly in the wide sense, if Hegel meant the Master-Slave
relationship to stand for some constants in human relationships, the Unhappy Consciousness to stand for man's relationship to God, and so forth.
Verene's deconstruction leads to this conclusion. But in the body of the
Phenomenology, one also comes across true metaphors, for example in
§622, where Hegel refers to natural drives as a "mainspring" for morality,

and describes Kantian morality's unsuccessful attempt to provide the "angle of inclination" for these drives.

But it is in the Preface to the *Phenomenology* that we find the main examples of metaphors. The Preface is not only replete with paradoxes, as was shown above, but is the unique locus in Hegel's opus where metaphors are rampant. It is as if Hegel, introducing a new approach to systematic philosophy to his contemporaries, was unable to find more precise "scientific" language to characterize his enterprise, and relied on the following series of metaphors (sometimes *mixed* metaphors) to persuade the public about its significance: Philosophical systems can be compared to flowering bushes in which buds give way to blossoms, which bring to fruition the salvageable essence of their forebears, though they appear to refute them (§2). Modern philosophy, like the Prodigal Son of the Gospels, impelled by guilt for squandering its birthright on the mere husks of truth, has been searching for consolation in the emotionalism of counterfeit philosophies, rather than in solid thought (§7). Former philosophies harbored a belief in a transcendent world, and they looked for threads of light leading to heaven (§8). Now, having renounced such otherworldly emphasis, contemporaries, like worms, are often content with this-worldly dirt and water (§8). And so the Spirit of the times is like a wanderer in the desert, parched with thirst, and easily satisfied with the modicum of refreshment that is supplied by purveyors of sublime feelings (§8). Thus philosophy is enshrouded in foggy mists which fall far short of the status of Science (§9), and deluded by practitioners who, like the "beloved faithful" of Psalm 127, think that God will give them wisdom in their sleep (§10). But our times are like the child in the womb, who develops slowly and almost imperceptibly, until at birth a qualitative change takes place, new life arrives; so also, changes have taken place in philosophy which are now coming to a head, and, like a flash of lightning in the darkness, are outlining the features of a new world (§11). The foundations have been laid for the new philosophical Science; but of course the foundation is not the building, just as the acorn is not the oak (§12). The current conflict between those who criticize the immature stage of the development of philosophy, and those who claim to have reached the zenith of that development, is the Gordian knot which "scientific culture" is now struggling to untie (§14). We have to avoid the error of the latter would-be "perfect" group, who try to give content to their very few insights by subsuming all sorts of materials into monochromatic formal structures, producing the Absolute as a "night in which all cows are black" (§16).

It goes without saying that if a reader used the Preface as an introduction to Hegel, and was not tuned to the literary devices, the metaphors would appear as poetic ambiguities and the paradoxes would appear as contradictions.

Syzygy:

"Contrast," as a literary device, is defined as "the juxtaposition of disparate or opposed images, ideas, or both, to heighten or clarify a scene, theme, or episode."[18] This definition is not quite strong enough to capture what Hegel does at certain special intervals in the course of the phenomenological dialectic. Perhaps a more accurate term would be "syzygy," the term for sidereal connections which Carl Jung borrows from astronomy to characterize "conjunctions of opposites" in personality development. As applied to Hegel, I am using the term to refer to occasional stages in his analysis of consciousness and Spirit in which the ongoing dialectic comes to a major conclusion or spiritual resolution with the unity-in-distinction of two paradigmatic or archetypal *Gestalten*. Two such instances have already been considered: The *Auseinandersetzung* of the "Beautiful Soul" and the Acting Conscience, in which saint and sinner, pure and impure, find unity in opposition, and merge in mutual forgiveness;[19] and the final confrontation between religion and scientific philosophy, laying the groundwork for "absolute knowledge."[20] I would point to one other development of this sort—easily missed because referred to only briefly by Hegel—drawing together figures from the beginning and the end of the *Phenomenology* into a final confrontation and dialectical rapprochement.

Happpy Self-Consciousness confronting the Unhappy Consciousness: Very early in the *Phenomenology*, chapter IV, Hegel presents to us the *Gestalt* of a self-consciousness striving with all manner of strategems for unity with the universal/unchangeable Substance; Consciousness, as an intrinsic relation to objectivity, is actually projecting itself and its fulfillment as this Substance. The alienation produced from this self-externalization finally gives way to the stage of Reason, in which the union of thought and reality, subject and substance, is seen in an abstract fashion; and then to Spirit, which entails a more concrete union, and in the aftermath of various cultural alienations arrives at the *Gestalt* of Conscience, and the vestibule of Religion, beginning in chapter VII.

But in religion, the counterpart of these developments takes place, beginning not with consciousness, but with *Substance* itself and moving in the opposite direction, towards *consciousness*. Initially, nature-religions encounter the Divine as substance and material, and prepare the way for the enhanced self-conscious developments of art-religion. Art-Religion achieves its culmination in comedy (the plays of Aristophanes are the obvious model Hegel has in mind); and the reason why this is the culmination is that in comedy all substantial realities—

---

[18]J. A. Cuddon, *A Dictionary of Literary Terms* (Garden City, NY: Doubleday, 1977).
[19]See earlier discussion, p. 32.
[20]See pp. 47–48.

including divinities as well as social customs and political establishments—are subjected to the overarching power of self-consciousness. The comic artist is one who, by satire, irony, ridicule, and other devices, in effect, subsumes substance and submerges it in self-consciousness.

But at this point—hundreds of pages after the analysis of the Unhappy Consciousness—the scene is laid for the ultimate stage of religion—Revealed Religion. Hegel in §§751–754 reminds us of the historical and social environment in which both the Happy Self-Consciousness and the Unhappy Consciousness had appeared: The Happy Self-Consciousness emerged at the apex of Greek art-religion, as Self-Consciousness in a sense attained to divinity by proving itself to be the power over the substantiality of the Divine; the Unhappy Consciousness developed in the aftermath of the "beautiful culture" exemplified by the Greek polity, as social cohesion was lost and replaced by the abstract legal persons exemplified in Roman culture and given philosophical expression in Stoicism. Thus (§755) the happy Self-Consciousness, in which Substance has alienated itself from itself and become self-consciousness, and the Unhappy Consciousness, in which self-consciousness in its alienation from the absolute Substance has become thing-like, and alienated from its own self-consciousness, turn out to be counterparts of each other and thus prepared for their unification. This takes place—according to Hegel's speculative reinterpretation of the birth of the God-man in Bethlehem—as the Divine Substance becomes manifest as a Self-Consciousness, and Self-Consciousness simultaneously encounters a Divinity from which it is no longer alienated (§§754-755).

Anomalies:

Anomalies or anachronisms "may be used deliberately to distance events and to underline a universal verisimilitude and timelessness—to prevent something being 'dated.'"[21] In artistic expressions, the appropriate comparison might be the Japanese artistic approach, *Sabi*, an intentional incompleteness, a perfected imperfection, meant to draw the attention and thoughts of the observer of the art object or painting away from, and beyond, the limited impressions actually encountered. The introduction of a wrong place or a wrong time in such cases is not a factual mistake, but geared to broadening the significance of the reference. The frequent inclusion of contemporary backgrounds and styles in Renaissance paintings of classical and Biblical subjects would be another example of the artistic use of anomalies. In Hegel's case, the intention seems to be to emphasize the universality of situations or

---

[21]Cuddon, *Dictionary of Literary Terms.*

figures. No commentator on Hegel points these anomalies out *as* anomalies or as mistakes, since, on the one hand, it is clear that Hegel's erudition was proof against inadvertently falling into such errors, and, on the other hand, the anomalies are effective for bringing out the universal import of the phenomenological *Gestalten*—in other words, the anomalies have been implicitly understood as *literary devices*. Some examples include the following:

> *Ceres and Bacchus*: Hegel refers in several places to the Greek "mystery" religions, in which sacrifices—bread and wine—were made to the gods. In chapter I, on Sense-Certainty, critiquing the view that particular sense objects are the most certain epistemological "givens," he suggests that proponents of such views ought to enter into the "ancient Eleusinian Mysteries of Ceres and Bacchus," so they might realize that sense objects are continually being annihilated as they are sacrificed to the higher powers of consciousness (§109). But with mention of the "mystery" religion connected with Eleusis in Greece, one might expect reference to the Greek god, Dionysius, and/or the Greek goddess, Demeter, rather than to Bacchus and Ceres, Roman counterparts of the Greek divinities. The anomaly reappears in chapter VII on Religion, where Hegel focuses on the ancient Greek mystery-cults as a stage of ritual in the development of Art-Religion, but again refers (§§718, 724) to Ceres and Bacchus. There were of course Hellenistic influences in Roman religion, and Greek gods were "adopted" by the Romans. But in these references, Hegel is not referring to hybrid Roman-Greek historical developments, but expanding the patterns to avoid pinpointing them historically.
>
> *The "Penates"*: In Hegel's discussion of the dialectical relationship between the divine law, connected with the rights of individuals and families, and the human law, dedicated to the preservation of order and the common good, although almost all of the imagery is Greek (Antigone vs. King Creon, the rivalries between Eteocles and Polyneices, the disintegration of the Greek polity, etc.), nevertheless the Penates, the Roman household gods, appear as an offshoot of the divine law. The imagery of the Penates (§§450, 457, 475) serves in Hegel's analysis to emphasize the alliance of the family with the divine law, and, in spite of its Roman character, to sum up the multiple examples Hegel gives in this section of the divine law operative within some paradigmatic characters of Greek drama—Antigone, Oedipus, Orestes, Agammemnon, and so forth.
>
> *Origen in the context of the French Enlighenment*: Origen is the Father of the Church who famously took the Gospel admonition literally to "make yourself a eunuch for the Kingdom of Heaven." In his analysis of the struggle of the Enlightenment with Faith, Hegel enters into the Enlight-

enment critique of attempts of believers to rid themselves of sensual desires by specific particular external acts, and Origen (one of the few people mentioned by name in the *Phenomenology*) becomes the prime example of this mistake (§570).

Judaism: Hegel's initial consideration of nature-religion begins with a segment on the divinity conceived as light—*das Lichtwesen*. Hegel emphasizes the abstractness and indeterminateness of the content of god-as-light, but attributes to this divinity some incipient determinations: The Deity "is clothed with the manifold forces of existence and with the forms of reality as with a selfless adornment; and these selfless forms are mere messengers of his will without any will of their own, evidence of his majesty, voices in his praise."[22] Hegel seems to be paraphrasing Psalm 104 of the Hebrew Scriptures: "Bless the Lord, O my Soul! O Lord, my God, you are great indeed! You are clothed with majesty and glory, robed in light as with a cloak. . . . You make the clouds your chariot; you travel on the wings of the wind. You make the winds your messengers, and flaming fire your ministers."[23]

The Black Stone of Mecca: In the discussion of nature-religion, with which chapter VII, "Religion," begins, Hegel analyzes the progression from the most "abstract" religions, such as the "religion of light," to gradual concretizations of notions of the divine in natural objects, plants and animals, and finally in the works of artisans. The implicit references are to ancient religions such as Zoroastrianism, Hinduism, and Egyptian religion, but towards the end he contrasts the external religious expressions with "simple darkness, the inert, the formless black stone"— referring to the black stone venerated by Muslims in the Ka'bah at Mecca. (§696). Hegel's intention is not to include Islam among ancient nature-religions; he was no doubt aware of the legends dating the black stone to Abraham, and the pre-Islamic pagan Arabic religious veneration of the stone. But he uses the black stone as an image of the inner nature of the divine essence which is still inchoate, and not yet fully united with its outer expressions (§707).

Shakespearean characters: In his analysis of the interplay of knowledge and not-knowing of characters in Greek tragedy, following oblique references to Oedipus, Orestes, the Delphic Oracle, Zeus, and other tragic personae, Hegel adds (§737) similarly oblique references to *Macbeth*

---

[22]§687 Dieses ist mit den mannigfachen Kraften des Daseins und den Gestalten der Wirklichkeit als mit einem selbstlosen Schmucke angekleidet; sie sind nur eignen Willens entbehrende Boten seiner Herrlichkeit und Stimmen seines Preises.

[23]*New American Bible* 4.

and *Hamlet*—the only references in the section on Art-Religion that depart from the all-pervasive Hellenic imagery.

As Hegel indicates in the very last paragraph of the book, his *Phenomenology* is not history, but history as subjected to the exigencies of conceptual comprehension. The juxtaposition of anomalies and anachronisms in the midst of rather pointed historical imagery is not just an exercise of artistic license, but offers judicious indications at certain points that this is history of a different sort.

Humor and Satire:

Hegel has a reputation for being dull, leaden and humorless; and of course humor, like beauty, is to some extent "in the eye of the beholder." But the following examples from the *Phenomenology* should offer some evidence to the unprejudiced reader that Hegel can indeed be witty and caustically so:

- §10 Philosophers who depend on feeling and intuition for their insights are like those about whom the Psalmist says "God gives them wisdom in their sleep"—and thus what they produce is only dreams.
- §73 Philosophers who think they can catch a glimpse of the Absolute by examining our powers of cognition first, are like the bird-watcher who thinks he can get closer to a bird by using a lime twig. But the Absolute, which is already at hand, makes fun of such strenuous efforts.
- §109 Those who wonder whether they can really know sense objects ought to consider the wisdom of brute animals, who don't just stand paralyzed before sense particulars but, without any further adieu, proceed to "gobble them up."
- §346 Nature itself has played a joke on us, since it "combines the organ of its highest fulfillment, the organ of generation, with the organ of urination."
- §665 No hero is a hero to his valet, since the valet is the one who sees him as a private individual eating, drinking and dressing.
- §803 The "absolute unity" of Schellingian "Substance" is an empty abyss into which all content is cast arbitrarily.

"Absolute Knowledge"
and the History of Modern Philosophy

The title of the last chapter of the *Phenomenology*—"Absolute Knowledge"—can conjure up in our minds some lofty images, no doubt stimulated by the lines, adapted from Schiller's poem, *Die Freundschaft*, with which Hegel ends this chapter and the entire book:

> Out of the chalice of this realm of spirits
> His infinity streams forth to the Absolute Spirit.[1]

Schiller's poem has to do with God creating innumerable spirits, and receiving from them companionship and the only possible reflection of his infinity. Taking our cue from this, we might interpret Absolute Knowledge, by analogy, to be—if not a mystical unity with the divine mind—something like an infinite comprehension, reflected in a final "absolute" Concept-of-all-concepts.

From the standpoint of someone who is suspicious, even fearful, of metaphysics, Hegel's "Absolute Knowledge" seems to represent an "I told you so," strengthening their resolve to avoid such thinking. As Walter Jaeschke observes, from the viewpoint of someone with an antimetaphysical bent, even the terminology seems highfalutin and off-putting:

> Whoever affirms the possibility of an "absolute knowledge" or ascribes such a knowledge to himself, will not have any further need to overcome his own ignorance: He has exonerated himself. The structure of the term, "absolute knowledge," contains not only a misunderstanding of the nature of all knowledge (since "knowledge" is always "determinate," mediated, and thus relative, and

---

[1] *Aus dem Kelche dieses Geisterreiches/schäumt ihm seine Unendlichkeit.*

can never be *absolute* knowledge). This construal stands as the height of philosophical hubris, and someone is always justified in avoiding, with a resigned 'a word to the wise suffices,' the type of person who maintains that an 'absolute knowledge' is possible and even claims it for himself.[2]

And some interpretations by Hegelian commentators tend to invite such caricatures of metaphysical sublimity.

INTERPRETATIONS OF ABSOLUTE KNOWLEDGE

Jon Stewart's interpretation of absolute knowledge falls into such a category. He characterizes it as a superseding and all-encompassing Concept:

> The absolute Notion is . . . the Notion which encompasses all other Notions within itself. It is the complete or exhaustive Notion. In other words, absolute knowing is the panoptic overview of all previous Notions. Hegel thus makes clear that absolute knowing is not the knowing of any particular fact or ultimate piece of wisdom but rather it is merely the grasping of the various forms of thought as a whole . . . Every individual truth or value must be understood in a larger context.[3]

The "larger context," for Herbert Schnädelbach, is a final comprehensive view of all the moments and stages that have been considered and superseded in the *Phenomenology*:

> [Hegel's chapter on Absolute Knowledge] can be characterized as nothing other than a summarizing overview of the whole process of the experience of consciousness, which the reader has endeavored to peruse. "Absolute Knowledge," according to Hegel, is the fully explicit self-knowledge of Spirit, that cannot as a result be distinguished from Spirit's process of knowing or experiencing.[4]

For John Russon, the "larger context" is not just the "various forms of thought"; it is primarily constituted by an intersubjective comprehension of being:

[2]Walter Jaeschke, "Das absolute Wissen," in *Hegel's "Phänomenologie des Geistes" Heute*, Andreas Arndt & Ernst Müller, eds. Deutsche Zeitschrift für Philosophie, Special Editiion #8 (Akademie Verlag, 2004), 194–195.

[3]Jon Stewart, "The Architectonic of Hegel's *Phenomenology of Spirit*," in Jon Stewart, ed., *The Phenomenology of Spirit Reader* (Albany, NY: SUNY Press, 1998), 471. This description is repeated in Stewart's *The unity of Hegel's Phenomenology of Spirit: a Systematic Interpretation* (Evanston, IL.: Northwestern University Press, 2000), 459, 465.

[4]Herbert Schnädelbach, *Hegel zur Einführung* (Hamburg: Junius Verlag, 1999).

Absolute knowing is the stance that sees metaphysics embedded within experience, and sees metaphysical—experiential—positions as intersubjective communications. . . . Absolute knowing, being—the "is"—is the enactment of intersubjective recognition itself. To say "is" is to say "successful communication" or "shared perspective."[5]

Robert Stern, emphasizing the overcoming of alienation, writes that for Science (in the Hegelian sense) to be possible,

Consciousness must have come to see, through a process of self-examination, that it can arrive at a view of the world that will make the world fully intelligible, where until then it has appeared alien to consciousness.[6]

Stern adds that this stage takes place in the *Phenomenology* only after the pictorial truths of the Christian religion have been demythologized, and cast in a more rational form.[7]

Henry Harris points out that this process of demythologization, in Hegel's account, takes place in the final stages of "Revealed Religion," after the death of the God-man, who is spiritually resurrected in the religious community. The community eventually attains a rational understanding of the spiritual events which have taken place in human consciousness. Many of these events have been charted in the process of Hegel's phenomenology of Spirit-as-consciousness (chapter VI), and Spirit-as-self-consciousness (chapter VII).

'Absolute knowledge' . . . has to be the knowledge expressed in the religion of a community that has arrived at a rational relationship with the world, and with itself; it is the knowledge that is finally and demonstrably necessary (in a logical sense, and not just as a matter of received general conviction) for the complete realization of human Reason.[8]

THE IMPORTANCE OF THE SUBJECT-OBJECT PROBLEMATIC

The common denominator in all these interpretations is that Absolute Knowledge is a state that results after following Hegel's analysis of all the states of consciousness and Spirit in the *Phenomenology*, and in particular the state discussed in chapter VII on Religion, which sets the stage for the appearance

---

[5]John Russon, *Reading Hegel's* Phenomenology (Bloomington and Indianapolis: Indiana University Press, 2004), 227.

[6]*Hegel and the* Phenomenology of Spirit (London: Routledge, 2002), 197.

[7]*Hegel and the* Phenomenology of Spirit, 195.

[8]H.S. Harris, *Hegel's Ladder* II (Indianapolis: Hackett, 1998), 709.

of Absolute Knowledge in chapter VIII, putting all the parts together, so to speak.

But as Jaeschke emphasizes, it is of the utmost importance to focus on the meaning that Hegel himself attached to the phrase, which has to be taken in the context of history, and the history of philosophy:

> In the conclusion of his Jena *Lectures on the History of Philosophy*, Hegel characterizes 'absolute knowledge' [as follows]: 'Absolute knowledge is this: to know opposition in unity, and unity in opposition.' But this knowledge of opposition in unity and unity in opposition is not—as it may seem at first—a playful and restless oscillation between these two poles—from unity to opposition, and then vice versa. Rather, Hegel next portrays this overcoming of bifurcation in a dramatic, even military fashion: "It seems that the World-Spirit has now managed to do away with all alien objective being, and finally to comprehend itself as absolute Spirit, and to produce out of itself what becomes objective to it, and to maintain this objectivity serenely under its control. The battle has ceased between finite self-consciousness and an absolute self-consciousness that appears as something external to the finite." Thus the message is about "reconciliation," since with the attainment of "absolute knowledge" this battle—whose staging ground is world-history and especially the philosophy of history—is over. Both have arrived at the point "where this absolute self-consciousness, the imaginative representation of which these histories possessed, ceases to be something foreign—and thus where Spirit is actualized as Spirit."[9]

As Charles Taylor cautions us,

> the common idea that "absolute knowledge is simply the whole content of the PhG" and that "the last chapter has meaning only as a recapitulation of the rest" is only partly true.[10]

The essence of what has been taking place throughout the *Phenomenology* and is finally brought to the fore in the standpoint of Absolute Knowledge is the following:

> The drama has been the split between subject and object, between consciousness and self-consciousness, certainty of self and truth. This is finally overcome at the end of the work.[11]

In other words, with Absolute Knowledge, a seachange has taken place. The phenomenologist has allegedly overcome all the subject-object di-

---

[9]*Hegel and the* Phenomenology of Spirit, 211–212.
[10]Charles Taylor, *Hegel* (London: Cambridge University Press, 1975), 214.
[11]Taylor, *Hegel*, 214.

chotomies prevailing in the Western philosophical tradition, and is ready to start again, no longer weighted down with such misleading presuppositions. As Hans Fulda observes, the "absolute" knowledge attained at the end of the *Phenomenology* is

> a knowledge absolved from the merest presupposition of an object. Such a knowledge has overcome the antagonism between subject and object, and simultaneously is an immediate—albeit unelaborated—knowledge of the Absolute.[12]

The real importance of Absolute Knowledge, in Hegel's estimation, is not so much that it is the end state which brings to a conclusion all the processes analyzed in the *Phenomenology*, but that it is the immediate, unelaborated, new *beginning* for the new approach to the Science of philosophy which Hegel was planning, and to which the *Phenomenology* was meant to be the introduction. This new beginning, as we shall see, was to find as its springboard the history of modern philosophy, and would bring to a conclusion the gradual refinement of the subject-object relationship that had been taking place in that arena. Absolute Knowledge, present now in its immediacy, presented the groundwork for Hegel's eventual elaboration of his philosophical system.

THE EMERGENCE OF ABSOLUTE KNOWLEDGE FROM MODERN PHILOSOPHY

Hegel situates his own project, and the future elaborations of "absolute knowledge," in his discussion of modern philosophy in §§802–804 of chapter VIII. This highly condensed sketch covers about two pages, summarizing the developments in modern philosophy which have prepared the way for the present stage of philosophical Science.

The brevity of this sketch of modern philosophy is of a piece with the brevity of this whole chapter. As is well known, Hegel, working on the manuscript of the *Phenomenology* in Jena, spurred on by a publisher's deadline and also by the news of the Napoleonic advances towards Jena, tried hurriedly to sum up the pivotal developments of the *Phenomenology* in his final chapter, making the chapter exceedingly difficult for subsequent readers, as well as for commentators, to disentangle. But with the short overview of the history of philosophy contained in this chapter, he sets the stage for his final arguments and his conclusions about the Absolute Knowledge that grounds scientific philosophy. The historical sketch is worth considering in some detail.

---

[12]Hans Friedrich Fulda, *Georg Wilhelm Friedrich Hegel* (München: Verlag Beck, 2003), 91–92.

Why does Hegel begin this sketch, not with classical philosophers like Plato or Aristotle, but with thinkers who are now considered luminaries of "modern philosophy"? For one thing, this indicates Hegel's preoccupation with distinctively modern epistemological and ontological problems: Cartesianism, dualism, the Kantian "transcendental turn," the problem of the thing-in-itself. These are issues that Aristotle, Plato *et al* never thought of, problems peculiar to the modern age, problems that we philosophers in our own time are still laboring on.

It should be noticed also—turning to Hegel's *Lectures on the History of Philosophy* for a comparison—that Hegel, at the very end of these *Lectures*, argues that although the absolute Idea had emerged in the philosophies of Plato and Aristotle, and had become concretized in the Neoplatonic philosophy, "the work of the modern age is to grasp this Idea as Spirit, and the Idea knowing itself."[13] This development of the self-knowledge of Spirit, in Hegel's estimation, is the special contribution of modern philosophy, its special "claim to fame," the final progressive development which capped off centuries of work by major philosophers. Then, continuing for a couple pages in this concluding section of the *Lectures*, Hegel offers an abbreviated sketch, a final summation, of the major developments in modern philosophy, mentioning Descartes, Spinoza, Leibniz, Kant, Fichte, and Schelling as the high points in the progress to Spirit's self-comprehension.

The sketch of modern philosophy at the end of the *Phenomenology* follows along these same lines and is similar in the thrust of its argumentation; but it begins with Francis Bacon rather than Descartes.

After overcoming the otherworldly alienations of medieval Christianity, says Hegel, "Consciousness discovers this present world as its own property . . . Through observation, consciousness . . . finds and grasps conceptually existence as thought."[14] This is the phenomenological stage which Hegel had already analyzed in great detail in chapter V of the *Phenomenology*, in the section on "Observation of Nature." The archetypal example of this mode of observation at the dawn of the modern age is Bacon, who maintained that there were laws and mathematical regularities in the physical world and that we could force nature to reveal these to us by painstaking observation and experimentation.

But this development was not without its dialectic antipode. The counterpart to Bacon's search for the lineaments of thought in nature was the

---

[13]G. W. F. Hegel, *Werke in zwanzig Bänden*, Vol. 20, *Vorlesungen über die Geschichte der Philosophie*, III (Frankfurt am Main: Suhrkamp Verlag, 1971), 458.

[14]§803. All references for this chapter are to G.W.F. Hegel, *Hegel's Phenomenology of Spirit: Selections Translated and Annotated by Howard P. Kainz* (University Park: Pennsylvania State University Press, 1994). The rendition of *Dasein* as "existence-here-and-now" in that translation has been shortened to "existence."

pathfinding investigations of Descartes, through whose work, as Hegel puts it, "consciousness finds existence within its own thinking."[15] This Cartesian endeavor was also charted at length previously in chapter V.B. of the *Phenomenology*, subtitled "The Actualization of Self-Consciousness through Itself," where consciousness searched for and eventually found a nonalien objectivity within itself, producing an absolute fusion of subjectivity and objective existence in a phenomenological *Gestalt* which Hegel designated *die Sache selbst*.

But the Cartesian reconciliation of thought and existence was imperfect and abstract. Spinoza came on the scene, and through his labor, says Hegel, "consciousness expressed abstractly the immediate *unity* of thinking *and existence*, of abstract essence and the self" in a monolithic divine substance incorporating and unifying even the immense diversity of subjective thoughts in its modes. There is also a stage corresponding to this development in the body of the *Phenomenology*. At the outset of chapter VI on Spirit, we find a reflection of this unifying substance in the development of an "ethical substance" unifying all individual consciousnesses—a *Gestalt* patterned after the Greek polity, in which unity was emphasized at the expense of particular individuality.

But such extreme Spinozan emphasis on the *unity* of thought and existence gave rise in the history of philosophy to an equal and opposite reaction on the part of Leibnitz, who, observes Hegel, shrank back from this "*selfless* substance" and "asserted the claims of individuality" against such overarching unity." Hegel's reference here is obviously to Leibniz's theory of the constitution of reality by monads endowed with perception or thought. This Leibnitzian movement towards individualization was carried forth by the individualistic *philosophes* of the French Enlightenment, such as Voltaire and Diderot, with whose help, according to Hegel, consciousness "externalized individuality in Culture." This individualizing process is also described in the *Phenomenology* in the sections on "Culture" which follow after the breakup of the "ethical substance."

The spirit of individualism develops further to an extreme degree, when individualistic thought is systematically propagated in the sphere of existence, so that even existent objects in the world must receive their meaning and value from conscious intentions; and this is the process whereby, as Hegel puts it, "consciousness comes to the thought of utility," that is, the philosophy of utility, proposed by Helvetius and other French champions of utilitarianism, whose attempts to project thought-designations on external objects is

---

[15]Hegel, *Selections*, §803.

discussed in the section on "the 'Truth' of the Enlightenment" (chapter VI.B.II.b) which comes at the end of the discussion of the Enlightenment in the *Phenomenology*. But this utilitarian phase, in which things are referred systematically to the human will, is not innocuous; when carried to its logical conclusion, it arrives at a tragic extreme and its final stage, where, Hegel says, consciousness comes to "grasp existence as its own will."[16] The main philosophical proponent of this new development was Jean-Jacques Rousseau, who thought that the ideal of a "General Will" could actually be put in control of the body politic. Rousseau's theories inspired utopians like Robespierre to attempt to implement politically the ideal of "Absolute Freedom," subjecting even the consciousness and wills of other persons to utilitarian manipulation. Such ideological excesses eventually led to a real-world terror, described by Hegel in chapter VI.B.III of the *Phenomenology*.[17]

Before proceeding any further, we might note that in this historical sketch we are considering, while there are many apparent references to developments in German and French philosophy, there are no discernible references to *British* philosophy after Bacon. The question naturally comes to our mind, what do Hobbes, Locke, Berkeley, Hume, and others contribute to this development of the self-consciousness of Spirit in modern philosophy? Apparently not much, in Hegel's opinion. If we look to Hegel's later *Lectures on the History of Philosophy* for evidence, we find that, while Hegel does treat of Anglophone philosophy there, he does so in a very patronizing manner, commenting, for example, that Locke's philosophy can at best be described as a "metaphysicizing empiricism,"[18] and that Hobbes' insights are "shallow and empirical."[19] Certainly Hume is important for rousing Kant from his "dogmatic slumber"; but in general it seems that, in Hegel's estimation, Anglophone philosophy had little intrinsic value.

Towards the end of the section on "Absolute Freedom" in the *Phenomenology*, Hegel indicates that when he is speaking about consciousness "grasping existence as its own will," he is referring not only to Rousseau but also to Kant, who, in Hegel's interpretation, extracted the essence of Rousseau's idea of a General Will from the political realm of the real world, where it had had such tragic consequences, and extrapolated it into the "unreal" realm of moral philosophy, the realm of thinking, where (it would seem) it would at least not cause any more heads to be cut off by the guillotine. As Hegel sums up the aftermath of the revolutionary spirit, at the end of the section on "Absolute

---

[16]Hegel, *Selections*, §803
[17]See earlier discussion, p. 28.
[18]Hegel, *Werke*, vol. 20, 223.
[19]Hegel, *Werke*, 227.

Freedom" in the *Phenomenology*, §595, "absolute freedom passes out of its self-destructive reality and over into another land of Self-Conscious Spirit, a land in which 'absolute freedom' in its state of unreality [i.e., as pure knowing] will count as 'the truth,'" i.e., no longer as a political agenda but as a moral imperative. The "land" is of course Germany. And here is where Kant's moral philosophy becomes the main focus. Hegel proceeds to his examination of Morality (chapter VI.C), at the outset of which he offers an intensive and detailed critique of the Kantian idea that the human will can and must legislate imperatives to be enacted in the natural world and to be implemented even in contravention of natural human inclinations. This was Kant's uniquely intellectualistic approach to expressing the *Volonté general* of Rousseau.

Hegel, along with many of his contemporaries, was appalled at the Kantian notions of morality, and at one place in the *Phenomenology* (§617) he refers to Kant's moral philosophy as "a whole nest of mindless contradictions." Clearly superior to Kant's moral system was the system of Fichte, with a consideration of which Hegel completes chapter VI of the *Phenomenology*, just before proceeding to chapter VII on Religion. Fichte's moral theory, emphasizing *Gewissen*, or "conscientiousness," was the logical or systematic conclusion of Fichte's *Science of Knowledge*, which is based on his insight about the self-identity of the pure ego. Thus Hegel, in his summation of the history of modern philosophy in the chapter on Absolute Knowledge, after commenting on the Rousseauean/Kantian development of the idea of absolute liberty, explicitly uses the Fichtean formula of ego-identity and says, "after all of this, consciousness publicizes the thought of its innermost depth, and expresses the essence as ego=ego."

Hegel then, with reference to the Fichtean dialectic of ego=ego, discusses the issue of the interplay of identity and difference and the relationship of identity and difference to time and extension, which were also important issues for Fichte. Hegel then proceeds to the dialectical stage at which the self-identity of the ego collapses into immediacy, such that subject becomes substance, and substance becomes the object of immediate intuition.

It is with this development, in his historical sketch, that Hegel arrives at the Schellingean problematic: Ego=ego has collapsed and become fused into substance. But how is this absolute substance, immediately intuited, related to the content of subjectivity and Spirit? This results in an impasse. Amid the grand unity of this absolute, where is the content? Hegel concludes, "If under such circumstances there should still be talk of a 'content,' it would be partly in order merely to cast this content (which, on its part, would be scared up in an external fashion out of sense-perception) into the empty abyss of the absolute" (§803). Hegel makes the same point in a stronger way a little later, when, in writing the Preface to the *Phenomenology* (§16), he refers to this sort of substantive, subject-less absolute as a "night in which all cows are black."

ABSOLUTE KNOWLEDGE AS THE GOLDEN MEAN
BETWEEN PHILOSOPHICAL EXTREMES

Having finished this capsule summary of the history of modern philosophy, Hegel then (in §804) situates his own position securely in the middle between Fichte and Schelling, as a kind of mediator between two extreme interpretations of the function of the ego:

The Fichtean extreme is described first: "The ego in the *form* of *self-consciousness* does not have to hold itself fast against the form of substantiality and objectivity, as if it had anxiety about being externalized." But the Schellingean extreme is equally unsatisfactory: "Neither is the ego some mediating entity [*ein Drittes*] that casts the differences back into the abyss of the absolute and asserts their 'identity' within the absolute." Then Hegel gives his own middle-of-the-road solution: "But knowledge consists rather in this apparent inactivity [of Spirit] that merely considers how what is differentiated moves itself in itself and devolves once again into its unity."

As Hans Fulda points out,[20] this is the paragraph in which Hegel presents Absolute Knowledge as the upshot of the prior developments in modern Western philosophy. Like Aristotle, portraying virtue as the rational middle-ground between two extremes, Hegel portrays absolute knowledge as a final moderate standpoint, avoiding the Fichtean dilemma of subjectivity trying in vain to avoid being immersed in external objectivity by holding on tenaciously to the determinations of the ego; but also avoiding the Schellingean impasse of asserting an absolute substantial identity of subject and object, and then discovering the embarrassing fact that there is no way to locate differences within the abyss of this absolute. Hegel's own "moderate" absolute insists on the recognition that the unity of the absolute is an identity of identity *and* difference, that the ego can situate itself at the *juncture* of thought and being, and that substance at its most concrete level *incorporates* subjectivity.

According to Hegel's interpretation of the history of Western philosophy, the main concern of philosophers from time immemorial has always been to coordinate being and thought. In modern philosophy since Descartes, the im-

---

[20]*Georg Wilhelm Friedrich Hegel*, 92.

portance of subjectivity has been more fully brought out, leading to the "Copernican revolution" of Kant. But now, in Hegel's time, the ground had been prepared for a more balanced, explicit, dialectical coordination of subjectivity and objectivity and interrelated oppositions. Hegel's *Phenomenology of Spirit* shows how the internal exigencies of knowledge had eventually led the way to this benign development; and the final historical sketch in §§803–804 of the *Phenomenology* emphasizes that "external" developments—the history of philosophy itself—have indeed created conditions ripe for the emergence of this new perspective. As he finished writing his *Phenomenology*, Hegel was making plans to demonstrate scientifically in his later system of philosophy just how Absolute Knowledge could coordinate oppositions in logic, nature, and the realm of spirit, systematically balancing unity with difference on these three levels.

Hegel's Absolute Knowledge is thus "absolute" in the sense that it is free and independent of philosophical extremes. This meaning of "absolute" is first adumbrated in the beginning of chapter V, Reason, where Hegel situates the "category" of true, authentic philosophical idealism between, on the one hand, the ten object-oriented Aristotelian categories and, on the other hand, the twelve subjectively conditioning Kantian categories and Fichte's Kantian revisionism in terms of the ego's self-identity:

> The *Category*, which formerly had the connotation of being the substantiality of what exists—either (indefinitely) the substantiality of existence-in-general, or the substantiality of existence over against consciousness—is now the *substantiality*, i.e. the simple *unity*, of the existent only insofar as it is a thinking-reality. . . . Only a one-sided, defective Idealism lets this unity come to the fore again as consciousness, on one side, and, over against consciousness, an in-itself. But the present Category, that is, the *simple* unity of Self-Consciousness and existence, has *difference* within itself. For its essence is just this: to be immediately identical-with-self in *otherness*, in absolute difference.[21]

The Categories relevant to Absolute Knowledge, in other words, will be distinguished by their focus on unities-in-differences, and their paradoxical coordination of opposites. As was mentioned in this chapter earlier, the Preface to the *Phenomenology*, written after the completion of the work, is notable for the

---

[21]§235 Die *Kategorie*, welche sonst die Bedeutung hatte, Wesenheit des Seyenden zu seyn, *unbestimmt* des Seyenden überhaupt oder des Seyenden gegen das Bewußtseyn, ist itzt *Wesenheit* oder einfache *Einheit* des Seyenden nur als denkende Wirklichkeit. . . . Nur der einseitige schlechte Idealismus läßt diese Einheit wieder als Bewußtseyn auf die eine Seite, und ihr gegenüber ein *Ansich* treten. Diese Kategorie nun oder *einfache* Einheit des Selbstbewußtseyns und des Seyns hat aber an sich *den Unterschied*; denn ihr Wesen ist eben dieses, im *Andersseyn* oder im absoluten Unterschiede unmittelbar sich selbst gleich zu seyn.

plethora of paradoxes it contains. But the most notable effects of Hegel's generation of paradoxical categories out of dialectical processes is to be found in his later systematic works—particularly his *Science of Logic* and *Encyclopedia of the Philosophical Sciences*. In Hegel's system, the reader soon becomes accustomed to paradoxical categories—being as nothingness, identity as a species of difference, essences as inessential, Nature as the transitoriness of the Idea, light as immaterial matter, the rational as the real, freedom as bolstered by determinations, and so forth.

Hegel insisted that philosophies are unavoidably products of their own times; and he would not consider his own philosophy an exception to this rule. The paradoxical categories that emerged under the rubric of "absolute knowledge" in his work brought together some of the opposing positions in his day regarding metaphysics, science, philosophical anthropology, political science, and other subjects. Contemporary thinkers trying to coordinate oppositions regarding mind and body, heredity and environment, freedom and determinism, duty and inclinations, religion and science, and so forth in our own era, might claim to be pursuing "absolute knowledge" in the Hegelian sense.

Works Consulted

Barth, Karl. *Protestant Thought: From Rousseau to Ritschl*. Translated by Brian Cozzens. New York: Simon & Schuster, 1969.

Cuddon, J.A. *A Dictionary of Literary Terms*. Garden City, NY: Doubleday, 1977.

Fichte, Johann Gottlieb. *The Science of Ethics*. Translated by A. E. Kroeger. London: Kegan Paul, 1907.

Fulda, Hans Friedrich. *Georg Wilhelm Friedrich Hegel*. München: Verlag Beck, 2003.

Goethe, Johann Wolfgang von. *Faust*. Translated by Walter Arndt. New York: W.W. Norton & Co., 1976.

Haering, Theodore. *Die Entstehungsgeschichte der Phänomenologie des Geistes* in *Verhandlungen des 3. Hegelknogresses*. B. Wigersma, ed. Tübingen, 1934.

———. *Hegel, sein Wollen und sein Werk: eine chronologische Entwicklungs- geschichte der Gedanken und der Sprache Hegels*. Stuttgart: Scientia Verlag Aalen, 1963.

Harris, H.S. *Hegel's Ladder II: The Odyssey of Spirit*. Indianapolis, IN: Hackett, 1997.

Hegel, G.W.F. *Early Theological Writings*, Translated by T. M. Knox. Philadelphia: University of Pennsylvania Press, 1971.

———. *Grundlinien der Philosophie des Rechts*. In *Werke in zwanzig Bänden*, Vol. 5.

———. *Phänomenologie des Geistes*. Wolfgang Bonsiepen and Reinhard Heede, eds. (Band 9 of the "Akademie" edition, *Gesammelte Werke*). Hamburg: Felix Meiner Verlag, 1980.

———. *The Phenomenology of Spirit*. Translated by A.V. Miller. Oxford: Oxford University Press, 1977.

———. *Phenomenology of Spirit: Selections Translated and Annotated by Howard P. Kainz*. University Park: Pennsylvania State University Press, 1988. (Abbreviated *SPK*.)

———. *The Philosophy of History*. Translated by John Sibree. New York: Dover, 1956.

——. *Philosophy of Nature*. Translated by A.V. Miller. Oxford: Oxford University Press, 1970.

——. *Philosophy of Right*. Translated by T.M. Knox. New York: Oxford University Press, 1967.

——. *Science of Logic*. Translated by A.V. Miller. Oxford: Oxford University Press, 1969.

——. *Spirit* (chapter VI of the *Phenomenology of Spirit*). Translated by Dan Shannon et al. Indianapolis, IN: Hackett, 2001.

——. *Vorlesungen über die Geschichte der Philosophie*, III. *Werke in zwanzig Bänden*, Vol. 20. Frankfurt am Main: Suhrkamp Verlag, 1971.

——. *Wissenschaft der Logik*. In *Werke in zwanzig Bänden*, Vol. 5. Frankfurt am Main: Suhrkamp Verlag, 1969.

——. *Hegel's Ladder I: The Pilgrimage of Reason*. Indianapolis, IN: Hackett, 1997.

Hösle, Vittorio. *Hegel's System: der Idealismus der Subjektivität und das Problem der Intersubjecktivität*. Hamburg: Felix Meiner Verlag, 1988.

Jaeschke, Walter. "Das absolute Wissen." In *Hegel's "Phänomenologie des Geistes" Heute*, Andreas Arndt and Ernst Müller, eds. Deutsche Zeitschrift für Philosophie, Special Edition #8 (Akademie Verlag, 2004).

James, William, *The Varieties of Religious Experience*. Cambridge, MA: Harvard University Press, 1985.

Kainz, Howard. *GWF Hegel: the Philosophical System*. Athens: Ohio University Press, 1996.

——. *Hegel's Phenomenology, Part I: Analysis and Commentary*. Athens: Ohio University Press, 1988.

——. *Hegel's Phenomenology, Part II: the Evolution of Ethical and Religious Consciousness to the Dialectical Standpoint*. Athens: Ohio University Press, 1983.

——. *Paradox, Dialectic and System: a Contemporary Reconstruction of the Hegelian Problematic*. University Park: Pennsylvania State University Press, 1988.

Kant, Immanuel. *Critique of Pure Reason*. Translated by Norman Kemp Smith. New York: St. Martin's Press, 1965.

——. *Fundamental Principles of the Metaphysic of Morals*. Indianapolis, IN: Library of Liberal Arts, 1949.

Kaufmann, Walter. *Hegel: Reinterpretation, Texts and Commentary*. London: Weidenfeld and Nicholson, 1966.

Kierkegaard, Søren. *The Concept of Anxiety: a Simple Psychologically Orienting Deliberation on the Dogmatic Issue of Hereditary Sin*. Translated by Reidar Thomte. Princeton, NJ: Princeton University Press, 1980.

——. *Either/Or*, Vols. I and II. Translated by Walter Lowrie. Garden City, NY: Doubleday Anchor, 1959.

——. *Fear and Trembling*. Translated by Walter Lowrie. Princeton, NJ: Princeton University Press, 1974.

——. *Søren Kierkegaard's Journals and Papers*. Edited and translated by Howard V. Hong and Edna H. Hong, Assisted by Gregor Malantschuk. Bloomington and London: Indiana University Press, 1970.

Labarrière, P. J. *Structures et Mouvement Dialectique dans la Phénoménologie de l'Esprit de Hegel*. Paris: Aubier, 1968.

Marx, Karl, *Capital*. Translated by Ben Fowkes. New York: Vintage Books, 1977.

———. *Critique of Hegel's "Philosophy of Right."* Translated by Joseph O'Malley and Annette Jolin. Cambridge:Cambridge University Press, 1970.

Meaney, Mark. *Capital as Organic Unity: the Role of Hegel's* Science of Logic *in Marx's* Grundrisse. Dordrecht: Kluwer, 2002.

O'Malley, Joseph. "Marx's Precis of Hegel's Doctrine on Being in the Minor Logic." *International Review of Social History*, Vol. XXII (1977), Part 3.

Pöggeler, Otto. *Hegel's Idee einer Phänomenologie des Geistes*. Freiburg: Verlag Karl Alber, 1973.

Russon, John. *Reading Hegel's* Phenomenology. Bloomington and Indianapolis: Indiana University Press, 2004.

Scheier, Claus-Artur. *Analytischer Kommentar zu Hegels Phänomenologie des Geistes*. Freiburg: Verlag Karl Alber, 1980.

Schnädelbach, Herbert. *Hegel zur Einführung*. Hamburg: Junius Verlag, 1999.

Souche-Dagues, Denise. *Le circle hégélien*. Paris: Presses Universitaires de France, 1986.

Stern, Robert. *Philosophy Guidebook to Hegel and the* Phenomenology of Spirit. London: Routledge, 2002.

Stewart, Jon. *Kierkegaard's Relations to Hegel, Reconsidered*. Cambridge: Cambridge University Press, 2003).

———, ed. *The* Phenomenology of Spirit *Reader*. Albany: SUNY Press, 1998.

Taylor, Charles. *Hegel*. London: Cambridge University Press, 1975.

Taylor, Mark. *Journeys to Selfhood*. Berkeley: University of California Press, 1980.

Travis, D.C., ed. *A Hegel Symposium*. Austin: University of Texas Press, 1962.

Verene, Donald Phillip. *Hegel's Recollection*. Albany: SUNY Press, 1985.

Voegelin, Eric. *Collected Works*, Vol. 12. Baton Rouge: Louisiana State University Press, 1990.

Westphal, Kenneth. *Hegel's Epistemological Realism*. Dordrecht: Kluwer, 1989.

Index

THE COMMUNIST MOVEMENT IN EGYPT

1920–1988

Tareq Y. Ismael
and Rifa'at El-Sa'id

SYRACUSE UNIVERSITY PRESS

Copyright © 1990 by Syracuse University Press
Syracuse, New York 13244-5160
All Rights Reserved

First Edition 1990

99 98 97 96 95 94 93 92 91 90   6 5 4 3 2 1

The paper used in this publication meets the minimum requirements of American National Standard for Information Sciences — Permanence of Paper for Printed Library Materials, ANSI Z39.48-1984. ∞™

Library of Congress Cataloging-in-Publication Data

Ismael, Tareq Y.
    The communist movement in Egypt, 1920–1988 / Tareq Y. Ismael and Rifa' at El-Sa' id.—1st ed.
        p. cm.—(Contemporary issues in the Middle East)
      ISBN 0-8156-2497-2 (alk. paper)
      1. Communism—Egypt—History.   I. Sa' īd, Rif' at.   II. Title.
III. Series
HX443.A6I86   1990   90-32961
335.43'0962—dc20   CIP

Manufactured in the United States of America

To Layla and Jacquie for enduring and unwavering support.

TAREQ Y. ISMAEL is Professor of Political Science, University of Calgary. He is the author of *Governments and Politics of the Contemporary Middle East* (1970); *The U.A.R. in Africa: Egypt's Policy Under Nasser* (1971); *The Middle East in World Politics* (1973); *Canada and the Middle East* (1973); *The Arab Left* (1976); *The Iraq-Iran War: Roots of Conflict* (1982); *Government and Politics in Islam* (1985); *PDR Yemen: The Politics of Socialist Transformation* (1986); and *International Relations of the Contemporary Middle East* (1986). He is also coeditor of *Canada and the Third World* (1976) and editor of *Canadian Arab Relations* (1984) and *Canada and the Arab World* (1985). His articles have appeared in the *Middle East Journal, Current History, Journal of Modern African Studies, Middle East Forum, Arab Studies, Europa Archiv, Arab Historian, Palestine Affairs, Canadian Journal of African Studies, Social Problems, International Journal.*

RIFA'AT EL-SA'ID is a historian with a Ph.D. and a doctoral degree in science from Karl Marx University in Leipzig. He played a leading role in the Egyptian communist movement in the 1950s and 1960s and spent fourteen years in prison for his political convictions. He is currently the secretary of the Central Committee of the National Progressive Unionist party and sits on the editorial board of the party's newspaper. He also is an editor with the Egyptian daily *al-Ahram* and has served as editor for the daily *al-Akhbar* and the well-known leftist journal *al-Tali'ah.*

Academically, he has devoted most of his work to the study of the Egyptian communist movement. He has published a number of authoritative works on the movement as well as works on the leaders of Egyptian political movements, including *Ahmed 'Urabi* (leader of the 1882 Revolution), *Sa'ad Zaghloul* (leader of the 1919 revolution and the Wafd party), *Mustafa al-Nahas* (leader of the Wafd), *Hassan al-Bana* (leader of the Muslim Brotherhood), *Ahmed Hussein* (leader of the Young Egypt party), and *Gamal 'Abd al-Nasser* (leader of the 1952 revolution). These and his other works have been published throughout the Arab world.

CONTENTS

FIGURES

Contemporary Issues in the Middle East

This well-established series continues to focus primarily on twentieth-century developments that have current impact and significance in one area or another of the entire region, from North Africa to the borders of Central Asia.

Selected titles in the series include:

The Arab Press: News Media and Political Process in the Arab World. William A. Rugh

Development and Social Change in Rural Egypt. Richard H. Adams, Jr.

The Egyptian Bureaucracy. Monte Palmer, Ali Leila, and El Sayed Yassin

Extremist Shiites: The Ghulat Sects. Matti Moosa

Family in Contemporary Egypt. Andrea B. Rugh

Islam and Politics. John L. Esposito

Khul-Khaal: Five Egyptian Women Tell Their Stories. Nayra Atiya

Reveal and Conceal: Dress in Contemporary Egypt. Andrea Rugh

Shahhat: An Egyptian. Richard Critchfield

The State, Religion, and Ethnic Politics: Afghanistan, Iran, and Pakistan. Ali Banuazizi and Myron Weiner, eds.

Women in Egyptian Public Life. Earl L. Sullivan

PREFACE

The development of communism in the Arab world is commonly explained by a conspiracy theory. This approach assumes that communism is a monolithic worldwide organization that is rationally structured along bureaucratic lines with hierarchical authority and communication patterns. Communists, then, are members of this organization committed to the accomplishment of organizational objectives, occupying statuses and roles within the bureaucratic hierarchy, and performing tasks dictated by and in service to the organization. Because the Soviet Union is conceived as the head of this organization, the term *the communists* is generally synonymous with the Soviet Union, and communists are considered its representatives or agents.

The conspiracy theory is most clearly manifested in the official perspective of Arab states. Intelligence and policy agencies in all the Arab states have pursued the investigation of communists and communist activity with the idea that they are manifestations of an alien organization involved in a Soviet-orchestrated conspiracy; as a result, intelligence and policy investigations have stressed the accumulation of information that will help substantiate such organizational ties. Thus government information sources provide a data base for verifying the Soviet penetration as a communist conspiracy. Studies relying on official data bases generally have not raised serious questions about the validity of the data and thus tend to perpetuate this paradigm of communism.

That the Soviet Union has made overt and covert efforts to foster and support communism is evident enough. But to attribute to the Soviet Union the degree of control over communism that this paradigm implies denies both the relevance and the viability of the communist model of social change and the ability of Arab political actors to act autonomously and rationally in seeking fundamental social change.

This study rejects the communist conspiracy paradigm as a mode of explanation and assumes that the validity of government data bases is suspect and therefore does not rely on them. Rather, the method employed here is to examine the development of communism in Egypt as a dynamic response to conditions in Egypt from three perspectives: the conditions in Egypt and the relevance of communist theory in addressing these conditions; Soviet policy toward Egypt and the role played by the Soviet Union in the development of communism in Egypt; and the communist movement in Egypt from the perspective of the principal actors — both the personalities and the parties.

Evidence of the potential value and utility of this approach is that such issues — rather than issues of party organization and Egypt-Soviet links — are stressed by the Egyptian communists themselves. In the interviews conducted for this study with Egyptian communist leaders and in the party literature, the paramount concerns of the actors have consistently been the social conditions of Egypt, the threat of imperialism, and the need to organize the workers and peasants to confront such challenges.

Many constituencies contributed to the realization of this project. Research is an arduous, expensive, and labor-intensive task as well as a labor of love. I wish to express my appreciation to all those who contributed to the task, in particular the University of Calgary (both my faculty and my department, and the Research Committee) and the Social Sciences and Humanities Research Council, and to acknowledge the Killam Resident Fellowship. I also want to thank Judi Powell, whose patience and skill transformed scribble to text; Mary Gray, whose care and fortitude made her a formidable taskmaster; and Ella Wensel, whose cheerful disposition brightened all tasks.

Finally, I want to thank my coauthor for working with me on this project. It has been a real pleasure to work together.

TAREQ Y. ISMAEL

Calgary, Alberta
1989

The Communist Movement in Egypt

1

Early Marxist Thought in Egypt

Although Marxism has been an active political force in Egypt at least since the turn of the twentieth century, there has been little systematic attention to the history, origins, and development of Egyptian Marxist thought. Most historians have instead focused on the later formations, ignoring the intellectual and organizational foundations of the communist movement in Egypt as largely inconsequential. Yet many of the difficulties and debates confronted by the movement in its later years were first established or encountered in its early years, making study of this period genuinely enlightening. Moreover, the foundations established during this early period were, as we will see, to play a significant role in the subsequent evolution of the communist movement in Egypt.

Socialist ideas were first introduced by Egyptian students returning from Europe. In 1908, about six hundred Egyptian students were in Europe, most of them in France. Others were distributed in Switzerland, Austria, Germany, and Britain. Socialist ideas were widely disseminated and debated in these countries, especially among students and intellectuals. The first Egyptian student organization abroad — called Jam'iyat al-Taqadum al-Misri — was established in Montpellier in 1893.[1] The association was founded by 'Ali Abu al-Futuh, who attended Montpellier in 1890–93. Abu al-Futuh led a campaign to change the bylaws of the university student association that forbade foreigners to become members of the executive committee. After returning to Egypt, Abu al-Futuh had a distinguished legal career culminating in his appointment as deputy minister of education in 1913. He died the same year.

In his memoirs, published in 1913, Abu al-Futuh noted of the association, "We ... decided to establish the Association of Egyptian Progress mainly for the service of the country. We did not want anything but

1

to bring together Egyptian patriots in order to spread education and support national projects as much as possible. . . . We support every national project which contributes to the country's progress."[2]

Between 1893 and 1920, seven associations were established in Britain, Switzerland, Germany, and France. According to a distinguished Egyptian student of socialist thought, Amin 'Iz al-Din, three factors are clear:

> The first which cannot be disputed is that the Egyptian student associations in Europe were in all cases political organizations in the fullest sense of the word. . . . It is our belief that the national and political trend in these organizations was a direct result of the close connection between the National party and its leaders before the first world war [al-Hizb al-Watani led by Mustafa Kamil, Mohammed Farid, and Ahmed Lutfi], who gave the student movement great attention and used the student organizations as the base for their call and activities for independence and as a home for the conferences they held in Europe.
>
> The second fact . . . is that the majority of these associations held close, strong, and fruitful relations with the socialist parties and associations, especially in France and Britain. That was very natural because the socialist parties . . . took more sympathetic positions toward the national questions of the time, such as the issues of Egypt, Ireland, and India. . . . We should not be astonished to find out, for example, that the students' association in London had close relations with the Labour party and the Fabian Society. In France, the student associations had close relations with the Socialist party, which opened its headquarters, newspapers, and conferences to them.
>
> The third and important fact is that some of the leaders of the student association did not cooperate with these socialist parties, organizations, and personalities only for the sake of winning support for the Egyptian question. Rather they went beyond that to the complete acceptance and propagation of socialist thought. They considered socialism as the logical and inevitable solution for the national question and the question of progress and justice in Egypt.[3]

Commenting on the political alliances of the student associations, Mahmud Abu al-Futuh observed that "experience taught the members of the Egyptian association in Paris that there is no hope that the rightist parties [would be sympathetic to the national question in Egypt] because they are after all colonialists in principle and the independence of Egypt does not coincide with their interests. Experience also taught them that the only help they could expect in France would come from the leftist parties because the defense of Egypt's rights follows from their principles, which call for the right of nations to live in freedom and cooperation."[4]

Among the Egyptian students who were active in the European student associations and later in the socialist and communist movements in Egypt were Salama Musa, who studied in England, 'Aziz Mirhum and Mansur Fahmi, who studied in France, and 'Ali al-'Anany, who studied in Germany. An early attempt to create a socialist party was made in 1918 by 'Aziz Mirhum and Mansur Fahmi after their return from studying in France. Their attempts were scuttled when Mahmud 'Azmi convinced Mansur Fahmi that Egyptian social and economic conditions were not conducive to the organization of a socialist party. In August 1921 Salama Musa and 'Ali al-'Anany helped establish the first Egyptian socialist party.

The socialist experience of Egyptian students in Europe provided an intellectual focus for the social consciousness already fomenting in them. These students were drawn mainly from the privileged classes; for those among them attracted to socialist thought, their privilege caused a crisis of conscience. Socialist thought provided an intellectual framework both to address and to redress the social ills of imperialist-imposed economic institutions in Egypt that preoccupied their political concerns. In this, it melded with the bourgeois nationalist aspirations of colonized elites and the social reform aspirations of idealists. The socialist student forums in Europe also provided a social framework for establishing political alliances with European groups and parties sympathetic to their nationalist and idealist aspirations. Many of the students, at the same time, learned from their European experience a fear of revolutionary socialism, which made them overly cautious about becoming identified with Marxist ideas and political activists. Salama Musa (1887–1958), one of the students who had a significant impact on the development of socialist thought in Egypt (indeed, throughout the entire Arab world), provides an example.

Through the publication of about fifty books on social, economic, and political issues over a fifty-year period, Salama Musa introduced several generations of young idealists to socialist thought. Musa's 1913 short monograph on socialism, *al-Ishtirakiyah,* is considered one of the first works in Arabic on the subject. It was widely distributed throughout the Arab world and reprinted many times. In its preface, Musa stated, "I am motivated to write this monograph because of the increasing absurdities and stupidities uttered against socialism." Musa's concern was triggered by an antisocialist campaign led by the journal *al-Manar* in 1910, edited by the prominent Islamic reformer Mohammed Rashid Ridha.[5] To dispel the myths and misconceptions being spread about socialism, he wrote *al-Ishtirakiyah* "to enlighten public opinion on the meaning of socialism and to explain the aims of socialists in Europe and America and point out their positive impact on legislation to improve the conditions of labor."[5]

Musa explained that socialism is an economic system based on the abolition of private ownership of productive resources. He identified such private ownership as the mechanism that serves the uninhibited greed of a powerful few at the expense and misery of the majority. The purpose of socialism, Musa explained, "is to create economic freedom in order to equalize opportunities among people."[6] Although Musa's works were diverse and the topics wide-ranging, two themes were consistently woven throughout them: the need to expose the nature and toll of human exploitation inherent in the capitalist system and to expose the exploitive nature of the Egyptian class structure. In Musa's own account of his work, given a year before he died, he said, "Twenty years ago, when I wrote my book, *Those Who Taught Me,* I mentioned twenty literary figures, philosophers, and scientists who had influenced my ideas and educated me. I did not mention Karl Marx, the propagator of socialism. Now [1957] I want to confess that there is no one on this earth who had a more profound influence than Karl Marx on my thinking and education. I used to avoid mentioning his name for fear of being accused of being a communist."[7]

The earliest formal presentation in Egypt of Marxist theory appeared in 1890 in an article in the influential journal *al-Mua'yyad.*[8] The anonymous author introduced Egyptian readers to the idea of Marxism in an analytical context. After surveying and critically reviewing different approaches to the concept of equality and social justice, the author proceeded to justify the ideas of Marx as the best means by which justice could be achieved. "Let us establish that the principle through which we attempt to achieve justice be that every man gets as much as he produces, not as much as he knows. This way we support the individuals while at the same time maintaining justice. . . . The social structure is required to divide money according to these standards of absolute justice. It is required to provide every individual in accordance with the benefits that accrue from his labor irrespective of his knowledge or luck."[9]

The author then introduced the principles of communism (transliterating the term *communism* directly into Arabic) and argued that

> some advocates of equality reject the equitable division of wealth because of the difficulties involved . . . and prefer collective ownership.

This doctrine is called communism. Let us not think that this cannot be achieved and do not assume that members of communist societies have to live in complete amalgamation and harmony. They could put their wealth in specific public places, and each one will take what he needs, just as happened in the Jesuit republics. . . . Those who oppose this doctrine claim that this will weaken production. But if we consider the response of the members of these [communities] . . . each one of them knows exactly what belongs to him because that is what he produced. There is no doubt that their conditions are much better than those of the worker who works for somebody else, as is the case for the majority of our social organizations.[10]

It was not until 1915 that a more elaborate and aggressive view of Marxism was presented by Mustafa Hassanain al-Mansuri (a twenty-five-year-old primary school principal who had never been outside Egypt and therefore must have become familiar with Marxism through Arabic materials). The book was entitled *Tarikh al-Mathahib al-Ishtirakiyah* (The history of socialist ideologies). Al-Mansuri was probably the first writer openly to declare his belief in Marxism and defend it against its opponents. He stated that "Marx without doubt is the greatest preacher of socialism and its most sincere advocate. It was he who supported the Democratic party which was established by Lasalle despite Bismarck's violent attacks against it. He was also the first to provide a program for a socialist party, and it was he who wrote the work *Capital,* which socialists call their bible. He wrote the constitution of the [first] international [socialist] association." Al-Mansuri went on to provide a summary of Marx's ideas expressing his admiration of them throughout his own book. "We have known how socialism evolved and spread in France, Germany, and Russia," al-Mansuri wrote, "however, it did not stop at the borders of these kingdoms in spite of the resistance of the governments and the rich. It was the facts that socialism incorporated and its display of the true sickness of societies that ensured its success. . . . A good idea cannot be prevented from spreading, and the truth—whatever the people with special interests may try to do—shall one day come out to the people." After presenting several definitions provided by socialist thinkers, al-Mansuri summarized his position and understanding of the socialist ideology:

Socialism is the orientation of those who claim that the social system lacks economic, managerial, social, political, and religious reform as a result of the defects which evolved from limitless competition especially after the discovery of steam power and machines which replaced workers and threatened the position of the laborers. These conditions multiplied the profits of the capitalists, who became extremely rich and controlled the workers, whom they treated cruelly and ruthlessly, cutting down their wages and prolonging their working hours. As a result, the conditions of the workers deteriorated, their morals broke down, and plagues such as TB became widespread among them.[11]

Complaints on behalf of the workers were completely ignored until Marx came on the scene and "was able to spread his ideas and form a strong labor party in Germany. He was also able to convene several international conferences of workers of different nations, after he faced many obstacles and was exiled from Germany to France and then Belgium. From there socialism started taking a scientific form, and its star rose when many of the most eminent thinkers, journalists, and writers advocated it, refined it, and rejected its impractical aspects, in addition to setting detailed programs for its implementation." After outlining his view of the principles and evolution of Marxist theory, al-Mansuri proceeded to delineate socialist goals and the means whereby they might be implemented. He did this by posing a question: if the capitalist exploits labor through the machine, "must we destroy the machine in order to return man to his lost paradise?" His answer: "There is no sane person who wants to return to the dark ages. . . . Thus, we have to have the machines serve man rather than compete with him. But how can we do this when the morals of the machines cannot be changed and the capitalists have total control over them and do not care except for their own interests at the expense of the pain and toiling of the laborers? . . . The only way to bring happiness to mankind is to abolish private ownership and to place capital in the hands of the workers themselves." Al-Mansuri argued that, despite the allegations of critics of Marxist socialism, such a goal need not come at the expense of nationalism, the family, or religion.

If socialists became internationalists as a result of the doctrines of Karl Marx, this does not mean that their national feelings have died away as some may have wrongly believed. Instead, these feelings tend to be aroused if someone attacks their country. They do not refrain from defending their homeland; however, they refuse to have a part in a war that seeks to deprive a weak nation of its freedom. . . .

As for the opinion of the socialists regarding the family system, it does not as a matter of fact differ from our own views [in Egypt]. Although some socialists call for the abolition of the family system and the replacement of the present marriage system with a marriage system based on love, this remains an individual opinion which does not hold on its own. The majority of the socialists agree that the family system is sacred and has to be preserved, though they call for the equality of men and women. . . .

There is no doubt that most of the socialists were influenced one way or another by materialistic principles and do not believe that religion is sufficient to reform society. In spite of that, however, we can see that religion and socialism are not contradictory and that both seek to support the weak. Anyone who looks at the facts of the Islamic and Christian religions could find many of the contemporary socialistic ideas such as "Zakat" (alms) which is equivalent to the income tax and which aims at reducing the differences between the rich and the poor. In Europe, on the other hand, several priests and clergymen in the nineteenth century considered socialism as part of the Christian faith and called upon people to believe in it and accept its principles.[12]

With regard to the implementation of Marxist socialism, al-Mansuri argued that socialism was flexible and that different forms of political activity were suited to different countries.

In democratic nations, for example, such as England and France the socialists present their demands to the government without adopting a hostile attitude toward it. In tyrannical nations, on the other hand, such as Russia, they tend to resort to violence and bloodshed because the authorities persecuted them and refused to address their demands. It is wrong, therefore, to perceive socialism as a set of static principles which cannot be changed or amended, or that its advocates should have the same appearance and opinions everywhere. The means can differ depending on the type of government and the social system in which they function, as long as all agree on the same goal.[13]

Al-Mansuri devotes two chapters to the application of Marxist ideas to the Egyptian context. In chapter 9, "The Chaos of Our Social System," he asserts that the Egyptian "social system has given rise to two opposing and conflicting groups. One group is that of the rich, who spare no effort to find means to subjugate and humiliate the people in order that they may have the final say and remain supreme . . . and the group of the poor who keep on searching for means to avenge themselves from the rich.''[14] Accordingly, al-Mansuri proposed a broad program, which if implemented would bring about social justice through a series of reforms.

In introducing his program, al-Mansuri states: ''Here are some of the reforms that can be sought in Egypt. . . . It is not my aim to have them as a program for an Egyptian socialist party as I believe the time is not suitable yet to achieve this step, which requires a level of scientific and literary maturity which is not yet available.''[15] In his concluding chapter, ''Egypt and Socialism,'' al-Mansuri proposes a comprehensive reform program for Egypt based on socialist principles (see Appendix A). In the program, al-Mansuri addresses the need to improve the status of women as well as demands for increasing pensions for senior citizens. His proposals directed toward women aimed at abolishing polygamy, emancipating educated women, and reforming the divorce laws and processes. Also included were provisions for opening government clerical positions to women and allowing married women to enter the teaching and medical professions.

In the field of education, al-Mansuri sought improvement in the standards and curriculum of private, religious, and public schools at every level. Central to these reforms was the need to expand free education. Moreover, primary agricultural schools should be established and control of education should be passed from government councils to a scientific committee under the authority of the legislature.

Al-Mansuri also urged democratic reforms at both the local and national levels. At the national level, he advocated a fundamental and wholesale change of Egypt's political process and institutions to establish responsible government, institute regular and free elections and proportional representation (based on the number of workers in every job), and ensure freedom of speech, press, and assembly. The national government should also take a greater role in the regulation of the Egyptian economy and society. For instance, the government was called on to become involved in operating railways and public transit and actively to encourage the formation of agricultural and industrial unions. Tax reform, land redistribution, the establishment of a national bank, and the regulation of foreign companies operating in Egypt were also demanded.

At the local level, councils should be formed to implement reform. The councils would be responsible for providing healthy and inexpensive housing to the poor and imposing a minimum wage for peasants and workers.

Al-Mansuri also included demands for judicial reform to accompany educational, social, and democratic reform. He believed that reforming the judiciary necessitated expanding the courts, introducing the jury system, and abolishing mixed courts, foreign capitulations, and case taxes. Reform in the philosophy of the judicial system was also needed: the system should no longer merely punish the criminal but reform him. To this end, al-Mansuri called for the abolition of the death penalty and the modernization of Shari'a law.[16]

According to al-Mansuri's biographer, Amin 'Iz al-Din, the book was unusual for a variety of reasons: the author was unknown in political, intellectual, and literary circles; the book did not address any of the contemporary political, social, or cultural issues that were the primary concerns of the intellectual media at the time; and the book was distributed in the markets of Damascus and Beirut rather than Cairo, where only a small number of copies were circulated. In addition, the book was unusual because it did not stop as other works did with theory and history. Rather, al-Mansuri analyzed Egypt's social realities. He examined social conditions and relations in a scientific framework and demonstrated the cleavages among social classes, particularly in their share of consumption, social position, and the exercise of power.[17]

Although his book was not widely circulated in Egypt and seems to have received little attention among intellectual and political circles at the time, al-Mansuri was treated as a conspirator, the book confiscated, and his house searched. He was temporarily arrested and charged with attempting to assassinate Sultan Hussein Kamil in April 1915, denounced by al-Azhar leaders for his educational reform program, and in 1930 permanently lost his job as an educator.[18]

In 1919, al-Mansuri published two books, one a translation of Leo Tolstoy's work under the title *Masawi' al-Nedham al-Ijtima'ie wa 'Ilajuha* (The evils of the social system and their treatment), and the other entitled *al-Taqadum wa al-Faqr* (Progress and poverty) based on a translation of the works of Henry George. The translations dealt with agricultural land distribution. In his commentary notes on the translations, al-Mansuri discusses Egyptian conditions in relation to the issues of the texts. For example, in his introduction to the Henry George translation he observes, "In the later part of the nineteenth century, Henry George spoke out to the people to explain the tyranny of private ownership of land and the poverty that it created among the majority of the people. . . . The misery of the workers and the increase of poverty among the people is a [direct] result of the monopoly of one group of people over the land. . . . The solutions introduced by the socialists to reform society will not produce results if land is not brought under public ownership."

Relating this to the Egyptian case, al-Mansuri observed that "the landownership system in Egypt is built on a base that cannot be called legitimate or just. ... The number of agricultural landowners is 1,455,000; among those, 1,190,000, or 91 percent, own less than five fiddans and own a total of 26 percent of agricultural land in the country. Forty-four percent of the [agricultural] land is owned by 12,400 people, whose average holding is greater than 50 fiddans: 1,600 of these are foreign owners. Is this a just distribution?"[19]

According to Amin 'Iz al-Din, al-Mansuri contributed to modern Egyptian and Arab social thought by specifying three principles of Marxist theory: "First, the necessity of public ownership of the primary means of production; second, the adaptation of socialism to the objective conditions of every country; third, the inevitability of socialist solutions." In addressing these principles, al-Mansuri "surpassed the utopian reformist framework."[20]

The next important Marxist thinker in Egypt was Nicola Haddad (1878 – 1954).[21] Haddad migrated from Syria to New York at the turn of the century, where he met the American socialist Eugene Debs. In 1910, together with Amin al-Rihani and Farah Anton (1874 – 1922), Haddad established an Arab socialist society in New York and published a magazine called al-Jam'ia. A few years later Haddad moved to Cairo, where he continued to preach socialism.

Haddad's writings are considered by many to represent the most sophisticated development of Marxist thought in the Arab world at that time. Typical of these was an article published in the Egyptian magazine al-Hilal in 1918. In this article, entitled "Socialism: What It Demands and What It Does Not Demand," Haddad responded to contemporary opponents of socialism. He also criticized reformists, who, in his view, sought to alleviate social pain without providing decisive answers to society's problems. Socialists, he argued, do not make this mistake; instead they propose radical solutions that address underlying social ills. He expanded on the socialist solution, stating that "socialist ideology is both logical and reasonable and is based on a fair socioeconomic tradition. It calls for the overthrow of the existing system and the implementation of a new one. This new system should be based on labor and its equivalent return instead of the accumulation of wealth. Thus, the system which the socialists seek is one in which the companies, utilities, and real estate become the property of the government so that they may benefit the whole nation rather than remaining a monopoly in the hands of a few owners."[22]

Haddad elaborated upon his analysis of the ills of modern society and his prescription for the future in a later book, Al-Ishtirakiyah, published in 1920. According to Haddad, capitalism (or for that matter individualism) refers to "the existing order which allowed to the utmost for competition among individuals so as to permit the powerful to enjoy the value of the toiling of the weak or at least provide him with the right to share the value of the latter's work. In other words, it allows the powerful to live in dependency on the poor. This is contrary to socialism, which rules that every individual should enjoy all the result of his labor on the basis that people who share labor should also share its fruits, each according to his work." Thus Haddad condemned a capitalist system that allowed five thousand Americans to own one-sixth of the wealth of the United States through the appropriation of the labor and effort of toiling workers. Within the capitalist system, he argued, "some people enjoy the fruits of the labor of the masses and are able to become lavish and extravagant, while the majority observe the fruits of their labor without being able to enjoy them. . . . The peasant raises the chicken and produces eggs but is unable to taste them; he produces cheese but is unable to eat it; he produces wheat and harvests it but eats only maize. . . . The capitalistic system therefore is unable to bring happiness to mankind despite the fact that mankind has a labor power which could bring happiness to double its *number.*"[23]

What, then, has the socialist system to offer? According to Haddad, socialism leads to the downfall of the capitalist state because all utilities and means of production are in the hands of the people. It ensures control over production and provides for every individual total security regarding work and means of sustenance. It also provides public services such as education and medical care to all people irrespective of their status or position in society. Such conditions and services could be provided only through socialism and not through any other reform measures.[24]

How is the transformation from capitalism to socialism to be achieved? Haddad identified two possible roads — evolution and revolution — and reviewed the ideological schism in socialist thought that had developed around this important question of strategy. Although he did not take an explicit position on this issue, he did consider capitalism unredeemable and socialism inevitable.[25]

The writings of al-Mansuri and Haddad introduced Marxist ideas in Arabic to the Egyptian public; their work was circulated outside Egypt as well as in the Arab world.

These early writings show that the introduction of Marxist thought was initiated by a critique of capitalism in terms of the social injustice it spawns. Al-Mansuri applied Marxist ideas specifically to analyzing the social conditions in Egypt and formulation of a program for their resolution. Haddad's work was more theoretical. Neither author dealt with issues of strategy. However, their concern with the fundamental injustice of existing social conditions reflects the reason Marxist thought became relevant to Egyptian intellectuals.

2

The First Movement, *1920–1928*

Although the early discussion of Marxist and socialist doctrine in Egypt provided the basis for later intellectual interest in a communist movement, the first organizational steps toward this goal were made by non-Egyptians. Communist activities began in Egypt surprisingly early. Documents prove that communist cells existed in the Greek communities of Cairo and Alexandria as early as 1894. An attempt by a Greek resident to distribute communist leaflets was recorded in Egyptian newspapers on March 18, 1894. The police arrest record described the literature as "anarchist leaflets" calling for the workers to celebrate the anniversary of the Paris Communes: "Workers . . . remember this day is the anniversary of the Paris Commune uprising. Let us, we oppressed workers, all unite, and let's shout together for the destruction of the greedy rich; long live the socialist revolution and long live communism."[1] Probably reflecting the activities of this early communist organization, in the same year Greek workers struck the Suez Canal Company.[2] One of the most important initiators of communist organization in the Greek community in Egypt was a sponge merchant, Sakilarides Yanakakis. He is credited with the establishment in 1895 of the first union in Egypt among shoe workers (the majority of whom were Armenians and Greeks). He continued to organize and finance the communist movement in Egypt's Greek community until the 1920s.[3]

There was also early activity within the Italian community in Alexandria, which alarmed the *khedive* of Egypt. He expressed his concern to his chief executive about the activities of the "international association."[4] There was a large community of Italian workers in Egypt, many of whom were sympathetic to or affiliated with the Socialist party of Italy. In 1882, the president of the Italian Workers' Association in Alexandria sent a letter to the prime minister of the revolutionary government of Egypt, Sami Pasha al-Barudi, declaring the association's support for the aims of the 'Urabi revolution and denouncing foreign intervention.[5]

A campaign to eradicate illiteracy among workers was established within the Italian community early in the century. The Free Popular League, the organization set up to conduct the campaign, had a board of directors composed of Italians, Greeks, Armenians, and Egyptians, according to a list it published on May 13, 1901.[6]

After the aborted 1905 revolution in Russia, a number of revolutionaries, including Bolsheviks, fled Russia. Many found their way to Egypt, where a Russian community already existed. In 1907, the Russian consul in Alexandria sought to have three of the revolutionaries extradited to Russia for execution, and in January 1907 they were arrested.[7] The foreign community in Alexandria mobilized in demonstrations to protest the extradition. The protests spread to Cairo.[8] Whether these protests were successful in forestalling the extraditions is not known, but the incident awakened the concern of British authorities in Egypt. A campaign of police harassment was initiated against the organizers of the demonstrations, and threats of extradition were used to dampen further activities.[9]

Although this activity was confined to the foreign community in Egypt, it did have an impact on the emerging Egyptian nationalist movement. The leading nationalist newspaper—the official organ of al-Watani party — al-Liwa' (Cairo), on February 11, 1907, lamented that no native Egyptians participated in the demonstrations. This, according to al-Liwa', proved that Egyptians "are still ignorant of what real freedom is and what constitutes human duties."

Most notable of the early foreign communist activists was Joseph Rosenthal. Although there were several communists in Egypt's foreign community at this time, Rosenthal was one of the first successfully to reach out to the native Egyptian community and to have an impact on the development of the Egyptian communist movement. Rosenthal settled in Egypt around 1899, acquired Egyptian citizenship, and became involved in labor union activism. Police reports on Rosenthal identified him as a Jewish Russian jeweler who had contacts with the Third International and with Bolshevik groups in Palestine. He has been credited with single-handedly founding communism in Egypt. The reports noted that Rosenthal, blacklisted by the police, had been under surveillance since 1901. He was an active labor agitator and maintained close relations with all workers' organizations in Alexandria. He was credited with organizing strikes in 1920 in Alexandria against rent hikes that were considered the best organized and among the first successful strikes in Egypt.[10]

As a result of Rosenthal's importance in the Egyptian labor movement, in 1921 Mustafa al-Nahas (the second man in the Wafd party after Sa'ad Zaghloul Pasha) visited Rosenthal "in his capacity as president of the workers' union," according to police records, "and consulted with him on a declaration Zaghloul intends to announce before the coming election."[11] Rosenthal himself summarized his activities in Egypt:

> Since my childhood, I was attracted by socialist principles. . . . My greatest hope was to see the conditions of the workers improve through the power of education and discipline. When I arrived in Egypt twenty-five years ago [1899] I began working to form unions. The first union in which I participated in its formation was the Union of the Cigarette Workers. After that I participated in the formation of several unions for the tailors, miners, and printers. These unions mostly belonged to foreign workers because the national workers at that time were a minority in all crafts and fields of work relative to their foreign colleagues.[12]

Constantine Weiss (alias Avigdor), the Comintern representative sent to Egypt in 1925, reported that communist cells were established among foreign workers in Egypt as early as 1917–18.[13] These cells had little impact and were apparently short-lived. By 1920, Rosenthal was active and influential in such socialist organizations as the Communist Club, the Groupe d'Études Sociales, and Groupe Clarté in Alexandria, made up mainly of foreign elements.[14] Alexandria at that time had a high concentration of foreign workers. Thus the earliest response to Rosenthal's initiatives came from the Greeks, Austrians, and Russians. The movement also attracted Armenians and Italians as well as a few native Egyptians, mainly workers and university students.

The 1927 census showed that there were forty-two thousand Italians, sixty-nine thousand Greeks, and nineteen thousand French in Egypt. British intelligence estimated the Armenian population in Egypt at about eighteen thousand and that of White Russians at about eighteen hundred.[15]

The main factor that contributed to the formation of these associations and facilitated their activities was that most of the members were foreigners who benefited from the system of capitulations, which provided special legal protections to foreign citizens. With the outbreak of World War I, however, most of the foreign workers left Egypt, and the dynamics of the labor movement changed accordingly. As Rosenthal explained:

When the Great War broke out, and the foreign workers were forced to leave Egypt, the local workers became a large majority in the working circles. This growth helped them to establish unions which were under the tutelage of different political parties concerned with national problems of the country, such as the Wafd, the National party, and others. I did not participate directly in the management of these unions. It was my opinion that we must establish centers to fight for the improvement of economic conditions of the working class and raise their intellectual consciousness. For that reason, in 1920 I issued a call to all the existing unions to establish a federated union. This call was responded to unanimously by the unions representing thirty-five thousand workers, and they sent representatives to Alexandria to discuss the idea. But the heads of these unions . . . feared that the establishment of true unions representing the interests of the workers would result in the loss of their own power. . . . This is why they worked very hard to convince their unions not to join. They continued to procrastinate on initial arrangements for a full year. In early 1921, we were able to establish the Union of Workers with only three thousand workers. Since the unions could not participate directly in political affairs because they were composed of different workers with conflicting political views, we thought of creating a political party to become the spokesman for the workers' unions, to defend their interests in parliament and elsewhere, and to work to force the government to issue social laws to protect the workers, who were left to the mercy of capitalism and its tyranny. To achieve this idea we created the Egyptian Socialist party.[16]

The size of the Egyptian labor force employed in modern production and transport industries was reported in the 1907 census to be 489,296. By 1917, it had increased to 639,929.[17] Within a decade, then, not only had the size of the modern industrial sector of the labor force increased, it had also become Egyptianized as a result of the emigration of foreign workers from Egypt. And unlike the foreign workers they replaced, the Egyptian workers were poorly organized, very poorly paid, and without the protection for labor activism that foreign status provided. There was no labor legislation to protect the working class from economic exploitation or political oppression; and from the time of the Russian Revolution in 1917 any efforts at organizing labor for improvement of its conditions were perceived by British intelligence and Egyptian security forces as communist subversion and harshly put down by the government. It was under these conditions that the labor movement came under the tutelage of the nationalist parties and fully participated in the nationalist struggle, culminating in the 1919 Egyptian revolution. In the after-

math of the revolution, the government set up the Labour Conciliation
Board (the official Arabic title was Lajnat al-Tawfiq bayna al-'Umal wa
As-hab al-'Amal), created on August 18, 1919, under the chairmanship of
a Britisher, Dr. Alex Granville, and composed of senior civil servants.
The board had no legal powers, and its official mandate was simply to receive and mediate labor complaints. Its latent purpose seems to have
been to monitor labor activity and defuse unrest.[18] But the revolution did
not produce any movement toward labor reform, and the alliance between labor and the bourgeoisie quickly dissipated.

In this setting of fundamental change in the demographic structure
of the Egyptian labor force, a nationalist revolution, and deteriorating
conditions for labor, Rosenthal continued his efforts to mobilize the labor
force in Egypt. Rosenthal and Egyptian intellectuals committed to the labor movement — among the most prominent were Husni al-'Arabi, 'Ali
al-'Anany, Salama Musa, and Mohammed 'Abdallah 'Anan — set out to
establish an Egyptian Socialist party (al-Hizb al-Ishtiraki al-Misri) with
Egyptian members who would represent the unionized workers.

Salama Musa stated that he and other young intellectuals — al-
'Anany, 'Anan, al-'Arabi, Sheikh Safwan Abu al-Fateh, Ahmed al-Madani, Anton Maroun, Hussein Nameq, Husni Muhaisin, and Sheikh 'Abd
al-Latif Bakheit — first formed a socialist society to study and investigate
the different orientations of socialist thought. Although all professed interest in and commitment to some form of socialist ideology, this early
group displayed considerable heterogeneity. Salama Musa, for example,
opposed both the Bolsheviks and revolutions. Husni al-'Arabi was at the
time busy translating a book written by Ramsay MacDonald, the leader
of the British Labour party.[19] 'Abdallah 'Anan sympathized with the
principles of socialism as delineated by the Second International, and
'Ali al-'Anany became a leftist Hegelian and adopted a moderate approach to change. Sheikh Safwan Abu al-Fatah and Anton Maroun were,
like Rosenthal, committed to more clearly communist principles.

One of the first steps taken by this group was to write to Rosenthal
as secretary of the foreign workers' socialist party to learn about the party's program. If they agreed with its principles, they would join it, but if
they found the principles to be incompatible with Egyptian national interests, they would form a society whose main objectives would be to study
socialism "rather than getting involved in politics."[20]

It was clear from the outset that this group of young intellectuals did
not intend to adopt Marxism uncritically. To the contrary, Musa stated
that "the members of this nascent society put Egypt's interests first. Its
aim shall be to Egyptianize the moderate [socialist] principles and en-

lighten the workers about their rights."[21] In other words, socialist principles were to be adapted to the conditions and circumstances of the Egyptian environment. Some members of the group subsequently opposed the formation of a new socialist party, either because they believed that such a party would compromise national unity or because they feared it would provoke a repressive response from Britain and hence delay Egyptian independence. The bulk of the group did participate in the creation of the Egyptian Socialist party, providing a strong impetus to the socialist movement.

Nevertheless, even among those who participated in the formation of the party, strong ideological differences existed, largely manifesting themselves as personality disputes. There was contention and confusion, for example, about who would be the secretary of the new party. On August 16, 1921, al-Ahram published an article which identified 'Ali al-'Anany as the party's secretary. Salama Musa denied this in al-Ahram the next day; and on August 19 al-'Anany's denial appeared. Then on August 23, Salama Musa sent a party declaration to the newspaper signed by himself as the secretary. When the party was officially declared in an announcement in al-Ahram on August 29, 1921, the secretary was identified as 'Abdallah 'Anan.

The Egyptian Socialist party, formed in August 1921, established its main office in Cairo and had branches in Alexandria, Tantah, Shebin al-Kom, and Mansorah. It soon thereafter applied for a license to publish a newspaper but was denied because of its opposition to British and government policy. The party responded by assuming the license of an existing paper, Jaridat al-Shabibah, which it attempted to transform into a party organ. Only one issue appeared, however, in the first week of July 1922, whereupon the government closed the paper and confiscated the issue. A further attempt to secure another newspaper was foiled by the authorities.[22]

The party's program was announced in a declaration in al-Ahram on August 29, 1921, signed by 'Ali al-'Anany, Salama Musa, Mohammed 'Abdallah 'Anan, and Husni al-'Arabi. Rosenthal did not sign, fearing that his "foreign name, in spite of my Egyptian citizenship, might be considered as a foreign intervention in an Egyptian issue."[23]

The declaration specified the following principles of the party:

Political Principles:

1. The liberation of Egypt from the tyranny of imperialism and the expulsion of imperialism from the entire Nile Valley.

2. Support for the freedom and self-determination of all people and brotherhood among all nations on the basis of equality and mutual interests.

3. Combat imperialism wherever it exists.

4. Resistance to militarism, dictatorship, and the arms race on land, sea, and air.

5. Opposition to aggression and offensive wars.

6. The abolition of secret treaties.

Economic Principles:

Work for the abolition of exploitation of one class by another, the elimination of class distinctions in society in natural rights, and the extinction of tyranny by exploiters and speculators. Work for the establishment of economic society on the basis of the following socialist principles:

1. The integration of natural resources into the public means of production for the benefit of the entire nation.

2. Just distribution of the products of labor in accordance with the law of production and personal ability.

3. Extinction of capitalist competition.

Social Principles:

1. Education must become a universal right of all members of the nation, both men and women, through compulsory, free education for the dissemination of true democratic teachings among all the classes of the nation.

2. To seek improvement in the welfare of workers through the increase of wages and the provision of salaries and settlements for disability and forced retirement.

3. Work for the liberation of Eastern women and their education.

The party will endeavor to achieve these principles through competition with other parties and peaceful propaganda through the following means:

1. The creation of agricultural syndicates, free industrial syndicates, and syndicates for production and consumption.

2. The preparation of socialist deputies for parliament and for representative local and municipal councils and others.

3. The liberation from restrictions, financial and others, on the right to vote and be nominated to parliament and the extension of these rights to both men and women whenever possible.

4. The dissemination [of the program] through publications and speeches.

Although the party's principles were grandiose in nature and scope, in practice the achievement of its organizational objectives was limited because of underlying conflicts between means and ends. Party praxis focused on two areas: the national question and labor mobilization. On the national question, the party assumed the role of handmaiden to the Wafd, simply supporting its initiatives.

Amid the rising nationalist fervor in Egypt, on December 14, 1921, when Wafd negotiations with the British for Egypt's independence were at an impasse, the party issued a declaration in support of the Wafd, calling for the creation of a national front in support of the Wafd party leadership.[24] In a manifesto issued in Cairo on December 22, 1921, the party reemphasized its commitment to struggle against British imperialism. At the same time, however, it declared that in its fight it would "integrally maintain its socialist programme and will not renounce its struggle against the Egyptian capitalist tyrants and oppressors, accomplices and associates of the tyrannic foreign domination."[25]

The party's lack of an independent agenda on the national question was obvious when the issue arose of who should represent Egypt at the Lausanne Peace Conference of November 20, 1922. The debate, led by the Wafd party, centered on whether a British client state government delegation or a nationalist delegation should represent the nation. The Egyptian Socialist party central committee issued a declaration on October 17, 1922, supporting a Wafd delegation.[26]

On labor issues, the Egyptian Socialist party took a vanguard role. In the industrial districts of Alexandria and al-Mahalah al-Kubra (a major industrial center in lower Egypt) the party was actively and intensely involved in mobilizing workers, organizing meetings, and recruiting members. Methods of mobilization and recruitment included organizing day and evening literacy classes for adults and children and establishing an association for industrial school graduates.[27] The major effort concentrated on the development of the General Union of Workers (Itihad al-Naqabat al-'Am), organized by Joseph Rosenthal in 1921. This union grew to include three thousand members from twenty different labor organizations.[28] Party-initiated activities were so prevalent that an *al-Ahram* correspondent observed (February 22, 1924, and March 29, 1924) that between fifteen and twenty thousand workers were influenced by the party's labor activism. The party, he noted, had sixty members in al-Mahalah al-Kubra organizing workers' associations and programs.

A main focus of mobilization activity was to articulate labor complaints and present them to the Labour Conciliation Board. From presentation of complaints to strike action, the process of mobilization was directed to improve the appalling conditions of labor. According to a report issued by the Labour Conciliation Board on its activities over the six months ending March 31, 1922, the number of strikes increased dramatically in the period. Eighty-one strike actions had taken place in fifty different industrial establishments. The longest of these strikes, conducted by the workers of the Suez Oil Refinery, was 113 days; the Cairo Tram Company had a strike that lasted 102 days; Warms and Company workers struck for 60 days; Alexandria Tram Workers went out for 42 days; Tura Alcohol workers were on strike for 32 days and Orwa el Waska Schools of Alexandria for 31 days; the rest of the strikes lasted less than a month. The board counted the number of workers' associations as thirty-eight in Cairo, thirty-three in Alexandria, eighteen in the Canal Zone, and six in the rest of the country. The report noted that wages had increased 85 percent since 1913, but the major portion of this increase took place during 1920–21.[29]

The party's activities reflected some of its internal ideological tensions between the primacy of socioeconomic and nationalist goals and between reformist and revolutionary means to their achievement. The professional and wealthier members of the party, concentrated in the Cairo organization, tended to favor the more moderate socialist course. Party radicals, however, resented the bourgeois element, seeing it as an obstacle to the further development of the party's socialist doctrine. Furthermore, the radical faction of the party had been recruiting members among the rank and file through union activities in the slums and factories of Alexandria, while the moderates remained isolated from the masses, largely restricting their activities to the fashionable Cairo coffee shops and literate circles of professionals such as lawyers, doctors, and teachers. By 1922, these tensions between the coffee shop intellectuals and the front-line workers culminated in the withdrawal of the former from the party. On July 30, 1922, a party conference convened in Alexandria and declared the Alexandria branch the party's headquarters.[30]

The party then proceeded to identify itself as "the Egyptian branch of International Communism." The party also decided to join the Third International. *Al-Ahram* observed that these steps were more than window dressing: "We are facing full-fledged Bolshevism." The moves were strongly opposed by moderates who thought they meant an abandonment of socialism for communism, which might have an adverse effect on the Egyptian national movement in relation to Britain. Salama Musa said that "our loyalty to Egypt should be greater than our loyalty to socialism. Our independence is our first goal, and socialism is the second goal."[31]

On October 20, 1922, the party declared itself "the true representative of the aspirations of the working class in Egypt." By late 1922, the Egyptian Socialist party, reportedly numbering four hundred in the Alexandria branch alone and a total of fifteen hundred in all branches, sent Husni al-'Arabi to Moscow to negotiate its recognition as the representative of the Egyptian proletariat and to join the Third International.[32] Al-'Arabi returned to Egypt in mid-December 1922 to report that the central committee for the Comintern required that the Egyptian party meet three specific conditions above the twenty-one general conditions imposed on all applicants: it must expel "undesirable elements" (which was understood to mean Rosenthal specifically); formally change the party's name from Socialist to Communist; and bring in any communist elements that were not already in the party. These conditions were to be met no later than January 15, 1923.[33]

In December 1922, the central committee of the now Egyptian Communist party accepted all the conditions of the Comintern. Rosenthal—who felt the time was not yet ripe for a socialist revolution in Egypt and who opposed some of the Comintern's twenty-one conditions—was expelled, and Ahmed al-Madani was appointed to replace him as treasurer.[34] Madani, however, resigned his position less than two days later, saying that "communism in this form is too much for Egypt, and the country is incapable of adopting its principles."[35] The majority of the central committee, headed by Husni al-'Arabi, thought that the time was suitable for social revolution and for the formation of a bona fide communist party.

Once the party became a member of the Third International, it presented a program to the party's general meeting of January 6–7, 1923. The program called for the nationalization of the Suez Canal, the liberation and unification of Egypt and the Sudan, repudiation of all state debts and foreign capitulation agreements, an eight-hour workday, and equal pay for Egyptian and foreign workers. Moreover, it called for the abolition of land tenancy by which peasants paid half of the crop on rented land, the cancellation of the debts of peasants who owned less than ten feddans, and the provision of basic human rights. It also called for the restriction of landownership to a maximum of one hundred feddans.[36]

Activity within the labor movement was intensified. The party advanced workers and peasants to its leadership ranks. According to the 1924 trial transcripts of the party leadership on charges of subversion, the party numbered fifteen hundred members, the majority of whom were workers. Party branches existed in rural areas as well as urban centers.[37] The party took complete control of the General Union of Workers, essentially absorbing its organizational structure: Husni al-'Arabi, general secretary of the party, was also general secretary of the union; Mustafa Abu Harjah, assistant general secretary of the union, was also a member of the party's central committee; the headquarters of the party and the union were the same. The union increased its membership to twenty thousand by 1923.[38]

BRITISH REACTION TO SOCIALIST ACTIVITIES

As early as the summer of 1919 the Foreign Office and British intelligence in Cairo were discussing the need to assign an officer trained in anti-Bolshevist methods to Egypt.[39] Two years later, a special bureau was established by the Egyptian Ministry of the Interior to monitor the activities of the nascent Egyptian Socialist party in Alexandria.[40] In their opposition to socialist activities the British found allies within the Egyptian bourgeois and religious circles. In June 1919 Sa'ad Zaghloul, leader of the Wafd party, was so concerned about such activities that he sent a letter from Paris to the central committee of the Wafd party stating, "The Wafd does not approve the leaflets which indicate that the Egyptians depend on the Germans and applaud the victory of the Bolsheviks. These leaflets benefit our enemies in their claim that the Egyptian movement has connections with the Germans and the Bolshevik movement."[41]

At the same time, however, a Wafd delegation to Europe in 1919 led by Sa'ad Zaghloul met with Russian representatives. According to Dr. Hafidh Affifi Bey, a member of the Wafd delegation, "The Russian Bolshevists promised the Sa'ad Delegation simply to help it to drive the English out of Egypt . . . by the money they have given to Sa'ad . . . and by the propaganda they are making directly and without our interference in Egypt."[42]

Fikry Abaza, a member of the National party, strongly attacked the formation of a socialist party; he wrote: "The economic position of the party can be summarized as a divisive force between the owners of money and the workers until the opportunity arises to redistribute property to everyone such that the wealth of the princes and the wealth of the poor will be equal."[43]

Members of the religious circles were also quick to condemn the new party. In 1919 the Grand Mufti of Egypt, Sheikh Mohammed Bakheit, issued under British prompting a *fatwa* (religious opinion) concerning Bolshevism. In it he provided a lengthy, complex, and discursive opinion, concluding that

> the "Way" of the Bolsheviks is one which destroys all Divine laws, especially the doctrines of Islam; and because it recommends what God hath considered illegal in His Book. It legalizes bloodshedding, allows trespass upon the property of others, treachery, lies, and rape, causing anarchy to spread among the people in their properties, their women, children, and inheritance until they become at last worse than beasts. God hath verily and plainly forbidden all these things, and such people are but apostates whose "Way" demolishes human society, destroys the order of the world, leads to apostasy from religion, threatens the whole world with horrible distress and bitter troubles, and instigates the lower classes against all systems founded upon reason, morals, and virtue.[44]

The British were overjoyed, and copies were made for distribution throughout the Muslim portions of the British Empire. It soon became apparent, however, that the *fatwa* had far from the desired effect. The Egyptian population, intensely suspicious of British activities, responded with increased interest to a hitherto largely unknown doctrine. Anything the British so disliked, they reasoned, could not be all bad.[45] In Iraq and India the *fatwa* could not be used because it was issued by a Sunni mufti and it made negative references to the Parsee community.[46] According to a British intelligence report, even the prominent conservative Islamic reformer Mohammed Rashid Ridha considered the *fatwa* a mistake. According to the report, Ridha maintained, "Nobody ever knew in Egypt so much about real Bolshevism before the publication of the *fatwa,* and the newspapers never wrote so much about Bolshevism before this publication."[47] Two years later, another prominent religious figure attacked the growth of Egyptian socialism. Sheikh Mohammed al-Ghoneimi al-Taftazani quoted the Koranic verse "Allah has preferred some of you upon others in wealth," and from it argued, "Praise God! As if we have finished all our affairs and as if we have finished building such that nothing remains but demolishing. Oh you who call for the new socialist party, it is enough what the East suffers from horrors and calamities, so do not tear it apart with this terrible Russian disease."[48]

As Sheikh Ridha had observed, public interest in Marxism and media attention to it increased as a reaction to British efforts to discredit it. The party seized the opportunity to explain to the public through the media the principles of Marxism as they related to Egypt's problem. Hassan Muheissan, for example, declared in *al-Ahram* (August 24, 1921): "We are asking for raped and lost rights. Regarding the political rights, we demand it from our English adversary; as for the economic rights, we demand it from our adversary, the owner of money, whether he is a foreigner or Egyptian. Let the proponents of justice and right stand up for us, and let the workers come in ranks under the banner of the socialist party in order to remedy what the old times and dark medieval ages have spoiled." The very next day, 'Abdallah 'Anan's explanation appeared in *al-Ahram:* "There is no better manifestation of the pitiful tragedy which is represented now by the individualistic regimes than the fact that the large majority in the present society have been deprived of ownership, and that a small group is monopolizing the joys of private ownership when most of its members are drowned in achieving their base lusts and are performing nothing for society."

Egyptian socialists as a whole — not just the Marxists — took the opportunity to use the media to disclaim the charge that socialism conflicts with religion.

The Marxist response was received by the public with more enthusiasm than generally greeted Marxist publications. This provided the Marxist groups with the opportunity to explain their much maligned position on religion to the public: "Bolshevism, Oh our Sheikh, is not as described by the inquirer — anarchic, irreligious, and immoral. On the contrary, it is justice and liberty and does not oppose the Islamic religion in any way. It is a power which God has sent upon earth, when the world became wicked, in order to restore to Islam its old form and its famous justice so that no hypocrite Mufti like you or irreligious Sheikh . . . should exist, God has sent Bolshevism."[49]

Later, Hussein Nameq in his book *Khulasat al-Iqtisad wa Nubtha Min al-Tarikh al-Iqtisadi* posed the question, "What is the relation of socialism to Islam?" His answer was that "the basis of socialism is consoling the poor and equality in rights. The Islamic religion imposes the alms and forbids evil and calls for harmony among all classes."[50] The most im-

portant defense of socialism, however, came from Sheikh 'Abd al-Latif
Bakheit, a legal scholar and a member of the Socialist party, who stated,
"Being in a high religious school, I challenge those who claim that socialism contradicts religion to produce a verse [from the Koran] or a Had-
ith [by the Prophet] that conflicts with socialism. On the contrary, the
spirit of the Koran and the Suna is consistent with socialism." In direct
response to Sheikh al-Taftazani's charge, Nicola Haddad wrote in *al-
Ahram* (September 13, 1921): "Socialism is a social doctrine, not a religious one. It has nothing to do with religion." 'Aziz Mirhum also responded to al-Taftazani, stating: "I didn't think that fanatic support of
the principle of private property could lead one to claim it as one of the
pillars of religion because morality and self-control are the foundations
of religion."[51]

Al-Ahram allotted space in three issues (September 1, 12, and 13,
1921) for the conservative-socialist debate sparked by al-Taftazani's
charge against socialism. At least one prominent conservative, Hanna
Androus, accused *al-Ahram* of allowing the socialists more space than
they deserved.[52] Newspaper attention to the topic ceased immediately,
and the interest of party spokesmen and leaders subsequently diminished
significantly. Because of all the attention given by *al-Ahram* to the debate
on Bolshevism initiated by the *fatwa*, more powerful pressures than
Androus's complaint were likely exerted on the newspaper.

CONFRONTATION AND SUPPRESSION

By 1923, the Egyptian constitution had been declared, martial law
abolished, and Sa'ad Zaghloul returned from exile to lead his party into
the elections and win a decisive majority. On January 28, 1924, Sa'ad
Zaghloul became the new prime minister, heading the first Wafdist government. Following the elections, the Communist party (which had not
participated in the election) asked the governorate of Alexandria for permission to convene a conference there on February 23 and 24, 1924. The
request was rejected. This episode ended the party's public operation.

The new Wafd government represented bourgeois landowner and
upper-class interests and aspirations. The composition of the Wafd leadership and the organization of the party circumvented the possibility of
any participation by nonelites. All of the so-called popular committees
that were constituted in the villages and towns during the events leading
up to the 1919 revolution evolved into district branches for the central
committee of the Wafd. These committees were composed of local elites,

not members of the district's popular classes. The inequality among classes in Egypt was so great that even local elites were far removed in social distance from the population they lived among.

The Wafd, then, was populist in the sense that it represented a broader spectrum of the population than the ruling elites. But the Wafd was not popular in the sense of representing the grass roots of the population — the broad base of poverty-stricken rural peasants and urban workers. In its nationalist struggle, the Wafd party reflected the ideological aspirations of the petite bourgeoisie for independence from foreign domination of the economy. In this way it coincided with the anti-British sentiments and national aspirations of the popular classes. But the Wafd's bourgeois interests in creating political, economic, and social conditions to benefit Egyptian entrepreneurs were antagonistic to the interests of the peasants and working classes in creating political and economic conditions that would improve their social circumstances. Once the Wafd party achieved power, the coincidence of interests dissipated. The Wafd was inherently hostile toward the labor movement and adopted the British intelligence image of it as a communist conspiracy propagated by foreign agents and national traitors to incite the "naturally patient and docile" workers against law and order.[53]

A British intelligence report dated February 28, 1924, reflected this common image of the labor movement and the coordination of strategy regarding it between the otherwise antagonistic British High Commission and Wafd government:

> Sa'ad Pasha discussed the whole question [of the labor strikes] with me yesterday and informed me that he intended, after waiting for about a fortnight to let things quiet down, to deal with the various Russians and others concerned by having them deported from Egypt; he was thinking out means of dealing with communists of Egyptian nationality, such as Husni al-'Arabi and Sheikh Safwan, and thought the Parliament would not find it difficult to deal with communism on the grounds of its being opposed to the principles of Mohamedan religion. I spoke to him as regards the necessity of legislation to regulate the relations between employers and employed; he told me that this was one of the matters with which he considered Parliament should deal as early as possible.[54]

The main issues of interest to the labor movement were wages, working hours, and working conditions. Workers toiled for insufferably long hours for barely subsistence wages in abysmally unsanitary and unsafe conditions and without any job security. The labor movement grew quickly but made little progress through negotiation and conciliation in the face of the combined power and hostility of British industrialists (and the British High Commission, which protected their interests) and Egyptian entrepreneurs. Following World War I, the workers' standard of living deteriorated even more as a result of inflation in the cost of living.[55] This deterioration galvanized the labor movement into more militant action by 1924.

As a result of a long and bitter labor dispute at Filatures Nationales d'Egypte of Alexandra over the company's effort to cut wages by 10 percent, on February 22, 1924, the company's 1,200 to 1,500 workers went on strike and occupied the work premises. About the same time, workers at the Egyptian Oil Industries (Egoline) went on strike and also occupied their work premises. On February 26, Egyptian Salt and Soda Company of Alexandria workers presented wage demands to the company. Two days later, workers at Kafr-El-Zayat Cotton Company of Alexandria went on strike for shorter working hours and better working conditions. On February 29 a strike occurred at the Abouchanabs Oil Works in Alexandria, where 250 workers shut themselves up in the factory and declared their intention to remain there until demands for increased wages and shorter working hours were met. Throughout 1924 the strikes continued to spread.

The inevitable clash between the Wafd government and the Communist party as the vanguard of the labor movement was accelerated by these events. British Foreign Office records show that Sa'ad Zaghloul was in consultation with the British on the labor problem, and both the Wafd government and the British authorities were using a communist conspiracy theory to explain the labor unrest. A handwritten note from one British diplomatic staff member stationed in Cairo to another, dated March 7, 1924, for example, said, "Are you reporting to the F.O. about the recent strikes in Alexandria? I think the communist colour ought to be emphasized."[56]

The paranoia of the British diplomatic and business community in Egypt regarding the Egyptian labor situation became evident on March 21, 1922, when the British High Commissioner's Office reassured the British Union in Egypt (an association of British businesses) that "His Excellency will take such action as he considers necessary to deal with such signs of Bolshevism as may manifest themselves in this country." With the intensification of labor activism in early 1924, on March 28, 1924, the president of the British Union in Egypt sought further assurance from the British High Commissioner that action would be taken because "recent events have shown that in the intervening period the movement has grown and has manifested itself to a degree which threatens European interests, and it is a matter of general concern to employers of labour."[57]

The government responded to the strikes with force. On March 24, Sa'ad Zaghloul issued a statement warning the striking workers: "If you respect the property of others and walk out of the premises voluntarily, you shall be treated as loyal to the law and country. If you refuse but to occupy the property of others by force, you shall be treated as transgressors and outlaws." The Wafd government thus prepared to crush the movement by force if necessary. Communist gatherings were forbidden, and on March 3 many leaders, including Husni al-'Arabi, Anton Maroun, and Sheikh Safwan Abu al-Fatah, were arrested. They were charged with, "first, the spread of revolutionary ideas contradicting the principles of the Egyptian constitution . . . and encouraging change of the basic social systems by force and terror, and other illegitimate means, through selling and distributing printed leaflets advocating this. Second, instigating the workers of some companies to commit the crime of using force, terror, threat, and illegitimate means and transgressing on the right of the aforementioned businessmen in work and threatening owners if they do not meet their demands."[58]

Joseph Rosenthal, who had been expelled from the party, categorically denied that such strikes were a prelude to a communist takeover. In his interrogation before the general prosecutor he stated: "It seems to me that the government confuses between striking by staying at the working place and deprivation of ownership. When the workers occupy the factory they do not ask to seize it; they are workers without weapons in front of the powerful factory owners, who could starve them and force them to accept harsh conditions. So if they happened to stand in their places inside the factory, it is because they found that to be the best way to hasten the solution of the problem and reach an agreement between them and the owners."[59]

In an effort to bring the labor movement under the political control of the government, on March 15, 1924, at the peak of the strikes, Sa'ad Zaghloul announced the creation of a General Syndicate of Workers (al-Naqbah al-'Amah lil 'Umal) under the direction of 'Abd al-Rahman Fahmi (secretary of the central committee of the Wafd). This group was transformed into the General Federation of Labour Unions (Itihad 'Am lil 'Umal). On April 18, 1924, the Wafd party published a workers journal, al-'Umal, which declared in its first editorial: "The duty of workers is to coalesce and bind together under one banner and one leadership and to seek reform through legitimate means. . . . Those who disagree with us and want to precipitate events . . . may force those in charge, even in the constitutional era, to clamp down on those who disregard law and order."[60]

By July 17, 1924, Fahmi had completed drafting the bylaws of the General Federation of Labour Unions in the Nile Valley, which called for the creation of labor unions all over Egypt to co-opt the labor movement and bring it under government control. It also gave the federation the right to declare a general or partial strike. Fahmi was about to present this law to the parliament, but the assassination of the British *sirdar* and the ensuing crisis (which led to the arrest of Fahmi himself and eventually the downfall of the Wafd government) aborted the effort, and the Wafd party made no change in the workers' conditions. Zaghloul's campaign against the communist movement, however, was successful in eliminating its leaders, who were either put in prison or forced to retire for safety. Zaghloul had dealt a severe blow to the communist movement in Egypt. Husni al-'Arabi admitted as much in a September 1924 report to the Comintern, noting that the government had broken up the communist-led trade union movement, infiltrated party ranks, and "pursues the party and monitors its members, so that at present it is very difficult for two comrades to meet together."[61]

In the aftermath of the decimation of the party, the Comintern immediately undertook to organize a new central committee in an effort to salvage party continuity and morale. With the most prominent of the Egyptian communist leaders imprisoned, the Comintern put together a new central committee from the remnants of the Egyptian Communist party still active and from new members essentially secreted into Egypt by the Comintern. In an obvious challenge to the government effort to suppress the party, the new central committee was announced on the same day the court sentenced Husni al-'Arabi, Anton Maroun, Sheikh Safwan Abu al-Fatah, Ibrahim Katsi, and al-Shahat Ibrahim, October 6, 1924.[62]

Rosenthal's son-in-law, Constantine Weiss (alias Avigdor), a Comintern specialist in Egyptian affairs, was sent to assist in organizing the new central committee. A new party organization — this time more tightly structured, with cells and a private printing press — was implemented in Cairo, Alexandria, and Port Said. A new party publication, *al-'Alam al-Ahmar* [the red flag], was produced. On March 6, 1925, the party acquired a small newspaper, *al-Hisab,* and put it under the editorship of a distinguished journalist of Lebanese origin, Rafiq Gabbour, a member of the party central committee. Despite harassment from the government (reported by Gabbour in *al-Hisab,* April 10, 1925) the paper managed to publish eight issues before it was shut down and its editors and staff jailed. Its last issue was published May 18, 1925.

From the first, the organizational meetings of the new central committee were infiltrated by British intelligence. An intelligence agent, Mohammed 'Abd al-'Aziz, became secretary general of the central committee in late 1927 and served in that post for four years. Authorities, then, were carefully apprised of every move the now clandestine organization made. According to an initial British intelligence report on the new party organization,

> From the enquiries made and evidence obtained in connection with the communist movement in Egypt, I have come to the conclusion that a communist party has again been re-organized in Egypt, with its headquarters in Cairo and a branch belonging to it at Alexandria.
> Those who re-established it included some of the foreigners and Egyptians who previously took part in the formation of the 1st Party, together with some of those who were convicted in the 1st Communist Case.[63]

The new communist organization was more directly influenced by the Comintern than was its predecessor and reflected the policy and objectives of the Comintern (and Stalinism, which was already manifesting itself at that time). Party control had shifted from Egyptian to foreign members, as was most directly reflected in its leadership, which was composed predominantly of foreigners sent to Egypt by the Comintern. According to a British intelligence report,

> Early in 1925 marked confirmation began to appear of reports received as to the intentions of the Comintern to start a movement in the Near East. In Egypt two distinct Communist movements became apparent. The first was a semi-secret movement under the nominal leadership of a certain Rafik Gabbour, a Syrian local subject, who worked with an Englishman who called himself Thompson who suddenly appeared in Egypt ... ; an Austrian called Weiss ... ; a Jew called Pollack ... and certain Egyptians who were employed to gain recruits, etc.
> The second and possibly more dangerous movement was that apparently headed by the so-called Prince Outchtomsky and including Russians, Jews and others, such as Andreyev, Vladislav, Resnikoff, Resnoff, etc.[64]

This effort by the Comintern was consistent with the conspiracy theory image of communism and was easily thwarted through arrests and deportations. On May 30, 1925, the government of Ahmed Ziwar Pasha arrested all members of the central committee. As a result of these arrests, it was discovered that this committee had connections with the communist movement in Palestine and that "other than the Egyptians, most of those arrested were from the Jews of Palestine."[65] Thereafter, Russian ships were not allowed to enter Egyptian ports, and many Russians were arrested and deported on suspicion of communist activity. Subsequent attempts by Comintern envoys were made to rejuvenate communist organization in Egypt. Alie Teper, vice-chairman of the Communist party of Palestine, arrived in Egypt in August 1928 with Youssef Ibrahim, an Egyptian graduate of the University of the Toilers of the East. Four months later, both were detained and deported. Next, Alexis N. Vasilev, a member of the executive committee of the Communist International, arrived in Egypt. He too was deported.[66] The Comintern subsequently ceased its efforts to rejuvenate the party and severed its association with it. The party essentially disappeared as an organization. At the Sixth Congress of the Comintern in 1928, the Egyptian Communist party was not directly represented but was represented by the Communist party of Palestine. In effect, the Egyptian party was placed under the stewardship of the Palestinian party.

3

The Second Movement, *1930–1950*

The communists in Egypt remained weak during the 1930s and depended to a large degree on foreigners who formed different cells and groups. The rise of Stalinism in the Soviet Union disenchanted socialist-oriented reformers; the rise of fascism in Europe enchanted tradition-oriented reformers. This change in the ideological climate was reflected in Egypt in the barrage of anticommunist, profascist propaganda in the press: "Fascism owes its success to circumstances and conditions. The investors in Italy panicked from the inability of the government to suppress the communist movement in the country and circled around the fascists, since they observed that putting the burden of chasing the communists on the shoulders of the fascists was better than leaving it to the government, which was blind, in addition to its weakness. There is no doubt that if fascism had not been formed by men of mighty strength and will, it would not have acquired that astounding victory in a short time."

Another journal indicated that "while Egypt is arming itself with what it has of written and unwritten laws to defend its entity against the communist conspiracies, it might be useful to look at the fierce war which the fascists in Italy had declared on the common enemy."[2] Within Egypt, Italian fascists established several organizations that further fostered the spread of anticommunist fascist propaganda.

Similarly, Hitler was lionized in the press. In a special supplement of *al-Fallah al-Iqtisadi,* Thabet Thabet, the editor, stated in his introduction:

> The Chancellor Hitler worked without rest in construction and education and in consolidating the power of the Reich and defending it against the Bolshevik danger. The Bolsheviks create obstacles to the

32

government by their terrorist activities and fake propaganda. Then came the incident of the parliament; it was the last incident of the communists' plot, and it was not the first. So Hitler saw that the Reichstag should be dissolved. On the 21st of March 1933 the new parliament convened and Hindenburg went to Potsdam Church, and there at the tomb of Frederick the Great he said his famous saying, "Germany has awakened to return to its old honorable traditions."[3]

As the non-Egyptian Left (from social justice reformers to Marxist revolutionaries) concentrated increasing efforts in the 1930s on fighting fascism, the British showed greater tolerance for leftist activities within the foreign communities, allowing them to function publicly and form organizations. Egyptian communist activities, however, focused primarily on labor issues, continued to be suppressed. Antifascist Marxist groups began to appear in the late 1930s organized within the European community in Egypt. These groups became the seedbed for a number of organizations.

ITIHAD ANSAR AL-SALAM (UNION OF PEACE PARTISANS)

One of the earliest such communist organizations was the Union of Peace Partisans (Itihad Ansar al-Salam), organized in 1934 by Paul Jacquot-Descombes, a Swiss engineer, whose father was active in Egyptian business. After finishing his education in Germany, Jacquot-Descombes returned to Egypt, worked with the Greek communist groups in Cairo, and then organized the union. This association joined the international organization Rassenlelewent Universel pour la Paux. It attracted middle-class intellectuals, Egyptians, and foreigners and included some Wafdists and women from the Union of Egyptian Women (al-Itihad al-Nisai'e al-Misri). It appears that Paul Jacquot-Descombes was planning to recruit Egyptianized elements to be entrusted with the responsibility of creating the seeds of a communist party. He discussed his plans only with three of his associates, who spoke Arabic and like him were extremely cautious. They were Sadiq Sa'ad, Youssef Darwish, and Ramon Duwaik.[4] With the outbreak of World War II, this association formally disbanded and its members continued their activities in other groups. Its property was transferred to one of these new groups, Jama'at al-Buhuth (the Research Group). The clandestine cell set up by Sa'ad, Darwish, and Duwaik continued to operate behind this new group.

AL-ITIHAD AL-DEMOQRATI (DEMOCRATIC UNION)

Al-Itihad al-Demoqrati (the Democratic Union), founded in early 1939 in Alexandria and Cairo, operated parallel to the Union of Peace Partisans, and the two had overlapping memberships. Its founders had wanted to participate in the union so as to Egyptianize it and give it a more clearly defined Marxist commitment. Jacquot-Descombes, however, had not responded to their initiative for fear of their radical Marxism. Rivalry was thereby created between the two groups. The basic aim of al-Itihad al-Demoqrati was to create an Egyptian Marxist group. Its bylaws required that a majority of the executive committee be Egyptian. It became a front organization for further clandestine Marxist cells. Shortly after its formation, al-Itihad al-Demoqrati established contact with a forum for Egyptian artists and intellectuals called al-Fan wa al-Huriyah (Art and Freedom). This forum, however, fell under Trotskyite influence, reflecting the factionalism within the Egyptian Left.

The most active organizers in al-Itihad al-Demoqrati were Henri Curiel, Hillel Schwartz, and Marcel Israel. Within a few years a conflict emerged and the three broke up to set up separate Marxist organizations. Interviews with associates of the three men indicate that the main reason for the split was a clash over strategy. Henri Curiel saw the necessity of immediately establishing a communist organization whose basic aim should be the Egyptianization of the movement. Hillel Schwartz, however, considered the Egyptianization slogan chauvinistic. He felt there should be no distinction between Egyptians and non-Egyptians in an international movement. Marcel Israel believed in Egyptianization but was so rigid that he prohibited non-Egyptians from participating in any leadership role. Curiel claimed that he and Israel differed on the question of religion. He maintained that Israel believed in the need to concentrate their attack on religion, whereas Curiel and his group rejected that approach because they were active among the students of al-Azhar.[5]

Henri Curiel established al-Harakah al-Misriyah lil Tahrur al-Watani (the Egyptian Movement for National Liberation). Hillel Schwartz established Iskra, and Marcel Israel established Tahrir al-Sha'ab (People's Liberation).

Thus al-Itihad al-Demoqrati became the seedbed for a number of activist Marxist organizations. For the nonactivists, the Social Cultural Club, al-Markaz al-Thaqafi al-Ijtima'i, emerged with the basic aim of promoting democratic antifascist activities. It was closely associated with Curiel's underground group. In early 1943, it was dissolved and was accused of being a communist front organization.

Similarly, Tahrir al-Sha'ab contributed to the establishment of two groups — one aimed at recruiting Egyptian workers called al-Khubz wa al-Huriyah (Bread and Freedom), the other, Thaqafah wa Faragh (Culture and Leisure), an extension of Curiel's activities, aimed at recruiting the Egyptian middle class. Both were banned in August 1941.

Meanwhile, Duwaik, Darwish, and Sa'ad established the Marxist intellectual study group Jama'at al-Buhuth (also known as the Groupe d'Études). Its basic aims were to acquaint foreigners in Egypt with the conditions of the country. In June 1943, the group published a book called *Egypt Now*. With the end of the war, it dissolved. Sadiq Sa'ad described the group:

> After a debate we decided to establish a secret organizational structure and we chose three for its leadership. This organization continued until 1942 . . . I used to attend the study circles regularly. In them, Marxist books were read and discussed. There I used to meet especially with Ramon Duwaik and Youssef Darwish, and I remember among important subjects we studied and left an impression in our minds of what we called the principles of secrecy and security, or the basic principles that protect the organization from police infiltration, and the stand we must take in interrogations and in court.[6]

Another group established by Duwaik, Darwish, and Sa'ad in 1940 was Jama'at al-Shabab lil Thaqafah al-Sha'biyah (Youth Group for Popular Culture). This was a popular organization aimed at organizing the masses. Literacy classes were organized in the poor areas of Cairo. It disbanded at the end of the war. Sadiq Sa'ad observed, "Our intellectual background directed us to search for mass action among the people — particularly workers and peasants. In that period, Youssef [Duwaik] had the opportunity to defend a worker's legal case. Through this he was able to establish contact with some leaders of the Union of Textile Workers. . . . His activities began to concentrate in that direction. He began missing the meetings of Jama'at al-Shabab lil Thaqafah al-Sha'biyah."[7]

Another significant Marxist group established in 1942 was Lajnat Nashr al-Thaqafah al-Hadithah (Committee for the Promotion of Modern Culture). Here several Egyptian intellectuals received their first Marxist lectures. Sadiq Sa'ad and Ramon Duwaik actively participated in its establishment but were subsequently expelled. Marcel Israel's group Tahrir al-Sha'ab also participated in it. Through this association Sadiq Sa'ad met Egyptian intellectuals such as Ahmed Rushdi Salih, 'Abd al-Rahman al-Sharqawi, Abu Sayf Youssef, Mohammed Ismail, and Sa'ad Makawi, who became prominent in the Egyptian communist movement in the 1950s (with the exception of al-Sharqawi and Makawi, who ceased organizational association in the 1940s). The association established a publishing house, Dar al-Qarn al-'Ashrin, managed by Ramon Duwaik, which became a center for publication and distribution of Marxist publications from Iraq, Lebanon, and Palestine, as well as Egypt. Similarly, Dar al-Abhath al-'Almiyah (House of Scientific Research) was established as a front for Iskra. It emphasized public education and was banned July 11, 1946.

By the early 1940s, all these fluid groups began to crystallize into more formal associations, making it easier for foreign Marxists to reach the Egyptianized elements and for them in turn to link with Egyptian intellectuals who sought to extend the movement into the ranks of the Egyptian masses. As a result, the labor movement again became more organized and more strident. By 1946, a series of student demonstrations and labor strikes united students, workers, and civil servants in organized protests. The government of Isma'il Sidqi Pasha was formed on February 27, 1946, with a mandate to crush the spreading social unrest. An ardent communist witch-hunter, Sidqi Pasha unleashed a campaign of harassment and suppression against communists, suspected communists, labor activists, and suspected sympathizers. Many clubs and associations were outlawed, 250 activists arrested, and the communist movement driven underground.

The transition from foreign Marxists to Egyptian intellectuals marked the initiation of the second communist movement. Figure 1 identifies the most significant groups and clubs that were spin-offs from the two founding associations. The most significant organizations to emerge out of the transition are discussed below.

JAMA'AT TAHRIR AL-SHA'AB (PEOPLE'S LIBERATION GROUP)

This group was formed in 1939 under the leadership of Marcel Israel, who had been a member of the Union of Peace Partisans. During that time, Israel called for Egyptianizing the union and forming a communist group. Jacquot-Descombes, however, being extremely cautious, refused and indicated that he would discuss nothing except the declared goals of the union. As a result, some of the members of the union became disenchanted and decided to split and form their own group. As Raymond Agion, a member of the union, stated,

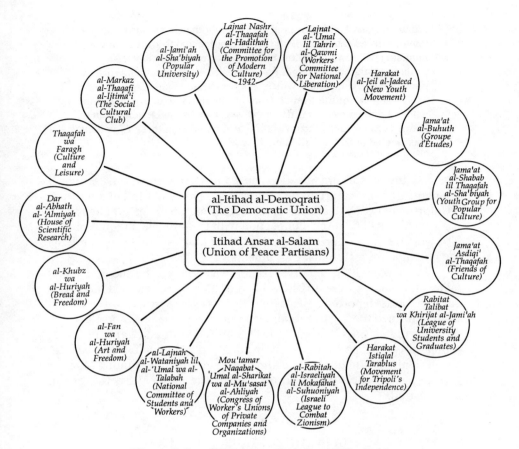

Fig. 1. Spin-off groups and clubs, 1936–1946.

In November 1939 I left the Union of Peace Partisans — me, Marcel Israel, Raul Curiel, and a Greek girl who was a journalist. Marcel was the most experienced among us. However, his experience was also modest, and when we had agreed to leave Paul Jacquot-Descombes's group, we were expressing our disenchantment with hesitation and fear and limiting the activities to foreigners alone and away from the Egyptians and the real problems of Egypt. . . . This disenchanted group then decided to form a Marxist group which concentrated on the Marxist formation of the Egyptian elements which were recruited . . . and studies in Marxism were organized in the Arabic language. In only a few months this group was able to recruit and

organize many Egyptians, and very rapidly the Egyptians became a
majority in its ranks. In 1940 this group decided to become a communist organization and convened a conference in which several reports about the situation in Egypt were discussed, together with a report on the organization, which was presented by an Egyptian who
was a member of the French Communist party. The organization,
whose establishment was declared, was named the Organization of
People's Liberation, and an executive committee of three Egyptians
was elected in addition to Marcel Israel.[8]

The activities of this organization caused problems, however, because it
concentrated on materialistic arguments. As Marcel Israel admitted,
"Unfortunately, these studies revolved around complicated ideological
issues which had no direct connection with the struggle's requirements.
The workers, for example, would start their Marxist studies by studying
the principles of materialistic arguments."[9]

In October 1941, the organization was attacked by the police and
many of its cadres were arrested. Most of them were released, and Marcel Israel was deported to Palestine. In 1944 he returned to Egypt and
again reformed the organization, claiming to be "the only non-Egyptian
member in its ranks." In early 1947 it united with Iskra and a smaller
group, al-Qala'h, to form a short-lived group called al-Tali'ah al-Mutahidah (United Vanguard). The aim was to create unity among Marxist
groups. With the formation of Haditu the same year, the group
disappeared.

AL-TALI'AH AL-SHA'BIYAH LIL TAHRUR (TASHT)

Al-Tali'ah al-Sha'biyah lil Tahrur, formally established in September 1946, evolved from an informal association that developed out of the
establishment of Jama'at al-Buhuth and the disbanding of the Union of
Peace Partisans. Figure 2 demonstrates the relationship of Tasht with associated organizations. With the encouragement of Jacquot-Descombes,
the cell in the defunct union was reconstituted as a clandestine organization within which Duwaik, Darwish, and Sa'ad established an Egyptian cell. By the middle of 1942, all the foreign Marxists left for Palestine
because of the encroachment of Axis armies on Egypt. Therefore, the
Egyptians functioned independently of non-Egyptian leadership for the
first time. After the war and the return of the non-Egyptian Marxists,
Sa'ad reports,

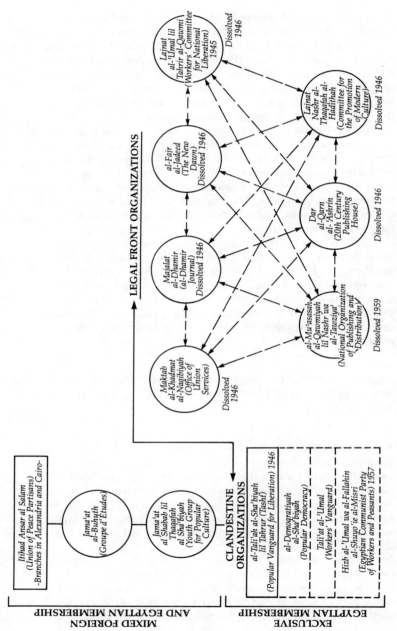

Fig. 2. Al-Tali'ah al-Sha'biyah lil Tahrur.

We decided to split. A motion to this effect was passed almost without debate and without political and intellectual differences. . . . As a result of the decision of the group, three of us [Duwaik, Darwish, and Sa'ad] held another meeting to discuss our future policy and program for our activities. We agreed on two decisions. The first concerned the policy of the cell. We decided it must have a dual purpose. On one hand, we must understand the Egyptian conditions so that we could draw the principles of Egyptian Marxist thought, which requires study of the Egyptian situation on a theoretical basis. It also requires mass activity either by joining existing legal organizations or if needed by creating others. . . . We were very convinced that information from books and sources cannot alone form the basis of knowledge. Rather, there must be a continuous integration of this and direct action among people. The Egyptian faith in socialism has its distinguishing features and specificity which makes its condition different than other countries. . . .

The second decision concerned the organizational structure. We decided not to establish a complete structure (not to recruit new members). . . . In the meantime, we decided to establish two cells — one, which includes Rushdi, Ramon, and me, to work among intellectuals; the second to specialize in activities among workers. We created a coordinating committee between the two cells. The development of our activities later on will determine the form of our organizational evolution.[10]

Thus the members of this group opposed the formation of a formal communist organization. The main reasons for such an attitude were given by Sadiq Sa'ad:

We had a dual goal: first, to understand Egypt on the basis of drawing what we called the Egyptian communist policy; that is, we were convinced that there does not exist "communism" in an absolute form, but instead there is a communism for every individual country. The principal mistake of the first communist movement in Egypt, together with the other communist activities which existed at the time, was that they did not understand the specific national characteristics and the particular identity specific to Egypt.

Second, we wanted to create popular relationships with the national popular movement and the Egyptian democracy. On these bases we conscientiously prohibited ourselves from declaring the establishment of a communist organization. We thought that establishment of a communist party at that time would involve us in organizational activities that would prevent us from achieving these goals.[11]

Jacquot-Descombes saw this organization as the fruition of his own work, which was to sow the seeds of Marxist thought, not to lay the foundations of organization. This he considered an Egyptian task, not one to be initiated by non-Egyptian elements. He thus considered his work in Egypt over by 1940, although he continued personal contact with his disciples until his departure from Egypt in 1946.[12]

Al-Tali'ah al-Sha'biyah owes its formation to four persons, Sadiq Sa'ad, Ramon Duwaik, Youssef Darwish, and Ahmed Rushdi Salih. Ahmed Rushdi Salih's father-in-law had some relationship with the Ministry of Interior and facilitated Salih's efforts to get a permit to issue the magazine *al-Fajr al-Jadeed* in his name. Sadiq Sa'ad, in his version of how Salih joined the group, stated that "in a meeting to discuss how to issue the magazine, Ahmed Rushdi Salih raised the question of finance and we told him that we shall try to solve this problem. Rushdi Salih insisted on knowing the source of finance and we had to explain the matter to him and our relationship with the secret foreign group which functioned behind the Jama'at al-Buhuth and how the group was going to finance the issuance of the magazine ... and Rushdi Salih agreed to join our small group."[13]

The magazine *al-Fajr al-Jadeed* came to life on May 16, 1945, on a biweekly basis. After twelve issues, on November 1, 1945, it appeared weekly. In the editorial of the first issue, the publication declared its Marxist orientation, attacked bourgeois intellectuals, and called for analysis of Egypt's concrete experiences. The publication's political program was published in the third issue (June 16, 1945): "Our national demand does not stop with political liberation or support for democracy. It does not even stop with the establishment of social justice or the improvement in the standard of living among the masses. It includes all that and adds to it a significant national demand. This is the adaptation of Egyptian heritage to our social and political needs."

By the appearance of the thirteenth issue (undated) the Marxist orientation of the magazine became even clearer. Sadiq Sa'ad, in an article entitled "The October Revolution ... A Stage of Transformation in Human History," stated:

> With the revolution of October, the proletariat — the class of the workers and the vanguard of toilers — controlled political power in Russia. That was the first time the masses took over political power. ... In the socialist society which was established by the October revolution, no parasitic class usurped the efforts of the toilers. Rather, the people produce for themselves and supervise the collective production because they own all means of production. ... [Oppressed]

people look up to the Soviet Union not because they are waiting for
the Soviet Union to "arrange" the revolution for them; rather these
people know with certainty that freedom cannot be imported from
outside. It must be built by them through their struggle.

In a content analysis of *al-Fajr al-Jadeed,* a student of Egyptian
journalism concluded that social issues received the most attention in the
journal. Education ranked first, then inequality among classes and social
justice, health and malnutrition, workers' conditions and issues, the
housing problem, and food supplies, in that order. [14]

Within a short time of its appearance, *al-Fajr al-Jadeed* was being
distributed all over the Arab world. It received financial and moral support from Arab groups and established contacts with Marxist and communist groups in Palestine, Syria, Lebanon, and Iraq. [15] In the meantime,
Sadiq Sa'ad published his celebrated book *Mushkilat al-Fallah* (The problem of the peasants), which identified the situation of Egyptian peasants
as a general national issue "crushing the landless peasant, the toiling
worker, liberal intellectuals, and the small owner." He identified the role
of imperialism in the Egyptian economy and described the reigning land
tenure system as "semifeudal." The consequent problems of the peasantry were fivefold: the limitations and rigidity of the agricultural economy, the inequitable basis of the present systems of "property returns"
(sharecropping and so on), the high price of agricultural products, the
backwardness of agricultural production, and the high price of land. In
Sadiq Sa'ad's opinion, "There are two points we consider to be at the
foundation of the problem. The first is the existence of a landowning class
which monopolizes agricultural land and agricultural production without
government regulation. The second point is the existence of a large class
of small farmers and agricultural workers who could not survive independently from the social, economic, and political influence of the landowning class." To deal with this situation, he suggested three necessary com-
ponents of agrarian reform: limitation of agricultural land ownership to
fifty feddans and redistribution of the rest to landless peasants, creation
of cooperatives to encourage production, and protection of peasants
through legislation. [16]

While Sadiq Sa'ad and his group were working among intellectuals,
Youssef Darwish was working among workers. On October 8, 1945,
Lajnat al-'Umal lil Tahrir al-Qawmi (Workers' Committee for National
Liberation) was created. This organization was not aimed at organizing
workers but at raising their political consciousness. Its founding pro-
gram, prepared by the al-Tali'ah al-Sha'biyah group, declared: "Do not

forget that the history of Egypt from the British occupation in 1882, the actions of political leaders from all ruling classes have been directed against the people. Do not forget that all your hopes of liberating Egypt from imperialism and internal exploitation can be achieved only by your own hands and through your leadership. ... This program is a popular program directed toward the Egyptian people and the achievement of their interests. ... This program will be achieved by the Egyptian nation spearheaded by the working class."[17]

According to Tariq al-Bushri, the program represented the first time that class struggle had been directly linked to national liberation. In articulating the comprador relationship between the Egyptian ruling class and British imperialism, the program maintained that "it is not possible to liberate the working class without liberating Egypt from imperialism."[18] Social demands, then, were delineated in the framework of the struggle against imperialism and foreign exploitation. These included the nationalization of public utilities, the liberation of Egyptian industry from foreign control, nationalization of all monopolies, and substantive agrarian reform, including the confiscation of large landholdings and their redistribution among the peasantry.

In late September 1945 the Workers' Committee for National Liberation initiated publication of a weekly journal, al-Dhamir. Only eleven issues were produced before the publication was banned by the authorities in July 1946. Directed at raising the political consciousness of Egyptian workers, the journal (like the committee) stressed the struggle of the workers in the context of national liberation from foreign domination. As one issue expressed it, "Imperialism is what is starving [the workers]. Imperialism closes the doors of science and knowledge. ... The workers more than anyone else are ready to make the sacrifice [for national liberation] because they understand well that imperialism has imprisoned them, deprived them of their freedoms, and armed their oppressors in order to weaken the struggle of the working class—the vanguard of the toiling masses."[19] Imperialism was directly linked to social exploitation, with the ruling class serving as its agents to oppress and impoverish the Egyptian people. The general secretary of the committee, Mohammed Youssef al-Mudrik, clarified this relationship in the November 14, 1945, issue of al-Dhamir: "The British discovered the existence of an exploiting class and became aligned with them against the people ... at the expense of the peasants and workers, in order to divide the spoils among themselves. Thus imperialism continues to protect the exploiters and oppress the workers." In the issue of December 5, 1945, al-Mudrik stated that "Egyptian workers have reached a degree of consciousness that qualifies them to lead the struggling nation. They are moving forward to achieve their aims."

Al-Mudrik was, in effect, advocating a workers' movement. In January 1946 he was arrested along with others associated with the journal for subversive activities. Commenting on their arrest in his memoirs, Taha Sa'ad 'Uthman (editorial secretary of al-Dhamir and a founding member of the Workers' Committee for National Liberation) declared that until he left prison in May 1946 he had no connection with any political organization.[20] In other words, 'Uthman, al-Mudrik, and others associated with the Workers' Committee were unaware of the committee's clandestine ties to the al-Tali'ah al-Sha'biyah group. On July 11, 1946, al-Dhamir was closed during the prime minister's crackdown against all leftist political opposition.

Following the suppression of al-Dhamir, Duwaik, Darwish, Rushdi, and Sa'ad decided to establish a clandestine political organization with members drawn from the Workers' Committee. According to Sa'ad,

> The cell decided that a new stage was beginning which required the establishment of a secret organization. We prepared some basic documents such as the political and workers' strategies and the basic by-laws. We had close contacts with a number of activists who cooperated with us during our public activities and agreed to join the organization. We organized in cells and elected a leadership. We held a founding congress in September 1946 which selected a three-person central committee. I was the political officer; Youssef Duwaik the organizational officer; and Mahmud al-'Askari the recruiting officer. The organization was named al-Tal'iah al-Sha'biyah lil Tahrur [Popular Vanguard for Liberation, popularly known by its acronym Tasht], which changed to al-Demoqratiyah al-Sha'biyah, then changed again to Tali'at al-'Umal [Workers' Vanguard], and finally in 1957 to Hizb al-'Umal wa al-Fallahin al-Shuyo'ie al-Misri [the Egyptian Communist Party of Workers and Peasants]. None of these changes had any effect on political or organizational matters. They were merely name changes for security reasons, not for political or ideological reasons.[21]

According to Abu Sayf Youssef, the founding congress identified two strategic aims for Tasht: to delineate the Egyptian road to socialism and to build strong relations with other revolutionary forces.[22] Tasht was organized into three distinct cells based on functional differentiation — mass work (recruitment and mobilization), political work (operationalization of the strategic aims), and organizational work (policy, planning, coordination, and the like). The functions of the three cells were coordinated through formal and informal communication. Policy issues were debated and decisions taken at meetings of cell leaders and central committee members, and these decisions were circulated through the organization in written communications. A system of color coding was used instead of names to maintain security. Out of this process, the post office developed as a fourth level of the organization, reflecting both the growth in organizational size and complexity and the centrality of the communication function.[23]

Tasht was organized on the principles of democratic centralism, with ultimate power vested in the membership and in principle exercised through regular congresses and other forums. Throughout its history, however, Tasht held only two congresses: the founding congress in 1946 and the 1957 congress at which the organization's name was changed to the Workers' and Peasants' Communist party. From 1946 to 1957, then, the policy-making body in the organization was the central committee, formed first by Sadiq Sa'ad, Youssef Darwish, and Mahmud al-'Askari, with Sadiq Sa'ad as the secretary general (1946 to 1948), then Ahmed Rushdi Salih (1948 to 1951), and finally Abu Sayf Youssef (1951 to 1957).[24]

The rigid policies and procedures of secrecy in the organization constituted a substantial obstacle to the democratic process. According to Abu Seif Youssef, "The true essence of the process of intraparty democracy is to allow the base to exercise a sort of control on the top. In the case of secrecy, the power cannot be full as not all members and officials are known to each other. Furthermore, secrecy breeds fear, suspicion, and lack of accountability. Secrecy may also make some officials reveal dictatorial tendencies."[25]

The organization made substantial demands on its members. The nomination process for a new member could take from six months to two years, during which time the nominee was investigated and tested. According to Helmi Yassin, "Membership in our organization resembled priesthood; moral stature was stressed. . . . The member had to be responsible in his private life, and the organization had the right to interfere in a member's private life."[26]

The organization issued two leaflets: an internal one, *al-Hadaf,* which published only fifty copies that were circulated among the members, then collected and destroyed, and a popular magazine, *Kifah al-Sha'ab.* Initially, the organization opposed any effort to unite with other communist groups, but in 1957 it changed this position and joined other communist groups in founding Hizb al-'Umal wa al-Fallahin al-Shuyo'ie al-Misri.

ISKRA

Iskra was formed in 1942 as a result of the split between Curiel and Schwartz. Its primary activities until 1946 were recruiting and educating intellectuals. Thus the organization's major aim was ideological education. According to Mohammed Sayyid Ahmed, one of Iskra's Egyptian leaders, Iskra believed that the development of class consciousness went through evolutionary stages beginning with foreign intellectuals, then progressing to Egyptian intellectuals from the upper class and well-to-do bourgeoisie, and finally reaching the working class. The children of wealthy Egyptian families were educated for the most part in the private French (*lycée*) schools. Some of the French teachers already had socialist political orientations. These schools were a primary arena for Iskra's recruitment of Egyptians. With the recruitment of students and Egyptian intellectuals, the second stage of Iskra was achieved. But the third stage of recruiting workers remained symbolic.[27]

Iskra was responsible for the creation of Dar al-Abhath al-'Ilmiyah, which was dedicated to publication of research on the political economy of Egypt. It organized lectures and discussion groups and established al-Jami'ah al-Sha'biyah to teach workers literacy, basic math, and foreign languages. One of the public activities of Iskra was Rabitat al-Talabah al-Misriyin, which was a student organization. According to one of its leaders, a prominent Iskra member, Sa'ad Zahran, Iskra established a student magazine named *Sawt al-Talib*, which played a very important role in mobilizing and organizing students and resulted in the creation of al-Lajnah al-Wataniyah lil al-'Umal wa al-Talabah in 1946.[28]

Iskra published a book by two of its most important leaders, Shuhdi 'Atiyah al-Shaf'ie and Mohammed 'Abd al-Ma'boud al-Gibayli, entitled *Ahdafuna al-Wataniyah,* in October 1945. The volume explained the aims and program of Iskra, identifying economic and political independence as the primary objectives. In explaining the contribution of this book to these objectives, the authors maintained in the preface:"The time has arrived for us to abandon an impulsive approach in delineating our national policy. At this critical historical moment, we require more than ever a clear definition of our national aims and the strategy to achieve them [based on] international developments enlightened by our past experiences. . . . This book is perhaps a humble contribution from us toward the [achievement] of this aim. However, this research . . . came as a result of previous studies of the international situation and a careful, detailed [examination] of the different social and intellectual currents.'' The first chapter identified the attainment of complete independence and popular democracy as the primary national goals to be achieved, "using all means of struggle appropriate to the international situation." It was argued that the international situation was right for the achievement of the national struggle, but any delay in moving vigorously would "result in grave harm to the Egyptian people and treachery to the national question."[29]

Achievement of the "national demands" for the evacuation of British forces and unification of the Nile Valley were rejected as inadequate for the achievement of independence.

> Neither these aims nor the means being used to achieve them truly reflect the national interest. They are also inconsistent with the international situation. Military evacuation alone will not guarantee the unity of the Nile Valley. We want economic, military, and political evacuation to build our independence on a solid foundation. We have seen many countries who have achieved complete military sovereignty . . . but in fact they are nothing more than economic and financial colonies. . . . As for the second demand, unity of the Nile Valley, while it appears logical and romantic, it has inherent within it great dangers that may be detrimental to the questions of both Sudan and Egypt: in the Sudan today there exists a movement which sees hiding behind the Egyptian demand imperialist tendencies emanating from Egyptian businessmen and industry who want to replace British imperialism with an Egyptian one. Insisting upon this unity gives a valuable opportunity to the British imperialists to encourage separatist movements. . . . The Egyptian people do not want to exploit anybody and demand a full Sudan, free of all kinds of imperialism.[30]

Chapter 2 related the Egyptian question to the international situation and the need to view Egypt's struggle in the context of international imperialism:

> There is nothing more dangerous to the Egyptian question than our insistence on the old approach in our struggle. [In this approach] we imagine that Egypt's relationship with Britain is the main issue, forgetting that the Egyptian question is an international issue and all the people of the world have a basic interest in solving the Egyptian question and realizing the aims of the Egyptian people. The international situation today no doubt strengthens our struggle against imperialism. This is why it is an imperative duty to connect our national struggle with the international struggle until we achieve all our goals.[31]

The program outlined an international strategy for the achievement of Iskra's national aims program:

1. Complete economic, military, and political independence through complete evacuation of British forces, nationalization of British shares in foreign companies operating in Egypt in payment of Britain's war debt to Egypt, and dismantling of British cultural, administrative, civil, and military controls in Egypt.

2. Secure the Egyptianization of the Suez Canal and Egyptian sovereignty over it.

3. Terminate all foreign capitulations immediately.

4. Establish control of Egypt's foreign policy.

5. Establish Egyptian and Sudanese unity in the struggle for military, economic, and political independence with democratic representation of the Sudan in all negotiations and agreements related to its independence.

6. Support the creation of the Arab League on the condition that it will be led by democratic governments.

7. "Support for the unity of Arabs and Jews in Palestine to struggle against imperialism and Zionism to achieve independence and democracy in Palestine."

8. Struggle against all fascist and imperialist attempts to create disunity among the Arab people by such foreign-sponsored schemes as "Greater Syria" and the Islamic League.

9. Support Egypt's participation in all international organizations such as the United Nations, Bretton Woods, and the international labor unions.[32]

In chapter 3, the authors outlined Iskra's democratic program:

If we fail to tie our external aims with a program for change. . . . and if the government does not have the real support of the people on the basis of a democratic program . . . this will lead to a gulf between the government and the people, the loss of the people's confidence, and the necessity to rely on an outside force to sustain authority. This will open the door to imperial conspiracies and manipulations. Thus the international democratic program is first and foremost the main aim for independence; second, it is the necessary means for the struggle to achieve independence; and finally it is the only means to protect this independence. What, then, is this program which will satisfy the majority of the people — workers, peasants, students, intellectuals, and small government employees? This program is a national imperative whose basic foundations are three democracies: economic democracy, political democracy, and social democracy.[33]

The basis of economic democracy was identified as improvement in the standard of living of the population. Industrialization integrated with agricultural development was considered essential, and the following program for a democratic government was outlined: progressive taxes on income and capital, economic development programs financed through internal and external loans, state ownership of key industries, participation of workers in management, the concessions of foreign companies not be renewed and upon expiration assets to be nationalized, and state encouragement of the development of democratically organized labor unions.[34]

In addition, the program called for labor legislation that would improve the working and living conditions of workers. Social insurance, unemployment insurance, old-age benefits, and workers' compensation were some of the programs advocated. A forty-hour workweek, a minimum wage, and union rights were also promoted.

Problems of agricultural reform and development were considered the most fundamental: "Without solving this issue, to address the basic interest of the millions of peasants, any independence Egypt may achieve is superficial and any democracy talked about is a democracy for the minority and a dictatorship over the majority which camouflages the worst kinds of exploitation." The following steps were considered essential to agrarian reform and development: land reclamation and improvement in irrigation; comprehensive land redistribution; organization of producer and consumer cooperatives; application of modern technology to agriculture; inclusion of peasants and agricultural workers under labor codes and social security programs; restructuring of agricultural debts; a progressive tax on agricultural incomes; and development of rural social services, including health and education.[35]

The industrial and agricultural programs constituted the economic dimension of democracy. The political dimension required development of representative institutions and participatory political processes at all levels of government from the village to the national level; the banning of particularistic interest groups because they create dissent and division in society, thus contributing to the maintenance of British imperialism; reform of public administration, especially the army and the police; and guarantee of basic freedoms. Social democracy required universal education; educational planning to be coordinated with economic planning so that education would serve development needs; a universal health care system and abolition of private medicine; greater attention to preventive medicine; equality between the sexes; equality among minorities; and freedom of worship, beliefs, and culture.

The authors concluded the chapter by observing: "These three dimensions — economic, political, and social — are the foundation of true independence. The struggle for them is an integral part of the struggle for independence. Independence is not an end it itself; rather, it is the means through which democracy is realized in all segments of Egyptian life, nurturing it until it becomes a popular democracy in the fullest meaning of the word."[36]

Although Iskra never directly put forward a program because of the ban on political activities, it disseminated its ideas through the publication of books and pamphlets. In April 1947, the weekly paper *al-Jamahir* became the unofficial organ for Iskra. Five members of Iskra, including the authors of *Ahdafuna al-Wataniyah* constituted the paper's editorial board. In addition, the heads of each section of the paper were the heads of Iskra's specialized cells. A coordinating committee worked between the newspaper's board and Iskra's executive board.

In its first editorial, *al-Jamahir* declared:

> *Al-Jamahir* is not only the newspaper's name. . . . It is the voice of the millions of workers, peasants, and intellectuals . . . who struggle against despised imperialism and hope for lofty independence. . . . *Al-Jamahir* declares a fierce war against all forms of imperialism, whether economic or cultural. The millions, including *al-Jamahir* will not accept anything but rapid and complete evacuation [of the British] from the Nile Valley from its source to the sea. *Al-Jamahir* will struggle against imperialism and will not forget the traitors, friends of imperialism, and the timid, frightened by imperialism. They hide behind their Egyptian identity but conspire with the conspirators [imperialists]. We will unmask all these and will expose them to the masses.
>
> *Al-Jamahir* will enter the fight for freedom and independence with a direction. We seek true democracy. Any reduction of freedom of expression, freedom of the press, or freedom of elections is a definite support for imperialism. . . . *Al-Jamahir* does not believe in

empty independence under which live millions of hungry, naked, ignorant, and sick. We want an independence that guarantees the individual the right to work . . . housing, food, medical care, education, and old age security suitable for human dignity.[37]

In the third issue, the editorial identified increasing U.S. imperialism as an emerging threat to Egypt. This was the first time in Egypt that the international basis of imperialism, rather than a specifically British dimension, was identified. Shuhdi 'Atiyah al-Shaf'ie, writing under the pen name of Mahmud Sandi, declared: "American imperialism sees itself as the only heir of the British Empire and the Hitler tradition. It seeks the domination of the world, including Egypt. Today it is satisfied with economic and political domination. And today it is working for a treaty that will protect its interest. We should not be surprised if tomorrow it sends occupation armies. . . . The nation does not want to exchange one imperialist for another or add another imperialism. . . . It demands complete freedom for Egypt and the Sudan."[38]

Iskra's effort to expand to its third stage of development — recruitment of workers — is reflected in *al-Jamahir*'s call for the creation of a workers' party. In a special issue to commemorate May 1, Shaf'ie declared: "On the first of May every year, workers all over the world define their program for the new year. For the Egyptian workers, let this year's program be to mobilize themselves and unite their voices under the leadership of a party of a new kind: a party that truly represents them; a party that is supported by millions of peasants, students, and intellectuals; a party that leads the unwavering struggle . . . and will lead the millions with determination toward freedom, democracy, and independence."[39]

AL-HARAKAH AL-MISRIYAH LIL TAHRUR AL-WATANI (HAMTU) (THE EGYPTIAN MOVEMENT FOR NATIONAL LIBERATION)

The formation of this movement had its roots in the differences between Henri Curiel and Hillel Schwartz regarding who should lead the communist activities. Whereas Curiel called for the Egyptianization of the executive levels so that most of its members would be Egyptians, Schwartz opposed this policy, accusing the call for Egyptianization of being chauvinistic. He maintained that in the development of Egyptian class consciousness, foreigners came at the first stage, then Egyptian intellectuals, followed by workers. His organization, Iskra, was constituted predominantly of foreigners.

As a result, Curiel attempted to form an Egyptian organization. After being released in late 1942 from al-Zeitoun detention camp, where he spent some time for his antifascist activities, Curiel said, "Immediately I started founding an organized Egyptian communist movement. I founded the Egyptian Movement for National Liberation [Hamtu] and contacted a group of Egyptian intellectuals. We proceeded rapidly with widespread activity, and we contacted many of the workers, the workers of the air force, the Sudanese, and the Nubians."[40] Curiel emphasized that the movement should not acquire a communist party name. As he explained later: "The fact is that many demanded declaring a party immediately; however, we saw that the declaration of a party that could really express the aspirations of the Egyptian people requires too much time and a greater effort and a political, material, and strategic preparedness that was not available to us. We were at the beginning of the road, and it was not easy to declare to the people that this weak formation was the ideal representative for the Egyptian proletariat. Thus, we declared that we were a national liberation movement that aims at achieving several goals, which are the formation of a communist party, land reform, and coordination of our common struggle with the Sudanese people."[41]

Before establishing a communist party, Curiel felt that a strong cadre should be built. To this end, he established al-Maydan Bookshop to disseminate political literature and create awareness among Egyptian intellectuals. Basic works of Marx, Engels, Lenin, and Stalin were translated under Salslat al-Kutub al-Khadra' (the Green Book Series) by Hamtu. Thirteen works in all were translated, the first time they were rendered accurately into Arabic. Curiel then organized a cadre school at his father's country estate in Mansoriya in January 1943, where Egyptian intellectuals taught workers, students, and petty civil servants the principles of Marxism, Egypt's history, and political economy. The first school had twenty-five pupils.[42] According to Henri Curiel's biographer, "the cadre training school . . . remained for Henri Curiel the most moving and inspiring episode in his long career as a militant."[43] Some of the graduates of the course joined the central committee of Hamtu. About the same time, Curiel was able to attract the remnants of the first movement, and Sheikh Safwan Abu al-Fatah and Sha'ban Hafedh, under the leadership of 'Abd al-Fatah al-Qadhi, joined Hamtu.

The basic foundations of Hamtu were Egyptianization, laborization, peasant mobilization, group organization, Sudanese mobilization, and ideological preparation. Curiel's theory of organization rested on the creation of cells organized around natural social groups. Hence there were occupational and ethnic cells to organize and mobilize at the grass-roots level to reach all groups among both labor and peasants. A central committee of four members provided the leadership. Curiel maintained that this method of organization was essential for any mass activities in the Egyptian milieu because there were no mass organizations, and so natural social groups were a place to start; most of the cadre came from these groups, identified with them, and could operate among them; and links could be built across ethnic and occupational groups as their consciousness increased, but it was essential that mobilization start from its natural base, not from an artificial one that ignored existing realities.[44]

The structure of the organization, then, was based on cells organized around natural social groups. Departments, directly under the authority of the central committee, were established to develop cells among social groups in the category designated as the department's responsibilities. The departments were air force, which organized cells among air force maintenance personnel (and later expanded to encompass the armed forces); al-Azhar, responsible for organizing cells among students at al-Azhar University; labor, responsible for organizing cells among workers in industry; community, responsible for organizing cells in poor neighborhoods in urban areas; rural, responsible for organizing cells among peasants; Nubians, responsible for organizing cells among the Nubians (a distinct ethnic group in Egypt); intellectuals, responsible for organizing cells among professionals and learned groups; and foreigners, responsible for organizing cells in the foreign communities.

The occupational arrangement of cells was criticized by many members of Hamtu because it diluted the role of the proletariat, confining it to one division; it also isolated the intellectuals, students, and foreigners in different sections, which allowed bourgeois tendencies to coalesce, intensify, and eventually fragment the organization.

According to Curiel, laborization meant bringing the labor vanguards together in the industrial centers so as to organize them. This issue became a major problem after Hamtu united with Iskra. As one of the members of the central committee, Sayyid Sulaiman Rifa'ie, put it, "Laborization was not merely a collection of workers, any workers. Instead there was a serious choice of labor cadres. However, after the union the slogan of laborization was smeared, and extortion took place under its name. Workers who were not competent for leadership nor had any weight arose, and when we tried to object, it was said we were against laborization."[45]

By the time of its merger with Iskra in 1947, Hamtu had between six hundred and seven hundred members. All but ten were Egyptians.[46] Thus Curiel's method of organization was successful as Hamtu was the largest, most organized communist movement among Egyptians and permeated all segments of Egyptian society.

Several small splinter groups emerged from Hamtu. First was Itihad Sho'ub wadi al-Nil (Union of the Peoples of the Nile Valley), a group with a strong religious orientation that was attracted to communist social principles. Its leader was 'Abd al-Fatah al-Sharqawi. Old-guard communists from the 1920s — most notably Husni al-'Arabi — joined with al-Sharqawi.[47] The group accepted the economic and social principles of Marxism but rejected the doctrine of historical materialism. Al-Sharqawi explained that he separated from Hamtu because of its antireligious orientation and the presence of non-Egyptian elements in the organization.[48] With the arrest of its leader in 1948, the group withered away. The second splinter group, al-'Usbah al-Marxiyah (Marxist League), founded by Fawzi Gurgis and 'Abd al-Fatah al-Qadhi, emerged in 1947 as a result of dissatisfaction over the role of foreigners in Hamtu and its method of organization. The split was catalyzed by disagreements over strategy precipitated by Prime Minister Sidqi Pasha's campaign against the communists initiated in 1946. While Hamtu's central committee advocated confrontation as a response to Sidqi's suppression, Gurgis and al-Qadhi advocated a more cautious, pragmatic response. At its formation, al-'Usbah disallowed any foreign membership. To ensure the dominance of the proletariat, the membership was regularly reviewed and the organizational structure modified. Cell organization on the basis of Curiel's natural social units was abolished. Al-'Usbah remained very selective and small, containing no more than sixty members at its height. By the end of 1949, the organization disintegrated as a result of disagreements between the founding members. Gurgis then established a new organization, Nawat al-Hizb al-Shuyo'ie al-Misri, as an extension of al-'Usbah al-Marxiyah both in its ideological and organizational objectives. Publication of al-'Usbah al-Marxiyah's news circulars al-Tali'ah (for public distribution) and al-A'jir (for membership distribution), was continued. Nawat advocated the unification of all communist associations into one party. It advocated the resolution of ideological differences among the associations that prevented unification by holding an all-parties congress with democratic participation and debate. For this reason, Nawat al-Hizb rejected the unification of Iskra and Hamtu. A fourth group, al-Tali'ah (of Alexandria), an Alexandria cell of Hamtu, led by Dr. Hasuna (an old comrade of the first movement cadres), broke away from Hamtu because of the role of foreigners.

NATIONAL STUDENT COMMITTEES

A final arena of Egyptian communist activity in the late 1940s was the growing Egyptian student movement, which was to furnish many of the communist leaders in the 1950s, 1960s, and 1970s.

During a meeting in the summer of 1945, leaders of the student movement met and decided to call for the formation of national committees to participate in the national movement. In their preliminary meeting they established a three-point program: "First, the struggle for the achievement of national independence is not only a struggle against military occupation, but also against imperial economic, political, and cultural domination. Second, it is imperialism—the feudalists and the large financiers — who are tied to the foreign institutions. Third, the route to resist imperialism is the route of national unity; the forces opposing imperialism have to unite in one wide front which struggles for the defeat of the colonial system." The most important slogan of the committee was, "Negotiation with the colonialist for the rights of the country is treason."[49] This slogan actually symbolized the end of one stage of struggle, which was based on negotiations and compromise, in favor of one that had the potential of leading to armed struggle. As such, this slogan was more powerful than that of the Wafd party, whose conventional means were negotiations, and the Nationalist party, which believed in no negotiations except after evacuation.

By early 1946, the student executive committee called upon all school and university students to arrange public meetings on February 9 to discuss the current political situation and oppose the principle of mutual defense, which implied imperial protection. It also called for abstinence from negotiations with the British except on the basis of a British declaration which accepted total evacuation. On the assigned day the general meeting took place at Fuad I University (after the 1952 revolution renamed Cairo University), where it was declared that negotiations were an act of treason and called for the abrogation of the 1936 treaty and the two agreements of 1899 pertaining to the Sudan; it also demanded the immediate evacuation of British forces. At the end of the meeting, one of the largest demonstrations since the outbreak of World War II took place. The demonstration was allowed to proceed to Kubri Abbas (Abbas bridge), which was surrounded by the police and then opened so that many students fell into the Nile. More than two hundred were injured.[50]

These casualties, however, served to exacerbate conditions rather than calm them, and between February 9 and 16 demonstrations took place in different parts of the country, resulting in numerous casualties.

A rumor about an attempt on the king's life was even circulated which further destabilized the shaky government of Mahmud al-Nouqrashi, leading to its eventual resignation.

Following the resignation of Mahmud al-Nouqrashi, the king appointed Isma'il Sidqi Pasha to form the new cabinet. After forming the government, Sidqi declared that he would allow the students to demonstrate though warning them against troublemakers. He even allowed one of his ministers to declare that such demonstrations helped the government in its negotiations.

The student executive committee issued a communique which stated that "the causes for which we began our struggle still persist, and that is negotiations should be on the basis of an officially declared communique on the British side, which recognizes our national right to total independence and the unity of the Nile Valley."[51]

On February 18, 1946, forty thousand demonstrators came together in 'Abdeen Square while fifteen thousand others grouped at the university, where pamphlets were distributed attacking British imperialism. Along with these demonstrations, representatives of both the workers and students met and formed the National Committee of Workers and Students (al-Lajnah al-Wataniyah lil al'Umal wa al-Talabah) with the aim of leading the struggle against the imperialists and their agents. The committee issued a statement declaring that the labor unions, university, and students would undertake a general strike on February 21, 1946. On the assigned day the general strike took place, and the demonstrations, though peaceful at the beginning, turned violent, leading to many casualties (about 20 dead and 150 injured). The student committee decided to make February 25 a day of general mourning for those who had been killed in the demonstrations. On that day a general strike took place, and again clashes with the police led to the death of 28 demonstrators and the injury of 342. Two British soldiers were killed and 4 injured.

According to Sa'ad Zahran, an activist in the national committee and later a leading communist, the national committee led a broad national front of communists (including Iskra and Hamtu), Wafdists, and independents who found common ground in the committee's action:

> The young leaders . . . were on the periphery of the ideological organizations. Their ideological age was not more than one or two years. They all came from the same social background and were bound by common daily problems and common political issues both in the university and in the mode of production. Those young people were motivated by the lofty moral, human, and cultural ideals of Islam and

socialism without falling into the dark pitfalls of ideological fanaticism or narrow partisanship. Those young men in these few weeks of
1946, perhaps for the first time in the history of contemporary Egypt,
[produced] a genuine honest leadership that was able to unify the
middle class freely springing from a national consciousness. . . . In a
rare historic moment, these young men accomplished a miracle of
sorts while their ideological leaders were unattentive.[52]

The national committee persisted in its opposition to the government policy and on July 8, 1946, issued a statement that was published in
al-Ahram calling for the cessation of negotiations and considering the
problem of the Nile Valley to be an international issue that should be put
to the attention of the U.N. Security Council. It also called for July 11,
the day Alexandria was shelled by the British navy in 1882, to be a day of
resurgence of the struggle.[53]

In a decisive attempt to crush the movement, on July 10 the government arrested hundreds of journalists, writers, intellectuals, and workers
and closed several newspapers. The National Committee of Students and
Workers was effectively suppressed by this action. Thus despite its effec-
tiveness in opposing the government policy, the national committee was
short-lived because of its many shortcomings. The committee confined
itself to the cities among the students and workers but ignored the peasants. Moreover, it did not organize itself so as to form entrenched cadres
among the people, and many divisions took place among its members.[54]
Nevertheless, and despite its mistakes and divisions, the committee, as
an opposing force, remained a part of the nationalist movement main-
stream.

AL-QALA'H

Al-Qala'h originated in February 1942 as an informal association
started by five senior high school students, an al-Azhar student, and a
skilled laborer. Outraged by British imperialism in Egypt and the country's social conditions, they initiated a Marxist critique of Egypt's problems and organized study groups and committees to solve community
problems. The group quickly expanded to involve the whole neighbor-
hood of al-Qala'h and became popularly known by this name. Although
the group did not have a formal organization or program, it advocated
political and economic independence and the "popularization" of the
economy.

Mustafa Haykal (a cousin of Mohammed Hussein Haykal, a leading figure in the Liberal Constitutional party) and 'Abd al-'Aziz Bayoumi, two of the founding members of al-Qala'h, entered the University of Cairo in the autumn of 1942 and continued their mobilizing and organizing efforts among the students. At its height, 1945–46, al-Qala'h had 150 active members, and its activities permeated the university and involved a far greater number of students. Thus al-Qala'h played a significant role in mobilizing the student movement. Through its activities in the movement, it established contacts with students from rural areas and with young officers in the military.

Because of its involvement with university students, every communist association wanted al-Qala'h to unite with it. In late 1946, Haykal contacted Henri Curiel in Hamtu and Shuhdi 'Atiyah al-Shaf'ie in Iskra to explore the possibility of unification. It subsequently united with Iskra, which was already in the process of uniting with Hamtu.

By 1947, there was a plethora of communist groups and splinter groups, all advocating similar goals and strategies but working independently and sometimes in competition with each other. The movement was highly fragmented. Cadres working in the university and in the labor movement began pressing for unification. Other communist parties outside Egypt also began pressuring for unification. As a result, the leaders of the various associations thought they should seek unity. By early 1947, the major groups took different positions toward the issue of unity. Hamtu, Iskra, and Tahrir al-Sha'ab strongly advocated unity and began negotiations to achieve it. They collectively issued a leaflet, *Wahda,* for the purpose of declaring their intention to unify and began coordinating their field activities. Al-Qala'h supported unity and joined Iskra. Al-Tali'ah (of Alexandria) agreed to unite under the condition that it be represented in the central committee. Al-'Usbah al-Marxiyah, Itihad Sho'ub wadi al-Nil, and Tali'at al-'Umal opposed unification on the basis that it was not a popular movement but a decision of leadership. Although unity took place in the field, three main issues caused tension among the leadership: democratic centralism and the means to achieve it; Egyptianization, which Hamtu considered the most urgent issue; and laborization.

Three coordinating committees were established, one for student affairs, one for workers, and one for intellectuals. A representative from Hamtu and one from Iskra served on each committee. Iskra, al-Qala'h and Jama'at Tahrir al-Sha'ab then declared unity and adopted the name al-Tali'ah al-Mutahidah. Its basic aim was to seek unity with Hamtu. Its leadership was basically that of Iskra plus Marcel Israel from Tahrir al-

Sha'ab. It established the journal *al-Jamahir.* Figure 3 illustrates the lines of fragmentation and integration of the communist movement over the decade.

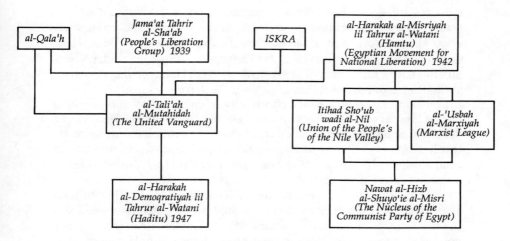

Fig. 3. Communist organizations, 1942–1947.

AL-HARAKAH AL-DEMOQRATIYAH LIL TAHRUR
AL-WATANI (HADITU)

This organization was formed in 1947 by the merger of Iskra, Hamtu, and several smaller communist groups. The merger created an organization with sixteen hundred members: seven hundred from Hamtu[55] and nine hundred from Iskra and Jama'at Tahrir al-Sha'ab (which had earlier united to form al-Tali'ah al-Mutahidah). Haditu brought together the foreign and Egyptian elements represented by Iskra and Hamtu. The four hundred foreigners and twelve hundred Egyptians were drawn from the circles of intellectuals and students. The Egyptian proletariat constituted a small minority. Within a few months of its formation, the membership of Haditu swelled to four thousand.[56]

At the time of Haditu's formation, its central committee was composed of eleven members — five from Iskra, five from Hamtu, and one from al-Tali'ah of Alexandria. Henri Curiel was the political officer and

Hillel Schwartz was the organizational officer. It was agreed that the cadre of Hamtu would be responsible for political and organizational activities; Iskra's cadre would be responsible for propaganda and popular action. The committee was subsequently expanded to seventeen. Haditu was organized on Hamtu's model of social groups. There were ten units: students, intellectuals, workers, foreigners, women, Sudanese, Nubians, army, Cairo neighborhoods, and districts, representing the major social areas Haditu worked in. Each unit was further divided into cells. Henri Curiel supervised nonworker units. The worker units were under Sayyid Sulaiman Rifa'ie, Mohammed Shatta (both from Hamtu), Shuhdi 'Atiyah al-Shaf'ie, and 'Abd al-Rahman al-Nasir (both from Iskra).[57]

Haditu concentrated its efforts on the mobilization and organization of laborers and students. Its success in organizing workers was reflected in September 1947, when the cadres of Haditu led a strike by the textile workers in Shobra al-Khaima which included twenty-seven thousand workers. In January 1948 the students of Haditu also organized a strike in Cairo University.

Haditu took over publication of *al-Jamahir* after unity in late June. The newspaper continued to call for a united struggle against colonialism. In one of its articles, it stated, "Remember that colonialism still occupies your land, sucks your blood, strangles your liberties, fights your constitution, and uses the same means of betrayal, treason, and conspiracy against you. Remember that nothing will dislodge it except your struggle, and your struggle shall never succeed except by your unity, workers, peasants, students, youth, and civil servants united in a great mass under the leadership of a sincere national front. Purify the court of traitors and rise against the archenemy—colonialism."[58]

The national front was to work toward breaking off negotiations with the British, abrogating the 1899 agreement and the 1936 treaty with the British, organizing an armed struggle against colonialism, rejecting U.S. loans and military mission, and attaining closer relations with the socialist camp. The national front was to constitute both Haditu and the Wafd party. "The alliance between the labor movement together with its conscientious vanguard and the Wafd is a necessary condition to restore the people's stolen liberty. The common struggle of the workers and the Wafdist masses in the cities and villages is the only way to break the chains that strangle our liberties."[59]

The attack on colonialism was not restricted to England; colonialism in general, including the growing American influence in Egypt, was to be swept aside. In an article in *al-Jamahir* (July 28, 1947) under the title "We do not want any colonialism, whether British or American," Shuhdi

'Atiyah al-Shaf'ie wrote: "Throwing [ourselves] in the arms of a new master, the American colonialism, this is the dangerous orientation that some Egyptian politicians follow. The head of the public relations office in the Prime Minister's Office is American; the principal counselor to the Egyptian delegate going to the Security Council is American; the Egyptian defense ministry presents a note which suggests a military mission of high-ranked Americans to reorganize the Egyptian army."

In spite of the early success of Haditu and its increasing influence, it soon began to fragment. In less than a year after Haditu was founded, divisions and polarizations began to appear. The main problem was that unity took place without agreement on basic aims and strategies. Fundamental ideological differences were exacerbated by the social differences within the membership, which consisted of foreigners, students, and intellectuals from petty and upper bourgeois backgrounds, and workers. Furthermore, the long-standing conflicts between Curiel and Schwartz were intensified in this setting.

The crisis in Haditu came to a head with the preparation for a conference organized to determine the group's ideological and strategic program. Curiel prepared a working paper that came to be known as "The Direction of the National and Democratic Forces." The problem emerged as a result of several statements in the program, one of which indicated that the party being founded would represent the proletariat and the national democratic forces. Curiel's opponents accused him of attempting to compromise the role of the proletariat with bourgeois elements. In defense of his opinion, Curiel argued, "The conditions of the post – World War II world have created a new status quo that attracted to the revolutionary work in Egypt non-labor-class forces; that is, the proletariat is not the only revolutionary class in Egypt; there are other revolutionary forces. While admitting the leadership of the proletariat, the party has to be a party for all the revolutionary masses — within this stage — a party for all of Egypt, that is, all the people should feel that the party belongs to them and not to the proletariat alone." As a result, factions and divisions developed. Curiel explained that "the reason for the spread of polarization and division was the domination of the petty-bourgeois elements who were terrified that the communist tide was receding and that a period of oppression was approaching in the wake of the Palestine war."[60]

When the leadership of Haditu attempted to confront the divisive factions, it fragmented into two opposing factions along the lines of Iskra and Hamtu. Henri Curiel (code name Younis) led the Younis faction, composed primarily of the Hamtu wing. The other wing, called the 'Adil faction, was led by 'Abd al-Ma'boud al-Gibayli (code name 'Adil) and in-

cluded 'Abd al-Rahman al-Nasir and 'Abd al-Mon'iem Ibrahim from Iskra, 'Adli Gurgis from Tali'at al-Askandiriyah, and Mohammed Shatta
and two others from Hamtu. The central committee of Haditu was then
enlarged to keep a balance between the two factions, with the Younis faction having one vote more. Eventually this factionalism went down to the
cadres, creating splinter groups within Haditu. One of the first was called
al-Takatul al-Thawri, which advanced the idea that the only way out of
the crisis was to hold a congress for open discussion to determine the line
of the party. Another was called Sawt al-Mo'aradhah; it condemned both
the 'Adil and Younis factions. Sawt al-Mo'aradhah considered itself a forum inside Haditu and issued only a leaflet.

The majority of the leaders of Sawt al-Mo'aradhah were from the
intellectual, student, women, and foreigner sections. According to one of
the Sawt leaders, Mohammed Sayyid Ahmed, they opposed the line of
national democratic forces espoused by Curiel and emphasized that only
workers should be recruited.[61]

Sa'ad Zahran, one of the leaders of a dissident splinter group from
Haditu, al-Takatul al-Thawri, explained that the problem was the contradictions between the views of the Egyptian and foreign executives. The
Egyptian intellectuals felt that the Haditu leadership with its foreign composition was incapable of understanding the strong national feelings involved in the Palestine issue. He also indicated that the splinter group felt
the authorities would use the excuse of the leadership being Jewish to
crack down on the communist movement and taint its goals as Zionist-
inspired.[62]

The struggle within the leadership of Haditu sparked an effort to remove control of *al-Jamahir* from Shuhdi 'Atiyah al-Shaf'ie. As a result,
he broke away from Haditu to form al-Takatul al-Thawri. This was the beginning of the fragmentation of Haditu into more than twenty splinter
groups within less than a year. Figure 4 reflects this fragmentation, identifying the major groups that separated from Haditu and factions that remained within Haditu.

AL-TAKATUL AL-THAWRI (THE REVOLUTIONARY BLOC)

Shuhdi 'Atiyah al-Shaf'ie announced the creation of al-Takatul al-
Thawri after receiving Curiel's report, "The Direction of the National
and Democratic Forces." Anwar 'Abd al-Malik, Sa'ad Zahran, and Hussein al-Ghamry, with Shuhdi—all former Iskra leaders—constituted the
leadership of this splinter group. Mohammed Sayyid Ahmed explained
the reasons for the split:

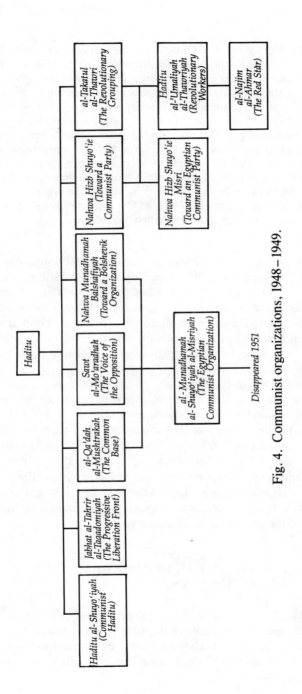

Fig. 4. Communist organizations, 1948–1949.

I had not heard of "The Direction of the National and Democratic
Forces," and it was presented for discussion only to the leadership. I
think Shuhdi did not even participate in the discussion. . . . Anwar
'Abd al-Malik contacted me in November 1947 inviting me to join the
group. I think that Shuhdi had wanted to break away and he used the
report to justify his group. The revolutionary group followed an ad-
venturous course in expropriating the printers, the technical equip-
ment, and the libraries [of Haditu] and accused anyone who opposed
that course of being a bourgeois with no class consciousness. With
this, the group laid the seeds of bad traditions among the communists. The strange thing is that they sabotaged the organization and
tore it down with great enthusiasm. The more they tore it down the
more they felt they had accomplished their aim.[63]

Sa'ad Zahran, on the other hand, explained that the splinter reflected fundamental cleavages in Haditu among young revolutionaries, old-guard
armchair Marxists and Egyptians, and foreigners. The old-guard foreign
leaders were content with critiquing the system and extolling class struggle, but the young Egyptian revolutionaries had grown impatient with discussion and wanted practical action. Curiel represented the old guard,
and his report reflected the foreign elements' hesitation to act and their
authoritarian style of leadership.[64]

Many other splits in the organization followed al-Takatul al-Thawri's secession. On May 15, 1948, a police campaign against dissident
groups was launched in conjunction with the declaration of war in Palestine. Curiel and other leaders were among the first to be arrested. As a
result, Haditu's leadership, along with its conflicts and contradictions,
fell in the hands of less experienced people. Haditu nearly disintegrated.
But with the defeat of the Arab armies in Palestine and the spread of national revolutionary feelings against the palace and the British, remaining
cadres of Haditu were quick to respond and to reorganize themselves to
recompose the organization and resurrect it.

HADITU AL-'UMALIYAH AL-THAWRIYAH
(REVOLUTIONARY WORKERS)

In July 1948, the Curiel faction expelled the 'Adil faction in a central
committee decision by a vote of five to four. The 'Adil faction then established a committee to prepare a conference for Haditu to determine the
direction of the party and elect a new central committee. The committee

affirmed its commitment to laborization and democratic centralism. It called for the election of the leadership by the cadre and for continued efforts to create a unified communist party. When the conference took place in July 1948, it announced the birth of Haditu al-'Umaliyah al-Thawriyah as an organization independent of Haditu. The major aim of this association was to create a preparatory committee for a conference to found an Egyptian communist party. All Egyptian communist organizations must be represented on the committee. It set a target date for the conference of December 31, 1948. A short while later, a majority of the leaders were arrested. A new committee led by Marcel Israel continued to work toward the formation of the preparatory committee. On March 19, 1949, the preparatory committee was formed from this new committee, Tasht, al-'Usbah al-Marxiyah, some members of the old Tahrir al-Sha'ab who had rejected unity with Iskra in 1947, and Nahwa Hizb Shuyo'ie. The preparatory committee issued a circular to direct the ideological conflict and disseminate ideas among the cadre in addition to suggested programs, but the police arrested Marcel Israel and the preparatory committee disintegrated.

After being released from prison, the labor cadre of al-'Umaliyah al-Thawriyah established al-Najim al-Ahmar in 1950. This organization continued until 1955, when it joined al-Hizb al-Shuyo'ie al-Misri al-Muwahad. Jabhat al-Tahrir al-Taqadomiyah [Gat] was one of the smallest offshoots of Haditu. It united with al-'Umaliyah al-Thawriyah when that organization was established but survived when it disintegrated and rejoined Haditu in 1950. Gat remained a small insular group even into the 1950s but had no distinct impact on the communist movement. Only one of its members, Ahmed Taha, became a member of Haditu's central committee.

NAHWA HIZB SHUYO'IE MISRI (NAHSHIM)

This organization was formed under the leadership of Hillel Schwartz, who withdrew from Haditu, taking with him some former Iskra comrades. A circular was issued under the new association's name announcing in the first issue, "Our aim is the creation of a communist party. . . . Yes, our purpose is to unify all the revolutionary socialists . . . to create the Egyptian Communist party."[65] Schwartz called for a conference of all the organizations.

Some of the old Iskra and Hamtu members primarily from the labor cadres in Alexandria and Shobra al-Khaima struggled to keep Haditu alive and decided to rename the organization communist Haditu (Haditu al-Shuyo'iyah). They evaluated the experience of Haditu[66] and rejected the natural social group organization system of Curiel.[67]

The student section of Haditu was repulsed by the factional infighting among the leadership. It criticized the secrecy of the leadership and demanded democratic participation in decision making. As a result, al-Qadah al-Mushtrakah was created as a forum within Haditu that demanded full participation. This in turn led to the formation of Nahwa Munadhamah Balshafiyah, which based its platform on the proposition that the cadre must be informed and allowed to participate in making decisions. This group called for a conference to make the leadership accountable and to make it 100 percent proletariat in composition.[68] The conference was held on December 28, 1948, and lasted four days. It was attended by forty-two delegates. When the leadership did not respond to the demands of this conference, Nahwa Munadhamah Balshafiyah and Sawt al-Mo'aradhah united to form al-Munadahmah al-Shuyo'iyah al-Misriyah.

Elected to the leadership were Odet Hazan and her husband, Sidney Salmun (non-Egyptian), Fatima Zaki (university assistant), and Michel Kamil (student).[69] Odet Hazan was the most powerful figure in the new organization. An extremist, she issued regulations that all recruits had to be workers and the membership must begin an active drive to recruit workers. She also demanded that members devote full time to the party.[70] She formulated thirteen conditions as essential and nonnegotiable for any other association to join with this one.[71] All others were considered agents of the police.[72]

At its inception the organization had five hundred members, but within three months, this number was reduced by half.[73] By the end of the first year, only ten members were left.[74] In mid-1950, Odet Hazan and her husband left Egypt, and the organization disappeared.

On September 8, 1948, Nahwa Hizb Shuyo'ie, some members of al-'Umaliyah al-Thawriyah, and the remnants of al-Takatul al-Thawri united to form Nahwa Hizb Shuyo'ie Misri under the leadership of Hillel Schwartz. In its first internal party circular, the aim of the new organization was declared to be "the removal of all the elements that do not meet our criteria; the strengthening of all committees by the expulsion of all weak elements; and the assignment of the central bureau to investigate all the suspicious elements in order to get rid of all spies and to watch over all the cells, committees, and members and to create a file on every member."[75] By December 1949, the central committee reported the expulsion of fifty-one members.[76] Dissatisfaction with the leadership increased. In a cadre circular, *al-Kader al-Shuyo'ie,* the issue was voiced and the proposition presented of "why we should expel the existing leadership."[77] The leadership maintained that its main purpose was to concentrate on preparation for the preparatory conference, permit the dissemination of all opinions related to unification, and publish the party circular weekly, ensuring its distribution to all members and organizations.[78] On March 14, 1950, the police arrested Hillel Schwartz and uncovered the organization.

The 1940s witnessed the renaissance of the communist movement in a variety of organizational forms. Driven underground by suppressive laws and police harassment, the movement evolved in an environment of secrecy and conspiracy, which permeated the process of development as suspicion and fear displaced camaraderie, and surreptitiousness became an end in itself. Such an environment seriously handicapped the movement toward organizational integration. Haditu, which had represented the culmination of that movement over the decade, was fragmented by ideological and personality rivalries before the end of the decade. Nevertheless, integration remained the persistent aspiration of the front-line members and indeed became their overt demand as Haditu dissipated into almost a dozen splinter groups.

4

Changes in the 1950s

The Palestine war had a profound effect on the Egyptian communist movement. The wholesale arrest and imprisonment or deportation of the leaders of the movement removed many of the old-guard leaders, both foreign and Egyptian. New leaders emerged from the cadres of students and worker activists recruited in the 1940s, and the movement was both renewed by their commitment and enthusiasm and fragmented by their inexperience and impatience.

The Palestine debacle triggered strong Arab nationalist outrage. The debate over nationalism versus internationalism within the communist movement in Egypt became a fundamental ideological issue. Furthermore, the heightened nationalist consciousness of the Egyptian masses as a result of the Palestine war made the issue a central one in terms of the movement's legitimacy. The government's successful identification of the communist movement with Zionism resulted in public suspicion of communism, which was exacerbated by Haditu's acceptance of the U.N. Palestine Partition Plan as a solution to the Palestinian question.

Thus the Egyptian communist movement entered the 1950s with its leadership ranks decimated, its ideological foundations fundamentally challenged, and its relevance to the Egyptian milieu seriously compromised.

Nevertheless, conditions at the turn of the decade provided the movement with the opportunity to reestablish its legitimacy. This opportunity centered on the issue of Anglo-Egyptian relations. The return of a Wafd government in January 1950 resulted in the liberalization of Egypt's political climate. The Wafd attempted to harness the rising nationalist tide to its political leadership and allowed an open forum in the press. In this liberalized atmosphere, the communist groups were able to publish their program on the national question and reassert their vanguard role in the national struggle. Two communist newspapers in particular—*al-Bashir* and *al-Malayeen*—became prominent in the Egyptian national struggle in this period.

Following is an overview of the most important groups in the period.

HADITU

In the early 1950s, Haditu experienced a resurgence amid the general political malaise following the Palestine war. It attracted members from all segments of society, including the demoralized Egyptian army, and had contacts with the free officers' movement. In fact, Haditu was the only political group that had organized branches in the military. Its membership increased to about three thousand by 1952.[1]

There were numerous reasons for Haditu's revitalization in the early 1950s. Haditu's experience with the press provided an avenue for mobilization of political discontent in the period after the war. It issued several magazines, including *al-Bashir, al-Mustaqbal, al-Malayeen, al-Wageb, al-Ghad,* and *al-Midan,* which published the work of many of the most eminent writers, journalists, and artists in Egypt.

Haditu also played a pioneer role in adopting and promoting the call for peace. Although initially it sought to cooperate with the world peace movement, the Egyptian National party, and leftist Wafdist elements, this was impossible because the movement was perceived as a socialistic endeavor. *Al-Bashir* promoted the cause of peace as part of the struggle against imperialism: "The struggle for peace is basically a struggle against imperialism. . . . The defense of peace displays and uncovers the advocates of [war]; it is the destructiveness of imperialism which creates wars; it is a continuous struggle against world monopoly, against the oil thieves and weapon merchants.[2]

Haditu's position toward the peace movement was that it should be public, legal, and legitimate; it should incorporate influential members from all social classes, provided that they were against war; and Haditu could not attain a leading role simply through numerical majority but rather through diligent and influence-promoting activities. Haditu, therefore, concentrated on recruiting public figures—artists, writers, movie stars—to the peace movement.[3]

Haditu's struggle for peace came under attack from various sectors, even from other communist groups. The Egyptian Communist party organization (known as al-Rayah after its party newsletter), Popular Democracy (PD), and the Red Star organization united in opposition to a signature-collecting campaign, accusing Haditu of indirectly serving the police by creating a list police informants could use. Instead, al-Rayah wanted any peace movement to operate clandestinely, while PD declared that such a movement had to be solely of the proletariat class since peace was the cause of the labor force. Such a position, underscoring the latent hostility toward popular activities, induced a harsh overreaction from Haditu, embodied in a violent public campaign. Haditu was yet to face its main challenge, however, the 1952 free officers' movement.

Despite these difficulties, the Peace Partisans' Movement provided Haditu with important contacts with other mass movements. Peace Partisans became the representatives of Haditu in Egyptian politics. The journal of the peace movement, *al-Katib,* became very popular among intellectuals. The Peace Partisans' Movement played a prominent public role in all political forums.

Haditu had focused the majority of its attention on the labor force, particularly Egyptian unions. Its underlying goal was to unify these groups under the banner of one organization, the Labour Union's General Federation of Workers (al-Itihad al-'Am li Naqabat al-'Umal), which was to be guided by principles rather than personalities. The resulting concentration of activities, as Haditu realized, would place the exercise of power within its own confines.

According to this plan, elements of Haditu, along with other union leaders, eventually formed the Preparatory Committee for the Labour Union Federation. Haditu not only took the initiative but also played the leading role in the process of building the federation. According to Tareq al-Bushri, 104 unions with approximately 65,000 workers joined the preparatory committee, totaling some 50 percent of the workers in unions.[4]

Having achieved such success, it was decided that a General Federation Foundation conference would be convened on January 27, 1952; but the day before, the Cairo fire occurred, and the conference was postponed. The preparatory committee distributed pamphlets condemning the fire and accusing the colonialists of igniting it.

On July 23, 1952, however, the army took power and subsequently released a great number of political prisoners. Many of these were members of Haditu, who immediately formed the Founding Committee for the Labour Union General Federation of Workers (al-Lajnah al-Ta 'sisiyah lil Itihad al-'Am li Naqabat al-'Umal), declaring their support for the army movement.

Early in August of the same year a new crisis occurred. A huge fire erupted in Kafr al-Dawar as a result of labor protests, and the founding

committee, under pressure from Haditu, promptly issued an announcement which was later to have serious adverse effects on Haditu. The announcement said, "Certain individuals—enemies to the workers and the
country — have attempted to discredit the patriotism of the working
class, instigated by the remains of reactionaries and imperialism. . . . This
authority, in the name of the workers, condemns these criminal acts
which benefit no one except the enemies of the nation. It also hopes that
those criminals responsible will be severely punished."[5]

Two union activists were later found guilty and executed; all the
blame fell on Haditu. Both the federation and Haditu were soon to clash
with the new military regime. On January 1, 1953 — the month that witnessed the beginning of the clash— al-Wageb magazine issued, under the
slogan "Workers of Egypt Unite—Workers of the World Unite," violent
attacks on the new regime's policies, declaring that the main problems
the workers faced were job security and intervention in the affairs of the
union. It related these conditions to the increase of American influence,
the deterioration of national industries, and the fall in the purchasing
power of workers and peasants.

Challenging these conditions, Haditu presented a charter for the
working class in an attempt to identify the goals of the movement as well
as clarify its own position toward different issues. The charter called for
"(1) total evacuation from Egypt and Sudan and the rejection of any alliance with the imperialists; (2) immediate parliamentary elections; (3)
aboliton of martial law and all other emergency laws; (4) support for the
demands of the General Federation for Sudanese Labour Unions regarding evacuation first and then self-determination; and (5) the protection of
developing national industry by limiting the entrance of foreign capital
and abolishing all treaties and agreements that facilitate such foreign
entrance.[6]

The charter then presented its demands regarding the improvement
of labor conditions. (1) establishment of a minimum wage limit; (2) insurance against unemployment, sickness, disability, and old age; (3) abolition of laws that prevent the operation of the Founding Committee for the
Labour Union General Federation of Workers; (4) the amendment of all
labor laws, supervised by labor representatives; (5) widening the rights
and freedoms of workers, the most important of which is the right to
strike; (6) providing workers the right to form their own unions and fed-
erations, democratically and free from government interference; (7) providing agricultural workers the right to organize themselves, free of the
interference and persecution of management.[7]

Haditu thus attempted to organize more unions as well as increase
its activities among the students. When land reform finally allowed agri-

cultural workers to form their own unions, Haditu attempted to oversee this growth and succeeded in doing so in many villages. In the universities, during the 1952–53 academic year, a student organization named the Communist Students' Organization — Haditu (Rabitat al-Tulab al-Shuyo'ieen — Haditu) was formed. Students from Cairo University, 'Ain Shams University, and Alexandria University joined. The group experienced several clashes with the police, as well as internal divisions, and eventually dissolved.

Haditu's relationship with the army began among the air force mechanical school graduates, through whom Haditu was able to create new cadres among the lower ranks, army sergeants, and eventually army officers. In many cases, Haditu had direct or indirect contacts with members of the free officers' movement, though it was shrewd enough to keep some of its own officers from joining the movement so as to allow for a measure of safety and security. Even Nasser did not know of Youssef Seddiq's relationship with Haditu until after the revolution.[8]

Haditu infiltrated both the army and the free officers' movement and was observing the Moslem Brotherhood, which was steadily gaining influence. Nonetheless, although it appeared that both the Haditu and the Moslem Brotherhood were sufficiently well organized and popular among the people to lead a movement, they lacked impetus.

Haditu's failure to take power was a result of the wide gulf between its political influence and its actual power; this situation was further exacerbated by the presence of the Moslem Brotherhood as a competing element and an obstacle. Also after the Cairo fire, most of Haditu's cadres were in prison. Nevertheless, Haditu was quick to express its support of the army movement, not recognizing that the free officers were also connected with the Moslem Brotherhood as well as the United States. According to Khalid Muhiyi al-Din,

> Colonel Evans [of the U.S. Embassy in Cairo] was acquainted with 'Ali Sabri, who in turn was acquainted with Abd al-Latif al-Bushri and the air force group among the free officers. Through these connections, Aly Sabri attempted to make sure of the American position —in case a movement within the army took place—as well as exactly where the British were in the Suez Canal, as the possibility of their intervention was especially feared. As I heard it, a contact did occur three or four days before the movement to make sure of the American position. Evans's reply to Aly Sabri was that if the movement was not communist, the United States would not intervene against it. On the night of the revolution, once everything had started, Aly Sabri informed Evans of the movement.[9]

Haditu twice helped the army movement achieve success, once directly, through positive participation and support, and once indirectly, through its activities, which frightened the Americans, driving them to support anything that would save them from the "red tide."

Haditu's support for the army movement proved to be an exception among communists everywhere. Both the Soviet Union and the international communist movement, with the exception of the Sudanese Communist party, condemned the movement. According to Henri Curiel, "[They] had an analysis of the army groups: soldiers — basically peasants; army workers — workers; volunteers — petty bourgeois; officers — middle bourgeois; high-ranking officers — bourgeois tied to royal and property interests."[10] The army movement was thus to the communists a middle bourgeois movement which represented only the interests of that class. Moreover, the relation of the movement to the United States exacerbated the suspicions already held by communists in general.

Soon after the revolution, all political prisoners were pardoned except communists on the pretext that communism is a social crime, not a political one. Relations between Haditu and the army movement quickly deteriorated. Only communists were detained as political prisoners, and state police soon concentrated the majority of their raids and arrests on Haditu members. The crucial turning point, however, came with the execution of the workers Khamis and al-Bakri in Kafr al-Dawar, which, according to Khalid Muhiyi al-Din, was opposed only by himself, Nasser, and Youssef Seddiq. Thus as the confrontation between Haditu and the army increased in intensity, the former was quick to withdraw its support for the regime and instead launched violent attacks on it.

The relationship between Haditu and the world communist parties began and was fostered within the peace movement, the world union movement, and the World Democratic Youth Federation. Attempted relations with the French, Italian, and British communist parties, however, did not meet with such success.

Haditu's interest in the issue of unity derived from the conditions that communists faced at that time. Criticizing its own initial ambivalence on this matter, Haditu declared that the goal of its struggle was the unification of those "true fighters" who believed in Marxism-Leninism-Stalinism. Furthermore, no preconditions to unity would be accepted, barring those of the Leninist principles of unity of will and action.

A unified front would necessitate basic agreement on any tactics it adopted, and Haditu declared itself willing to compromise — provided it was not at the expense of basic communist principles — to facilitate such a merge in the name of peace and in opposition to military dictatorship. Differences soon emerged with the Egyptian Communist party organization, however, over what kind of front should be formed. Whereas the latter called for a popular front, Haditu preferred a democratic one. The difference represented a fundamental disagreement on strategy. The Egyptian Communist party at this stage refused any cooperation with the political parties and other public associations such as unions, maintaining that they were bourgeois organizations. For this reason, the party called for the formation of underground workers' and peasants' unions and peace committees. It was from such underground organizations that the party wanted to create a popular front.

In an article in *al-Malayeen* (a Haditu weekly established in mid-1951), under the title "A Democratic Front Not a Popular Front," Haditu expressed its belief that the basis for the formation of a popular front did not exist because there were no parties truly representing the different social classes and that the existing movements, though having a revolutionary potential, did not crystallize enough to undertake such an endeavor. A "democratic" front, however, was viable—indeed, the article stated that "everyone who opposes [a democratic] front is a traitor whether he knows it or not."[11] These arguments were basically aimed at the other communist movements, which preferred a "popular front." As a result of their strong reaction, Haditu was forced to attempt to ameliorate its criticism, especially regarding the Socialist party led by Ahmed Hussein. Thus in the following issue, *al-Malayeen* stated that it did not mean to attack leaders such as Ahmed Hussein or Fathi Radhwan or other revolutionary elements "who did not accept submission to tyranny and injustice. We talked to many of their leaders and found ourselves the truthful motivations which drive them toward struggle. Many of those heroes knew how to highlight the revolutionary aspect of Islam." In defending its earlier article, the newspaper stated that it was not directed at anyone "except at the clowns in the labor movement [meaning the Marxist movement], those whom we know well and from whom we receive news day after day despite the fact that we don't deal with them directly." In clarifying its position, *al-Malayeen* emphasized that "we do not fight a foolish economic war but a conscious political one. Because of that we need a political democratic front and not an economic committee to nationalize oil. The nationalization of oil is part of the program of this front which has to be formed first and which knows when these issues could be raised and prepare what needs to be prepared." Unhappy with these arguments, Ahmed Hussein, the leader of the Socialist party, published an article in the same newspaper under the title "A Popular or Democratic Front," in which he stated that *al-Malayeen* was simply provoking a linguistic argument. "What is important," he said, "is the program that

shall be agreed on, which is fighting imperialism, consolidating the constitutional basis, and fighting corruption."[12]

At the same time, Haditu attempted to expand its relations with
other political forces, managing to attract several of their leaders to its
ranks. From Young Egypt, both 'Adil Hussein (the brother of Ahmed
Hussein, the leader of the organization) and 'Abdel Mune'in al-'Ayyashi
joined Haditu. Several members of the National party, such as Youssef
Helmi, Ahmed Sadiq 'Azzam, Sa'ad Kamil, and Ahmed Naguib, also
joined its ranks.

Following the abrogation of the 1923 constitution, a three-year tran-
sitional period was declared, to last from January 17, 1953, to January 16,
1956. All political parties were dissolved and banned and the military
junta declared itself on February 10, 1953, a Revolutionary Command
Council, concentrating all powers in its hands. Haditu greatly expanded
its opposition to the new regime and its policies. One of its pamphlets
published in this period, for example, stated: "The military dictatorship
has begun a new chapter, aimed at consolidating its absolute tyranny and
autocracy through the declaration of the Republic. The aim of the declaration is to limit popular freedoms. . . . Naguib has decreed himself its
president, becoming, in essence, an absolute military dictator. The people will not recognize the establishment of an Egyptian Republic unless
it comes as a result of a direct popular referendum in which the workers,
peasants, merchants, and all groups of people participate."[13]

Haditu's actions posed a particular threat once the organization
called upon students and all political forces to form a national front. In a
leaflet addressed to the students, it advocated "a more intensified struggle, strong unity, and stubborn resistance against the tyranny, which had
exceeded its limits." Furthermore, it called for a unification of ranks —
whether communist, Wafdist, Brotherhood, or socialist — to form a general federation.[14]

State security forces were ordered on August 10, 1953, to crack
down on Haditu. Twenty-one of the party leaders were immediately arrested, pending their presentation to the Revolutionary Court. The government, however, later retreated from that position and instead decided
to present them to a military tribunal, which passed extremely harsh sen-
tences on them. On December 16 of that year, fifty more members were
arrested by the security forces.

In retrospect, 1953 was an extremely trying year for Haditu, even
though the regime failed to suppress its activities totally. By early 1954,
Haditu's activities gained in intensity, and on January 12, 1954, al-Kifah
(The struggle) magazine again began production. On its first pages, al-

Kifah showcased the December arrests, stating that "this very thing was happening while the leaders of the gang were addressing the people, advocating their own sham democracy and concern for the restoration of the constitution, as well as demanding from every Egyptian not to be 'afraid.' Oh citizens, intensify your struggle to uncover the conspiracy driving the leaders of your national movement to the American scaffold named 'Revolutionary Court,' and demand the release of all political prisoners."

In subsequent issues, Nasser himself was branded as a traitor and American puppet, but in the fifteenth issue, which appeared August 20, 1954, *al-Kifah* launched its most violent and radical attack on the regime. In an article entitled "Fight the Treaty of Treason, Imperialism, and War," it declared: "Finally the military junta has taken off its latest mask, which had covered its treacherous nature, and signed with the imperialist British. This, under the guidance of its American masters, has created a treaty of disgrace and humiliation, a treaty of treason, imperialism, and war. The treacherous junta is not shirking its basic role, that of subjugating our people to American imperialism forever." The magazine then called for an armed uprising — against both the British and the regime itself — and urged the peasants to cease paying taxes to the state.

HADITU AL-TAYYAR AL-THAWRI
(HADITU REVOLUTIONARY CURRENT)

Differences and divisions were quick to erupt in Haditu, largely, according to Mubarak 'Abdu Fadhil, because of contradictions between the three leaders who came after Curiel, namely, Sayyid Rifa'ie [Badr], Mohammed Shatta [Hamido], and Kamal 'Abd al-Halim [Khalil]. What were these contradictions? According to Fadhil, "Badr launched a violent campaign against the intellectuals (Kamal 'Abdel Halim, Zaki Murad, and Ahmed al-Rifa'ie) because of their involvement in the public and popular activities of the peace movement and their lack of concern with the internal activities of the party. In this, Badr had actually collided with two basic pillars of Haditu, popular activities and activities among the intellectuals."[15]

Haditu had initially supported the role of the army in the 1952 revolution; but soon after the revolution, the military regime began an attack on the Left, including Haditu. As a result, by December 1952 Haditu adopted a position condemning the role of the army and calling for the formation of a national democratic front. Badr, who as Haditu political chief had personally approved the army's role, superseded the Haditu position of advocating a national democratic front by calling for the nationwide organization of secret revolutionary base committees.

These differences intensified to the point that on June 28, 1953, after a majority vote, Badr and his supporters were suspended from the central committee. This group, however, was quick to react and soon formed a new movement which they called the Democratic Movement for National Liberation—the Revolutionary Current (DMNL-RC).

According to Badr, there were four basic issues of contention between Haditu and the DMNL-RC. First, DMNL-RC maintained that public activities sapped the resources and energy of the organization and should be dispensed with. Second, Haditu was the party, and others were welcome to join it, but there should be no negotiation for unity. Third, the majority of the central committee was calling for a national front that would include the Wafd and other progressive forces. Badr and Muslim rejected the Wafd because, they maintained, it had no role in the national struggle. Finally, the majority of the central committee agreed that the time was right for armed struggle against the British and began gathering arms. But Badr and Muslim thought that conditions were not right for such a confrontation.[16]

Badr and the others received little support for their actions and instead were largely condemned by the imprisoned members of the central committee. The DMNL-RC, nevertheless, was sustained by both the support of the Sudanese Communist party and many Sudanese students in Egypt.[17] According to Farouk Abu Issa, one of the Sudanese communist students, these students were instructed by the secretary general of the Sudanese Communist party, 'Abd al-Khaima Mahjoub, to join Haditu. Upon their arrival in Cairo, one DMNL-RC member spent two nights with them to convince them to join the DMNL-RC.[18]

The DMNL-RC soon published three leaflets—al-Tali'ah (The Vanguard), al-Kader (The cadres), and Sawt al-Talib (The voice of the student). Each leaflet was directed at a particular audience and carried the party message to it. Al-Tali'ah, targeted at intellectuals, served as a sounding board for ideological issues; Sawt al-Talib focused on student concerns; and al-Kader carried the official organizational positions to the rank and file in the organization. In one of its issues, al-Kader indirectly delineated the role of these newsletters in explaining the tasks facing the organization: ''In the present circumstances, the Egyptian working-class vanguard faces a serious task, which is to delineate the path for the struggle of the working class. It also requires the vanguard to specify for the working class all forms of struggle, organization, and principles which allow and enable [the working class] to mobilize its forces to lead all popular forces."[19]

One of the main functions of *al-Tali'ah* was to announce the theoretical, strategic, and tactical differences between the Revolutionary Current and Haditu. The Revolutionary Current adopted a hostile attitude toward the Moslem Brotherhood, whereas Haditu attempted to include them in a national front. In a subsequent edition, *al-Tali'ah* published an article entitled "The Moslem Brotherhood Betray," stating that the party served only the people's enemies. "But of course treason does not declare itself; instead it puts on a glamorous cloth to lead the masses and their leaders to destruction. The Moslem Brotherhood has chosen religion to cover its reactionism and treason."[20]

The Revolutionary Current also adopted different tactics to deal with the national problem. Whereas Haditu advocated the formation of a national front, the Revolutionary Current called for the formation of revolutionary committees composed of workers and peasants dedicated to organizing strikes in the factories. It rejected any form of alliance and instead adopted a hostile attitude toward all other forces in the political arena. The Revolutionary Current's isolation, followed by state arrests of some of its members and the withdrawal of the Sudanese cadres, led to its joining the movement toward unification into the Unified Egyptian Communist party.

AL-NAJIM AL-AHMAR (RED STAR)

The origins of the Red Star can be traced to 1948–49, when the communists from al-'Umaliyah al-Thawriyah were in prison; disagreement regarding the future of Haditu led to a division in its ranks. After their release from prison, most of the group went back to Haditu. A small faction, under the leadership of 'Adli Gurgis and Ahmed 'Ali Khadhir, formed the Red Star. Its guiding principles were the necessity of operationalizing socialist goals into programs of action; of armed struggle to expel the British from Egypt; of the nationalization of productive resources, especially land; of a Marxist-Leninist party under the leadership of the proletariat allied with the peasants; and of having 75 percent of its membership come from proletarian ranks.

The political program for labor was to achieve independence of the labor movement and its freedom of action, a forty-hour workweek, equal rights and wage parity between the sexes, child care for working mothers, and unemployment insurance. The political program for peasants was to achieve redistribution of all farms over fifty feddans to landless peasants, development of model farm cooperatives from confiscated land, compensation for nationalist landowners who did not oppose the revolution, and raising the rural standard of living.[21] After their release in 1950, the faction not only formed the Red Star but also began publishing a magazine of the same name. The organization consisted of between forty and fifty members, 60 percent of whom were workers.

In 1951, however, 'Adli Gurgis was arrested again, and after the Cairo fire in 1952, other members were also arrested. By the time the army movement took over, the Red Star was supporting its policies regarding land reform as well as the expulsion of the king, although the group did advocate more radical reforms and called for the king to be tried.

The most important contribution of this organization to the communist movement in Egypt was its efforts toward unification. Between 1953 and 1955 the organization advocated the cause of unity among the many factions that made up the movement.

NAWAT AL-HIZB SHUYO'IE AL-MISRI (THE NUCLEUS OF THE COMMUNIST PARTY)

This group was formed in late 1949 and, less than two years after beginning its activities, it became the target of police investigations and raids. The program of this organization was presented in a pamphlet that it distributed: "(i) to eradicate the monarchical capitalist system and domination by the world colonial forces — both of which support the existing regime in Egypt — by armed revolution, and (ii) the establishment of the Popular Democratic Republic — composed of a popular front of workers, peasants, revolutionary intellectuals, producers, and cultivators — under the leadership of the labor class and guided by the Communist party."[22]

The official policy of this group was to support the army movement, but an internal leaflet — discovered by the police on September 27, 1952 — showed that this was merely an opportunistic position. The leaflet stated: "As long as the bourgeois army movement presents slogans which the people aspire to, at a time when there is no deep-rooted Marxist leadership among the masses, it would be absolute folly to raise hostile slogans against it."[23]

It went on to depict the tactics that the group would apply in dealing with the regime should the opportunity arise. The growing authoritarianism of the new regime, however, soon forced the nucleus to turn to direct opposition. Thus one finds, in the editorial of *al-Nasr,* a pamphlet for popular distribution, "The military junta's treachery began with its persecution of the Egyptian labor class, exemplified by the hanging of two of its members — al-Bakri and Khamis — and then culminated in the isolation of the labor class. This treacherous gang, which has been imposed upon us, cannot — in its stand regarding the British colonialists and our national cause — but take the position of treason and compromise."[24]

By the end of 1954, even though the organization had been subjected to more police raids and many of its principal cadres had been arrested, it still continued to function. By 1955, however, the nucleus sensed the extreme danger to the communist movement as a whole and became more inclined toward unity with other organizations.

AL-HIZB AL-SHUYO'IE AL-MISRI AL-MUWAHAD (THE UNIFIED EGYPTIAN COMMUNIST PARTY)

The earliest attempts at unity took place in late 1953, when the Committee for Unification first met to discuss the issue of a united communist movement. One of the basic preconditions for unity was that Haditu would not obtain a majority in the leadership of the new party.

The proposed unification was based on two documents: the first was political, which condemned the army movement, accusing it of being an American scheme; the second was organizational, full of liberal ideas. This development could be construed as a political defeat for Haditu because it supported the army movement. Nevertheless, in 1955 five communist groups merged: Haditu, the Nucleus, the Red Star, the Communist Vanguard, and the DMNL-RC. Figure 5 shows the divisions in the movement and the lines of unification to form the new organization.

The new party presented a program calling for concentration of power in the hands of the people; nationalization of utilities and major companies; confiscation of land from large landowners, followed by its distribution among the peasants; separation of religion from the state; the abolition of all imperialist treaties; the improvement of economic conditions for both men and women; and the establishment of special relations with the Soviet Union. In its attack on the army movement, the party declared: "The military junta has solved its 'national problem' by signing an Anglo-American imperialist treaty which relinquishes control of our

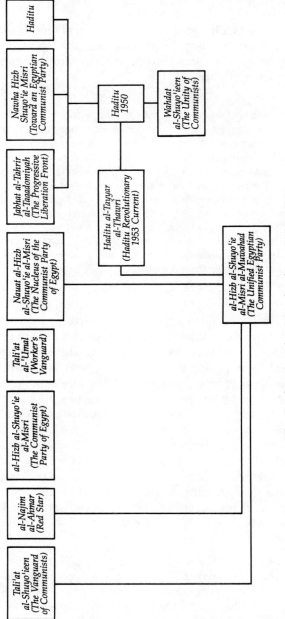

Fig. 5. Communist organizations, 1950–1955.

own country. What does it matter that the people are succumbing to misery, hunger, worry, and a fear of the future?''[25]

The situation soon changed. Nasser's change in foreign policy was an important element in shifting the orientation of the Egyptian communists, impelling them to reassess their position toward the government. M. S. Agwani contended that

> The Czech arms deal marks a watershed in the history of the modern Arab East. It destroyed many a time-honoured assumption and illusion about the pattern of politics in the area and created new ones. Among the illusions destroyed was the belief, common to Western circles, that nationalism in the area could be propitiated by marginal concession within a paternalistic framework designed to protect foreign strategic and economic interests. On the other hand, the Soviet bloc was not a little taken aback by the unsuspected potentialities of the so-called *bourgeois* Arab nationalism. The most confounded lot of all, however, were the Arab Communists whose copy-book maxims about the chronic ailments of the national *bourgeoisie* — vacillation and betrayal being the most notorious among them—stood utterly exposed.[26]

The position of the Unified Communist party was contradictory; one group would choose to support Nasser's policies and another would dogmatically refuse to reassess its position, notwithstanding the changing conditions. The opposing faction's stance was exemplified in one pamphlet: ''Our support for the positive side of the dictatorship's foreign policy does not imply, by any means, the overlooking of the reactionary and treacherous aspects of the government's internal policy and its relationship with the imperialists.''[27]

In contrast, the supporting group (led by Kamal 'Abd al-Halim) strongly vindicated the army movement through propaganda activities, and even the communists who were in prison expressed their support for Nasser's policies. For example, in April 1956, the Unified Communist party issued a statement under the title ''Imperialism Is the First Enemy,'' declaring its support of Nasser's policies:

> There is no doubt that the government of 'Abdel Nasser has taken the right position. It has opposed the Baghdad Pact—collaborating with the other Arab countries against it—and has offered Arab assistance to Jordan in order to relieve imperialist pressure on Amman to join the pact. Nasser has also clearly stated that he is going to oppose Zi-

onist aggression and that he shall defend Egypt and its independence, as well as the Arab East and its independence. There is no doubt that Nasser's Czech arms deal was a consolidating step toward our independence and the independence of the Arab people ... therefore, there is no doubt that we support Nasser's government in its peaceful and independent steps. We support it strongly and honestly against all imperialist conspiracies, whether they be external attacks or internal intrigues.''[28]

The statement, nevertheless, called upon Nasser to mobilize the nation into a popular front to face the foreign aggression.

Following the nationalization of the Suez Canal and the tripartite aggression in Egypt, many cadres of the Unified Communist party were quick to volunteer for the front lines. They convened a mass popular gathering at the cemetery of the martyrs in Port Said, where Ahmed al-Rifa'ie declared: ''The enemy, after his failure and defeat, is trying to conspire anew; he is attempting to create a rift between us and our heroic leader, Nasser. Yet we all know who Nasser is: he is the decisions of Bandung and Brioni; he is the high dam and the nationalization of the Suez Canal; he is the destruction of feudalism and the defeat of monopoly. Nasser is the glory and history of Egypt.''[29]

TALI'AT AL-'UMAL (THE WORKERS' VANGUARD)

This group was founded in September 1946 by about seven people, including Sadiq Sa'ad, Ramon Duwaik, Youssef Darwish, Mahmud al-'Askari, and Ahmed Rushdi Salih. For security reasons, the name changed a number of times, as indicated in Figure 2. The executive committee consisted of Sadiq Sa'ad (political chief), Youssef Darwish (organizational chief), and Mahmud al-'Askari (popular activities chief). The total number of members of this new organization varied between twenty-five and thirty.[30]

The basic program of action provided by this group called for the expulsion of the British from Egypt and Sudan, with the right of the Sudan for self-determination; support for the peace camp headed by the Soviet Union; the establishment of a popular democratic republic; the nationalization of monopolies; distribution of land among the peasants; and equality between men and women. To achieve these goals, this group's main aim was to ''isolate the treacherous bourgeois from their leadership of the popular masses—who were aspiring to freedom and independence

— and instead gather the popular masses around the labor class, as the new leader of the revolution."[31]

The Workers' Vanguard, therefore, adopted a hostile attitude toward the existing parties and, in a pamphlet dated July 24, 1950, it stated, "The rule of the large property owners and financiers — whether Sa'adist or Wafdist — is characterized as the rule of bribery and embezzlement."[32] This statement led, a week later, to the political police raiding the premises of the PVL (Popular Vanguard for Liberation) dealing a severe blow to the group.

How, then, did things go with the July 23 army movement? Helmi Yassin recalls that the Workers' Vanguard was the first to support Nasser in his opposition to the Baghdad Pact and his plan to go the Bandung conference, thereby coming under violent attack.[33]

Hence the initial position of the Workers' Vanguard toward the government was hostile. A leaflet issued by the vanguard stated:

No day passes without the military dictatorship showing its clear aggression toward the freedoms of the people and their rights. After having abolished the parliamentary system and the constitutions — in order to suppress the voice of the people and deprive them from practicing their natural right — and after having dissolved the parties — specifically to destroy the Wafd and disguise its own treachery — the government immediately began to direct its blows against the free and struggling people, throwing them into prison for nothing other than their refusal to substitute British imperialism with American imperialism. Down with the military councils and Naguib's fascist and treacherous government. Long live independence and freedom.[34]

Even the confiscation of the wealth of the royal family was considered to be no more than a decision "taken by the high fascist council, the council of the alleged revolution and reactionary coup."[35]

The position of the Workers' Vanguard began to shift, however, after Nasser's opposition to the Baghdad Pact and subsequent participation in the Bandung conference. Thus, on August 5, 1956 — less than two weeks after the nationalization of the Suez Canal — the vanguard distributed a pamphlet entitled "To the Courageous Egyptian People," which stated that "the nationalization of the canal was a new blow received by the imperialist camp from the Egyptian people. It was a blow that rendered him unconscious and drove him insane, after it eliminated his influence in our beloved country." The imperialists, however, "shall not waste any opportunity to use base conspiratorial means to deprive us of our freedom, steal our food, and topple our national government, that same government which has not only struggled at Bandung and Brioni but is still struggling for peace, the right of the people to self-determination, the dissolution of imperialist pacts, and no more foreign interference in the internal affairs of sovereign states."[36] The pamphlet went on to pledge the vanguard's support to Nasser.

After the end of the tripartite aggression, and within the context of overwhelming national euphoria, most of the cadres of the vanguard were released. Public action could then develop within the confines of the state institutions such as the national assembly.

AL-HIZB AL-SHUYO'IE AL-MISRI
(THE COMMUNIST PARTY OF EGYPT)

The Communist party of Egypt was founded by Fuad Morsi and Ismael Sabri 'Abdullah after their return from studying in Paris in late 1949. They teamed up with a breakaway faction from Haditu led by Mustafa Tebah, Dawod 'Aziz, and Sa'ad Zahran. The party was declared on January 1, 1950, listing a membership of about twenty. The party presented a fourteen-point program, as follows:

1. Independence and liberation from foreign domination whether British or American and the evacuation of the British forces from Egypt and the Sudan.

2. Resistance to the conspiracies of world imperialism led by the United States, to launch a new world war against the people, and the elimination of the conspiracies of the reactionary classes to involve the Egyptian people in imperialist-inspired military adventures.

3. Joining the ranks of the peoples who struggle for their freedom and liberty, peace and democracy, under the leadership of the Soviet Union and China.

4. The elimination of the large landownership system and of the capitalists and monopolists who rely on the armed power of the colonialists and the adoption of a democratic system in which power belongs to the workers, peasants, nationalists, and democrats.

5. The sequestration of large agricultural holdings (more than fifty feddans) and redistributing it among the peasants.

6. Nationalization of monopolies, banks, public utilities, and colonial institutions so that they may be led by the workers.

7. Expansion of political liberties such as freedom of writing and speech, freedom of religious belief, and freedom of demonstration, striking, and gathering, in addition to the formation of political parties.

8. The creation of a popular democratic army that includes all the people.

9. Improving the living standards of the workers and other social classes, especially peasants and white-collar employees, as well as social insurance and the limitation of hours of work to forty per week.

10. The imposition of progressive taxes on income profits and inheritance. Workers, peasants, and junior employees were to be exempted from direct and indirect taxes.

11. Education should be made free and a right to every Egyptian.

12. Emancipation of women and establishing their equality with men in all economic, social, and political aspects. They should also enjoy equal pay with men for the same work.

13. The freedom of the Sudanese people and their right to self-determination. Egyptian and British forces were to evacuate the country.

14. The freedom of the Palestinian people, their right to self-determination, and the formation of an independent Arab democratic Palestine. All Arab armies were to withdraw from Palestine.[37]

The party was highly secretive and devoted much of its attention to the covert building of its intellectual and organizational structure. It refused to admit foreigners. According to Morsi, this party "was the first to provide an analysis of the role of the feudal class in Egypt as well as the first to analyze its relation to the British and the monarchical system. It also played an important role in Egyptianizing and Arabizing the communist movement."[38] The central committee of the party was composed of four people: Fuad Morsi (secretary general), Mustafa Tebah (organization), Dawod 'Aziz, and Sa'ad Zahran. Tebah was arrested on July 17, 1952 (a few days before the revolution), and Zahran was arrested on February 28, 1953.

Their arrests necessitated the formation of a new leadership, which consisted of Fuad Morsi [Khalid], secretary general, Dawod 'Aziz [Ghaleb], secretary for propaganda, Ismael Sabri 'Abdullah [Assem], secretary for the organization. In spite of several blows to its security, the new party not only survived but proved capable of competing with the largest communist group, Haditu, although it did concentrate more on clandestine activities. Also contrary to Haditu, the party raised the slogan, "no communism outside the party." It opposed any unification attempts, at least until 1957, when finally the currents for unification were so strong as to force it to abandon this slogan.

The party adopted a radically hostile position toward the Wafd and, later on, toward the army movement. In the first issue of *Rayat al-Sha'ab*, it stated: "The Wafd government has compromised with the imperialists and has, furthermore, accepted their existence and verdict. Let us, instead, unite in a popular republic to face the enemies of freedom and evacuation. Let us come together around the party which struggles for the people and independence from colonialism."[39]

When the army took over in July 1952, *al-Haqiqah* (the internal circular of the party) presented an article written by the secretary of the party, entitled "The Great Fraud—A Military Fascist Coup to Drag the People into War."[40] In reflecting the party's hostile view of the new regime, the article described the new regime as a fascist movement supported by imperialism. It also attacked Haditu for supporting the military coup. Naguib was considered to be an American puppet, and even the conflict between Nasser and Naguib was interpreted as "competition and difference, only serving the imperialists and negatively striking the people."[41]

While Nasser was still at Bandung, *Rayat al-Sha'ab* caustically used words such as "the bankrupt fascist of Egypt seeks glory in Bandung," "the atrocities of the bloody Nasser," and "Nasser is the enemy of peace.''[42] Following the tripartite attack on Egypt in 1956 and Nasser's consequent great popularity in Egypt and the Arab world, in addition to his increasingly active leadership of the Third World anti-imperialist movement following Bandung, the party was forced to revise its assessment of the regime. It eventually joined the trend toward unification of the communist movement.

5

The Communist Movement
and Nasserism

The 1952 Egyptian revolution considerably changed the environment of the Egyptian communist movement. Although at first the new regime appeared to represent more of a palace coup than a transformation of Egypt's political system, this image changed in the turbulence of 1955–56. As a result of the Bandung conference of April 1955, the Czech arms deal in September 1955, nationalization of the Suez Canal in July 1956, and the Israeli-British-French invasion of Egypt in November 1956, Nasser emerged as an international spokesman, an Arab leader, and an Egyptian hero. More significant for the communist movement, Nasserism began to unfold as a consistent if not a coherent ideology. The fundamentally humanistic concerns of the new regime became manifest as events precipitated revealing responses.

The two central tenets that became the core of Nasserism revolved around the issues of Arab unity and Palestine. The communist movement's position on these issues was problematic on two counts. First, there was ideological factionalism on both issues within the movement. Second, the popularity of Nasser reflected the importance of these issues to the Egyptian public. The problems of the movement in dealing with these issues indicate its difficulties in responding to its environment. The newspaper *al-Fajr al-Jadeed* gave special attention to the issue of Arab unity. From the beginning the newspaper considered the foundation of the Arab League as a positive step and one of the Wafd's democratic accomplishments. It warned, however, that those in charge of the Arab League should "make the Arab people feel that the policy of the league is run for the good of the masses . . . [and] the good of the people and not for the interest of a small group of them who do not care except for exploitation and getting rich."[1]

The policies of the Arab League, however, were quickly to come under fire. It was accused of being "a league of states and not a league of people, which represents exclusively the ruling classes."[2] The league was further accused of being "a British instrument" and condemned for ignoring the cause of Palestine and the problem of the Sudan. "The league is going its own way. As for the people of the East who aspire to freedom, they do not expect something from it unless it becomes a league for the Arab people in which the people of the Arab East are rightfully represented, and [it] endeavors to strengthen the ties among these and consolidate against imperialism."[3]

Al-Fajr al-Jadeed's sister journal *al-Dhamir* played a leading role in calling for the unity of the Arab labor movements and frequently provided space for Arab unionists such as Palestinians Mokhlis Amr and Boules Farah and Mustafa al-'Arissi, a Lebanese. It was also the first leftist labor forum to call for establishing an Arab labor federation. In 1945, in describing the convention set by the Alexandria workers for the Arab delegates to the Paris summit, the paper noted that the workers who attended the celebration expressed "the necessity of forming a general federation for the workers of the Arab East."

Iskra's position on the Arab world in general and the question of the Sudan in particular was indicated by Shuhdi 'Atiyah al-Shaf'ie and Mohammed 'Abd al-Ma'boud al-Gibayli in their book *Ahdafuna al-Wataniyah*. They stated that "Egypt cannot secure its independence unless the Sudan is completely liberated from the British colonialists, whose remaining in the Sudan is a continuous threat to Egypt's independence directly and indirectly. . . . The Sudan alone will not be able quickly to get rid of the British colonialists unless its people participate in a united front with the Egyptian people to struggle against the common colonialists." The writers also attacked the reactionaries who called for "Egyptian-acquired rights in the Sudan" and used popular slogans such as the unity of the Nile Valley to hide their colonial schemes. They declared that the Egyptian people "respect the right of the Sudanese people to total political independence and their sincere wish to get rid of foreign colonialism whether British or Egyptian."[4]

The Iskra program, as put forward in *Ahdafuna al-Wataniyah,* also strongly endorsed Egypt's participation in the Arab League:

> The Egyptian people are very committed to the Arab League but refuse firmly . . . to have the Arab League become a tool in the hands

of the imperialists to smother the liberation movement and to stop democracy from growing. The Arab League will never become an instrument of struggle unless all the Arab nations demand democratic governments . . . to increase the spirit of struggle for Arab unity, popular participation must be increased and representation should not be for governments exclusively but should include labor and student unions, organizations representing intellectuals, peasants. . . . The Egyptian people will call upon all the Arab nations to form a united front for the struggle against imperialism, the achievement of true democracy, and economic integration and close cooperation. . . . The Egyptian workers' unions and university students can play a decisive role in this respect by calling for unity and organizing continuous communications so that no action can take place in one country without producing a reaction in all other [Arab] countries.[5]

The program strongly cautioned against the idea adopted by the "colonialists and their treacherous agents" of endowing the league with a religious overtone, "diverting attention from the nationalist characteristic of the league and its foremost duty toward national struggle." Such a scheme, in their view, threatened to create divisions in society and provide insecurity for different minorities:

There is nothing more dangerous to the question of Arab independence than those voices that ask for the transformation to an Islamic League. That means

1. Diverting attention away from the nationalist struggle against imperialism which is the foremost struggle for every Arab whether he is a Moslem, Christian, or Jew.

2. Frightening all the religious minorities . . . with this religious fanaticism and persecution, thus separating them from participation in the struggle against imperialism which will weaken the Arab national movement. . . .

3. Providing imperialists with the opportunity to interfere under the pretext of protecting the minorities. . . .

4. Splitting the nationalist movements all over the world by including Moslem minorities in this Islamic League. This will have a negative impact on the liberation movements. For example, including 90 million Indian Moslems in the proposed league means separating them from the rest of the Indian nation in their common strug-

gle against imperialism and diverting them toward unity of the
Islamic countries, thus weakening the nationalist movement in India.
This will strengthen the position of imperialism in that country and
thus strengthen imperialism at the international level. This is a strike
against liberation movements everywhere.

     5. Losing the sympathy of international public opinion, which
today supports all national liberation movements but will certainly
refrain from supporting any national liberation movement that
smacks of religious fanaticism and sectarianism. . . . The loss of public opinion will be a great loss to the Arab nationalist movement.[6]

     The program also rejected the "Greater Syria" proposal that ad-
vocated the unification of Iraq, Syria, Lebanon, Palestine, and Transjor-
dan into one state. It argued that "British imperialism is behind this project, supporting it fully" as a strategy for checking French colonial
interests in the region and consolidating British control over it. The authors of the Iskra program maintained: "We do not object to unity among
the Arab nations in their struggle against imperialism . . . but we strongly
object to a plan . . . which imperial designs are behind . . . and which
is supported by a small group of reactionaries in the different Arab
countries."[7]
     Regarding the position of Haditu concerning Arab unity, al-Malay-
een declared in its seventeenth issue under the heading "To the Millions
of Arabs": "Yes. We are those 70 million who live in the Arab lands east
and west from Iraq to the Levant, and from Najd to Egypt, Libya and Mo-
rocco. We are a standing and strict unity for thousands and thousands of
peoples whom the colonialists wanted to paint in black their days and
years and to colonize them." It continued,

     If we are not a racial unity tied by one origin, one language, and one
     history, then we are a tremendous emotional unity, the origin of
     which is deprivation of all dignified human rights; its language is the
     inevitable hatred against the tyrannical rulers, and its history is those
     scandals and tragedies which are committed in our countries by the
     allied colonial bloc. The unity of those millions of Arabs shall not be
     useful to them in winning the battle for a modern free life if it remains
     only a unity of complaints and indignation. If they do not proceed to
     the positive field, the field of mutinous struggle, which cannot take
     place except through scientific and practical organization, a unified

organization in all means of national struggle, a unity through which the unified popular organization could relentlessly drive and penetrate all the obstacles which the colonialists put in the way of our goals, and burn their colonial bases at the same time. This way we prepare the great machinery for the break loose uprising from slavery and tyranny; the uprising of freedom and progress; the great uprising.[8]

EGYPTIAN COMMUNIST ORGANIZATIONS AND THE PALESTINE QUESTION

The earliest position adopted by Egyptian communist organizations on the question of Palestine dates from the 1920s, when the Egyptian Communist party expressed its concern and opinions on the issue through the pages of *al-Hisab*. Under the heading "Balfour visits his victim, and Palestine meets him with a general strike," the paper described Arthur Balfour as having made "the famous declarations which he issued in the name of the British government, and according to which Palestine was given to the Jews and Zionism despite the will of its inhabitants and against every tradition, custom, or law." It proceeded to state, "When Balfour visited Palestine in April 1925 in response to the invitation of the Hebrew University, the inhabitants met him in every place he went by all means which expressed their frustration, anger, and disgust concerning his visit, which resembles the visitation of the murderer to the family of the deceased and the aggressor to his victim." The article concluded, "We salute this magnificent uprising in Palestine and hope that the honorable Palestinians persevere in their glory and struggle for the independence of their country. They as exhausted innocent [people] should put their hands in the hands of every labor class in any country, for the labor class is exploited everywhere, and the exploited are kinsmen."[9]

Two decades later, the two major organizations that expressed staunch opposition to the Zionist and imperialist activities in Palestine were the *al-Fajr al-Jadeed* group, the Workers' Vanguard organization, and the Democratic Movement for National Liberation, Haditu.

Thus on June 16, 1945, *al-Fajr al-Jadeed* condemned Zionism as "an imperialist movement which in practice is no more than an old form for the exportation of capital, overtaking the markets and monopolizing as much as possible the sources of primary resources on behalf of the huge imperialist companies. The [Arabs'] struggle against Zionism [however] does not mean a struggle against Jews."

Mokhlis Amr, a Palestinian Unionist leader, wrote an article which called upon the Arab workers to unite "to fight Zionism among the ranks of workers, displaying it as a capitalist colonial movement."[10]

Despite its virulent attack on Zionism, *al-Fajr* strongly condemned the discriminatory actions against the Jews who lived in Egypt, which were mainly led by the Moslem Brotherhood. Ahmed Rushdi Salih (Jihad) wrote about the attacks against property in the Jewish community: "We believe that fighting Zionism is a glorious patriotic effort that we should undertake both strictly and forcefully. Zionism is a capitalist colonialist movement that both the American and British imperialists use now to consolidate their pillars in the Arab countries." There were some reactionary currents, however, which "met on a common goal in turning our nationalist movement from its current flow against the British colonialists and reactionary tyranny into a racial movement. The leadership of the November 2 strikes was in the hands of these reactionary groups, and as such it did not benefit the popular bases at all, benefited the colonialists much, and consolidated the government better than ever before." He further stated that "Zionism benefited from the directing of our movement on November 2 in the wrong direction. It acquired strong proof against the Arab people that they do not respect the rights of the Jewish minority and that the Jews cannot be safe unless they are grouped in one country."[11]

Al-Fajr also published the full statements of the "Anti-Zionist League in Iraq." On the anniversary of the Balfour declaration, the league issued the following statement: "We, being Jews and Arabs at the same time, declare our condemnation of and objection to the Balfour declaration, and we call upon every citizen to struggle for the total independence of Palestine, the formation of an Arab democratic government in it, the prohibition of Zionist migration to Palestine, and the cessation of transferring lands to the Zionists."[12]

In a study presented in the name of *al-Fajr al-Jadeed,* Rushdi Salih declared: "Colonialism, the Zionist capitalists, and the Arab feudalists are the ones responsible for the repeated massacres which the Arab people committed against the Jews. The winners from these massacres and religious hatred are the colonialists who succeeded in diverting attention from them; it is the Zionist capitalists who succeeded in attracting the sympathy and enthusiasm of the Jewish masses, throwing them into the battle in order to consolidate the Zionist exploitation of Palestine; it is the Arab feudalists who threw the Arab people into turmoil, while at the same time dealing with the colonialists and selling Palestine's land to the Zionist brokers."[13]

Further examination of the Palestine question was provided by Sadiq Sa'ad of the *al-Fajr al-Jadeed* group. In his *Falastin fi Makhaleb al-Isti'mar,* Sa'ad asserted that the cause of Palestine was a cause of national liberation from foreign colonialists and from the reactionary rule imposed on the people. He concluded that the Palestinian cause "is not different in essence from the cause of our country [Egypt]." What was different, however, was the means by which the British used Zionism to consolidate their position in Palestine. Sa'ad perceived Zionism "not an instrument in the hands of the British colonialism yet not entirely separated from it. Zionism is a partner of the British colonialism in Palestine and its offspring, both exchanging help and sharing the benefits."[14]

To explain the emergence of the Zionist movement, Sa'ad undertook a brief examination of Jewish social, economic, and political history from which he concluded that Zionism served the interests of Jewish capitalists, not those of the broader Jewish masses. Zionism sought to link Palestine to the world capitalist system through colonial means. Thus for Sa'ad Zionism was "a colonial movement whose economic goal is to export capital to Palestine and its neighboring countries, making them a market for investment and consumption of commodities. It is from here that the most harm and danger may emanate, not only in Palestine but in the economic life of all the Arab countries, especially the emerging national industry in every Arab territory, and Lebanon in particular because of its proximity to Palestine and its relatively low immunity against Zionism." Thus the Palestinian cause was

> a nationalistic and democratic cause in the first place; that is, a cause of persecuted, enslaved people who struggle against the foreign imperialists, and the British imperialists in particular. It is the same cause as that of all other colonies, the sacred cause of the right to self-determination for a persecuted people who do not govern themselves. The issue of Jewish migration to Palestine is simply a side and secondary point with respect to the principal and essential point, which is the fall of Palestine into the paws of foreign colonialism [i.e., Britain]. . . . Since British colonialism in this small area of the Arab world enables Britain to control Egypt, Iraq, Syria, Lebanon, and the Arabian Peninsula, the Arab people feel the common danger which threatens them continuously, and you find them showing strong solidarity with the nationalist Arab movement in Palestine.[15]

How, then, did Sa'ad perceive the solution to the Palestinian problem? As he put it,

The solution of the Palestinian cause is not unique. It is the solution
of the problem of colonies, that is, it cannot come about except
through the complete liberation of these brother countries from colonialism, and for Palestine to be ruled by a democratic, popular rule
that emanates from the people and their will. When we say the people
of Palestine, we mean its Arabs and Jews. There is no doubt that this
solution, which is the only feasible solution, imposes upon the Jews
of Palestine the duty to liberate [themselves] from the hands of Zionism in order to form with the Arabs of Palestine a unified nationalist
democratic front, without which Palestine cannot be liberated from
colonialism and exploitation. As to the solution of the world Jewish
problem, it is not a unique solution; instead it is the [same] solution
as for the other millions, or hundreds of millions, of persecuted, en-
slaved, and exploited [people]. The problem of the Jews does not differ in principle from the problems of the blacks in America or South
Africa. It does not differ in principle from the case of the toiling persecuted classes in the colonies. We say to all those persecuted "that
the only solution to your sufferings is the correct and right democracy; to fight for it." This slogan applies to the Jews too.[16]

The Workers' Committee for National Liberation also gave special
attention to the Palestine question through the pages of its journal *al-
Dhamir*. In an article under the heading "You Shall Not Pass," Khairy
Mahmud (Youssef Darwish) wrote: "This is the word that the Spanish
Republicans cried out in 1936, when world fascism attacked them with its
tanks, weapons, and Nazi and fascist money. This is the same word which
the peoples of the Arab countries cry out today in the face of Zionism."
He continued:

Fascism and Zionism come from the same origin in colonialism, exploitation, and greed. Fascism is the instrument of the rotten capitalism which resorted to intervention and terror to continue the exploitation of the working people. Zionism is the instrument of world
imperialism which resorted to lying to the peoples of the world and
the toiling Jews and resorts to terror today, enslaving the Arab people. Zionism finds fertile soil for spreading its principles among the
Jews in the countries where terror rule predominates. Both it and fascism are strongly tied together and cannot be detached except by
struggling against the cause of persecution and injustice and defending freedom and democracy. . . . Zionism does not solve the problem
of 16 million Jews. The Jewish problem is simply an indivisible component of all the peoples' struggle, irrespective of religious creed, for

the sake of their freedom and democracy. . . . The Arab peoples, at
the head of which is the Palestinian people, are determined through
their unity, organized ranks, and dependence on the other democratic people to stop the overwhelming Zionist danger.

The article blamed the Arab League for its indecisive position regarding
the Zionist danger: "If the Arab League did not undertake the decisive
and strict position which was demanded of it in such an issue, the Arab
people, represented by the delegates of the Arab workers in the world labor unions conference in Paris, were able by their consensus to make
world laborers feel the danger of Zionism to humanity, and enabled them
to prevent the participation of the Zionist labor representative in the Executive Federation Committee."[17]

Another article written by Mahmud al-'Askari under the heading
"No Racialism among the Workers" stated that Zionism is "the immediate danger which not only threatens the toiling people in our Arab sister
Palestine, but also threatens the lives of the toiling people in the Middle
East in particular and the peoples of the world in general. It also threatens
the cause of world peace because Zionism is the rotten colonial Jewish
capitalism which misguides the toiling Israeli people, whether workers or
agriculturalists, to exploit them. . . . It puts poison in the honey by raising
the racial persecution complex . . . blinding their sight from the truth in
the interest of a group of tyrannical Zionist capitalists."[18]

Iskra's position on the Palestine question was set forth by Shuhdi
'Atiyah al-Shaf'ie and Mohammed 'Abd al-Ma'boud al-Gibayli. In dealing with the Palestinian cause the authors' analysis was based on three
main points. First, "Zionism is no less dangerous to the independence of
Palestine than any other kind of colonialism. It is a terroristic colonialism, totally tied to the world imperialists. . . . [Its] danger is not confined
to Palestine alone but threatens the independence and freedom of all
other Arab countries." Second, distinguishing between Zionism and Judaism and considering the former to be an enemy of both Jews and Arabs,
Jewish workers, peasants, and intellectuals should "form a unified front
to struggle against colonialism and its Zionist instrument." Third, they
attacked "the Arab reactionary elements," which "refuse to recognize
the right of the Jewish people to cooperate on equal terms with the Arab
people to achieve independence and democracy which give Zionism the
chance to cheat the Jewish masses in the name of nationalist sentiments,
and the British colonialists to assign themselves as an arbiter in every dispute that erupts." They perceived that a "Palestine liberated from colo-

nialism of all kinds is capable of solving its problems by establishing a democratic government in the shadow of which Arabs and Jews cooperate."[19]

Iskra also contributed to the struggle against Zionism through support of anti-Zionist activities by Egyptian Jews. In October 1946 party leaders brought to the attention of the nationalist newspaper *Sawt al-Umma* the formation in Cairo of an anti-Zionist Jewish organization, the Democratic Israeli Youth.[20]

Iskra's message stated: "We have received from the 'Democratic Israeli Youth' in Cairo word which mentions that their group has emerged from among the people and that their goals are summarized in fighting racism and struggling against colonialism and its Zionist offspring." It further stated that this group, "which speaks in the name of the free Egyptian Israeli community, and which reaches about 100,000 citizens, opposes Zionism and its unjust goals, which do not solve the problem of the dispersed Jews." Later, this group became known as the al-Rabitah al-Israeliyah li Mukafahat al-Sihuniyah (Israeli League for the Struggle Against Zionism), its principal aim being to "fight Zionism and its malicious propaganda among all the Israelis living in Egypt."[21] The league also declared that "most Jews do not accept Zionism and perceive it as a ploy in the hands of the colonialists to consolidate their position." The statement then ended by stating that "it is our indomitable feeling that our Egypt today is in most need of grouping all the sincere nationalistic elements to destroy colonialism, defeat Zionism, and bring to existence a free independent Arab East sheltered by tolerance and the fraternal atmosphere which purifies us from the hateful fanatic vision behind which no one stands to gain but the occupier."[22]

The secretary of the league, 'Izra Herari, further accused Zionism of attempting to "tie the Jews to the imperialist wheel and make them slaves to implement its contemptuous aim through the policy of divide and conquer which it presents in Palestine. Through the policy of creating a Zionist Jewish state in Palestine, it becomes a colonial spearhead against the peoples of the Arab countries."[23] The league further condemned the Jewish migration to Palestine and expressed its rejection of "a policy of migration which is opposed by most of the inhabitants of Palestine and practically leads to results which are in contradiction with the claimed humanistic aims. We are in no need of a migration that leads our Jewish brethren to live in an atmosphere of civil war in Palestine, that is, if it does not lead them to the notorious Cypriot camps behind barbed wire. However, we are sure that a free independent Palestine shall participate in goodwill with the other democratic countries in sheltering the dispersed Jews."[24]

In reference to the Jews who were still in the concentration camps in Western Europe, the league accused the Zionists of refusing "to think of any solution for these miserables except going to Palestine. This way they increase their sufferings in order to exploit them within the confines of the interests of the Zionist party." To solve the problems of the Jews, the league suggested that they return "to the countries from which fascism has expelled them." As for those who did not want to return to such places, "we see that it is the duty of all countries, especially the vast [in area] among them to receive those dispersed [ones] and help them to settle."[25]

The league also condemned the Zionist terrorism in Palestine, calling it "a fascist movement directed basically against the Jewish masses, which serves no one except the colonialists, who found the terroristic movements under the cover of maintaining security—a legal argument in appearance—to transform Palestine into an armed camp serving their aggressive projects, and a moral justification to subdue the inhabitants to a system of persecution and perpetual tyranny." It concluded that the "formation of a unified front with the Arab liberation movement for the sake of a free, independent, and democratic Palestine is the only salvation for the Jewish masses in Palestine." The solution offered by the league thus was manifested in the following statement: "The Palestinian problem, basically, is the problem of the liberation of Palestine from persecution and colonialism. The only course the Jews of Palestine should pursue is to come to an understanding with the Arabs and unite with them to liberate Palestine from the yoke of colonialism. A free democratic Palestine is the only [condition] which could guarantee the Jewish inhabitants a prosperous, free, and fruitful life."[26]

On the issue of Egyptian Jews, the league maintained:

We announce that the only path left for Egyptian Jews is to join the Egyptian national movement and completely support it until it achieves all its aims. The interests of the Jewish masses are no different from the interests of the rest of the Egyptian people. It is not possible for Egyptian Jews to live in equality with the rest of the population unless Egypt is independent and democratic. The Israeli League for the Struggle Against Zionism realizes that in its struggle against the detrimental Zionist influence it serves the interests of the Jewish communities as well as the interests of the Egyptian citizen.[27]

This position of the leftist-oriented Israeli League inevitably led to violent clashes with the Zionists in Egypt, which were expressed in the struggle for power in the Jewish Makkabi organization for *al-Dhaher* in April 1947.[28] In this organ, the Zionists attempted to lobby to expel the Jewish democrats from its board of directors. As the newspaper *al-Ja-mahir* expressed it, "They met by night planning and conspiring under the leadership of Clement Chicorel, who gathered in the day preceding the convention of the general board of this club (Makkabi) tens of Zionist youths and some employees of his well-known store. They planned the conspiracy to expel the democratic Israelis. Their leader told them, 'fear nothing for the Egyptian police answer the least sign from my finger! We have agreed with them on everything!' On the assigned day of the convention of the general board, Chicorel mobilized his group and was able, after forging the list of the club members, and by means and ways opposed to the laws of societies, to appoint a Zionist board-council." The newspaper then expressed its amazement that a policeman obstructed one of the young democratic Jews telling him that "it is not the right of anyone to speak in the name of the club except Khawajah [foreigner Chicorel]."[29]

The expelling of the communists from the Makkabi club initiated a massive press campaign on the part of the league against the Zionists. *Sawt al-Umma* was the main organ active in this campaign, with Mustafa Kamel Muneib the most vocal writer. Under the heading "Zionist Dens in Egypt," he wrote an article warning against the danger of Zionists who used the Makkabi as a base from which to organize their destructive activities. He further stated that those who ran the club were "in totality a group of wealthy Jews who became rich by sucking the blood of Egyptians and standing on the side of the British colonialists in fighting the nationalist, democratic movement in Egypt."[30] Two days later, an article under the heading "A Blatant Zionist Conspiracy" discussed what happened in the Makkabi of al-Dhaher between the Zionists and the democratic Jews and condemned the wealthy Jews who benefited from exploiting the Egyptians and the country's national cause. On April 24, 1947, the conflict culminated in armed clashes when Jewish members of the league attempted to enter the Makkabi and were obstructed by the Zionists. The leftists, however, were able to force their way in. *Sawt al-Umma,* commenting on this incident, expressed its amazement at the impertinence of one of the Zionists named Albert Hatchwell, who "declared in front of the police that he was a Zionist flesh and blood, that he belongs to the Stern Gang, and that he is going to pursue his way and no power shall be able to obstruct his work."[31]

The press attack, however, put the Zionists on the defensive. Clement Chicorel sent a letter to *Sawt al-Umma* in which he denied that Makkabi was a Zionist den and that the club encouraged its members to become involved in political issues. Instead, he stated that its policy "aims at opposing any political activity . . . [and] that some rioting elements which attempted to impose their will on the Makkabi Club were pushed aside and are now trying to fish in troubled waters." The newspaper, however, indicated that Chicorel did not state his opposition to Zionism in his letter, whereas the Jewish communists sent a letter "declaring their opposition to Zionism and their total support for our first campaign against Zionism."[32]

By mid-June 1947, however, the Israeli League was informed by the Ministry of Social Affairs that it opposed the formation of the league "for security reasons." And despite their protestations to the al-Nouqrashi government, many members of the league were arrested and expelled from the country, while the Zionists continued to enjoy their privileges.

Haditu, through *al-Jamahir,* wrote calling for the evacuation of the British from Palestine and attacking Zionism, the agent of colonialism. It also mentioned the activities of the democratic Jews in Egypt who opposed Zionism.[33] Addressing itself to the Anglo-American Investigation Committee, *al-Jamahir* stated: "The Palestinian cause is clear and is in no need of committees, research, or proposals. The Palestinian people want to rid themselves of your imperialism, exploitation, injustice, and terror. The Palestinian people want their independence and freedom; they want democracy and equality, which all citizens, Arab and Jews, would enjoy. The independence of Palestine necessitates a continuous struggle on the part of the inhabitants of Palestine, the unification of their ranks, and getting rid of the Zionist influence, the instrument of imperialism on one hand, and the Arab reactionary, the lackey of imperialism, on the other hand. The Palestinian cause could be summarized in the words struggle for evacuation and democracy."[34]

In a caricature drawing, *al-Jamahir* provided a picture of the Palestinian people chained by Zionism with the aid of Harry S. Truman and Ernest Bevin. The caption stated, "This is what the Anglo-American imperialists and their Zionist lackeys want for the Palestinian people; but the people are determined to break their chain."[35]

Al-Jamahir attempted to provide a scientific study of Zionism. It stated that "the world imperialists used the Jewish capitalists to permeate the poison of the racial Zionist theory among them [i.e., the Jews], misguiding them as being people who cannot be assimilated by other people, and that the solution to their problem and the abolishing of their persecution could come only through the formation of a Jewish state in Palestine." The paper then predicted the outcome of the creation of such a state. If and when established, this state would become "a strategic point which the imperialists shall exploit in order to destroy the Arab liberation movements and an imperialist castle against the people. Zionism shall provide the chance for the exploitation of British and American capital by enslaving both the Arab and Jewish workers and peasants and ravaging the natural wealth in the Arab world, especially oil and minerals." The paper then rhetorically asked for the solution. It answered: "The problem of the Jews is divided into three parts: (1) the problem of the persecuted Jews in different countries; they must participate in the struggle with their people to achieve democracy; (2) the problem of the dispersed Jews; they should be provided with the means to return to their original homelands. It should be clear that Palestine cannot solve the Jewish problem, and any attempt to show Palestine as the solution to the Jewish problem simply complicates the two problems; (3) the problem of Palestine; its solution is bounded in the common struggle between the Jewish and Arab people together to get rid of Anglo-American imperialism and create a free, democratic, and independent state."[36]

Al-Jamahir also criticized the reactionary governments because they "fight the anti-Zionist movements while turning a blind eye to the Zionist movements which shed the interests of the homeland, at a time when we all know that Zionism is an aggressive terroristic movement that is based on the principles of terror and aggression."[37]

Al-Jamahir attempted to extend its activities among the Jews who lived in Egypt to isolate them from the Zionist movement. It declared that "lately an Israeli League has been formed to fight Zionism." In an interview, 'Izra Herari, the secretary of the league, stated that "the goal of the league is to fight Zionism and its misguiding propaganda among all the Israelis living in Egypt." In response to why the league was formed at this particular time, he answered, "because the poisonous Zionist propaganda has become highly active in Egypt lately, which threatens the relations between the Arabs and Jews by poisoning the atmosphere in a country like Egypt where Jews lived for many generations in the best of conditions with their Egyptian compatriots." He also stated that "Zionism is a colonial instrument which is attempting to attract the Jewish people in order to achieve the aims of the imperialists in creating a Jewish state in Palestine that would help [them] to consolidate their position in the Middle East."[38]

In a later issue, *al-Jamahir* published a call from the Israeli League, which was also widely distributed among the Jewish population of Egypt: "O mothers we want to protect your children from the glamorous lies of the Zionist propaganda, which aims at sending your children to live in Palestine amid the enmity of the majority of the population, and in a system that is totally tyrannical and persecutory. O Jews, O Jewesses, Zionism is trying to drag us into a dangerous adventure. Zionism is contributing to making Palestine an uninhabitable country. Zionism wants to isolate the Jews from the masses of the Egyptian people. Zionism is an enemy to the Jews. Down with Zionism. Long live the Arab-Jewish fraternity and long live the Egyptian people."[39]

When the U.N. partition decision was declared, the Workers' Vanguard immediately condemned it and supported the declaration of war against the Zionist state. Haditu, however, supported the decision and opposed Egypt's involvement in the war. Its position was based on the claim that Palestine was declaring a religious war "from which only the imperialists would benefit." It believed that the armed struggle against the colonialists and the mobilization of Arab armies should be undertaken against Britain and not for a war in Palestine.[40] The movement justified its support for the partition by stating, "We do not want to take Palestine away from the Arabs and give it to the Jews, but [we want] to take it away from the imperialists and give it to the Arabs and Jews. We do not accept the partition except forcibly as a basis for the independence of Palestine; then a long struggle would start to narrow the differences in the points of views in the two states, the Arab and the Jewish."[41] The movement thus was strongly opposed to the call for *jihad* in Palestine. "Let's turn the arms against the colonialists in Fayed, the Suez Canal, and the Sudan. It will not be possible to liberate Palestine with our backs uncovered to the enemy. Let's liberate the Nile Valley so we can liberate the whole East."[42]

Haditu issued a statement in which it accused the Arab governments of attempting to "stop the rising tide of the nationalist movements and the transformation of our sacred war against colonialism into a racial-religious war which consolidates the position of the colonialists. They also aim at distracting the attention of the toiling masses from the struggle for the sake of their standard of living toward an external issue that would make them forget this struggle. They aim at transferring the attention of the nationalist democratic opposition from the ruling reactionary areas in the Arab East and their conspiracies in order to group them in a strategic coalition subject to the imperialists."[43] Following the establishment of the state of Israel, *al-Malayeen* condemned the treatment that Jewish citizens were receiving at the hands of Arab governments.

> The Jewish citizens experienced the worst from the governments of the perished era and during the racial Palestinian massacre. They were arrested, had their money sequestered, were thrown into con-

centration camps, and sent into exile at al-Tor. The tyrannical authorities forced them to leave and did not give them a passport but only a small deportation paper which made them international refugees carrying no citizenship. We did not believe that the Wafd government would perpetuate this undemocratic process, but it did. The last of those tragedies was the tragedy of Ninette Belaish in the foreigner's prison, where they tried to force her to sign the deportation request, but she did not want to leave her homeland, Egypt, and remained attached to the floor of the prison and the land of her dear homeland.[44]

Haditu thus condemned the creation of Israel but also opposed the deportation of Jews to the new state and considered such a policy a conspiracy to support Israel. In its twenty-first issue *al-Malayeen* stated, "Some Zionist agents contacted some Egyptian authorities to sign a treaty between Egypt and Israel. These authorities rejected the offer because it does not differ from the 1936 treaty. We have known that those agents are negotiating now with Haykal Pasha and some Egyptian pashas to conclude this deal through them."[45]

Egyptian public opinion, however, was strongly in favor of intervention, especially since nationalistic and religious sentiments were at a high peak. Many people perceived the Palestine war to be a war against imperialism in general, and the opposition of the communist groups sharply reduced their popularity.

The Egyptian Communist party, however, not only opposed intervention but supported the partition resolution (although condemning those responsible). It believed that the solution to the Palestinian problem was to accept the U.N. resolutions, that Egypt's involvement in the war was an attempt to divert attention from the country's internal problems, and that the army was simply an instrument of the government to whip the people rather than fight for the motherland. The state of Israel was considered a manifestation of British and American imperialism rather than a threat in and of itself. The party, in other words, considered the real fight to be against the former rather than the latter.

In their failure to respond to public opinion, the Egyptian Communist party and others reflected the world communist position on the issue. After the partition took effect, for example, the British Communist party newspaper the *Daily Worker* expressed its support for the decision and stated that the British and American imperialists were "regrouping their forces and uniting their ranks in order to forestall the partition while the leftist Soviet bloc, which supported its wish that the spirit of progress in the two new states in Palestine, would proceed forward in its way." The newspaper attempted to highlight the progressive nature of the new state by saying that British policy was clear in its opposition to the partition and that the United States was beginning to oppose it too.[46] In a different issue, the same newspaper attacked the Arab leaders and called them fascist feudalists who cooperated with the imperialists. It also accused the Arab League of attempting to "transform the sentiments against imperialism toward fighting six hundred thousand Jews."[47] In March 1947 the communist parties of the British Empire convened in London, where they condemned Zionism, Anglo-American imperialism, and the Arab reaction. They called for a common Arab-Jewish struggle in Palestine against the imperialists. The conference declared that "a free and independent Palestine shall be ready, in partnership with other free countries in the world, to extend the hand of help, and to maintain security for the victims of fascism and Nazism." It also declared its support for the struggle for independence in Egypt, Palestine, and eastern Jordan and its opposition to colonial projects such as Greater Syria, the Eastern coalition, and the committee of common defense between England and the Arabs.[48]

6

Dissolution of the Egyptian Communist Movement

On January 8, 1958, a united Egyptian Communist party was declared. Nevertheless, it was clear from the meetings and discussions that preceded the declaration and from the minutes of the first meeting of the selected central committee (in which acute disagreements occurred between the various groups) that what had emerged was a fragile alliance rather than solid integration and unity. Each group brought with it into the new formation its own perceptions, perspectives, and ambitions. The laborious and controversial debate over the different groups' assessments of Nasser's policies was by no means near its end. Disagreements over the Marxist analysis and interpretation of Nasser's regime and its capacity to achieve the tasks of the national democratic revolution were immense. It has been argued that external factors played a major role in all stages of the development of the communist movement in Egypt between 1957 and 1965 and were related to the split, the unification, and the eventual dissolution of the party. Another important factor was the controversy over the nature of Nasser's regime.

After the 1956 Suez crisis, the tripartite aggression of Britain, France, and Israel against Egypt and Nasser's declaration of his socialist-oriented economic reforms, Nasser had become a symbol for Third World liberation movements. This instigated heated discussions, not only among Egyptian communists but among communists throughout the world over the role of the national bourgeoisie in economic and social transformation.

The impact of Nasser as a charismatic national anti-imperialist leader who might be able to achieve the task of the national democratic

106

revolution outside the classical Marxist formula of the proletarian revolution has been immeasurable. The idea of unifying the Egyptian communist groups was initiated by Nasser's achievements as explained by Sa'ad Rahmi: "The unification process corresponded to a rise in a new Nasserist trend. It was a new ideological creation . . . a new blossom flourishing in the brightness of Nasserism. These circumstances dictated it [i.e., unification]. In other words, had the negative aspects of Nasserism continued, the future of the unified party would have been different. The fact is that we and the others all met on the platform of fascination with Nasserism."[1]

Mubarak 'Abdu states in his manuscript "History of the Communist Movement in Egypt": "In 1957 a high tide of unity was flowing: so high that one can say the year 1957 was devoted to the accomplishment of the task of unity. This wave of unity was swept forward by the peoples' national battles of 1956–57 and the clearness of Nasser's policies, which demanded absolute support of the Egyptian communist movement."[2]

Other communist parties (especially in the Arab world, the Middle East, and Mediterranean countries) were important influences on the Egyptian communist movement from 1957 to 1965. The Iraqi and Lebanese communist parties were particularly influential, especially at the stage of unification, which they enthusiastically supported. The Italian Communist party also played a prominent role in the unity process in 1957–58 and in the dissolution process in 1964–65. Impressed with President Nasser's socialist experiment, the Italian Communist party, through its branch in Egypt's Italian community, influenced Egyptian communists to support Nasser first by uniting in 1958 and later by dissolving in 1965. Dina Forte, an active member of Egypt's Peace Partisans' Movement in the early 1950s, was prominent in the Italian Communist party in the 1960s and provided the special link between the Italian Communist party and the Egyptian movement.

Fakhri Labib in assessing the unification process stated: "I believe that some brother parties played a role in pressuring us to unite and that some members accepted the unity with great embarrassment. In other words, there was no real conviction. I believe that the Italian Communist party played a major role through comrades Baieta and Spano."[3] The final factor of particular significance in this period was the relationship between Nasser and the Eastern bloc, which was established in September 1955 by the Czech arms deal and continued to grow until its zenith with the Soviet agreement to build the high dam. This relationship not only strengthened Nasser's own belief that he could build socialism without a proletarian revolution but likewise seems to have convinced Soviet officials and scholars. A number of publications by Soviet scholars began advocating this new theoretical trend within the Marxist context. One work, translated from Russian to Arabic, entitled "Nasser and the Battle for Economic Independence, 1952–1972," declared:

> The liberation movement of the people of Asia, Africa, and Latin America plays the major role in the weakening of capitalism. The main direction of this movement at the present indicates that the struggle for liberation in many countries is turning, in practice, into a struggle against all exploiting relations of production be they feudal or capitalist. The second important feature of the contemporary liberation is that its vanguard is the countries that adopt noncapitalist modes of development, in other words, those countries which have followed the road toward the horizon of socialist society. Egypt is one of the first countries that has followed that road.[4]

To investigate the development of the united party, whose unity ended up being a path to dissolution, it is important to know not only how each group perceived, interpreted, and reacted to Nasser's proclamations and actions but also how far each was influenced by external factors, regional and international.

At the time of the impetus toward unity, there were three main Marxist organizations in the political arena: the Unified Communist party, the Communist party of Egypt (popularly known as the Banner after the name of its party circular), and the Workers and Peasants party. There were also two smaller groups: the Unity of Communists and the group of Fawzi Gurgis, which grew from a splinter group of the Unified Communist party to revive the former al-Nawat organization (see figure 6).

When representatives of those groups sat together to negotiate the proposed unity, it soon became clear that all they agreed on was the necessity for unity. There was no general agreement among them, and there were many points of disagreement on theoretical and ideological issues. There were even many clashing views in regard to what strategies and tactics the united party should adopt. It was agreed that these disagreements be shelved to achieve unity at any price. Unification was hastened by elements who wanted to guarantee the support of all Egyptian communists to Nasser, either because this was something they believed in or, according to members of the Banner, because they were weakened by the years of prison and torture and wanted to put an end to any confrontation with the authorities.

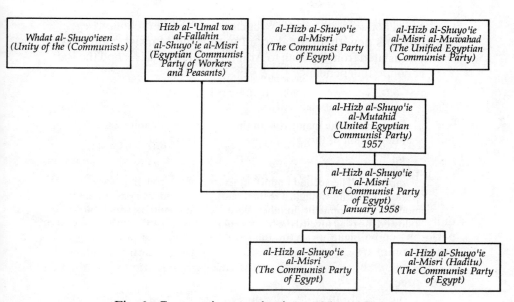

Fig. 6. Communist organizations, 1956–1959.

AL-HIZB AL-SHUYO'IE AL-MUTAHID
(UNITED EGYPTIAN COMMUNIST PARTY)

In this atmosphere, a coordination committee was formed consisting of Mahmud al-'Alim from the Unified Communist party, Helmi Yassin
from the Workers and Peasants party, and Sa'ad Zahran from the Banner.
The committee held several meetings and sometimes invited other members from the three organizations. At the first meeting of the committee,
representatives of the Workers and Peasants party, the Egyptian Communist party, and the Unified Communist party discussed the agenda,
which included the task of the committee and its limits and the committee's direct responsibilities.

The Egyptian Communist party's view, as recorded in the minutes
which were published by the Unified party, was that

> the task of our committee is to coordinate the people's activities. I
> therefore suggest in these circumstances of invasion and with the
> tasks of defense it poses to establish, besides our secret underground
> committee, another public committee to be called the Progressive

Committee for National Consolidation to rally the masses for the national battle. We believe that this public coordination will be a step toward the comprehensive unity for which our party strives. We believe that unity can be achieved in these phases:
1. Coordination in public activities.
2. Narrowing ideological differences.
3. Organizational unity.[5]

The representative of the Workers and Peasants party said: "The task of our committee is to take collective positive actions as a step toward comprehensive unity." The representatives of the Unified party stated: "The objective of our committee is to liase our activities in the struggle into collective unified activities as a step toward comprehensive unity. Although we do not believe in phases, we believe that a collective performance will lead us to the best ways of achieving unity. As for the public committee, we think that leaflets should be circulated to the masses signed by comrades from the three organizations and not by a committee.[6]

In the second meeting, the question of the public committee was once again raised. Representatives from the Banner seemed to have accepted the committee as a compromise though members of the Workers and Peasants party were against the idea. The representatives from the Workers and Peasants party stated: "With reference to the discussions in the previous meeting, our organization thinks that we should limit ourselves to our secret committee. The proposal of a public committee, we believe, is advanced for the current situation and it is against our strategy, which is to operate from within the governmental platforms under all circumstances and irrespective of all difficulties." The representative from the Unified party said, "We believe in the possibility of establishing a public committee together with our secret committee to coordinate our struggle in different fields.[7] Members of the coordination committee were endeavoring to solve organizational problems to achieve unity. Ideological and political disagreements were as great as organizational ones. Nevertheless, an attempt was made to gloss over these differences to achieve unity.

The first attempt in this direction was made by the Italian Communist party. Alberto Yako Fello asked members of the coordination committee some questions; he considered the answers to be a common assessment of the current situation in Egypt. These answers were published in the Italian communist newspaper.

There are two characteristic features of the current phase; on the one hand, the national bourgeoisie is seriously engaged in the struggle against imperialism. On the other hand, imperialism is using all means to try to defeat the struggle and topple 'Abd al-Nasser's government. Such a government cannot survive without the support of socialist countries and without receiving the support of a broad national front.

Unity has become possible now because differences between the organizations have greatly diminished. These differences were directed toward the role of the national bourgeoisie in the nationalist movement. Well . . . today we all agree on one central point which is manifested internally and internationally. The point is that the national bourgeoisie is spearheading the struggle for national independence.

The committee then outlined a common program for the three organizations: "The protection and enforcement of national independence and active defense of peace enforce the unity of liberated Arab countries which abolish the remnants of feudalism, put an end to monopolies, respect and consolidate democracy, build a progressive modern national economy, improve the standard of living of the masses, and make social and cultural reforms." The committee's answers concluded: "A characteristic feature of the current regime is the great victories which the nationalist movement in Egypt has achieved. For the first time in the modern history of Egypt we find a national government which is defending the rights of the country. It is supported by a broad alliance which includes the working class, the petty bourgeoisie, and the national bourgeoisie and is headed by 'Abd al-Nasser's government, which was able to head a victorious struggle against imperialism."[8]

The statement issued by the three organizations, the Banner, the Unified party and the Workers and Peasants party, embodied more or less the same concept:

The historical role of the Egyptian government is not limited to its stand alongside masses in the National Front to defeat imperialism in our country. It is also offering an influential contribution in the struggle against imperialism in all Arab countries. Egypt is setting an example for all Arab countries who are struggling for liberation and independence. Imperialists conspire and use the meanest devices. They persistently circulate rumors in an attempt to undermine the

great achievements which Egypt has accomplished and is accom-
plishing every day. They try to create doubts about the government's
stance, which is not questioned except by biased elements and imperialist agents.

The statement proceeds to refute allegations that the government is not
capable of solving its economic problems, especially that of unemployment. It attributes these problems to the war and emphasizes that "the
government is making great efforts to put an end to these difficulties." It
referred to the issues of individual liberties and human rights, which were
capitalized on by anti-Nasser elements: "The imperialists and their
agents shed crocodile tears about what they call a violation of human
rights and individual liberty, ignoring the fact that the Egyptian people
and Egyptian nationalists have never enjoyed the freedom and liberties
which they enjoy today. The only groups who have lost their freedom are
the imperialists and their hired agents and the reactionary fundamental-
ists." The statement then pleads for the release of the communists still in
prison, whom it describes as "the citizens best able to understand the
government's nationalistic policies, the elements most capable of defending this policy and rallying the masses around it."[9]

The statement concentrated on politics, mainly praising and affirm-
ing support for Nasser and his government. Ideological and theoretical
disputes were either glossed over or ignored. Each organization sought
to ensure that it would control the new formation when it materialized.
The Unified party, dominated by the Haditu element, which outnumbered
the other small groups forming the party, accused the Banner of trying to
control the new party's central committee. The representatives of the
Banner asked for equal representation. This was refused by members of
the Unified party. The Unified party nominated four members who were
in prison, however, whereas all those nominated by the Banner were
available so the latter had the majority of votes in the central committee
when it was actually formed. Members of the Unified party accused the
Banner of lacking popular support and having a very small membership.
This opinion was expressed by al-Rifaʻie: "The surprise was when we
found that the total number of members presented by the Banner did not
entitle them to more than one member in the central committee. In many
places the membership of the Unified party did not find anyone to unite
with."[10] Saʻad Rahmi of the Unified Egyptian Communist party, however,
contradicted this view: "I make testimony for history; there were lies regarding the subject of members. Their lists were a mere legend! I headed

a leading committee for the United party in Alexandria. The committee was composed of ten members, five from the Unified party and five from the Banner. The Unified party presented eighty members while the Banner presented only five in addition to the five members in the leading committee.[11]

Similar allegations were made a year later by Anwar Ibrahim from the Egyptian Communist party of Workers and Peasants against the Unified party, mainly Haditu. Ibrahim described the situation in Alminia: "In Alminia, the available leadership was from the Party of Workers and Peasants and the Banner while the Unified party was weak. But at the grass-roots level there was an urge for unity. There was no cheating in the lists of membership, as far as I know, in the provinces of Alminia and Beni Swafe. In Alminia the Banner presented forty members whereas the Unified party presented only ten."[12] On balance, the internal and external pressures toward unification overcame the ideological and organizational obstacles. In February 1957, the United Egyptian Communist party was announced by the Unified party and the Banner with the hope that the Workers and Peasants party would join at a later stage. A declaration statement was issued.

The declaration proclaimed that for the first time in its modern history, Egypt had become an independent republic and defender of the struggling people and bearer of a brave army. The nation was praised as united, strong, and the protector of the independence of the Egyptian people. The Egyptian state was glorified as entering a new parliamentary democracy with the expansion of political freedom and the furtherance of trade unions in the interest of the working class. The declaration called for greater unity among the communists, the working class, and even the national bourgeoisie, which had advanced the national revolution against the imperialist forces. Of particular significance, the communists were declared the most dedicated combatants in defense of the government. Moreover, President Gamal 'Abd al-Nasser was hailed as the national hero. Finally, the declaration affirmed the party's commitment to achieve unity with the Workers and Peasants party in the near future. The latter joined sooner than expected. A statement on January 8, 1958, declared the birth of al-Hizb al-Shuyo'ie al-Misri (the Communist party of Egypt), "the fruit of revolutionary unity between the Workers and Peasants party and the United Egyptian Communist party."[13]

AL-HIZB AL-SHUYO'IE AL-MISRI
(COMMUNIST PARTY OF EGYPT)

Reflecting on the unification of the Banner, the Unified party, and the Workers and Peasants party, Ahmed al-Rifa'i later observed: "It is possible to say that during 1956–57 the Unified party was dominated by the practical practices of Haditu and supported the twenty-second revolution of Haditu while the elements of the smaller organizations that joined the Unified party were not able to deal with Nasser, especially inasmuch as they had earlier devoted all their time and effort against Haditu and against its support for the movement of the army."[14] Similarly, Sa'ad Rahmi said, "The Banner imagined that the Unified party was a body without a head and that the thinkers of the Banner could ride onto that body and become its head."[15]

Not surprisingly, then, the first meeting of the central committee was more of a confrontation between the different factions than the inaugural session of a united party. Mohammed 'Ali 'Amir describes this confrontation: "In the first meeting Ahmed Khadhir delivered a speech in which he hailed unity and welcomed the comrades, but he criticized the comrades of the Banner for not nominating workers for the central committee and said that our future task should be to ease our orientation toward the workers. Comrades of the Banner responded angrily, and the inauguration turned into a confrontation."[16]

The central committee decided to divide the country into fifteen party districts. A committee was organized for each district with a central bureau for all. A journal, *Itihad al-Sha'ab,* and a bulletin were to be published regularly.[17]

The organizational disagreements actually represented ideological and political disputes which mainly revolved around the question of the party's relationship with Nasser. These disputes fell into two categories: disagreements between the various factions within the United party over the concept of Arab nationalism as represented by Nasserism and different concepts of the national democratic revolution and consequently different interpretations of the term *new democracy.*

Before the unity with Syria, the communists' concept of nationalism had differed totally from Nasser's. They viewed Arab nationalism as one phase in the long process of liberation and anti-imperialist activities. They never viewed it as an ultimate end in itself, whereas Nasser had always regarded Arab nationalism as the ultimate goal of the struggle. The communists considered the nation as a characteristic feature of the victory of capitalism over small feudal states, which would give way to internationalism when socialism prevailed in the future. This view emerged before the unity of the party, and the unity between Egypt and Syria, which happened at the same time, led to increased tension between Nasser and the Egyptian communist movement. It also augmented tension between hard-liners and moderate elements in the movement who were prepared to go halfway to meet Nasser's nationalism. Nasser's attitudes toward hard-liners were tough, and these people were subjected to oppressive measures. He was suspicious and mistrustful of moderates. Even when they tailored Marxist interpretations to defend his nationalist ideas, he insisted on drawing a clear demarcation between communism and nationalism.

The new party found itself lagging behind the nationalist torrent which was sweeping away all obstacles to the unity between Egypt and Syria. That unity appeared to be a practical manifestation of the correctness and validity of Nasser's ideals and the erroneousness and invalidity of the communists'. At the same time, it seemed that the moderates had a clear grasp of the situation and a clear vision of the direction in which the society was moving.

No matter how positively moderate communists spoke about him and praised his achievements, Nasser was always suspicious that they would jump on him at a certain point. He therefore always tried to guard his domain against them. His suspicion was manifestated in the attitude of the regime toward the new United party. Although the new party supported Nasser's internal and external policies, he did not show any change of attitude toward it at that stage; its members were even denied the right to stand for election to the National Union, which occurred at the same time as the unification of the party.

Political and theoretical disputes instigated a quick revival of the preunion differences. The rifts that were hurriedly patched up in the declaration of unity became apparent at their weakest point, that of organization. The first meeting of the central committee of the United party was devoted to overcoming the acute difficulties and to forming the politburo. It issued a declaration and other statements in support of Nasser on various occasions, particularly on the formation of the National Union and the unity between Egypt and Syria, irrespective of the unresolved differences in the party regarding both of these events. The central committee also discussed two organizational issues: the finance office and the problem of full-time party officials. According to former Haditu members, who composed the bulk of the Unified party, members of the Banner and members of the Workers and Peasants party were trying to curtail the influence of the elements of the Unified Party, particularly Haditu. Fakhri

Labib concluded that the conflict had reached crisis proportions. For instance, full-time officers were labeled as "tramps" and were made to appear to be an organizational problem when in fact they were a political problem because the majority of the full-time officers were drawn from the Unified party. Further, when these officers stopped receiving wages, some members of the Unified party reacted by ceasing their financial subscriptions and donations. They also established their own budgets and their own finances, thus creating an overlap. What was significant in this crisis was that the attempt to limit the influence of the Unified party, which was really a political issue, took the form of an organizational problem as a way of justifying the actions taken.[18]

Those on the opposite side also agree that it was a political issue but emphasize that Haditu was trying to dominate the new party through its large numbers of full-time officials. Helmi Yassin said in retrospect, "I would like, after all this time, to state the fact, which is that we were surprised immediately after the unity by comrades of the Unified party presenting immense numbers of full-time officials both in leading bodies and other ones, and we felt that the Unified party wanted to control all aspects of the party activities. It wanted to have all the full-time officials, and these are the ones who are necessarily the most influential members."[19]

Fawzi Habashi also states that it was a political confrontation and that the question of the full-time officials was just a guise. He maintains, "It is not true that the battle started because of the full-time officials. The battle within the party started because of a political confrontation over the question of unity between Egypt and Syria, and when the political differences started, the confrontation took different shapes. The issue of the full-timers emerged and the imaginary lists of full-time officials were discovered and consequently the comrades of Haditu started to flock together and refused to hand over their membership."[20]

These political differences, which took organizational form, became more acute, parallel with the mounting tension in the relationship between the regime and the communists over the questions of nationalism and democracy, especially after the army movement in Iraq. Some elements among the Egyptian communists, namely those of the Banner, saw in the collaboration between Kassem and the Iraqi communists an ideal that Nasser should follow in his relationship with the Egyptian communists. This aggravated the feeling of suspicion and mistrust toward the communists which Nasser had always fostered. Furthermore, Nasser viewed the communists' turning toward Kassem as an immediate threat to his position as the sole leader of the Arab nation. An attack launched against the communists reached its zenith in January 1959, when the authorities began taking measures to crush the communist movement. Under these circumstances a split occurred in the new party, and the two central committee meetings that were held emphasized factionalism rather than unity. A split was inevitable, and most speculations as to the real reasons for the split have some foundation. It is true that moderates wanted other elements to make concessions to Nasser in order to find a place for the communists in the state apparatus so that they could participate in policy making and thus in working toward political and social change. There is also some truth in the story that the hard-liners wanted to obtain recognition from Nasser and gain respectable conditions for collaboration. There also is some truth in the version that some elements felt worn out by repression and wanted an honorable surrender. All different factions, no matter what their real motives, blurred their problems with a screen of ideological, political, and organizational justifications.

After the confrontation over the issues of finance and full-time officials, four members of Haditu compiled a report under the title "The Facts of the Crisis Which Our Party Has Undergone." The report, written by Farouk (Fuad Habashi), Akif (Ahmed al-Rifa'ie), Ahmed (Shuhdi 'Atiyah al-Shaf'ie), and Khalil (Kamal 'Abd al-Halim), accused the members of the Banner and the Workers and Peasants party of being opportunists. It describes how they tried to control the new party and direct a severe blow to Haditu elements. The report accuses the Banner and the United Party of wanting to liquidate Haditu and affirmed that Haditu's victory lay with the masses, which fought to defend the unity against the accused. Moreover, the report rejects the claim that only the Banner represented true communism. But Haditu proved the victor because it made concessions to achieve unity. Thus the Haditu faction changed its political defeat to an organizational victory by obtaining a majority in the central committee of the new party. The report indicates that members of the Banner demanded nine seats out of nineteen on the central committee and threatened to secede from the party if their demand was not met. They were able, however, to conduct separate negotiations for unity with the Workers and Peasants party, which resulted in the Unified party gaining eleven seats, the Banner nine, and the Workers and Peasants fourteen.[21]

The report accuses the Banner and the Workers and Peasants party of opportunism and says that they always supported the nationalist government and that they were, in a way, supporting imperialism and its agents:

Those who opposed the revolution from its very first day, analyzing it as fascist, changed their stance after seven years of criminal acts. They made this change without seriously criticizing themselves and without admitting their mistakes in front of the masses. These were the people who are trying now to draw the party back to a position of enmity to nationalist rule and to the policy of emphasizing points of disagreement with the government rather than points of agreement and alliance. Their policy is one of creating doubts about the government's strength against imperialism, claiming that it has relations with the Eastern socialist bloc only to put pressure on imperialism to reach an agreement with it.[22]

The report went on to reveal what happened in the discussions of the politburo, quoting members of other groups, especially in regard to the relationship between the party and the government. The report even mentioned the pseudonyms of the speakers, which then became known to all, especially to security forces.

Members of the Banner and the Workers and Peasants party justifiably considered the report, which was published outside organizational channels and organs, not only as counter to the organization's interests but also as perfidious. Even some members of Haditu condemned the report.

In response, the politburo called for a meeting at which the majority of its members decided to expel the four members who wrote the report. They were accused of stealing one of the party's printing machines and of acting to sabotage the party, of which the report was an obvious demonstration.

Haditu could not afford this decision, especially after the dissolution of the Rome group, which consisted of some members of Haditu under the leadership of Henri Curiel, who lived in France at this time. He formed the group to gain outside material and moral support for the party. This was lost with the dissolution of the Rome group. Thus Haditu reacted vigorously to the expulsion decision. Shahata al-Nashar described the situation as extremely critical. Enormous pressures were brought to bear, and the Haditu group was subject to expulsion from the party. A series of meetings and negotiations was launched in an attempt to avoid a split because Haditu did not want one. In particular, al-Nashar tried to ensure that no split occurred. Moreover, violations of party discipline began to surface, thus prompting a meeting with the Unified party in Cairo, which was attended by fifteen members, including Fawzi Habashi, 'Adli Gurgis, Mohammed Hijazi, Marie Papaduponlas, Mohammed Osman,

and al-Nashar. Fuad Morsi of the leadership defended the decision to expel members and suggested that they had brought their problems upon
themselves. The split thus became a reality.[23]

Al-Nashar was responsible for the finances and the printing machine in the Cairo area. He was forced to surrender his responsibilities in
addition to handing over the membership list to a member of the Workers
and Peasants party. He refused. Al-Nashar claimed that the Workers and
Peasants party was anxious to expel the leadership of Haditu. Four prominent members were subsequently expelled in addition to perhaps the
most important one, Gamal Ghali, who was responsible for Giza. Gamal
al-Sharqawi described the response of Haditu elements to expulsion of
the members in similar terms.[24]

THE PARTITION OF AL-HIZB AL-SHUYO'IE AL-MISRI

At the second and last meeting of the central committee of the
United party it was decided to split: "The central committee got together
in its second separatist meeting. All the sick in summer resorts, the
sleepy and the pregnant turned up to put their mark on the decisions of
the politburo. Thus the central committee emphasized its determination
to put an end to the political dispute by its revengeful actions. It emphasized its determination to create a split."[25]

Members of the Banner and the Workers and Peasants party accused members of Haditu of treachery and expelled them. Even those
who accepted the decision and remained in the central committee were
soon expelled. The accusation was not without grounds. Ahmed al-
Rifa'ie admits that they were moving actively in liaisons with expelled
elements of Haditu. He maintains that expelled members remained de
facto in the party. For instance, Mohammed al-Zubayr was made responsible for the printing machine and Fuad Habashi was given the task of securing a place for it. There was no intention of forming an independent
organization, but prison conditions decided otherwise. No independent
organization was formed outside the prison. Leading members such as
Mubarak 'Abdu Fadhil, Bahig Nassar, Mohammed al-Gundi, Ahmed
Khadhir, and Mohammed 'Ali 'Amir continued the operations of the
party. Its public activities continued. Members participated openly in
trade unions and among the students. Moreover, the publishing house at
Dar al-Fikr operated as usual, and independent publications bearing the
name of the party were undertaken. Al-Rifa'ie points out that other members began to take tough measures against comrades who stayed with

them and even began to expel large numbers of the cadres. This situation persisted until they were all arrested in January 1959 when they declared an independent organization.[26]

Obviously, members of the Banner and of the Workers and Peasants party had their suspicions about the remnants of Haditu and worked together until they got rid of them. Members of the Workers and Peasants party turned to the members of the Banner, the weaker partner in the alliance against Haditu. Fakhri Labib described what happened:

> After the comrades of Haditu had gone, attacks were directed against the Banner because of its "rightist" stance. . . . After Haditu had gone, the party suffered many organizational problems, but in spite of that we succeeded in joining together and, to a great extent, the wounds were healed. A clearer and better defined political line crystallized, and we began to discuss and practice approaches to reach unity and confrontation . . . but soon differences between us began to become very acute. Comrades of the Banner agreed on that approach, but they were accusing us — the Workers and Peasants party and the remnants of the Unified party — of being ultraleftists and saying we were more for confrontation than unity. With the beginning of the arrests in September, when some comrades were arrested because they shouted in public meetings slogans such as "Like Kassem, O Gamal!" or "Like Iraq," differences over the political line of the party became more acute.[27]

In this atmosphere, a decision was made to reduce the number of members of the central committee to thirteen, distributed as follows: Abu Sayf Youssef, Helmi Yassin, Fuad 'Abd al-Mon'eim Shuhto, Louis Ishaq, Hassan Sidqi, and Mohammed Badr from the Workers and Peasants party; Mahmud al-'Alim, Sa'ad Rahmi, Fakhri Labib, and 'Abd al-Mon'eim Shatlah from the Unified party; and Fuad Morsi, Ismail Sabri, and Sa'ad Zahran from the Banner. Remnants of the Unified party took the side of the Workers and Peasants party against those of the Banner, and the Banner found itself squeezed. Abu Sayf Youssef of the Workers and Peasants party was elected secretary general of the party. The permanent committee was dissolved, and a secretariat of five members, including the secretary general, was formed. The other four members were Fuad Morsi (Banner), 'Abd al-Mon'eim Shatlah (Unified party), Fakhri Labib (Unified party), and Helmi Yassin (Workers and Peasants).

This was the situation when the government launched a massive campaign on January 1, 1959, against all communists. This date is generally accepted as the day the split was publicly voiced and Haditu declared itself an independent party, the Egyptian Communist party. The group, to some extent, felt secure and did not anticipate actions against them. Feeling secure, they proceeded with a planned meeting at 7:00 A.M. on January 1 at Mubarak 'Abdu Fadhil's place, which was clearly known to the police. As a result, when the police cracked down, all the leading figures were arrested. The only exceptions were Kamal 'Abd al-Halim, Fuad Habashi, Mohammed Youssef al-Gundi, and Ahmed Khadhir. Thus Haditu elements found themselves in a difficult situation, and they may have been expected to rescind their support for Nasser. Nevertheless, they continued to support the Nasser regime and affirmed their allegiance in writing personally to Nasser in September 1959.

The other groups in prison were two small organizations, the Unity of Communists, which was a splinter from Haditu, whose members had walked out in protest against Haditu's support for Nasser in the early days of the army movement, and a splinter group from al-Nawat, which had refused, under the leadership of Fawzi Gurgis, to join the Unified party when al-Nawat united with Haditu. The other major group was Jama'at al-Hizb al-Shuyo'ie al-Misri, members of the Banner and the Workers and Peasants party who remained in the United party when the Haditu element left. They continued, before the period in prison and after it for a while, to follow a hard line against Nasser's policies.

DISSOLUTION

Within two years of the harsh crackdown against the communists, two developments occurred in Egyptian politics that had a significant impact on the relations of the communist movement to the state. These developments were the manifest pursuit of a socialist transformation of the state and the manifest pursuit of a single-party state through absorption of progressive political forces into the state apparatus.

The socialist transformation of the Egyptian state was initiated in July 1961 with the following measures: (1) profit sharing, whereby 25 percent of profits in all enterprises were to go to workers; (2) participatory management by which four employees (at least two from labor) were to be elected by employees to the management boards of all enterprises; (3) a ceiling of 5,000 Egyptian pounds was placed on annual wages; (4) a progressive income tax was enacted to increase to 100 percent of income over 10,000 Egyptian pounds and 149 companies, including 15 banks and

17 insurance companies, were nationalized; (5) 51 percent of 91 companies not nationalized was to be publicly owned; (6) mass transportation
was taken over by the public sector; (7) the maximum amount of agricultural land that could be owned was limited to 100 feddans; and (8) all rents
were permanently frozen.

These sweeping measures were followed in 1962 by the nationalization of pharmaceutical companies, flour mills, and other essential
goods producers. The National Charter, adopted May 21, 1962, proclaimed Egypt to be a socialist, anti-imperialist, and Arab nationalist
state. This philosophy was subsequently embodied in the new constitution proclaimed on March 25, 1964. Article 1 stated: "The United Arab
Republic [UAR] is a democratic socialist state based on the alliance of the
people's working forces." This was further elaborated in Articles 3, 9, 12,
13, and 14. Thus the socialist character of the state was established in
principle, law, and policy.

The socialist character of the Egyptian state was formalized in the
international sphere as well. In the East-West competition, Egypt's increasingly friendly relations with the Soviet Union culminated in Nikita
Khrushchev's three-week visit to Egypt in May 1964 to open up the first
stage of the high dam. In addition, by the mid-1960s the UAR had become
a strident leader of Afro-Asian liberation. In one four-month period, for
example, the UAR hosted an African summit conference (July 1964), an
Arab summit conference (September 1964), and a nonaligned nations
conference (October 1964).

The creation of the Arab Socialist Union in 1962 inaugurated the
state's effort to absorb all progressive political forces into the state system. It was natural for Nasser to approach Haditu elements in seeking
communist cooperation. Ahmed Hamroosh states:

> Gamal 'Abd al-Nasser called 'Ali Sabri, Mohammed Hussein Hay-
> kal, and Ahmed Fuad for a meeting in June 1962. . . . Nasser asked
> every one of them to contact those whom they trusted to form cells
> of not more than ten persons for a vanguard organization. He said to
> Ahmed Fuad that he wanted a disciplined organization like the com-
> munist organization and one that did not have basic disagreements
> with Marxism on social and economic matters. Ahmed Fuad con-
> tacted me, and I started building a cell whose members were all pro-
> gressive revolutionaries. We formed a leading committee with
> Ahmed Fuad, al-Gibayli, and myself (all three ex-members of Had-
> itu). A number of communists who were released from detention
> joined us.[28]

Thus the idea of the dissolution of independent organizations and their integration in a vanguard organization of Nasser's was developing. In April 1964, Nasser released all communists from prison. A committee was appointed to help them find employment. On December 13, 1964, a new General Secretariat of the Arab Socialist Union was appointed with six of its sixteen members communists and socialists. Shortly thereafter, Nasser created a secret vanguard unit in the Socialist Union to lead the socialist transformation of Egypt. This unit, known as al-Tandhim al-Tali'i, included some leading communists.

A two-pronged approach was used to assimilate communists into the Socialist Union. In the first prong, Zaki Murad, Mohammed Shatta, Sharif Hatata, and others were seduced into joining the vanguard unit, provided they renounced their affiliation with the Communist party. The second prong was to convince the remaining party members to dissolve the party and join the Socialist Vanguard. Thus the communists found themselves in a very poor position: half of their leaders had already joined the vanguard organization while they were still negotiating, which weakened their negotiating position.

For the Communist party, Haditu, negotiations took place in several stages. Several meetings took place between al-Ahmed al-Rifa'ie, Mahmud al-'Alim, Fuad Habashi, and government elements (mainly represented by Mounir Hafez, one of the aides of Sami Sharaf, Nasser's secretary of information). At that point, it was agreed to merge the party and the vanguard unit and unify them at all levels. That agreement, however, lasted only a few hours. The communist representatives were then summoned to be told that Nasser was angry because they violated the secrecy of the agreement and that Field Marshal 'Abd al-Hakim 'Amir and other army leaders objected when they learned of it. So the agreement was canceled. The negotiating position of the Haditu group had become even weaker, and eventually it had no weight at all. At last, its members agreed to dissolve the party.

In tracing how the process was finalized, each group should be considered separately. Ahmed al-Rifa'ie described the process in Haditu:

> After the release some contacts were made between Zaki Murad and Mahmud al-'Alim on one side and Mounir al-Hafiz on the other. Al-Hafiz was known to belong to a group very close to Nasser which supported the idea of unifying the communists and Nasser's men in one organization. Then a meeting was held at Alexandria. It was attended by Ahmed Hamroosh and 'Abd al-Ma'boud al-Gibayli from

the vanguard organization and Fuad Habashi, Zaki Murad, and me.
The topic of the meeting was unity with their organization and the
organization of leadership in the different areas. We insisted at that
stage that we should have members on all committees in all regions
and districts.[29]

Nasser not only refused the idea but he also refused the idea of
amalgamating them all together.[30] What was the next step? Eid Salih answers this question: "After his release from prison, the engineer of the
dissolution was Kamal 'Abd al-Halim. "Comrade Khalil (Kamal 'Abd
al-Halim) attended the meeting of the committee of the Alexandria area
and discussed with them the idea of dissolution and the report which
would be presented to the conference of the party. When he felt the objec-
tions of myself, Sabir Zaid, Sayid Hassan, and Mohammed Younis, he
said, 'We are not actually going to dissolve the party. We are only going
to pretend to do so in order to get rid of the pressures from suspicious
elements.' He said that we should delegate him to negotiate with the government and he could go and negotiate while we went ahead to form a new
party."[31]

The conference met in September 1964, but no decision was made.
Another conference was called for March 14, 1965. By that time, it was a
matter of formalities for the decision had already been made. Most of the
prominent leaders such as Zaki Murad, Mohammed Shatta, Ahmed al-
Rifa'ie, and Sharif Hatata did not attend the conference because they had
already joined Nasser's vanguard organization. The junior cadres came
to the meeting, but the decision had already been made. Kamal 'Abd al-
Halim was delegated by the conference to finalize the process. He sent
the following telegram to Nasser, who had been reelected president:
"The most beautiful thing we present to you on this historic occasion is
the information that the representatives of the Egyptian Communist
party Haditu in their meeting held today decided to put an end to their
independent organization because of their belief in your call for the unity
of all the socialist forces in one revolutionary political organization, and
that this one party under your leadership is the substitute for our independent organization."[32]

Thus the Egyptian Communist party Haditu was dissolved. Fakhri
Labib reveals how the Banner and the Workers and Peasants party were
dissolved. "After our release, the bulk of our program had been achieved
while we were isolated. Nobody had or could suggest an alternative to
Nasser or even develop on his stance. A strange situation was reached:
the existence of a party formation without a program or independent ban-

ner. That was the basic reason for dissolution. I also want to put on record here that there were strong pressures and even threats from ex-Marxists who were more enthusiastic about the idea of dissolution than the men of the regime themselves. Some of those ex-Marxists were explicitly threatening a choice between 'dissolution or prison.' " Labib said that a conference was called: "There was no real discussion. The conference was not called for discussion. It was called to emphasize the dissolution. I know that some members were against the dissolution, but they voted for it to get rid of the leadership and build a new party."[33]

Sa'ad Rahmi corroborated this version of the dissolution: "After the release, the central committee met and responsibilities were distributed, but everything was going on behind the back of the central committee. The idea of dissolution began to be discussed at the zenith of our fascination with Nasserism. Haditu had dissolved itself, and I remember that an ex-Marxist [he refrains from mentioning the name] was pressuring and threatening us. A conference was called. It was attended by members of the central committee and a number of cadres. The rightist wave was very high. I admit that I voted for dissolution, as I was not far away from that wave of rightism. The dissolution was finalized without any serious discussion."[34]

Finally, Fuad Morsi contends that although dissolution might not correspond to the principles, it was an urgent necessity. There were many deserters, and only few comrades stood to defend communism. Moreover, Morsi pointed out that the Nasser regime had co-opted the policy of the Communist party and proclaimed the building of a socialist society based on scientific socialism. Indeed, Nasser was enlisting members in a vanguard party to lead the Socialist Union. This situation, Morsi argues, necessitated a pragmatic approach, one that stood in contradiction to the principles of communism and what the Communist party stood for. The only practical recourse was dissolution.[35]

On April 25, al-Ahram, the semiofficial newspaper of the Egyptian government, announced that it had learned that the "secret political organization which calls itself the Communist party of Egypt had decided to dissolve itself." In the final communique issued by the central committee, the reasons for the decision were outlined. The communique included self-criticism of the entire communist movement in Egypt. It also included a detailed assessment of the "deep-rooted social transformation that took place in Egypt under Gamal 'Abd al-Nasser's leadership of national alliance forces in the Socialist Union." The communique continued by expressing hope for future political action in Egypt, "which cannot be shouldered by anybody else but the Arab Socialist Union as the only organization that can carry the responsibilities of continuing the revolution in all national patriotic social, economic, and cultural spheres." It concluded that "this is the first time in history that a communist party ends its independent existence and accepts the leadership of the national socialist revolutionary forces."

7

The Third Movement, *1975–1988*

After the party formally dissolved itself in 1965, its members were totally demoralized. Those who believed that the dissolution of the party would result in their direct participation in the intellectual leadership of the socialist transformation of Egypt soon discovered that they were isolated, quarantined, and contained. A secret report to Nasser from a member of the central committee of the Arab Socialist Union on the dissolution of the communist parties reflected the suspicion that surrounded the communists. The report concluded that (1) The Communist party did not really dissolve itself and cease its activities. The declaration of dissolution only committed the party to dissolve its independent organizational structure. (2) The communists were said to be continuing to maintain that they were Marxist-Leninists. This meant that their ideas were in fundamental conflict with Arab socialism and the National Charter. (3) The dissolution was a pragmatic response to political conditions rather than an ideological commitment to the principles of the July 23 revolution. (4) The communists did not recognize the socialist achievements of the promulgation of socialist measures in 1961.

Thus although the prominent intellectuals of the party were given some avenues of intellectual expression such as editorship of the journal *al-Tali'ah,* they were emasculated politically. Many were absorbed in Tali'at al-Ishtirakiin, popularly known as al-Tandhim al-Tali'i, but they were not allowed to participate. In fact, the Nasserized leadership of al-Tandhim al-Tali'i successfully isolated the communists and immobilized them. Nasser's trusted friend and minister of various portfolios from 1964 to 1971, Sha'rawi Jum'a, was secretary general of al-Tandhim al-Tali'i. He insisted that serious attempts were made to integrate the communists into the organization but at the same time to make sure they did not take it over.[1]

They were absorbed into the organization as individual Marxists but were treated as potential co-conspirators. According to Sha'rawi Jum'a,

> I remember that President Nasser during his meeting with the members of the Executive Bureau of Cairo and Giza in March 1966 answered a question in regard to the stand of the Executive Bureau toward communists, stating, "As for the question on the communists, they have good people among them. Prior to the 1952 revolution, they could not find another avenue to fight for the freedom of this country and its independence." The Marxists were given the opportunity to join the agencies of the vanguard organization from its inception. When I assumed the office of general secretary of the Socialist Vanguard [1964], I knew a great deal about the communists and their capacity for political action. Thus I suggested the inclusion of the outstanding elements among them to work with us in the Executive Bureau. When I submitted the names to Nasser, he did not object to any of them and did not add any to the list. This is clear evidence that there was no deal between Nasser and the Marxists. The choice was personal.[2]

The split vision of the role of former communists in the political process is reflected in the following incident:

> When the new building of al-Ahram was opened in 1966, Nasser visited al-Tali'ah there and met with the staff, the majority of whom were formerly prominent members of the communist party. During the visit, he listened to their concerns about their level of participation in the leadership of Egypt's socialist transformation and what they perceived to be the deliberate effort to isolate them. They pointed out that not one former communist was elected to any prominent post in the Socialist Union. Nasser turned to the distinguished communist leader Abu Sayf Youssef and asked, "Did you run for any post?" Abu Sayf Youssef replied no, and Nasser responded, "You are very smart." Turning to the group, he noted, "Your role is like that of St. Peter; you are to propagate, not lead."[3]

The story shows that Nasser envisioned a specific role for the former communists and had no intention of allowing them to take over the political leadership of the Socialist Union. He wanted them in the service of the state, not in its vanguard, as the communists anticipated.

Gradually, the former communists withdrew from active public participation. Sporadic attempts to reorganize the Communist party were quickly squashed by the powerful intelligence and security agencies. Even the slightest suggestion of reorganization was met with harsh measures. The intelligence agency tactics were termed *al-Dharabat al-Ijhadhiyah* (abortive strikes), a term used by the security agencies to describe the policy of preemptive strikes against any indication of organized political activism.

In the last days of Nasser, as a result of the shake-up following Egypt's disastrous defeat in the 1967 Arab-Israeli war, the communist movement was revitalized. Three different streams can be identified: the Marxists who participated in but became disaffected with Nasser's political institutions; old-guard communists who never accepted the dissolution of the Communist party; and young militant university students.

Among the first stream, initiated by Marxists disillusioned by their efforts to cooperate with Nasser, three main circles emerged, then consolidated into one. The largest, most effective, and longest lasting of these circles was called Jama'at Bila Isim (Group without Name). For purposes of secrecy, the group never carried an official name, although it published some founding documents under the name of Ahmed 'Urabi al-Misri. It was well known that this was a new organization, but the style of its publications led many to believe it was led by the old guard. But the group was so secret that nobody could even guess at the membership.

The other two circles were smaller and had fewer resources. One of them issued a single publication, *al-Shurooq* (The Sunrise), but the group was immediately discovered by the police and its members arrested and harassed. The other circle, also without a name, was composed of a limited number of old cadres.

Under pressure from the harsh security screen against communist activities, the three groups united into one in April 1972 and published under the name Ahmed 'Urabi al-Misri reports analyzing Egypt's socioeconomic and political problems. During the October 1973 war with Israel, the group began issuing a leaflet called *al-Intisar* (The victory) for public distribution. The leaflet was initially published irregularly in response to issues that arose. By the end of 1984, *al-Intisar* was being distributed outside Egypt. From issue 122, it was distributed internationally from Cyprus. The successful repeated clandestine publication of the leaflet and its widespread distribution and circulation reflect a sophisticated organization and experience leadership.

The first document issued by the founding central committee of the newly united group, *Min-al-Tajmi' ila Bina' al-Hizb* (From the gathering to the building of the party), published in January 1974, addressed the minimum conditions required for the establishment of a communist party. The publication declared that the goal of unification was ultimately the creation of a communist party but identified the basic conditions in the internal and external environments that had to be achieved before the goal could be realized. The internal environment was defined as the basic political, organizational, and philosophical foundations of the party. A basic requirement was a skilled cadre with an advanced level of theoretical sophistication. Another requirement was the development of an administrative apparatus for managing information and communications systems. In the external environment it was necessary to achieve a level of contact and direct involvement with the working class and poor peasants, as well as a presence within the national and democratic forces in the country.

The second document published by the unified group, in August 1974, was called *Mashrou' Barnamij 'Amil lil Qewa al-Sha'biyah al-Misriyah* (A draft program for action for the Egyptian popular forces). The document presented a national program with ten basic aims: /

1. The liberation of Sinai and the Arab lands occupied by the Israeli enemy in 1967 and supported by American international imperialism.

2. A just solution to the Palestinian problem based on the rights of the Palestinian people to self-determination on their land and the establishment of a completely sovereign national state.

3. Strengthening and defending the political, economic, and cultural independence of the nation.

4. The achievement of comprehensive and substantive democratic transformation in all aspects of political, social, economic, and cultural life.

5. Defense of the progressive social accomplishments of the July 23 revolution and the struggle for their development.

6. Achievement of comprehensive economic development in the shortest possible time.

7. A fundamental social and economic reform and more decisive attention to the solution of people's problems and raising their standard of living.

8. The achievement of comprehensive and substantive cultural transformation and the eradication of illiteracy in five years.

9. Support for and unification of all Arab forces struggling for liberation, social progress, and unity.

10. A foreign policy to serve national and progressive aims based on strengthening friendly relations with all the forces of progress and peace in the world.[4]

The second stream in the revitalization of the communist movement was initiated by the old-guard communists who never accepted the dissolution of the party and never participated in the Socialist Union. A small, committed core, this group initiated an ultrasecret and tightly knit circle. The circle had no name until 1975, when it declared itself to be al-Hizb al-Shuyo'ie al-Misri: January 8.

The final stream was composed of newcomers to the political scene, mainly young university students, unseasoned in politics and impatient for change, who grew out of a group called Kutab al-Ghad (Tomorrow's Authors), which became very prominent during the student movement of 1972. From Kutab al-Ghad developed a communist circle characterized by left extremism, condemnation of the earlier communist movement, and contempt for the 1965 dissolution decision. In 1975, this group declared itself Hizb al-'Umal al-Shuyo'ie al-Misri.

Thus by 1974, these three streams were engaged in organizational activities independent of and in competition with the others. The communist movement at the beginning of the last quarter of the twentieth century was considerably different in configuration and context from its predecessors but still displayed the fragmentation that characterized the movement from its inception. This fragmentation became manifest with the rebirth of three separate communist parties. The next section of this chapter examines the doctrine and strategy of each of these parties from the political documents they produced.

JAMA'AT BILA ISIM DECLARES ITSELF THE EGYPTIAN COMMUNIST PARTY

On January 1, 1975, a workers' strike took place in Helwan, Egypt's major industrial center. It quickly spread to Cairo, where demonstrations in the Bab-Alouq area turned violent and looting took place. The government accused the communists of leading the strikes and demonstrations and arrested about five hundred communists, leftists, and Nasserites. The arrest campaign concentrated on the largest communist group, Jama'at Bila Isim, which produced *al-Intisar* and the Ahmed 'Urabi al-Misri papers. Among those arrested were some of the leading communist figures, including Nabil al-Hilal, Zaki Murad, Mubarak 'Abdu Fadhil, and Mohammed 'Ali 'Amir.

The arrests failed to paralyze the group, however. It continued its activities and did not delay the planned announcement of the rebirth of the Egyptian Communist party. On May 1, 1975, announcements were sent to all communist and workers' parties throughout the world to proclaim the new party. The announcement stated the objectives of the party:

1. The total liberation of all Arab land occupied as a result of the 1967 aggression.

2. The guarantee of the legitimate national rights of the Palestinian people and their right to self-determination in their own land and the rejection of all partial, bilateral, and capitulatory solutions.

3. Resistance to all imperialist conspiracies that aim to push the country into surrendering to the imperialist designs, to isolate it from the anti-imperialist and anti-Zionist Arab camp, and to open the door to imperialist capital in order to regain its control over the foundations of the economy.

4. Resistance to the reactionary and right-wing conspiracies to cooperate with imperialist designs, to regress in the field of economic development, to retract the social and economic progress, and to destroy the achievements of the workers and peasants.

5. The completion of the aims of the national democratic revolution and the march forward on the road of social progress toward socialism.

6. Continuation of the struggle for the achievement of a comprehensive democratic transformation which guarantees the fullest democratic rights to the masses of the people.

7. Continuation of the struggle to achieve the daily economic demands for the masses of workers, peasants, revolutionary intellectuals, and toiling masses.

8. Continuation of the struggle to achieve national, progressive, and democratic Arab unity.

9. Resistance to the attempts of imperialist and local reactionaries to weaken and strike an alliance with the socialist camp and its vanguard, the Soviet Union; and to struggle to strengthen friendship and cooperation with the Soviet Union and the socialist countries.[5]

Writing on the fourth anniversary of the party's founding, Zaki Murad (Salah) noted:

We refused to allow it to come into the world without securing its survival and [guaranteeing] the conditions for its growth even in the face of increasing difficulties and obstacles. For that reason, its birth was delayed a few years. That is because we insisted that prior to its coming to life, it must be a strong structure that can resist the storm its rebirth will create, the inevitable and natural logic of class struggle. Imperialism and its agents, who were secure since the 1960s because of the disappearance of the forum for the independent revolutionary Marxist-Leninist working class, will not stand idle in the face of the return of the strong enemy of its designs. The Egyptian bourgeoisie, including the national bourgeoisie, was forced to take a negative stand toward the creation of the new independent forum of the working class because this bourgeoisie failed completely in leading the Egyptian national movement at this new historic stage. . . . Thus the infant from the moment of its birth must be strong . . . and able to respond to blows without being destroyed. The early comrades may remember that for years we insisted on refusing to give our organization the name of a party, even though the circles were united [and agreements were reached] on the basic political and philosophical foundations for the new structure. Rather, we preferred to continue being a Marxist-Leninist organization without a name until we could attain the conditions to secure its continuity, vitality, and ability to withstand the most severe blows. A barrier against independent political activity had been firmly established in the country for almost a quarter of a century. Even the Marxist-Leninist party that for a while challenged the barrier eventually surrendered to it and withered away. . . . The control of the security agencies was great, the imperialist reactionary right-wing alliance was moving quickly to impose its absolute control over the country after aborting the struggle of our people and army. . . . Under these conditions we refused to bear the responsibility of declaring a party. . . . In this new stage, we must be

careful to avoid all the mistakes and the main pitfalls of the previous
[communist movements] whether in policy, organization, or the
spheres of the international proletariat and the revolutionary solidarity to the movement of the Arab working class (the communist movement in the Arab countries and the Arab liberation movement in
general).[6]

In July 1975, the party issued its first political program report.[7] The
document concentrated on internal, national, and regional Arab conditions and the nature of the Sadat regime. The program of the party was
delineated in terms of the concrete conditions facing Egypt and the Arab
world. The most significant conditions were identified as the American-
Saudi alliance of reactionary forces; the American-Israeli alliance of
imperialist-colonialist forces; and the emerging American-Egyptian alliance under the policies of the Sadat regime, which placed Egypt on the
axis of the American-Saudi and American-Israeli alliance systems. Thus
a direct consequence of Sadat's policies was the increasing isolation of
Egypt from the Arab world, which increased Egypt's dependence on the
United States and its acquiescence to Israeli policies of colonization of
the occupied territories, suppression of the Palestinian resistance movement, and aggression against Lebanon.

All opposition within Egypt to Sadat's policies was fully suppressed, and a de-Nasserization program undertaken to dismantle all
progressive programs and remove all obstacles to rapacious profit-taking
by internal reactionaries in alliance with multinationals. "There is a fierce
conflict going on today between the forces of imperialism, Zionism, reactionary, and right-wing forces in our country on one side, and the
masses of our people with all their national democratic and progressive
forces on the other side. The last campaign of arrests is an integral part of
the conflict; it serves the interests of the aggressive alliance and paves the
way for destroying all national and social gains [made during the Nasser
era], for pushing through the 'American solution,' and for assuring
Egypt's isolation and abandonment of the Arab liberation movement."[8]

At this stage in Egypt's history, the tasks of the party were identified
as exposing the U.S.-sponsored policies of capitulation and pacification
in the Arab-Israeli conflict; exposing and resisting the effort to isolate
Egypt from progressive Arab forces and the anti-imperialist camp; defending the rights of workers and peasants and mobilizing them "to
counter any encroachments on them or any violations of democratic liberties"; establishing a worker-peasant alliance and a front of popular
forces; and transforming the party into a mass party by establishing "the
closest ties of struggle between our party and the masses."[9]

The party's tasks were delineated based on the membership's analysis of the political trends emerging under existing internal and external conditions. The two most significant trends were identified as the integration of the Egyptian economy in the international capitalist system and the isolation of Egypt in the Arab and international spheres.

The open-door policy constituted the practical means of Egypt's integration into the world capitalist order. The outcome was predicted as the increasing dependency of Egypt on the international capitalist order, the progressive underdevelopment of Egypt's productive forces through this dependency, and the progressive impoverishment of the masses as a consequence of the deterioration of productive forces:

> Open door is the policy of one segment of the Egyptian ruling bourgeoisie in the sphere of economic development dependent upon foreign and local capital in order to strengthen capitalist production relationships within the framework of imperialist dependency, in other words within the framework of international capitalism. The Egyptian bourgeoisie offers this policy as the only alternative left for the Egyptian economy to get rid of the difficulties of the years following the June 1967 defeat. Resorting to this choice in economic policy is based mainly on the encouragement of foreign, Arab, and private Egyptian capital. This capitalist development policy is not a solution we were forced to adopt. Rather, it is a conscious choice coinciding with the selfish interest of the Egyptian bourgeoisie ruling class.[10]

Settlement with Israel constituted the practical means of isolating Egypt from progressive Arab and international forces. The predicted outcome was the integration of Egypt into the American alliance system. At the regional level, this would effectively subordinate Egypt to the American-Saudi alliance of reactionary forces and at the international level to the American-Israeli alliance of imperialist/colonialist forces.

> A partial bilateral, incremental agreement between Israel and Egypt will isolate Egypt from the Arab liberation movement and split Arab solidarity. This campaign is executed under the aegis of very close relations, a strong alliance, and coordinated planning with the most reactionary and regressive forces in the region (Saudi Arabia, Iran, Jordan, the Gulf states, and Oman). The timing coincides with the diligent efforts to undermine relations with our most sincere and dependable allies; in their forefront is the Soviet Union. All this is taking place while the reactionary and right-wing forces and the influence of parasitic capitalists increase inside the state institutions.[11]

The party politbureau met in June and July 1978 to formulate a program of action to respond to the deteriorating economic conditions in Egypt and Sadat's initiatives vis-à-vis Israel. An urgent program for action was announced in July in which the party's immediate tasks were identified as the overthrow of the "parasitic capitalist regime," the rejection of the capitulation policy with Israel, the mobilization of the masses to liberate all occupied Arab land, return of Egypt to the progressive Arab camp, the end of the open-door policy, and democratic reforms in Egypt.[12]

By the time the Camp David Accord was signed in November 1978, the party's predictions appeared manifest. In December 1978, the party issued the following announcement: "These agreements . . . are a completion of the aims of the 1967 aggression and a continuation of the policies of the May 1971 regime which aims at moving Egypt from the camp of national liberation to the camp of dependency and client status to American imperialism and Israel. . . . The parasitic ruling capitalists of Egypt welcomed . . . their new role as the humble servant of American imperialism and international Zionism in exchange for their support of this regime against the increasing anger of the popular masses."[13]

In the same declaration, the party identified the aims of the Camp David Accord to be the creation of a tripartite detente between Israel, Egypt, and the reactionary oil-exporting regimes. In sponsoring the accord, the declaration argued, the United States was seeking to reduce the threat posed by the Arab-Israeli conflict to the security of petro-dollar flows from the Gulf to the West. In this context, the Camp David Accord was viewed as the first stage of the strategy; it was anticipated that the reactionary oil-producing states would join the Camp David process in the second stage.[14]

In January 1980, a detailed report on the Egyptian situation was issued summarizing the politbureau's meetings of December 1979. The meeting was held to consider the internal situation in Egypt in light of the local, parliamentary, and union elections held the previous summer. The report maintained that internal developments verified the predictions of the July 1979 politbureau meetings. The Sadat regime had isolated Egypt completely in the regional and international spheres. Even the reactionary oil-producing states rejected the Camp David Accord and distanced themselves from Egypt in the tenth Arab Summit Conference in Tunis in November 1979. Thus the American strategy had failed, leaving Egypt isolated in the Arab and international spheres, totally dependent on the United States. Negotiations between Egypt, the United States, and Israel to implement self-rule for the Palestinians in accordance with the Camp

David Accord had failed because of Israeli rigidity and Sadat's capitulations. In fact, as a result of the Camp David Accord, Israel was able to increase its rate of settlement in the occupied territories. Economic conditions in Egypt had deteriorated, contrary to Sadat's promises of improvement as a result of American financial assistance after Camp David, and the masses became disillusioned with the Sadat regime. The open-door policy produced rapid inflation, unbridled consumerism, multinational penetration of the economy, and the destruction of local industry. These conditions thus contributed to the greater exploitation of labor. Finally, the regime had become more oppressive against all democratic forces.[15]

In reviewing the situation of the party, the report identified two imperative tasks. The first was to transform it into a mass political organization; the second was to form an Egyptian national democratic front. "While these two main duties are closely connected ... the first duty should receive our greatest attention. Thus the creation of a mass-based communist party is our path to the formation of the national democratic front. The front is the foundation that we cannot do without if we really aim to establish a national democratic front government and system on the ruins of the existing regime."[16]

In September 1980, the party held its first congress. The congress produced five documents: the party program, its bylaws, an organizational report, and two working papers — "The National Democratic Front in Egypt" and "Consolidation of the Egyptian Communist Movement."[17] The program declared:

> The Egyptian Communist party has not emerged from a vacuum. ...
> It is an extension of the Egyptian national revolution; it inherits its
> accomplishments, is proud of its culture, and enriches it. ... It is a
> continuation of the revolutionary march of the Egyptian communist
> movement from its initiation in the 1920s. It recognizes the achieve-
> ment and successes [of the movement], and it does not disassociate
> itself from the deviations and failures [of the movement]. ... The
> Egyptian Communist party, then, is the fruit of more than half a cen-
> tury of the Egyptian communist struggle. ... The Egyptian Com-
> munist party is the party of the Egyptian working class ... but this
> does not mean that the party supports only the interests of the work-
> ing class. Our party is required to play a leading role in the entire na-
> tional and class struggle in society. ... The Egyptian Communist
> party is an integral part of the Arab national liberation movement and
> one advanced vanguard of it.[18]

The program declared the party's doctrinal basis to be Marxism-Leninism. It emphasized that theoretical principles of this doctrine were modified in their application to the specificity of the Egyptian national struggle and historic tradition. Thus, although the ultimate aim of the party was to establish a communist society, this long-term goal must be achieved through a chain of social, political, and economic transformations.

> Thus this program which our party presents today is not a program for building socialism in Egypt, because the main immediate aim which is now pressing the Egyptian working class and its allies is not building socialism; rather, it is specifically the necessity of saving the nation from the counterrevolution, alleviating the destructive impact of [the counterrevolution], and overthrowing the counterrevolutionary regime [of Sadat] . . . and to continue the completion of the aims of the national democratic revolution.
>
> On this basis, the Communist party of Egypt clearly delineated its program to be to thwart the counterrevolution and to achieve the aims of the national democratic revolution.[19]

The report provided a detailed analysis of the historic evolution of the Egyptian national movement and then addressed the current circumstances and tasks of the Egyptian national revolution, starting with the party's position vis-à-vis the international situation.

> 1. The Egyptian democratic national revolution is taking place in an era of transition toward socialism.
>
> 2. The major contradiction in the current era exists between the world socialist system and the world imperialist system.
>
> 3. The world revolutionary process in the current era will be consummated through combative solidarity among three major revolutionary forces—the international socialist system, the revolutionary working-class movement in the advanced capitalist countries, and the international movement of national liberation, in which the working class is playing a growing role.
>
> 4. This era is witnessing the fragmentation and collapse of the world's imperialist system and a deepening of the general crisis of capitalism.

5. Nonetheless, the phenomenon of fragmentation and the crisis world imperialism is suffering from do not in any way mean the elimination of the danger of American imperialism.

6. The contradictions among imperialist countries are becoming increasingly aggravated.

7. International developments underline the decisive role the world communist movement is playing in the world revolutionary process.

The program moves on to discuss "the Egyptian national revolution and the Arab situation." It deals with the Middle East problem, the scheme of imperialism, the main contradiction, the dangers of apostasy, the export of counterrevolution, the victories of the Arab liberation revolution, and the faltering of the Arab revolution. On the Palestine issue, the party declared a strong nationalist position, advocating "the establishment of a strong secular state on all the Palestinian soil" as an ultimate aim (see Appendix D). Although this was the party's position at the time, it conflicted with the position of the Palestinian Communist party when it was subsequently established. But the Palestinian party did not exist in 1980 when the Egyptian party's program was formulated. The Egyptian party later modified its position, yielding to the Palestinian party on issues related to Palestine. Joint statements were issued by the parties in regard to the Palestine issue and the Middle East situation.

In a report entitled "Report on Unity: A Look at the Path to Unity," the program emphasized the importance of unity in the communist movement. Although this party identified itself as the main body of the movement in Egypt (recognized locally, regionally, and internationally), it also recognized the existence of other Marxist cells and groupings in Egypt and dedicated itself to cooperation and coordination with these groups, striving for unity of action and eventual unity of organization.[20] By the end of 1987; circumstances in the Egyptian communist movement dramatically changed and resulted in a reexamination of the unity issue.

For the first time, the party officially recognized the serious error of the 1965 dissolution. In a report in the program entitled "Our Party Possesses Potential for Development into a Mass Party: The Dissolution Decision of the Egyptian Communist Organization Was a Grave Political Mistake,"[21] the program examined the negative consequences of the decision and evaluated it as

a great gulf between old-guard communists and the Egyptian youth
who began adopting Marxism in the mid-1960s. This produced fragmentation in Marxist circles later. Some exploited that gulf in order
to isolate the party from the youth and push the youth toward extreme Marxist groupings that adopt adventurist positions in both policy and organization.

No doubt the departure of the old guard from the party and the
withdrawal of the youth from it weakened the possibility of our party's transformation into a mass party.

Outside Egypt we notice that the dissolution of the communist
organization encouraged Numeiri to exercise the same pressure on
the Sudanese communists to dissolve their party.[22]

Facing the problem of how to build a mass party, the program re-
iterated the December 1979 politbureau report. It recommended seven
steps in the building for mass organization: strengthen and support the
central committee of the party; build political organizations in working-
class areas; create new cadres in the different regions of Egypt and
strengthen existing regional leadership; increase the number of full-time
party organizers; devote more attention to youth; expand party membership; and implement party bylaws.[23]

Although information on the actual activities of the party is not
available, the above list provides an indication of the direction of party
praxis in the decade of the 1980s. Further indications of party activity are
indicated by a report issued in February 1983 (see Appendix D for full
text). The report examined international, regional, and internal conditions. Reviewing Egypt's circumstances since the coming to power of
Mubarak, the report noted no basic changes in the class nature of the regime. In effect, the open-door policy continued, and the regime had become more oppressive toward the working class and small peasants as
economic conditions deteriorated and private concentration of wealth
continued. With the party in the vanguard of opposition, consciousness
among the masses and intellectuals was increasing, and the natural link-
ages between internal conditions and external events (especially Israel's
invasion of Lebanon) were more clearly perceived. The class struggle
going on in Egypt has been distinguished, in 1988, by

an incipient surge toward national struggle, an awakening in the national struggle thanks to the parties, the national and progressive
forces, the labor and professional unions, and committees with the
character of a front, such as the National Committee to Support the

Palestinian and Lebanese People and the Committee to Defend the National Culture. This struggle has started to create a qualitative transformation in the consciousness of growing sectors of the people and in the mass atmosphere in general toward Camp David and normalization, and the effects of the al-Sadatist brainwashing and his psychological war against Arab affiliation and national affiliation have started to disappear.

An escalation of the democratic struggle, embodied in the broad campaign against the continued state of emergency and its extension for another year, the demand for the release of prisoners, the campaign against torture, and the enlarged lawyers' movement for the restoration of legitimacy to the Lawyers' Union.

The growing economic and social struggle, embodied in a series of workers' and students' strikes and sitdowns and a fierce struggle in defense of the public sector and the gains of the workers and peasants.

In all these struggles, our party has played a vanguard, innovative, effective, and growing role.[24]

An abridged version of the report set forth the immediate tactical objectives of the party:

The national-democratic forces of Egypt must forthwith draw up a realistic minimum program of national salvation based on three fundamental principles:

1. The ensuring of freedom of national expression of will and the restoration of national sovereignty and of the country's political and economic independence.

2. The satisfaction of the people's socioeconomic demands.

3. The achievement of an all-embracing turn toward democracy.

These three principles are interrelated and complement each other. None can be separated from the others or put into effect while ignoring the others. Our party is therefore opposed to all calls for pushing any of these three crucial tasks into the background.[25]

In 1984, the party held its second congress, reflecting its continuing development and vitality. That the party could hold a second congress inside Egypt in extreme secrecy is evidence of its organizing and security abilities.

Writing in 1987 in the *World Marxist Review,* Mohammed Magdi Kamal, a member of the central committee politbureau of the party, stated:

Although participation in a strike is an offence punishable with 25 years of forced labour, strikes do not cease. In 1985–1986 alone some 100,000 people took part in more than 40 strikes. Unrest has spread to the state apparatus as well. In February 1986 a mutiny broke out in the security forces (these troops are used for punitive purposes). All these actions were brutally supressed by the authorities. Many strikers, including members of our party, were imprisoned. The government usually accuses Communists of organising strikes.

Although the leadership of the Egyptian Federation of Labour (EFL) submits to the government and is connected with the ruling party, pressure from the working masses has forced it to oppose the dismantling of the public sector, privatisation and affiliation with the International Confederation of Free Trade Unions, contacts with the World Federation of Trade Unions are beginning to be restored.

Industrial unions and committees have assumed a patriotic stand. The Helwan Steel Works local can be cited as an example: it firmly opposed a visit to the enterprise by the President of Israel. The Left scored a major success in the 1983 elections to union committees and boards. However, intervention by the current EFL leadership and the security service prevented the elected candidates of the left to win seats on ruling trade union bodies.

Our comrades have sponsored the establishment of the Union of Egyptian Peasants which unites several thousand agricultural labourers, owners of small land plots and tenant farmers. The union has branches in all provinces, fights against the onslaught on the gains of the peasants won as a result of the agrarian reform, and together with the working class, strives to deliver the country from imperialist slavery.

There is also growing opposition to the policy of the authorities on the part of other mass organisations, such as unions of lawyers, journalists, physicians and actors, clubs of college and university teachers, the committee for the defence of national culture, as well as youth, student and women's associations.

Resistance has frustrated all attempts at forcing the Egyptian people to accept normalisation of relations with Israel. Significantly, not a single candidate of the ruling National Democratic Party dared support the Camp David Accords in the recent elections to the National Assembly. Hostility to the US presence on Egyptian soil and to Egypt's ''special ties'' with the United States is growing.

The Egyptian Communist Party, still having to operate underground, is playing a prominent part in directing these actions. *Al-Intisar,* its clandestine newspaper, exposed imperialist and reactionary
schemes and calls on the people to fight for a programme of national
salvation. Striving to consolidate its ties with the masses, the party
issues numerous leaflets on vital issues of concern to them and uses
every opportunity for legal forms of political work among the working people. . . . The demand that the ban on the Communist Party be
lifted is heard increasingly, supported by all opposition parties. In
connection with the recent verdict in the "Trial of the Egyptian Communist Party" which sentenced 34 Communists and patriots to
prison terms, the leaders of these parties and of the lawyers' and
journalists' unions sent a message to the President of Egypt insisting
that the sentence be revoked.[26]

In the April 1987 elections to the Egyptian parliament, the party
nominated four of its well-known leaders as candidates. Because the
party was banned from running in the election, the candidates, as individuals on nonparty lists (according to the Egyptian electoral law), were
supported by the Tagamu' party through the publication of the campaign
literature in its newspaper. In addition, the Tagamu' party did not run its
candidates in these districts so as not to compete with the communist
candidates. The Tagamu' party is a political party made up of an alliance
among independent Nasserists, nationalists, socialists, and Marxists.
The Tagamu' party was formed in 1977 when its members disaffiliated
and disengaged from all other political organizations to create an independent progressive political party. The four communist party candidates in the election ran as independents, espousing a communist party
program. No communist candidates won a seat. This was anticipated, but
the campaign provided a public forum for their views, and this was the
purpose of the exercise. Tagamu's party paper, *al-Ahali,* published the
programs of its candidates, including the communists. Thus the election
campaign provided an opportunity to voice the party views in public forums.

The communist election program set out the platform of the party.
Four basic principles were stated in this platform. First was commitment
to the liberation of Arab lands from Israeli occupation and to the liberation of the Palestinian people, through the repeat of Camp David, and the
call for the end of political, economic, and military dependency on the
United States; the reevaluation of all international economic, political,
and military agreements conducted by the Egyptian regime since May 15,
1971; complete support for the rights of the Palestinian people in self-

determination and sovereignty; the achievement of Arab unity, strengthening relations between the progressive Arab forces; and the end of inter-Arab conflicts. Second was commitment to a neutral, progressive, anti-imperialist foreign policy. Third was the necessity of rebuilding the Egyptian economy to free it from dependency. Finally, the party pledged to struggle for a comprehensive, democratic transformation in the Egyptian political system.[27]

These views were expressed in the campaign slogan "Socialism is Egypt's future." This slogan represented a response to the slogan of Islamic groups that "Islam is the solution."

Although no leftist candidates were elected, the Communist party politbureau considered the election evidence of growing public suspicion of government interference in the elections and increasing skepticism about the legitimacy of the outcomes. In union elections that shortly followed the parliamentary elections, the Left in general, and communists in particular, did very well. The Communist party politbureau considered that this election accurately reflected the popular appeal of the Left.[28]

In January 1988, the politbureau met to review the party's activities. The report issued after this meeting examined the international, regional, and internal spheres in the light of recent events, the most important of which was the stock market crash of October 19, 1987. In examining the impact of the crash on Egypt, the report noted: "The economy was strongly affected by this as a result of the deepening relationship between the international capitalist system and Egypt. This is a result of the dependency policy adopted by the ruling capitalist alliance from 1974 to the present under the open-door policy."[29]

The loss in the value of Egyptian oil exports, whose price is calculated in U.S. dollars, was estimated at $300 million as a result of the decline of the U.S. dollar. In addition, the cost of imports from Japan and Western Europe increased because their currency had increased relative to the American dollar. Also, the cost of servicing Egypt's foreign debt increased as 36 percent of the debt, $54 billion, is held by Western Europe and Japan. Finally, according to government statistics, the value of investment in foreign stocks by Egyptian financial institutions had declined by 35 percent, and the exchange value had decreased by another 20 percent. The total loss for Egyptian investment in stocks on the international market was estimated at $500 million. Another billion dollars was lost in related investments.[30]

The report noted that regional conditions had deteriorated. American penetration and Israeli aggression were unchecked; earlier progressive reforms in Iraq, Syria, and Algeria had been rolled back; the significance of the Palestine issue in Arab politics had been successfully diluted, as reflected by the emergency summit conference of Arab leaders at Amman in November 1987, which gave equal billing to the Iraq-Iran war and the Palestinian problem and the normalization of relations with Egypt.[31]

In light of international, regional, and internal circumstances, the party identified its immediate tasks in the Arab sphere to be to intensify the struggle against the Camp David Accord to contain its acceptance in the region; to emphasize the unity of progressive Arab forces against the alliance of reactionary Arab forces with imperialism and Zionism; to support all efforts to stop the Iraq-Iran war and the return of both belligerents to their prewar borders; and to oppose the involvement of Egypt in the Iraq-Iran war.[32] In the internal sphere, the tasks were identified as the need to prevent further deterioration of conditions of the working class; widen the base of the democratic movement by participating in all elections and activities; combat the influence of the Islamic movement in professional associations and among peasants and youth; build the Egyptian Left as a nucleus of the national democratic front and coordinate activities with the Marxist elements to unify them in the framework of the party; and fight against normalization with Israel, combat dependency conditions by working against the American and Zionist presence in the country, publicize the issue of foreign debt, and expose the special relationship with the United States.[33]

The report signaled a fundamental change in the party's practical position on Arab issues, particularly the Palestine issue. Contrary to its past practice, the party participated with Palestinian fighters in resisting Israeli occupation of Beirut in 1982. A list of party member casualties was published.

AL-HIZB AL-SHUYO'IE AL-MISRI: JANUARY 8

Shortly after Bila Isim declared itself to be the communist party, the old-guard communists who had rejected dissolution in 1965 reacted by declaring this party. This group's main focus was opposition to the communists who had collaborated with the Nasser regime. In declaring themselves a party, the group remained reactive to the collaborationists. Even the name — January 8 Communist party of Egypt — reflected the symbolic continuation of the United Communist party formed on January 8, 1958. Although this party showed some initial success in its first year as its membership increased rapidly, by the second year a serious split on strategy and tactics began to appear within its leadership. In 1985, one faction published two reports in which it announced publicly the organization's structure and problems and revealed the real names of the secretary general and all members of the politbureau in the opposing faction. This virtually destroyed the organization, and it quickly disappeared. Its leadership split into opposing Marxist circles.

HIZB AL-'UMAL AL-SHUYO'IE AL-MISRI

Also in reaction to Bila Isim's declaration, the young extremist group Hizb al-'Umal al-Shuyo'ie al Misri[34] also declared itself a party. Shortly after its birth, the party began issuing a journal, *al-Shuyo'ie al-Misri,* which carried the subtitle "The Official Theoretical and Political Spokesman for the Workers' Communist Party of Egypt." The first issue appeared in September 1975 in Egypt (it was published in Beirut two months later), announcing the party's bylaws and theoretical position on both international and Egyptian issues. It announced that from 1972 to 1975 the group had been publishing position papers under the pen names Shuyo'ie Misri and Ismail Mahmud in *al-Hadaf, al-Rayah,* and *Dirasat 'Arabia,* all published in Beirut, and *al-Tali'ah* in Kuwait. The first issue's editorial declared:

> Now we have our own special forum. . . . It is one of the political means of our revolutionary struggle. . . . The journal will try to distinguish our intellectual, political, organizational, and popular positions, and will play a role in debating issues relevant to this. On the one hand, it will present positions on fundamental issues of ruling-class conditions and authority; the nature of revolution, class alliances, the national issue, and the problem of democracy in our country. On the other hand, it will relate these issues to current events. . . . The journal will not limit itself to the issue of the Egyptian revolution for this is tied to the Arab revolution. . . . Our revolutionary responsibility requires us to participate in the Arab revolution's development and leadership. . . . It is natural that the Palestine issue and the means of facing Israel on both tactical and strategic levels will be among the most prominent concerns of this journal. . . . The journal will not abandon its international role, specifically in relation to the tragic current situation of the international communist movement. This requires us to clarify our position on this in this debate in all its forms, shapes, and manifestations, particularly on the right-wing Soviet revisionism and the left-wing Chinese revisionism. Our journal

must emphasize the Marxist revolutionary line that has been distorted by the conflicting revisionists. . . . As for the true Egyptian and Arab revolutionary forces, this journal will be the means of intellectual struggle on principles in order to correct it and modify it to achieve the correct and mature positions to deal with the problems and theoretical issues, propose solutions, resolve differences, strengthen agreements, and share experiences. . . . It is an intellectual struggle . . . a debate on principles between revolutionary forces and a struggle of ideas, positions, and means to arrive at correct stands.[35]

This group challenged the legitimacy of the communist movement on the national, regional, and international levels and took a vanguard role in the reform of the movement. Its program represented a radical platform based on disassociation with the past and rejection of the legitimacy of the existing establishment with the communist movement.[36] The journal constituted the theoretical arm of the party's program. It continued publication in both Cairo and Beirut until the Cairo uprising in January 1977. The party played a prominent role in the uprising, organizing students and workers. The police and intelligence responded with mass arrests of party members and supporters. Confessions and disclosures obtained from those arrested resulted in further arrests. The party was reduced to scattered Marxist circles, and the journal ceased publication.

AL-TAYYAR AL-THAWRI (THE REVOLUTIONARY CURRENT)

Al-Tayyar al-Thawri was composed of a group of old-guard communists who had rejected dissolution of the party. It was led by Mohammed Abbas Fahmi, Tahir al-Badri, Ahmed al-Qassir, and Sidqi al-Qassir, who tried to collect the disaffected elements of the movement. They believed that because of the special influence of Mohammed Abbas Fahmi and Tahir al-Badri, a commitment to Stalinism was clear. This was manifested in the rejection of "moderate" Soviet positions such as detente, the Cuban missile crisis of 1961, and the Soviet position vis-à-vis Nasser and the Palestinian issue. They criticized Soviet theories regarding states of the Third World, the noncapitalist road to development, and the new democracies. Their strongest criticism was directed at the position taken by international communism in general, the Arab communists in particular, toward the Palestinian issue and Israel. They also condemned the moderate position of the Palestine Liberation Organization. They expressed complete support for the Chinese position both theoretically and practically.

Despite the group's insistence that it was not a political party, intelligence forces broke it up into three groups — two very small and inconsequential and the third under the leadership of al-Badri and Fahmi.

Following the death of Nasser and the rise of Sadat, a new al-Tayyar began to emerge whose basic ideology was that Egyptian communists are tools in the hands of the Soviets. Soviet policies are reformist and reject the establishment of the dictatorship of the proletariat. It was a grave mistake to support the reforms of Nasser, his nationalization, and even his anti-imperialist positions because they were only band-aid solutions to reform the capitalist society and prolong its life.

Complete support was given to Sadat because of the belief that he was building a democratic society in which revolutionary forces could function. The group also supported Sadat because he opposed Nasser and the Soviet Union. Confusion over its ideological position caused the membership to decline radically. Because the group supported Sadat through Mahamud al-Khafif, the brother-in-law of ʻAbdul Salam al-Ziyat (for a while the closest man to Sadat), a deal was worked out with Sadat's police agencies whereby this organization was given support and the freedom to work openly as long as it maintained its anti-Nasser, anti-Soviet position.

Two grave mistakes resulted in the discrediting of this organization. First was Sadat's involvement in the July 19, 1971, coup in the Sudan and the group's support for the execution of the popular secretary general for the Communist party and the labor leader al-Shafiʻ Ahmed al-Sheikh on the charge that they were Soviet agents. The second mistake was when the security police arrested Fahmi in January 1975 thinking he was a member of the Egyptian Communist party and found a printing machine in his possession. He informed the intelligence that the machine had been provided to him by the other state security agency. After Camp David, more members left the group and more splits took place. When Fahmi died, the group became weaker. During Mubarak's day, it continued to support the regime on the basis that democracy brings freedom of organization and work and openly published a circular called al-Haqiqah.

Al-Badri became the main leader. Others were ʻAbd al-Monʻeim Talimeh, a university professor, and Badr ʻAql, a bank worker. In the 1984 election, they supported the Wafd party on the basis that it defends democracy. Their basic theory was Wafd democracy, freedom of work, and revolutionary awakening.

In 1985–86 al-Tayyar tried to declare itself a political party. On the specified date of the meeting at the residence of Talimeh, while 'Aql was carrying the last issue of *al-Haqiqah* from the press, he was met by rival intelligence agents with photographers and the press. They were all arrested but released immediately. By 1989 they claimed to be a current, not an organization.

Thus the party organized by Bila Isim was the only one to survive. It established and maintained a viable organization and network and was the first party since the 1920s to be recognized in international and regional communist forums.

In February 1988, it issued a report entitled "Toward a Correct and Realistic Understanding of the Question of the Unity of Egyptian Communists." The report declared that the call for unity in 1980 did not stem from equality with the other groups. Rather, the party "is the only one capable of unifying Egyptian communists within its framework. It is not just one of the Marxist groups which can disintegrate and fragment." The report based this claim on the party's having survived the 1981 police campaign of suppression and holding a congress in 1984. It also participated in the parliamentary elections of 1984 and 1987 and achieved some success in the labor union elections of 1987.

The report argued that the political map of Marxist groups had changed. As a result, new strategies were needed for unity, which could be achieved through coordination with the Egyptian Communist Workers party, cooperation among the former members of dissolved and defunct Marxist groups, and publication of a bulletin directed to these two audiences to create an intellectual dialogue with them on "the nature of the current revolutionary stage and what relates to it in terms of criticizing and refuting the thesis that the current stage is the stage of socialist revolution; on the nature of the current authorities, criticizing and refuting the thesis that the current authorities are a part of the national democratic front; on the position of the national democratic front, criticizing and refuting the idea that the necessary front is only a popular front; on the position toward the communist party's existence and dissolution."

The report emphasized that there was no contradiction between this position and its current position on the question of unity and the commitment to build a national democratic front among the progressive forces in Egypt. These forces were identified as being the Tagamu', the Nasserites, and themselves. A month later, their internal party leaflet emphasized the call for the building of a national front.

In the classical tradition of the Egyptian communist movement, the party's elaboration of doctrine and strategy emanated from two foundations—ideological principles and practical politics. Party praxis, derived from this foundation, focused on public consciousness raising through the dissemination of political documents and a regularly issued series, *al-Intisar;* collaboration with other progressive forces such as al-Tagamu' and al-Hizb al-Ishtiraki al-'Arabi al-Nasiri; and public mobilization and action such as the public protest in January 1977 against Sadat's efforts to remove government food subsidies.

By 1988, there were indications of the emergence of a united or common front of progressive forces. This front includes three main groups: al-Hizb al-Shuyo'ie al-Misri, al-Tagamu', and al-Hizb al-Ishtiraki al-'Arabi al-Nasiri. This apparent unity is a new development in the strategy of the Left.

8

On the Origins, Evolution, and Role of the Egyptian Communist Movement

This study of the Egyptian communist movement has revealed a number of characteristics about its origin and evolution. This chapter will identify these characteristics and examine them in an effort to understand the nature of the movement in terms of its role in Egyptian politics.

ORIGINS

The communist movement in Egypt dates back to the turn of the century. Its intellectual roots were in European socialist thought, and the movement never really transcended these roots. This conclusion is based on an assessment of the movement's role in Egyptian politics over its history. Socialist thought emerged in Europe in response to the development and conditions of urban-industrial society. It addresses issues related to the management of human affairs organized in the framework of urban industrialism. So it is not surprising that the communist movement in Egypt emerged in response to conditions in the industrial sectors in Cairo and Alexandria. Before World War I, the industrial labor force was predominantly foreign — especially Italians and Greeks. When these workers left Egypt on the eve of the war, their ranks were filled by Egyptians. Although much less politicized or mobilized than the foreign workers, Egyptian workers were even more vulnerable to exploitation than their foreign counterparts. Furthermore, they were unprotected by the capitulations agreements, which limited persecution and suppression of foreign labor activists. In the context of excessive exploitation of Egyptian factory workers and suppression of labor activists or reformers, the principles and methods of communist labor mobilization were relevant and adaptable. Furthermore, since the turn of the century Egyptian students had brought back from Europe the doctrines of European socialism generally and Marxism specifically. Several Egyptian intellectuals applied Marxist ideas to Egyptian social problems when the Egyptianization of the industrial labor force occurred. They immediately became involved in labor activism and contributed substantially to the initiation of an Egyptian labor movement. Indeed, the origins of the labor movement in Egypt cannot be separated from the communist movement.

Thus the theory and practice of communism were transplanted from industrializing Europe to the industrial sectors of Egypt unimpeded by obstacles of relevance and relativity. But the industrial sector in Egypt was and has remained a small segment of its economy. Before World War I less than 5 percent of Egypt's labor force worked in the manufacturing sector, and this sector still accounted for only about 20 percent of workers in 1986. The industrial sector in Egypt, then, has been small and isolated and nonrepresentative of the economic, social, and political patterns and problems that faced most Egyptians in their everyday lives. Yet Marxist thought in Egypt never transcended the boundaries of analytic categories formulated to examine the transition from rural-feudal to urban-industrial life and to manage the affairs of urban-industrial relations.

Although there have been many theoretically sophisticated Marxist analyses of Egyptian social problems by participants in the Egyptian communist movement, the Egyptian experience has made no evident contribution to communist thought. In other words, there has been no significant or profound Egyptianization of communist thought.

This is only one indicator that the Egyptian movement failed to transcend its intellectual roots in seeking a communist praxis in the Egyptian milieu. A more significant indicator is the failure of the movement to make itself relevant to Egypt's peasant base. The appeal of communism in Egypt has remained urban throughout the history of the movement, and even in the urban centers, its appeal has been largely confined to intellectual elites and industrial workers.

Another indicator was the ongoing conflict the movement experienced in its relationship to nationalism and nationalist issues. When addressing the issues of imperialism, the orthodox communist concept of imperialism provided the movement with the ideological framework for direct action in mobilizing Egypt's anti-imperialist struggle. Indeed, it was in the spheres of labor mobilization and anti-imperialist mobilization — both categories rooted in orthodox communist ideology — that the Egyptian communist movement was most active and played a vanguard role.

On nationalist issues, however, the orthodox communist concept of nationalism remained fundamentally problematic in the Egyptian context, indeed in the Third World context. The Egyptian communist movement never resolved this problem ideologically and hence was never able to formulate a consistent position or program on nationalist issues. The movement wavered on fundamental issues, and leadership fell to other forces. This problem was most apparent on the issues of Palestine, Arab nationalism, and Nasserism.

As a social movement, communism in Egypt did transcend its European origins early in its history. Communist activism in Egypt was initiated within the foreign labor communities, but the movement did not spread to Egyptian workers. It was initiated by a group of European-educated Egyptian intellectuals who organized the Egyptian Socialist party in 1921. The point of transcendence is marked by the transformation of the party into the Egyptian Communist party in 1922. The name change reflected the shift in party leadership from the Western-educated intellectual elite to front-line labor organizers and activists.

The party was so successful in mobilizing labor that the labor movement was born in this period. By 1924, labor represented a real force in Egyptian politics. Between 1920 and 1924, the scope and magnitude of labor mobilization and strike action dramatically increased. To crush the labor movement and bring unions under the tutelage of the government, in that year Egypt's first nationalist government cracked down on the Communist party. Wholesale arrests of leaders and members, confiscation of party property, and an intense propaganda campaign against the party decisively suppressed it. The party was declared illegal. Thus the first phase of the communist movement in Egypt was brought to a close by outright suppression.

Although the origins of the communist movement in Egypt are European, and the movement seems to have been circumscribed to the ideological terms of references of this origin, the movement was from the beginning an Egyptian social movement. It was the product of Egyptians seeking solutions to Egyptian problems for the betterment or benefit of the Egyptian people. The communist movement in Egypt, then, was not the creation or tool of some external power. Neither the First International nor Stalin's Comintern ever controlled the movement.

The dualistic nature of the movement's origins (European roots/ Egyptian ontology) is reflected in a problem that plagued its organizational efforts throughout the second phase (1930 – 65) and revolved around the role of foreigners in the movement. Some factions advocated equality among Egyptians and non-Egyptians; others insisted on the exclusion of non-Egyptians. And a variety of positions existed between these two extremes. The European roots of the communist movement in Egypt presented a problem for its advocates in a period of emerging nationalism. And one manifestation of this problem was the debate over the role of non-Egyptians.

EVOLUTION

The suppression of the communist and labor movements in Egypt initiated in 1924 continued unabated throughout the 1920s and 1930s. As a result, the Egyptian communist movement was driven underground. In contrast, the official tolerance of the antifascist activities of foreign socialist organizations in the 1930s resulted in a resurgence of the communist movement within Egypt's European community. This combination of conditions profoundly affected the development of the communist movement in Egypt over the next several decades.

First, it set the evolutionary basis for fractious organizational tensions related to the dualistic nature of the movement's origins. The movement was revived from within the European community and spread from there to Western-educated Egyptian intellectuals. The old-guard leadership of front-line labor organizers and activists was displaced by an intellectual elite involved more with cultural activism than with labor activism.

These conditions set the basis for ideological tensions related to issues of nationalism versus internationalism. The debate over the role of non-Egyptians in the movement was only one manifestation of these tensions. Another was the role of rank-and-file members; yet another related to tensions over the class origins of the leadership.

Underlying such tensions was the fact that Western-educated participants in the communist movement in Egypt tended to have a European orientation to the concept of nationalism and therefore to reject it in favor of internationalism. Furthermore, Western-educated Egyptians, as well as those from European backgrounds involved in the movement (for example, Jacquot-Descombes, Curiel, and Schwartz), had upper-class backgrounds. They were thus distanced intellectually and socially from the nationalism rising throughout the Third World generally and Arab nationalism rising in Egypt and the rest of the Arab world specifically. Nowhere was this intellectual and social gulf more profoundly demonstrated than on the Palestine issue.

Finally, the government's tolerance of antifascist activism at the same time that labor activism was suppressed bred suspicion between different groups and individuals within the movement. The covert and clandestine nature of the movement in the second phase contributed to the intensification of the role of personality in organizational establishment and maintenance. In this atmosphere, ideological and organizational tensions showed up as personality disputes, and personality disputes were played out as ideological conflicts.

One of the most prominent characteristics of the communist movement in its second wave of development, 1930–65, is the process of organizational fragmentation. Promoted by fractious organizational and ideological tensions, and intensified by covert and clandestine processes, the movement in this period was constantly fragmented. The result was that at any given time there were at least three major associations (and usually a plethora of minor splinter groups), all with similar goals and strategies, yet each claiming sole ideological legitimacy. What prevented total atomization of the movement?

Pressures toward reintegration represented the other prominent characteristic of development in this period. These pressures were produced by the front-line cadres who were more concerned with organizational praxis than with the doctrinal debates that preoccupied the leadership cadres. Such pressures, of course, worked against the tendency toward fragmentation. Thus the splinter and spin-off groups that were continuously generated by the forces of fragmentation were also always in the process of regrouping and realigning to form new coalitions and unions. For example, in the 1940s, two major organizations in the movement, Iskra and Hamtu, united to form Haditu; other organizations joined the union. Haditu then proceeded to fragment, producing a plethora of splinter groups. In the 1950s, fragments of Haditu regrouped and united with others to form the Egyptian Unified Communist party. This, too, then began to fragment. The fragments subsequently regrouped and united with the Egyptian Communist party of Workers and Peasants (formerly Tasht) to form the Communist party of Egypt, which then began to split up.

The processes of fragmentation-reintegration ultimately dissipated the energies of the movement. In this light, it is not surprising that the movement voluntarily dissolved itself when the opportunity seemed to present itself in 1965 for members to play a vanguard role in the Arab Socialist Union. Thus the second wave of the communist movement in Egypt was brought to a close by voluntary dissolution.

The communist movement remained dormant for the rest of the decade. By the early 1970s, however, several different groups had reemerged. Only one demonstrated the political and organizational ability to survive a combination of strident police suppression and fratricidal intergroup competition. In 1975, this group declared itself the Egyptian Communist party. Throughout the 1970s and 1980s, the party worked to rebuild front-line cadres in urban and rural centers and to build an organized front of progressive forces.

Thus the third wave of the communist movement in Egypt represents a more mature organizational form than its predecessors. Organizational survival and task performance are the criteria for this assessment. The Communist party of Egypt has survived intact for over a decade and has functioned effectively clandestinely in the hostile environment of political suppression.

In its evolution over the twentieth century, the communist movement in Egypt has moved through three distinct stages. Each stage is marked by distinctive organizational forms and activities. And each stage was brought to a close by a principal limiting condition which the form or structure of the movement in that stage could not overcome. In the first stage, the organizational form was a centralized party with front-line activities concentrated in the labor movement and controlled from the top. The limiting condition was political suppression. In the second stage, the organizational form was multicentered, with diffuse front-line activities controlled from different, uncoordinated, often competing centers. The principal limiting condition was structural fragmentation.

The third stage, of course, is still in process so its ultimate limiting condition is not known or evident. Its organizational form is a decentralized unicentered party with diffuse front-line activities. If successive stages in the process of development suggest an overcoming of limiting conditions, however, it may be inferred that the communist movement in Egypt by this stage has overcome, through organizational adaptation, the environmental problem of political suppression and the structural problem of fragmentation.

ROLE

The communist movement in Egypt has been a significant political force in the country's politics throughout the century. Its significance derives from its vanguard role in mobilizing popular classes, organizing them as political actors, and articulating their political interests and will. Each stage in the evolution of the communist movement in Egypt is characterized by different manifestations of this role in terms of the primary audiences and issues addressed. In the first stage, the industrial working class was the primary audience. The communist movement played a vanguard role in mobilizing labor, organizing the labor movement, and articulating labor's interests in wages, job safety, and security.

In the second stage, the primary audience was the cultural working class — the intellectuals, artists, and skilled artisans who worked in Egypt's cultural industries (education, journalism, literature, cinema, art). The explosion of cultural clubs in the 1930s and 1940s reflects the role of the communist movement in mobilizing this class. The communist movement played a vanguard role in organizing the cultural working class in the anti-imperialist struggle for national liberation.

The third stage is difficult to assess because it is still in process and the party has been very clandestine so little is known about its activities. Thus any representation made is based on speculation. Party publications and documents provide the only clues. They indicate that the party is focusing on the two areas of strength from the past — the labor movement and the anti-imperialist struggle. Furthermore, party documents suggest that it has adopted more of an Arab perspective on fundamental nationalist issues than the movement has expressed in the past. This is reflected in such issues as Palestine, Camp David, and Middle East politics.

In a very concrete sense, the communist movement has brought the public into the political process in Egypt. Through its various organizing and mobilizing activities, the movement penetrated into the popular classes and politicized their social problems. In this way, the movement played a vanguard role in politicizing groups and issues.

Although the movement never achieved any formal power, it has influenced the direction of change of politics in Egypt. The formal political actors in Egypt have had to respond to the movement's initiatives, whether positively or negatively. These initiatives focused on the need for labor legislation and agrarian reform in domestic affairs and the need for independence and sovereignty in international affairs. The communist movement heralded these issues long before they became historical inevitabilities. Although change on these issues has never been far-reaching or comprehensive enough to satisfy the revolutionaries (or even the reformers) or to solve the social problems, the point is that the communist movement's initiatives made change inevitable for they forced other political actors to deal with the issue and with the expanded public consciousness of the issue.

The communist movement in Egypt is more of a social conscience vanguard than a revolutionary vanguard. The movement has been more focused on the politics of social issues than on the politics of revolution. Hence the role of the revolutionary vanguard — a role certainly paved by the communist movement in its politicizing and mobilizing activities — has been picked up by others: first, by the free officers and more recently (but less successfully) by the Islamic fundamentalist revolutionaries.

APPENDIXES
NOTES
INDEX

APPENDIX A*
Egypt and Socialism

I. GENERAL REFORMS

1. The decision of the legislature should be final.
2. The cabinet should be responsible to it.
3. The enactment of laws which guarantee free elections.
4. The dissolving of the legislature every three years.
5. Distributing the seats according to the proportion of workers in every profession.
6. Increasing the numbers of members of the legislature so that it may include a representative for every 100,000 people.

II. SOCIAL REFORMS

1. Enacting a law which prohibits polygamy unless the first wife was barren or crippled, and the punishment of anyone who breaks this law by imprisonment or financial penalty.
2. Requiring divorce to take place before a judge, and strong reasons should be given as to why the husband wants to divorce; otherwise his request is to be rejected.

*A selection from Mustafa Hassanain al-Mansuri, *Tarikh al-Mathahib al-Ishtirakiyah (Cairo: N.p., 1915), pp. 110–17.*

3. The emancipation of women after education has been spread among them. Their emancipation right now may lead to social chaos. Schools should also instruct them in matters of virtue.
4. The enactment of a law which prohibits early marriages such that a young man could not marry before twenty-five years and a young woman not before sixteen years. Anyone who breaks the law should be punished by imprisonment or financial penalty.
5. The government should impose a large tax on the bachelors who are capable of marriage, equal to one-fourth of their income.
6. Poor women should be helped at the time of their marriage with a bonus of not less than LE30.
7. Pensions should also be provided to senior citizens.
8. The government should accept women in clerical jobs.
9. The government should enact a law that does not prohibit female doctors and teachers from marrying since this is against human nature and calls for vice.

III. DEMOCRATIC REFORMS

1. Local councils should be spread all over, even in villages.
2. These councils should build healthy housing and rent it at low rates.
3. They should also impose a minimum wage for the farmers and workers so as not to go below five piasters. Any employers breaking the law should be punished by imprisonment or a financial penalty.
4. Barren land should be distributed among poor peasants on the condition that it does not belong to individuals. Instead, it should be given to them for long periods such as twenty to thirty years.
5. A progressive tax should be imposed on income if it exceeds LE200 annually.
6. An inheritance tax should also be imposed, which increases the further away the inheritor is from the deceased.
7. Lowering the transportation costs in railways.
8. All railways and tramways should belong to the government or civil councils.

9. The government should encourage people to form agricultural and industrial unions.

IV. EDUCATION

1. Educational curricula should be improved by introducing chemical and physical sciences.
2. The abolition of arts departments in secondary schools and teaching history and geography in the science departments.
3. The opening of primary agricultural schools which should be free.
4. The improvement of al-Azhar and other religious institutions by introducing modern science in their programs.
5. An annual subsidy of LE100,000 should be provided to the Egyptian university.
6. The university should provide special attention to the science department.
7. The expansion of the free education system in all schools.
8. The imposition of laws for the private schools which guarantee the competence of the teachers.
9. The government should create technical firms for soap, paper, glass, and tannery products.
10. Teachers' conditions should be improved, both financially and in prestige.
11. Education responsibility should be taken away from the government councils and put in the hands of a scientific committee which is a member of the legislature.

V. THE JUDICIARY

1. The expansion of the courts and the introduction of the jury system.
2. Allowing for a jury in the national courts.
3. The abolishment of the mixed courts.
4. The abolishment of foreign capitulation.
5. The abolishment of case taxes.
6. The reform of the Shari'a law so as to conform with the modern times.

7. Relaxing the strictness of the law so as to reform the prisoner rather than impose revenge upon him.
8. The abolishing of capital punishment since it is an indication that the government has failed to rehabilitate the criminal.

VI. OTHER DEMANDS

1. The abolishment of ranks and conferring them only on the most efficient.
2. The enactment of a law which imposes a maximum in profits so that it does not exceed 5 percent.
3. The imposition of a law which protects children who have been deserted by their parents.
4. The government should enact a law which requires foreign employers to hire national workers, up to 50 percent of the total employees.
5. A high tax should be imposed on alcoholic beverages and the properties of gambling casino owners should be sequestered.
6. Prohibit immigration to the country unless the person has a skill.
7. Closing the gap among the government employees. No employee should earn more than LE100 per month or less than LE5.
8. Military education should be mandatory in schools in order to be able to abolish the army in the future. The pension law should also be reformed in favor of small employees.
9. A maximum should be imposed on the value of the medical clincial service so as not to exceed twenty piasters.
10. Governorate councils should impose a maximum on land rent so that it may not exceed LE10.
11. The establishment of a national bank.
12. The abolishing of any laws which restrict freedom of speech, press, or meetings.

APPENDIX B*
The Honorable
Sayid Hassan Mohammed Asks...

What is your judgment concerning the "Way" of the Bolsheviks which is spreading and doing harm everywhere these days? The chief points in their "Way" are anarchy, corruption, denial of the religious, legalizing the illegal (antinomianism), freedom from any creed at all, trespassing on the property of others and denying individuals' right to hold property, holding it to be allowable to every man to seize what he wishes from whomsoever he wishes, legalizing the shedding of man's blood, denial of rights of husband and wife and of the legitimacy of their children which they claim as the property of the state, thus demolishing the fence guarding family life, no distinction between Halal and Haram, every woman is the common property of each of them without any marriage contract, any woman attempting to defend her honor forfeits her life, unmarried women are often forced to prostitution, and married women to be unfaithful to husbands and children: in a word they allow everything that God's Laws prohibit.

Give us your Fatwa, and God reward you.

Our Judgment: We say that this is an ancient "Way" and it is the creed of a Persian hypocrite from Fassa named Zoroaster.

*British Foreign Office, F/O 141/779, File 9065. As translated in Foreign Office Records.

He improvised his heresy during the era of the Magians when it met with the approbation of the people, but it was a man from Mazria called Mazdaq who spread it later on among the masses. He taught communism of property and of persons and put it in their mind that this, although it might not be from religion, was at least honorable in the doing. Thus he provoked the villeins against the nobles and facilitated violation for violaters, oppression for oppressors, and adultery for adulterers so that they obtained possession of such gentlewomen as they had never dreamed of, with the result that an unprecedented deluge of distress embraced the whole country. This had taken place during the reign of King Qebaz-ibn-Fairuz, son of Yezdegird of Persia and after a reign of twenty years, the heads and chiefs of his country unanimously agreed to depose him from the throne on account of his siding with Mazdaq and his followers, who claimed that God furnished the means of living to be divided equally among the people, but that people treated one another wrongfully making some rich and some poor. They decided to take from the rich and give to the poor and that property and women should be common to all. The masses seized this opportunity and sided wholeheartedly with Mazdaq and his followers aiding them in all their views. They grew so strong that they dared to attack a man inside his own door, encroaching upon his property and his women without his being able to withhold anything from them. They induced Qebaz to welcome their heresy threatening to depose him in case of disobedience. Very soon the people became like beasts and the son ignored his father and the father his son, his wife and all his relations, and none could possess anything of what he had. They put Qebaz in a place beyond the reach of everyone besides themselves and said to him, "You have done iniquity in the past and you cannot be saved and purified except by making your women public property," and they also seduced him to offer himself as a sacrifice to fire.

Zarmahr, one of Qebaz's helpers, seeing what these people had done, attacked them with some of his nobles who followed him, and killed many of Mazdaq's followers, and restored Qebaz to his throne. Afterward the followers of Mazdaq continued to excite Qebaz against Zarmahr until he killed him. Qebaz was one of the good-hearted Persian kings, so that it was easy for Mazdaq to influence him; with the result that anarchy prevailed everywhere and corruption embraced the whole country. The case continued to be terrible until Kisra Anoushirwan (Khosroes), son of Qebaz, sat on the throne, and ordered his people to abandon the views of Zoroaster and Mazdaq. He put to an end all their false doctrines and killed many of its followers. At last he utterly annihilated this sect and reconfirmed the creed of the Magians who were still clinging to it.

Islam was introduced and swept this false Way aside. God the Most High had caused His Book to decend upon His apostle (upon him be prayers and peace) ordering the people to do all that was good and avoid all evil. He also commanded them to believe in the right doctrines concerning His truth which is worthy of His Deity and Lordship. Regarding the truth of the apostles, he commanded us to believe in their sinlessness and their abstaining from committing any evil. He instituted the law of contracts for transferring the rights of property by sale, endowment, will, and so on; also explained the question of inheritance and the share of each heir. In His precious Book He made it clear that He Himself undertook the distribution of the means of living among His creatures by saying, "We divided up their livelihood among them" and "God gives the livelihood to whom He wishes from among His servants," and so on.

The prophet (upon him be prayers and peace) also said in his farewell sermon, "Praise be to God; we ask His forgiveness and repent towards Him of our evils and sins; and anyone who loses the way of God can find none to guide him. I testify that there is no Deity but God and that Mohammed is His servant and Apostle. O! servants of God I recommend to you His fear and piety and urge you to obey him. Ye people! hearken to my words, for I know not whether, after this year, I shall ever be among you here again. O! people your lives and property are sacred and inviolable among one another, until we meet your Lord exactly as this day of this month. O! Lord! I beseech thee bear Thou witness unto it, anyone of you who has anything entrusted to his care must give it back to its owner. Be sure that illegal profit is but an innovation of the era of ignorance, the first of this sort being that of my Uncle al-Abbas-ibn-'Abdul-Muttalib. Also revenge for blood is an innovation of olden days, the first of its sort being that of Amer ibn Rabia ibn el-Hareth ibn 'Abdul Muttalib. Also the memorable deeds of the era of ignorance are but innovations (the service of al-Ka'aba, and giving drink are excluded). Willful murder of a soul involves punishment, and manslaughter, such as killing by sticks or stones involves an indemnity of one hundred camels; but anyone who exceeds this amount is considered to be one of the people of ignorance.

Ye people! truly Satan despaireth of being worshiped in your land, but if in some indifferent matter, which ye might be disposed to slight, he could secure obedience, verily he would be well pleased.

Ye people! to carry over a sacred month to another is only an increase of unbelief. They who do not believe are led into error by it. They allow it one year and forbid it another, that they may make good the number of months which God hath hallowed, and they allow that which God hath prohibited. Verily the number of the months with God is twelve months, according to the book of God, on the day in which He created the Heavens and the earth. Four of them are sacred, three successive and one single: Zul-Kida, Zul-Hujja, Moharram, and Rajab.

O Lord! do Thou witness unto it. Ye people! ye have rights demandable of your wives and they have rights demandable of you. Upon them it is incumbent not to violate their conjugal faith, neither to commit any act of open impropriety; which things if they do, ye have authority to shut them up in separate apartments and to beat them with stripes, yet not severely. But if they refrain therefrom, clothe them and feed them suitably. And treat your women well: for they are with you as captives and prisoners, they have not power over anything as regards themselves, and yet have verily taken them on the security of God; and have made their persons lawful onto you by the words of God.

O Lord! do Thou witness unto it. Ye people, all the believers are but brothers; none is allowed to encroach upon the property of another except at his will.

O Lord! do Thou witness unto it — Ye people! beware lest ye become pagans after I leave you and kill one another. Verily I have left among you the Book of God and (the example of) my family — which, if ye hold fast, ye shall never go astray.

O Lord! do Thou witness unto it — Ye people! Thy Lord is one and ye all have one father—Adam—and Adam is of dust. The most honorable before God is the most pious. An Arab has no superiority over a Persian except by piety. O Lord! do Thou witness unto it. Ye People! let him that is present tell it unto him that is absent. Ye people! God hath ordained to every man the share of his inheritance: a testament is not lawful when it exceeds the third.

The marriage bed is for children but the violator of wedlock shall be stoned. Whoever claimeth falsely another for his father, or another for his master, the curse of God and the angels, and of all mankind, shall rest upon him.

Peace be upon you and the mercy of God and His blessings.

It is known from all that the "Way" of the Bolsheviks is one which destroys all Divine laws especially the doctrines of Islam; because it recommends what God hath considered illegal in His Book. It legalizes bloodshedding, allows trespass upon the property of others, treachery, lies, and rape, causing anarchy to spread among the people in their properties, their women, children, and inheritance until they become at last worse than beasts. God hath verily and plainly forbidden all these things, and such people are but apostate whose "Way" demolishes human society, destroys the order of the world, leads to apostasy from religion, threatens the whole world with horrible distress and bitter troubles, and instigates the lower classes against all system founded upon reason, morals, and virtue.

Accordingly every true Moslem ought to avoid such people and their misguided views and false doctrines and deeds, because they are undoubtedly apostates, who do not follow any of the *revealed religions* nor do they recognize any order of society.

In short, even Kisra Anoushirwan, who was a Magian, a worshiper of fire, did not approve such views, which are contrary to justice and order. Then, is it not far more necessary that Moslems do the same, whom God hath commanded in His Book by his prophet, saying: "Verily God enjoineth justice and the doing of good, and bestowment of goods to kindred; and He forbiddeth wickedness, wrong, and oppression. He warneth you that haply you may be mindful."

4 Shawal 1337   Signature and seal of
                                                MOHAMMED BAKHEET
(July 2, 1919)   (Grand Mufti)

APPENDIX C
Egyptian Communist Party
Political Report*

[Text of the political report (al-Taqrir al-Siyasi) of the Egyptian Communist Party Central Secretariat in which the party "announces its return to action eleven years after its dissolution in July 1964"—dated July 1975]

World imperialism and local reactionaries have lately buffered a continuing series of defeats in the economic, political, and military domains. The national and progressive forces and people are scoring victory after victory day after day and wrestling away positions out of the claws of their enemies.

This is headed by the crushing defeat of U.S. imperialism in Vietnam and Cambodia and includes the collapse of the military dictatorship in Greece, the overthrow of the fascist regime in Portugal, the termination of the agent imperial regime in Ethiopia, the foiling of the imperialist plan against Makarios's legitimate government in Cyprus, the overwhelming success of the Italian Communist party in local elections, the intensification of contradictions inside NATO, the aggravation of unemployment and inflation and the escalation of the strangling economic crisis in the capitalist world, and the mounting revolutionary tide in the Latin American countries.

*Al-Safir (Beirut), August 4, 1975, p. 4.

However, the ruling authority in Egypt insists on challenging the march of history and adhering to its line of retreat and setbacks in the various domains in line with the "step-by-step" method.

IN THE NATIONAL ISSUE

— The ruling authority is betting on the U.S. role in the area and aligning itself with the attempts to reach a U.S. solution of the crisis.

— It has recognized the state of Israel in stages and is preparing to coexist with it in the area.

— It does not mind accepting a separate partial settlement with Israel for the sake of kilometers in the Sinai Desert.

IN FOREIGN POLICY

— The ruling authority is increasingly abandoning the slogan of "the strategic alliance" with the Soviet Union, and it has launched continued slander campaigns against the friendly Soviet Union and worked to diminish Egypt's relations with the socialist bloc countries.

— It is working continuously to make U.S. imperialism appear blameless. It considers its sabotage role against peace and its imperialist depletion of the peoples' resources as "efforts to serve world peace and prosperity." It depicts the United States as the best friend of Egypt and the Arabs.

— It is strengthening its relations with the regimes which are agents of U.S. imperialism, such as Iran, and it even did not hesitate to dispatch an official friendship delegation to Chile, thus participating in breaking the isolation of the fascist clique.

IN ARAB POLICY

— The ruling authority is increasing its cooperation with the reactionary Arab regimes and establishing a Cairo-Riyadh axis at a time when its relations with Syria are lukewarm and its relations with the Palestinian resistance are deteriorating, in addition to the escalation of its conflict with Libya.

— Its trend toward relinquishing its national commitments is intensifying.

— It has covered up the imperialist-reactionary plot against the unity of Lebanon and the Palestinian resistance by taking a neutral attitude toward the agent reactionary forces on the one hand and the democratic and national forces and the Palestinian resistance on the other.

IN THE ISSUE OF DEMOCRACY

— The ruling authority has squashed movements of the masses (the war factory workers on January 1, 1975, the al-Nahallah workers, and the peasants' movements in Dikirnis and others).

— It has launched a war of attrition against the left-wing forces by launching continued arrest campaigns against the left-wing forces in Egypt.

— It has suppressed the progressive press (suppressing al-Katib Magazine, strangling al-Tali'ah, and suspending the al-Mansura university magazine).

— It has handed the leading positions in the press over to right-wing and agent elements while banishing progressive journalists.

— It has ignored the choices of the Press Syndicate Council regarding press representatives on the higher press council.

It has ignored the student list approved by the General Conference of Egyptian Students. It has imposed a list which ignores the students' democratic rights and intensifies its guardianship of the students' movement.

— It crossed several progressive elements off the list of candidates for the Arab Socialist Union.

IN THE SOCIAL AND ECONOMIC FIELD

— The ruling authority has increased private sector investments from 30 million pounds in 1974 to 100 million pounds in 1975.

— It has allowed the private sector to own tankers of up to 40,000 tons, cargo ships of up to 15,000 tons, and passenger ships, and to participate in the land transportation of passengers.

— It has raised the maximum limit for deals between the government and private sector contractors from 100,000 pounds to 500,000 pounds.

— It has granted Egyptian contracting companies and consultation firms the same tax exemptions given to Arab and foreign capital.

—It has given the Egyptian private sector all of the privileges given to Arab capital.

—It has put public sector shares up for sale and liquidated some of its holdings or sold them to the private sector. It has given up several large trade centers which were owned by the public sector.

— It is moving toward dissolving public institutions and disintegrating the public sector by following the principle of the independence of each economic unit.

— It has allowed foreigners and Arabs to purchase real estate, which has decreased Egypt's sovereignty on its national soil and raised the price of land, thus leading to a hike in housing rents.

—It has moved toward lowering taxes on the higher strata in order to encourage foreign investors.

—It has opened the door to monopolist companies by allowing them to establish joint companies.

—It has allowed the return of trade agencies.

— It has allowed the establishment of foreign banks for dealings with the local money market, thus threatening Egyptian banks with unfair competition from foreign banks and the establishment of joint Egyptian-foreign banks, which facilitates the control of banking business in Egypt by the foreign banks.

—It has established markets and moves toward the gradual transformation of Egyptian ports into free zones.

—It signed twelve agreements with world oil companies, eleven of which were American, during 1973 and 1974.

—It amended the agrarian reform law to increase the leasing of agricultural lands, allow the expulsion of lease holders from their land, and disband the committees for resolving disputes.

— It has exempted companies established in accordance with the foreign investment law from adhering to labor legislation.

—It has sought to tie the Egyptian economy to the international imperialist economic bloc (the EEC).

This flow of trends and successive measures raises the following important questions: Are we on the eve of a sudden counterrevolution? Has any change occurred in the nature of the class system of the ruling authority in Egypt? Has the ruling authority in Egypt lost its national feature? The exact, scientific reply to these questions is the important basis for understanding the dimensions of the current situation and defining the sound revolutionary position in the current stage.

Actually, what is happening in our country today is the natural and logical result of the line that has been adopted by the ruling authority in Egypt since May 15, 1971. In the wake of striking at the Nasserite left in

May 1971 — whose leadership represents the bureaucratic bourgeoisie [al-Burjwaziyah al-Buruqratiyah] who are linked with, profit from, and adhere to nationalization measures and the leading role of the public sector — the authority became dominated by a class alliance which includes the following classes and groups:

1. The rural bourgeoisie (the rich of the countryside) whose cadres dominated most of the ASU command posts and the majority of the seats in the People's Assembly [Sayyid Mar'i, Mohammed Hamid Mahmud, Youssef Makadi, Mahmud 'Abu Waifyah, Ahmed Younis, Mohammed 'Uthman Ismail, Ahmed al-Qasabi, and others).

2. The upper strata of the bureaucratic and technocratic leaderships in the state organs, the public sector, and the political system who profited from their high wages, representation allowances, rewards, commissions, embezzlement, and bribes. These strata accumulated funds and began to invest them in trade, industrial, and parasitic activities. Their interests were linked to the private sector. They became fed up with the restrictions imposed on private activity and began to look forward to openness toward the capitalist West in order to benefit from commissions granted by capitalist companies.

3. Commercial, real estate, and parasitic capitalists who make quick profits through competition and trafficking in the black market and smuggled goods and not through productive operations.

In the battle waged by this alliance against the Nasserite left, it tried at the beginning to neutralize the Marxist Left by choosing several Marxist elements to occupy leadership posts in the ASU and the cabinet (ministers, general secretariat members, and members of a general committee). The ruling alliance also tried to approach the old classes and groups which had been affected by nationalization and guardianship measures. This alliance issued successive decisions pardoning some of their members and lifting the guardianship decisions.

Following the October War in 1973, particularly after Kissinger's visit to the area and the signing of the first disengagement agreement, and after the authority adopted the policy of betting on the U.S. solution and economic openness, new social forces joined the ruling alliance:

1. Big capitalism, whose representative, 'Uthman Ahmed 'Uthman assumed the responsibility of housing, building and reconstruction.

2. Big capitalists and traditional owners of agricultural land who were hurt by the nationalization and guardianship measures, and the traditional agents of U.S. imperialism.

3. Neocompradoric groups composed of the sons, sisters, and relatives of senior state officials. These began to be established inside the class stratum and groups of the alliance. They procured the services of

big monopolist companies and began to play the role of commission agents for these companies.

These transformations that occurred in the ruling alliance were the result of several important political and economic factors:

1. Feudalists and big agricultural landowners were allowed to sell their surplus land in accordance with the agrarian reform law. This led to a great increase in the size and importance of the rural bourgeoisie.

2. The middle bourgeoisie increased. Particularly the commercial sector greatly developed and moved into positions of the upper bourgeoisie because of the fantastic profits made through competition, the black market, illegal operations, smuggling, bleeding the public sector by buying goods from it and then selling them at exorbitant prices, and because of the failure to take deterrent or preventive measures to stop the growth of these social groups.

3. The nationalization and guardianship measures that have come about since July 1961, and which did not harm the essence of capitalist relations in society, drove the Egyptian bourgeoisie to transfer its investments to nonproductive and parasitic fields which were not affected by the nationalization measures (real estate ownership, taxis, services, trade, competition, furnished apartments, and others). All this led to the development of these bourgeois sectors and the increase of their economic influence.

4. Increasingly, strata of the bureaucracy and technocracy have begun to link their class interests with private activity and have begun to enter into joint projects with the private sector.

5. Marriage ties and relationships began to appear among the ancient class families and those of the ruling alliance. As a result, this led to a link in class interests among them.

6. The reactionary Right and the Nasserite Right exerted increasing pressure on the authority in an attempt to stop independent development and impose retreat and setback by:

A. Attempting to exploit the crisis of the Nasserite regime following the 1967 setback (the unsuccessful military coup of the field marshal), and asking Zakariyya Muhiyi al-Din in the Supreme Executive Committee to stop development, expand the private sector, and follow the policy of openness.

B. Attempting to grasp the opportunity of 'Abd al-Nasser's death (the attempt of the old revolution council members to revive the council and hand over authority to it and the famous memorandum of the ten submitted to al-Sadat).

C. Investing the October War achievements in the interest of the right (the frank call to condemn Gamal 'Abd al-Nasser, liquidating the

July revolution, canceling the public sector and the labor and peasant gains, and so on and so forth).

Although the attempts of the Right in 1967 were unsuccessful due to the massive upheaval on July 9 and 10 and the resistance of Gamal 'Abd al-Nasser and the Left to the scheme, the Nasserite regime offered concessions to the Right that strengthened its arm (permitting the private sector in 1968 to export all nontraditional goods). The value of the commodities produced and exported by the private sector reached 4.27 million pounds in 1967–68, that is, an increase of 1.716 million pounds over 1966–67.

7. Gamal 'Abd al-Nasser's disappearance from the scene, the Nasserite Left's lack of entrenched popular roots, its lack of belief in the democracy of the popular masses, and its determination to settle accounts with the Nasserite Center and Right without relying on the masses, all led to settling the dispute within the ranks of the authority, not in the interest of the Nasserite Left.

8. The asset gained from the October War facilitated the authority in gradually peddling its defeatist scheme.

9. The active role played by U.S. imperialism in the area following the October War to exploit the results of this war has strengthened the positions of the agents of imperialism and the reactionary social forces and enabled them to take steps in the direction of regaining several of its old positions (returning 'Ali and Mustafa Amin and Ahmed Abu al-Fath to the press, the return from abroad of the leaders of the Moslem Brotherhood and pardoning them, and the appearance of the cadres of the old classes).

The deviation of the ruling authority from the progressive nationalist line which was pursued by the Nasserite regime, its relapse from the economic and social measures of the July revolution, its downgrading the masses, gains, and its increasing connection with the world capitalist regime have become clearer every day.

But does this mean that the ruling authority in Egypt had fallen in the pitfalls of agentry, a matter which makes it incumbent upon us to wage the struggle in order to bring about its collapse?

Actually, while appraising the ruling authority and defining our stand toward it, we must avoid falling into two deviations:

1. An adventurist left-wing deviation that would jump to the conclusion that the ruling authority as a whole has betrayed the national issue and will accordingly call for its collapse.

2. A lackey right-wing deviation which turns a blind eye toward the continued deviations which are taking place in the authority's nature. Changes took place and are still taking place in the balance of forces in-

side the ruling alliance and the increasing alliance of the authority with the imperialist plans in the area. This deviation considers the authority as a whole a nationalist authority.

Each of the two deviations stems from ignoring objective reality and does not pay attention to the fact that the ruling alliance includes unharmonious elements and several social groups and classes. Some of these have actually reached the extent of treason and agentry.

By virtue of the dual nature of the national bourgeoisie, others try to conclude a truce with imperialism, desperately struggle for reaching a compromise with it, and dream of playing the role of its small partner in the area. This occurs under the influence of increasing fear from the political and social consequences of a long-term war with imperialism and Israel, from the repercussions of such a war on the class struggle in the society, and from the increasing weight of the progressive role being played in the Palestinian resistance in the Arab homeland.

In addition, there are quarters in the ruling alliance which still believe, in one way or another, in the national Nasserite line and try to adhere to this line to an extent that does not drag it into a conflict with the ruling alliance.

It is our duty to realize the differences between attitudes of the various alliance quarters and to point out the contradictions which take place among these quarters. Although they are secondary contradictions, still we cannot deny or ignore their significance so long as they reach an extent which requires from time to time a political liquidation inside the ranks of the alliance commandos (alienating the 'Aziz Sidqi group and then the 'Abd al-'Aziz Hijazi group).

We, however, should not turn a blind eye toward the fact that the agents and reactionary forces are the ones whose influence is continuously increasing inside the alliance, whereas the size, weight, and influence of the national forces are continuously diminishing.

In the face of these specific circumstances, accusing the authority — with all its classes — of treason and calling for overthrowing it is an adolescent attitude which ignores the fact that there are still patriotic elements and groups inside the authority. On the other hand, this attitude also ignores the fact that some quarters of the alliance have a hesitant nature, although today they are going along to a great extent with the agentry trends and are quickly endeavoring to make a compromise with imperialism and Zionism. These quarters might turn away from their attitude tomorrow if the U.S.-Israeli arrogance continues and if the masses succeed on the Arab and local levels in resisting the schemes of capitulation and apostasy.

It is a simplification for us to imagine the ease with which the ruling authority—regardless of its intentions—can reach an overall settlement with the Zionist enemy and U.S. imperialism, because the attitudes of the various sides in such a deal are governed by contradictions, struggles, and the balance of several forces.

Within the United States there are forces desiring a settlement of the issue which would enable the United States to depend on protecting its interests in the area on Israel and on friendly Arab regimes at the same time. However, there are also other forces which adhere to absolute support for Zionism and Israel.

In Israel there are extremist Zionist forces—the weight or effect of which should not be minimized—which opposed the attainment of a compromise with the Arabs regardless of the extent of concessions on the part of the Arabs.

In Egypt the ruling authority cannot discount completely the patriotic trends within the Egyptian armed forces and the reactions to any submissive settlement among the ranks of the Arab masses in Egypt and the Arab world. Likewise, the ability of this authority to make concessions decreases with the passage of time since the October War, because the credit with which this authority emerged after this war decreases daily. On the other hand, the aggravation of the crisis of the world captialist system in general and the aggravation of the political and economic crisis of U.S. imperialism in particular tend to minimize the extent of the benefit derived by the ruling authority from the policy of attachment to the United States and from the economic open-door policy toward the West, and tend to dissipate a great deal of the dreams of the social forces which place their stakes on the U.S. horse.

In the opposite direction, turning a blind eye to the dangerous pitfall toward which the ruling authority is taking the country and attempting to defend the policy of a setback or regret, while justifying the steps and actions of the authority and stressing the patriotic nature of the ruling alliance as a whole is a lackey rightist attitude.

It is our duty to expose and denude all the measures or attitudes involving a retreat or reversal from the patriotic line or a jeopardy of the gains of the workers, peasants, and the toiling masses.

While the authority continues to draw away from the patriotic and progressive line, emphasizing the patriotism of the authority cannot be anything other than a kind of camouflaging and misleading which would make the masses lose their alertness and distract them from the responsibility of resisting the pacification and capitulationist trends.

Briefly, our attitude toward the ruling authority in Egypt is specified as follows:

— We will struggle to strike at the agent forces in the regime which seek to implement the imperialist designs and will remove these forces from the ruling alliance.

— We seek to paralyze the hesitation of the hesitant forces which are increasingly leaning toward the pacification of imperialism.

— We will induce and encourage the patriotic elements and factions in the authority to resist the submissive inclinations and the pacification inclinations which equally foster the U.S. plan in the area.

Our tasks are the following: Being guided by the Marxist-Leninist teachings, our party is required to forecast all the possibilities in the coming stage and prepare for facing them.

The fierce onslaught being launched by the ruling authority against the gains of the workers, peasants, and the toiling masses and the escalation of inflation and the aggravation of the cost of living tend to create sudden explosions of the social contradictions in the cities and the countryside.

Accordingly, it is the duty of our party not to be taken by surprise by these events, to be prepared to face them and direct them in a vigilant manner, upholding the appropriate revolutionary slogans.

The announcement of the establishment of our party and its increasing activities, in addition to the aggravation of the class struggle, will induce the ruling authority to escalate the war of attrition which it is waging against the progressive forces in Egypt.

It is the duty of our party to be prepared to avoid the blows, benefiting from the past experience. We must speed up the completion of the party's structure, adhere to the rules of safety, and protect, strengthen, and deepen the party's ideological and organizational unity.

The increasing activity of the reactionary rightist forces and of the extremist religious groups and the Moslem Brotherhood's regrouping and intensification of activities portend the possibility of fascist coup d'état activities.

It is the duty of our party to warn of these dangers and to prepare to face and resist them. It is also our party's duty to make good use of all the forms of struggle and to be prepared to work under various circumstances.

Some sides of the ruling alliance are pushing with all their strength in the direction of proceeding along the course leading to a capitulationist settlement at the end of the road. Other sides entertain naïve hopes for what is called "the reassessment of U.S. policy in the area." Under such circumstances, it is possible that the ruling authority will attain a partial U.S. settlement. It devolves on our party to expose and denude the attempts made by the Right and its propaganda in this respect.

The U.S. government is dragging its feet in proclaiming its new policy in the area. However, the features of this policy have begun to be clearly manifested through the feverish imperialist and reactionary attempts to prepare a new massacre for the Palestinian resistance, to fragment Lebanon's unity and to attempt to divide its territory, to foment a civilian, sectarian war in Lebanon, and to escalate Israeli acts of aggression against southern Lebanon.

THE EXPOSURE AND DENUDING OF THE U.S. POLICY

The new U.S. policy in the Middle East will reflect the stability of the imperialist struggle in the area along with a change in its tactics and methods. It is imperative that our party expose and denude this fact and foil the misleading attempts which will be made by the trumpets of the reactionary right wing in lauding this policy by proclaiming it.

The attitude of our party toward any expected U.S. settlements emanates from a constant and principled stand, namely, rejecting partial and unilateral settlements, refusing to recognize Israel or to reach conciliation with it, or making a commitment to any conditions tending to hamper the struggle of the heroic Palestinian people to recover their rights, determine their own fate on their national soil, and set up their democratic state over the liberated areas of their territories.

In the coming stage, the ruling authority might try to put a liberal touch to the regime by allowing, within limits, various platforms within the socialist union or by allowing the publication of some new newspapers. In such a case one should not exaggerate in applauding such steps or portraying them as democratic openness, because the ruling authority will make certain that these things take place within the narrowest limits, that is, within the framework of the classes and factions forming the ruling alliance in order to contain the political movement in Egypt. At the same time one should not take an isolationist or negative attitude toward these steps, but one should seek to benefit from them to the maximum extent.

The positive attitude of our party will help expose the false character of these steps if the authority refuses to establish a platform for the leftist forces, allow the publication of a newspaper for the Left, or provide a useful work opportunity for the progressive forces in the country in case the authority yields to pressure.

Our slogans and the forms and methods of our struggle in the coming stage must not be either above or below the level of the masses' preparedness.

THE TASKS OF THE COMING STAGE

Our party specifies for itself the following basic task in the coming stage:

1. Our party will expose the capitulationist and pacification trends. It will call for a unified struggle attitude for the revolutionary and patriotic forces in the domestic and Arab fields against imperialist U.S. designs and solutions.

2. Our party will expose and resist the tendencies seeking to bring about Egypt's forsaking of its pioneering pan-Arab responsibilities in the Arab liberation movement and will play a positive and effective role in unifying the Arab progressive forces. Our party will struggle for the betterment and bolstering of Egypt's relations with the progressive and patriotic Arab states which take an attitude hostile to the U.S. imperialism and its designs in the area (Iraq, Syria, Libya, Algeria, and the PDRY).

From this premise, we can condemn the suspicious campaigns being launched by the Egyptian information media against Libya, reiterating like a parrot all the lexicon of the arguments used by the trumpets of imperialist propaganda against Egypt when it broke the arms monopoly and established friendly relations with the Soviet Union and the socialist countries. At the same time it is incumbent on us to reject the course of personal vituperation and the call for overthrowing the regime in Egypt.

3. Our party must actively defend the gains of the workers and peasants and mobilize the masses to enable them to counter any encroachments on them or any violations of democratic liberties.

4. Our party must speed up the establishment of the workers-peasants alliance and building the front of popular forces benefiting from the appropriate circumstances created by the policy of the ruling authority and which will lead to the expansion of the social basis of the front.

The building of the front must take place simultaneously from the bottom through the joint struggle for the masses' daily demands and for the transfer of the leadership of the mass and trade unionist organizations to the hands of the struggling and revolutionary elements.

And from the top [it must build] through the intensification of the contacts with the various patriotic and democratic forces and the direction and ripening of the constructive dialogue with these forces.

5. Our party must seek to transform our party into a mass party by establishing the closest ties of struggle between our party and the masses.

In this critical and decisive stage through which the country is pass-ing—in which the positions of the rightists in the authority are strength-ening—in which the ruling alliance unilaterally acquires the right to the public political organization, and in which the fierceness of the onslaught against the gains of the workers, peasants, and toiling masses is intensi-fying — our Egyptian Communist party now appears in the arena in its capacity as the party of the working class, the peasants, and the Egyptian toilers as the sole organized political force in the ranks of the camp of the revolution, while the other patriotic and progressive forces lack political organizations capable of leading their class struggle.

Therefore our party, which had the honor to break through the wall of the ban on party activity, and which appeared as the independent ros-trum of the Egyptian working class, bears great historical responsibilities under the present circumstances, whether for preserving the national in-dependence and foiling the designs of imperialism and local reaction, leading the daily struggle of the working class, the peasants, and the toil-ing masses, or in arousing and helping the allied patriotic and progressive forces in closing their ranks and in their mobilization, organization, and the construction of the popular forces front.

Although it is the right of our comrades to be proud of having had the honor of setting up the independent organization of the working class, despite the terrorist and fierce harassment campaigns and face to face with these harassment campaigns, it is the duty of our comrades to un-derstand the heaviness of their responsibilities with an indefatigable or-der, confidence in which despair does not penetrate, insistence which does not accept capitulation, revolutionary patience, and a selflessness which does not anticipate results and which is not weary of difficulties. We are confident that our comrades, who have succeeded in transforming the scattered cells of the Egyptian Marxists into a party for the Egyptian working class, are definitely able to continue to march on the road of struggle until final victory regardless of the costly sacrifices.

[Signed] The Central Secretariat of the Egyptian Communist Party, July 1975.

Note: At its recent meeting the politburo of the Egyptian Communist party approved the outlines of this report and entrusted the Central Sec-retariat with drafting it.

APPENDIX D*
The Egyptian Communist Party's Political Report:
The Main Trends in the Domestic Situation

The political bureau of the Egyptian Communist party has issued a report titled "For the Sake of Real Change in Egypt and the Upsurge of the Arab Liberation Movement," consisting of three sections: international, Arab, and local. *Al-Yasar al-'Arabi* published excerpts from the part related to Egypt.

The report defines the basic situations after al-Sadat's death as follows. No change has occurred in the class nature of the regime and no turnover has occurred in the members of the ruling class alliance, in the spirit of the elimination of some al-Sadatist symbols and the prosecution of some members of al-Sadat's family.

Mubarak still is to one degree or another anxious to distinguish himself from his predecessor in conduct and practice and increasingly to express the interests of the productive segment of the ruling-class alliance.

Attempts to change the balance of forces within the ruling alliance by causing the retrenchment of the parasitic sector of the bourgeois ruling class are still proceeding falteringly and hesitantly, taking care to avoid infringing on this sector as a social force participating in the ruling alliance.

Al-Yasar al-'Arabi (Paris), No. 55, June 1983, pp. 18–20.

Some limited favorable changes are still being made which do not infringe on the essential features of the policies of apostasy.

The essential features of the policies of apostasy remain as they were.

In spite of all the official admissions of economic disaster, and in spite of all the media clamor about the need to correct the course of the economy, the regime has not adopted a single economic measure to help rid the country of the policies that brought about this disaster. Indeed, the regime has not taken steps worth mentioning even to guide or amend its policies.

The ill-starred policy of liberalization, in its al-Sadatist conception, is still the official policy of the government, in spite of all the noise about "orienting this policy." The system of importing without currency transfers is still in effect.

The new five-year plan (1982–87) reveals the ruling regime's adherence to the same objectives and orientations as those of the al-Sadat era in the area of economics. The plan is focusing its attention on the activities of the nonproductive private sector, and the proportion of private sector investment has dropped from 32 to 24 percent. The execution of the plan will further aggravate the disruption in the distribution of national income.

The regime has started to launch a vicious new attack against the rights of the poor and the small peasants in order to consolidate the positions of the big agricultural landowners and to serve the interests of large Egyptian and foreign agricultural capitalism, which has invaded the Egyptian countryside intensively in recent years. The People's Assembly is now debating proposed amendments to the Agrarian Reform Law which will constitute an assault on the peasants' gains and a regression from the Agrarian Reform Law. These amendments will demand that agricultural landowners be empowered to expel tenant peasants in the event that the landlord or tenant dies or the landlord wishes to sell the land, and they will also permit the landowner to transfer from cash rent to sharecropper rent. The regime's emphasis on basic commodities is still in effect, and the prices of goods are being raised wholesale without commotion.

Meanwhile, the wealth of a handful of parasitic millionaires is multiplying with every passing day. The proportion of Egyptians living below the poverty line in 1981 came to 33 percent in the urban areas, 44 percent in the rural areas, and 37 percent in the nation as a whole.

The regime is still anxious not to challenge parasitic capitalism as a social class, and it still adheres to it as a component of the ruling alliance, contenting itself with trimming its claws and reducing its political influence without infringing on its economic conditions, thus enabling parasitic capitalism to continue to grow and permitting it to consolidate its political influence and control or to affect political decision making.

Although the barbaric Israeli aggression on Lebanon and the escalation of the people's struggle in Egypt against imperialism and Zionism have made it mandatory that the regime be unenthusiastic over its relations with Israel, freeze some sections of its former agreements with it, go slowly with normalization procedures, stumble in the autonomy negotiations, and advance its dealings with the Liberation Organization, these are passing phenomena that are fated to disappear, as long as the regime's adherence to Camp David in platform and in text continues; as long as the regime's loyalty to its essential commitments relative to Camp David documents, among them the provision of Egyptian oil for the Israeli enemy, remain in effect; as long as the Israeli ambassador continues to lurk on Egyptian territory; as long as the regime continues its pressures on the Palestine Liberation Organization to urge it to follow the al-Sadatist platform, which is based on the grant of prior concessions and the unilateral recognition of Israel; as long as the regime continues to rush impulsively after American solutions, promotes the Reagan initiative, and urges what it calls the constructive role American imperialism is playing in the region; and as long as the regime imposes strict restrictions on any popular movement against American imperialism and Israel.

Mubarak's practices since his assumption of the presidency have created a relatively better political climate and have given the political opposition greater opportunities to express itself, but the regime is still adhering to antidemocratic policies and insists on continuing the state of emergency. It is packing its prisons with political detainees while continuing political trials of the people in opposition to it. It is adhering to the aresenal of laws restricting freedom, which al-Sadat issued. Mubarak himself has stood up to defend these laws and to justify their retention, has refused resolutely to abrogate them, has ridiculed the people who are calling for their abrogation, and has enthusiastically defended the Ethics Law, which all noble and democratic forces inside and outside Egypt have condemned and one of the prominent ruling party experts on law has called "a disgrace." The regime has interfered grossly in the student federation elections in the universities and is continuing its aggressive scheme against the Lawyers' Union.

Aggravated class struggle is the basic characteristic of the international situation. The class struggle going on in Egypt has been distinguished in the past year by the following events:

1. An incipient surge toward national struggle, an awakening in the national struggle thanks to the parties, the national and progressive forces, the labor and professional unions, and committees with the character of a front, such as the National Committee to Support the Palestinian and Lebanese People and the Committee to Defend the National Culture. This struggle has started to create a qualitative transformation in the consciousness of growing sectors of the people and in the mass atmosphere in general toward Camp David and normalization, and the effects of the al-Sadatist brainwashing and his psychological war against Arab affiliation and national affiliation have started to disappear.

2. An escalation of the democratic struggle, embodied in the broad campaign against the continued state of emergency and its extension for another year, the demand for the release of prisoners, the campaign against torture, and the enlarged lawyers' movement for the restoration of legitimacy to the Lawyers' Union.

3. The growing economic and social struggle, embodied in a series of workers' and students' strikes and sitdowns and a fierce struggle in defense of the public sector and the gains of the workers and peasants.

In all these struggles, our party has played a vanguard, innovative, effective, and growing role.

The class struggle in Egypt is taking place essentially between the ruling class alliance on one hand and the forces of change on the other.

In addition, a struggle is going on within the regime and the ruling alliance engendered by secondary contradictions between the forces that aim at establishing al-Sadatism without al-Sadat and the forces that have the goal of guiding the regime's policies and rectifying its practices.

In the past, the class struggle concentrated on a group of focal issues, foremost of which are the following:

1. The struggle over economic and social policy. This struggle has essentially centered on liberalization policy, conceptions regarding development, positions on parasitic capitalism and the spreading phenomenon of corruption, and positions on the masses' economic demands.

REGARDING LIBERALIZATION

The al-Sadatist forces have insisted on adhering to the policy of liberalization in the consumerist sense, which provides the best climate for the incubation, growth, and enrichment of parasitic capitalists.

The forces for guidance within the regime have called for the shift of liberalization to a "productive liberalization" to serve the interests of the major elements of productive capitalism.

Meanwhile, the forces of change have opposed the platform of the policy of liberalization from its very foundations and have demanded that it be abandoned, that the domestic economy be protected from infiltration by foreign monopolies, and that foreign investment legislation be abrogated.

The labor union movement has joined the forces of change. The general assembly of the General Federation of Workers' Unions has decided to demand that the establishment of any foreign company engaging in economic activity similar to [that of] any domestic firm be suspended.

REGARDING DEVELOPMENT

The al-Sadatist forces, which have wrecked development in Egypt, have spurned all efforts to develop production and have pursued nonproductive activities or activities that are at the margin of the production process.

The forces of guidance have concentrated attention on industrialization and increased production in accordance with a platform that separates development from raising the standard of living of the masses of the people so that increased production will be devoted to increasing the profits accruing to the coffers of the major capitalists at a time when the masses' suffering is intense.

The forces of change demand comprehensive economic and social development founded on planning that will take into consideration the interests of the masses of the people. This will put a limit to the parasitic plundering of the resources of the country, will reject the invasion of our economy by foreign monopoly, and will link economic growth with equity in distribution so that increases in national income will be directed to greater and greater basic social, cultural, educational, and medical services instead of flowing into the coffers of the exploitative, domineering few.

REGARDING THE DEMANDS
OF THE MASSES OF THE PEOPLE

The al-Sadatist forces have clung to their fixed position on this demand, which is rejection and repression by iron and fire — a position that manifested itself under al-Sadat's aegis in the crushing of mass movements and worker strikes by the tanks, helicopters, and military units of Central Security.

The forces of guidance have ignored the demands of the masses, have condemned the promotion of such demands, and have condemned "special interest groups." The new five-year plan has failed to find a solution to the everyday problems of the masses.

Meanwhile, the budgets of the security agencies and allocations to the Central Security forces are swelling year after year. The regime uses a paucity of resources and revenues as an excuse for failing to respond to the demands of the masses and tries to divert the masses with tranquilizers by means of superficial, formalistic, bureaucratic solutions to their problems, which are alien to the changes required by the social platform.

The forces of change have continued to struggle for the gains of the masses of the people, especially the workers and peasants. The working class has launched a series of strikes and sit-ins which have reflected the escalating spirit of struggle to gain better work circumstances and conditions.

REGARDING PARASITIC CAPITALISM
AND THE PHENOMENON OF CORRUPTION

The al-Sadatist forces have tirelessly resisted the escalating campaign against corruption and parasitic capitalism in order to preserve and strengthen their positions. These forces have started to accuse the forces of change of attempting to distort the image and reputation of Egypt.

Toward the end of 1982 the organizational secretariat of the ruling party issued a publication which clearly expressed the al-Sadatist forces' policy, accusing the opposition of creating illusory issues and alleged abberant acts with the objective of raising provocation, casting doubts, and exploiting the masses' sufferings.

The forces of guidance, for their part, have tried to portray corruption as the moral deviation of an individual character, and they have been anxious, to underline the change in their conduct, to prosecute occasional symbols of parasitic activities in an attempt to settle all scores against individuals. Each new prosecution of a symbol of parasitic capitalism has led to the involvement of additional government organizations and officials in those organizations, by virtue of the intermarriage and interconnection of the interests of parasitic capitalism and senior bureaucrats and technocrats in the government and the public sector.

The forces of change have demanded that class corruption, and not just individual corruption, be challenged and that corruption be treated as a social phenomenon that has become widespread under the aegis of the hegemony over the agencies and institutions of the government and [we must] confiscate the wealth of the parasites.

1. The struggle over the position regarding the public sector. For years, the al-Sadatist forces have worked ceaselessly to sustain a vicious attack against the public sector, with the objective of demolishing it, step by step, liquidating its role in society by shutting down some of its units on the pretext that they are incurring losses, selling its successful units or getting them involved in joint projects with foreign capital, liquidating its links by eliminating organizations, and constantly weakening it in the face of unequal competition from the Egyptian private sector and foreign capital.

In the wake of Mubarak's assumption of the presidency, the campaign directly to liquidate the public sector fell off somewhat, especially after it met violent resistance from the Egyptian working class and the forces of change. Following Mubarak's instructions, the government withdrew the draft law, and Mubarak declared his objection to the principle of offering public sector shares for trade on the stock exchange, expressed his interest in supporting the public sector, and proceeded to make inspection tours of the units in it.

The forces of guidance have elected to retain the public sector while guiding it in the direction of developing and expanding productive capital in Egypt.

The forces of guidance have started to promote bureaucratic methods to support the public sector, such as establishing holding companies or strengthening the grip of the government apparatus and ministers over public sector units.

The view of some bureaucratic and technocratic leaders of the public sector regarding the support and development of the public sector consists of liberating it from government tutelage, attaining independence of administration within it, and freeing it to issue bylaws, deal with workers, and reduce their rights and guarantees against severance.

The forces of change, for their part, have waged a successful struggle to defend the public sector in which the Egyptian working class has played a prominent, innovative, vanguard role, forming committees with the character of a front to defend the public sector at work sites under the initiative of the national and democratic forces. The union movement has played an effective role in the struggle, and the leaders of the General Federation of Workers' Unions belonging to the ruling party have not been absent from it.

Although this mass resistance has succeeded in blunting the vicious attack on the public sector and has obstructed efforts at direct liquidation, the elimination of the leading role of the public sector in the domestic economy is still continuing. This elimination will be achieved not merely by closing down or selling public sector units or offering their shares for trading but by more devious and dangerous means, by the mobilization of the public sector to serve foreign and Egyptian capital and to exploit its resources to finance projects of the private sector and investment companies. The role of the public sector as a basic investor in investment companies has been noticeably prominent in recent years. The liquidation of the public sector can be achieved in another area by liquidating it technically from within, by plundering its personnel and technical labor, enticing them to emigrate to work in the investment companies or encouraging them to hasten to find job opportunities abroad.

Therefore, our party is struggling for true, effective protection of the public sector and support for its true development, stressing its requisite national role.

It is not enough for the forces of change to succeed in preserving the public sector as an entity; rather, the test lies in the role this entity will play in the society and the interests it will serve.

2. The struggle over the position on imperialist hegemony. The al-Sadatist forces have continued to work to solidify the country's subordination to American imperialism. In September 1982 the government signed an Egyptian-American treaty to encourage and protect investment, which sanctified economic subordination to American imperialism.

The forces of change immediately took a stand against this conspiracy and took the initiative in divulging the essence of the agreement, which infringed on national sovereignty and was destructive of the domestic economy. It intensified the struggle to expose the role of American imperialism as the first and major enemy of the Egyptian people.

The forces of guidance, since Mubarak took charge, have been careful to modify the policy of blatant subordination to American imperialism which al-Sadat pursued, have tended to highlight nonalignment, and have declared that the restoration of normal relations with the Soviets is being studied. In the wake of the disclosure of the essence of the draft American-Egyptian treaty by the forces of change, Mubarak ordered that the procedures for approving it be suspended and that it be studied again, and some leaders of the ruling party have expressed numerous reservations over the provisions of the agreement.

3. The struggle over the position regarding the Israeli enemy. The al-Sadatist forces have called for a total literal commitment to the Camp David agreements and the peace treaty with Israel as policy, and the or-

ganizational secretariat of the ruling party, in its publication issued at the end of 1982, attacked the appeal to freeze the Camp David Accord and expel the ambassador.

The forces of change continued their struggle against the Camp David agreements and normalization and organized a mass signature campaign to demand the expulsion of the Israeli ambassador. Some successful forms of solidarity with the Palestinian and Lebanese people were also manifested in the days of the siege of Beirut.

The general conference of clubs of faculty members in Egyptian universities issued resolutions prohibiting dealings with Israeli universities, and committees of support against participation by Israeli professors in scientific conferences were active in the universities. More than one hundred university professors in Alexandria University sent cables of protest to the president and the president of Alexandria University, protesting the granting of permission to certain Israeli professors to take part in the activities of the international conference on photochemistry which the University of Alexandria had organized.

The guidance forces have adhered to their commitment to Camp David while attempting to slow down the normalization procedures in a quiet, undeclared, indirect manner.

4. The struggle over the position of democracy. The al-Sadatist forces have continued their efforts to disturb the relatively better political climate which Mubarak's actions since assuming the presidency have engendered, and they have exerted pressure on Mubarak from within the ruling party to resume al-Sadat's repressive platform in dealing with the opposition.

The forces of change are struggling to end the state of emergency and eliminate legislation restricting people's freedoms, especially that which restricts the right to form political parties, and are struggling to establish their own independent parties. They demand a comprehensive democratic transformation. The forces of change have succeeded in forming the Egyptian Committee for the Defense of Freedoms, which has unified the efforts of all the political forces in the area of the defense of democracy.

The forces of change have also succeeded in propelling the labor union movement onto the stage of democratic struggle. The general assembly of the General Federation of Workers' Unions recently requested a review of the Law Protecting the Domestic Front and the Ethics Law and asked that labor nominations in the coming elections not be submitted to the socialist prosecutor. They have also demanded the abrogation of all exceptional laws and the preservation of the independence of the union movement and have demanded that attempts by the ruling party to establish party committees for itself within productive units and worker groups be thwarted.

FAVORABLE CHANGES AND OUR POSITION ON THEM

The class struggle which the forces of change have led has realized some gains, and one can derive a major lesson from the developments of the past year, during which the masses have moved and have intensified their struggle and have made some gains and imposed setbacks on some aspects of the policy of apostasy.

In the current context of the balance of forces between the camp of revolution and the camp of counterrevolution, and in the context of the incomplete maturation of the subjective and objective elements needed to realize a comprehensive radical change, these limited changes are of importance, and one must deal with them intelligently and determine the suitable slogans and practices to exploit to the maximum so as to prepare the ground for the elimination of the policies of apostasy and surrender and provide the necessary circumstances for advancing the revolutionary process.

Our party considers that the national democratic parties have the duty of opposing every attempt to cause these changes to lapse so as to guarantee the continuation of the current climate, which is suitable for the mass struggle.

The protection of these changes will come about not by boasting about them or exaggerating their status, but rather by revealing their limited nature and by constantly struggling for more comprehensive, deeper changes.

Today, seventeen months after President Mubarak propounded the slogan "turning over a new leaf," the validity of the conclusions of our party's documents has been confirmed. These documents state that radical comprehensive change means a hard class struggle, which cannot be realized from above but is realized through organized, effective mass struggle under the leadership of a democratic national front in which the party of the working class plays a growing leadership role.

THE NATURE OF THE DESIRED CHANGE

The change the masses of our people demand is not the replacement of faces that have been discredited by ones that have not yet been, the

embellishment or enhancement or the ugly face of al-Sadatism, or the repair of the destroyed system of al-Sadatist subservience, and it is not an
artificial breathing spell or process of transfusion which will benefit the
moribund al-Sadatist alliance.

The change the masses of our people want is deliverance from the
policies of apostasy and surrender, which have brought our people to the
depths of the abyss, the elimination of the political, economic, and social
influence of the social forces these policies have brought to the fore; the
confiscation and nationalization of their fortunes, which were plundered
from the treasuries of the government and usurped from the blood of the
people and the sweat of the brow of the toilers; and the purging from the
institutions of government of the representatives of these social forces
and their hangers-on.

The change to which the masses of our people aspire is the repudiation of the road to subordination to neocolonialism and the pursuit of the
road to independent development. The ordeal our people are going
through is not the product of mistakes, poor evaluations, or the deviation
of one official or another, but is the natural and inevitable result of capitalist growth in the context of subordination to the system of neocolonialism, the bitter fruit of the policy of liberalization, and the surrender of
the keys to our economy to the multinational monopolies.

The ideas the masses of our people want are ones that can be translated into perceptible results, which will alleviate their suffering, will
limit the class differences between the parasites and big capitalists on one
hand and the workers, peasants, and intermediate classes of the people
on the other, and will be reflected in tangible measures that will inhibit
vile parasitical plunder and greedy capitalistic exploitation and raise the
masses' standard of living.

In brief, the desired change consists of a group of measures to be
taken in favor of specific social forces and groups against and at the expense of other groups and classes which are antagonistic to the people,
exploit them, and dominate them.

The salvation of the nation will not occur spontaneously, and the desired change will not be realized by administrative decrees from above.
It will take place through class struggle against the puppet class forces
which have an interest in the continuation of the old conditions.

Therefore, the instrument and strike force for the attainment of
change are the masses of the people, the masses of the workers, peasants,
the lower bureaucracy, and the national bourgeoisie. Thus it is impossible
for change to occur from within the ruling alliance or for the salvation of
the nation to come about as a gift from the regime that has caused the nation's ordeal, especially since time has revealed the inadequacy of the no-

tion the forces of guidance within the regime have adopted on change and their limited ability to bring it about.

The national alternative to the policies of apostasy will not be realized through the ruling al-Sadatist alliance but must be forged by the masses.

The mass struggle will not be effective and decisive in the battle for change unless it is furnished with the elements of awareness and organization and unless it is rid of haphazard conduct.

Therefore, we have been, and always will be, in favor of the enlightenment of the masses, the organization of their movement, and the escalation of their struggle to achieve their social, economic, and political demands.

In another area, the conversion of the masses of the people into an effective force in the struggle for change requires that these masses be politicized and that they be drawn to take interest in political issues and join the political struggle. That will not automatically be achieved by those masses but will be achieved through concentrated, organized, persistent daily activity within the ranks of the working class, the peasants, and the other forces which the policies of apostasy and capitulation are grinding down or harming, which are going through crisis, which are suffering from the ordeal, and which are aspiring to change. It is necessary to connect the particular problems of the masses with the general issues of the nation and enlighten the masses by linking the two in an inseparable manner.

It is also necessary to persevere to shift the movement of the masses and to advance it from a state of observing and waiting to a state of action, immersion, action, and conscious, organized activity. The masses will not move effectively in the pursuit of change unless they are organized in their political parties and mass organizations, unless they are closely attached to their vanguards, and unless these vanguards are capable of mobilizing these masses and providing them with a program for combat and appropriate combative slogans.

It is necessary that all the detachments of the Egyptian national movement join together in the context of a front. The national democratic forces have succeeded in forming numerous committees with the character of a front, but these committees act in the framework of partial issues, and front activity is still short of the level the stage demands. The national democratic forces must hasten in taking steps to build their strategic front, the national democratic front, and to declare their tentative front, the front of national salvation.

UNDERLINE OUR PARTY'S POSITION
ON THE RULING REGIME

Our party's position on the ruling regime is distinct from subservient right-wing hypotheses and secessionist left-wing hypotheses whose banner is borne by some political forces in Egypt. Our party, in determining this position, proceeds from four specific considerations:

1. The class nature of the regime. Our party's program has stated that the powers under al-Sadat's aegis embodied a reactionary subservient class alliance led by parasitic capitalism and containing the following class forces: parasitical capitalism, especially compradores; the higher levels of the bureaucracy and technocracy, which have connections with imperialism and international monopoly capitalism; industrial, commercial, and large agricultural capitalism, connected to foreign capitalism, foreign trade, and the export of crops; and feudalist cliques.

After the death of al-Sadat, the class nature of the regime did not change, and parasitic capitalism, which is a distinctive class of the large bourgeoisie, still holds the most powerful positions in the political, executive, and legislative institutions of the regime. It is the main power center among the authorities. That explains the survival of the essence of the al-Sadatist policies and the faltering and vacillating steps toward guidance. The al-Sadatist forces are still the most effective element in the ruling alliance. For all these reasons, our party's strategic position regarding the regime remains unchanged.

2. The distinctive view of the institution of the presidency. Our party, in March 1982, pointed out, in the report of its political bureau, that the institution of the presidency has been gravitating more and more toward the expression of the interests of the productive sector of the Egyptian bourgeoisie and the bureaucratic and technocratic bourgeoisie since the death of al-Sadat. The unfolding of events has underlined the soundness of our party's position of insisting on the importance of closely watching the phenomenon of the difference in conduct between the institution of the presidency and parasitical capitalism, within the context of the ruling alliance, when it stated that the significance of this difference was that the institution of the presidency no longer played the role it had in the past under al-Sadat, as a basic front-line bastion of parasitic capitalism and the spearhead of counterrevolution. At the same time, however, our party warned, and still is warning, of any exaggeration of the magnitude and scope of this difference in conduct and of any excessive description of the power or desire of the institution of the presi-

dency to strike out at and liquidate parasitic capitalism as a social force. The most that can be expected of the institution of the presidency, in the context of the retention by the ruling al-Sadatist alliance of its previous positions, is merely an attempt to create limited changes in the context of the guidance and programming of the regime's practices.

3. Trends in the indexes of the regime's relations with imperialism and Zionism. When our party defines its tentative position on the regime, it is taking into consideration trends in the indexes of the regime's relationship with American imperialism and Israel and its expectations of the developments in this relationship.

Though Mubarak started his term with the joint Bright Star maneuvers with American imperialism, the skies of Egyptian-American relations are no longer as clear as they were under al-Sadat. The first signs of a lack of mutual trust between Washington and Mubarak have appeared, especially since Mubarak has abandoned the al-Sadatist platform of abject subservience and has started to propagate the notion of a "special relationship" with the United States.

In the course of the past year, Egyptian-Israeli relations have continued to decline, and contractions between the Egyptian regime and Israel have grown, starting with the crisis of Mubarak's refusal to go to Jerusalem, then the problem of Taba, and proceeding through the events of Lebanon and the resultant recall of the Egyptian ambassador. Israel does not hide its uneasiness and anxiety over Egypt's position, and it does not cease to exert pressure on the regime to stimulate the faltering process of normalization.

4. Contradictions within the regime. With every passing day, the lack of harmony that prevails among the parties in the ruling alliance and the contradictions taking place at the apex of power, within the institutions of rule and in the ranks of the ruling party, are being reaffirmed.

These contradictions are secondary, are taking place within the context of the regime, and do not amount to a major contradiction among the parties to the ruling alliance, although they have been tending to escalate and become aggravated, and not to be resolved, under the pressure of the intensifying class struggle under way in the society.

In our party's report to the national and democratic forces, these contradictions and their nature must be apparent, and it is not permissible to ignore them, be indifferent toward them, or become engrossed in struggles among cliques in favor of one group against another.

THE CRYSTALLIZATION OF THE NATIONAL
SALVATION PROGRAM IS AN URGENT TASK

The national and democratic forces in Egypt must immediately crystallize a realistic minimal program for national salvation which will be based on three focal points:

1. The liberation of national will, the restoration of national sovereignty, and the restoration of national political and economic independence.

2. The fulfillment of the social and economic demands of the masses.

3. The attainment of a comprehensive democratic transformation.

These three focal points are sequentially connected, closely knit, and integrated; they cannot be separated from one another, nor can one be carried out while ignoring the others. Therefore, our party objects to all appeals to push any of these three tasks of the struggle into the shadows.

The masses of the people have been pushed to the brink, their daily sufferings have reached the peak, and their accumulated economic and social problems, which infringe on their standard of living, will no longer tolerate any procrastination or delay.

Solving the problems of the masses and responding to their demands will be realized only through the pursuit of an independent road to economic development which is aimed at realizing planned economic development with the goal of responding to the needs of the masses of the people and constantly raising their standard of living.

The effective struggle to realize this goal, against the social forces that are opposed to its attainment, especially parasitic capitalism, will be out of the question in the context of the destruction of democracy and the deprivation of the masses' right to think, express, organize their ranks, and establish political and union organizations capable of leading their political and economic struggle.

Saving the nation from economic ruin and delivering the masses from their economic, social, and democratic ordeal will be out of the question except in a national context that will save the nation from the abyss of subservience and replace the policies of apostasy and capitulation with a national policy which will rid the country of Camp David and its implications, will deliver Egypt's political and economic independence from the clutches of American imperialism and Zionism, and will restore to Egypt its Arab identity.

The basic link in the struggle to achieve a comprehensive transformation continues to be the acquisition of the masses' right to establish their independent party and organizations, liberated from all government control.

It is obvious that the national salvation program will be a limited one, capable of rallying the broadest front of forces aspiring to change in spite of their different ideological premises; therefore, the national salvation program will not be the end of the journey and will not bring about deep radical change in the society. Its only objective will be to end the terrible sequence of deterioration and start the country on the road toward a democratic national regime.

Our success in faithfully meeting all these responsibilities will depend on our party's success in developing its power, supporting its organizational structure, implanting its positions in the political life of the country, and turning it into a mass party with roots that extend far into Egyptian society and [forming] firm, deep relations with the working class, the peasants, the toiling masses, and the young.

This all makes it incumbent on our party in the coming stage that it involve itself to the maximum in the mass struggle, that it give priority to action at the base, in the midst of groups of workers and peasants, stimulate the political struggle in their ranks, and link their economic struggle to the current of general political struggle. It also demands the reaffirmation of our party's presence in all the national economic, social, and democratic struggles, its endorsement of the issues and daily problems of the masses, and its success in setting forth the requisite detailed programs for the various national groups and classes, in crystallizing and presenting power and suitable slogans, and in leading the daily struggle of the masses to attain their demands.

[Signed] The political bureau of the Egyptian Communist Party, February 1983.

NOTES

1. EARLY MARXIST THOUGHT IN EGYPT

1. Amin 'Iz al-Din, *Shakhsiyat wa Marahil 'Ummaliyah* (Cairo: Kitabat, Jumhoriyah No. 16, May 1970), pp. 74–75.
2. Quoted in ibid., pp. 74–75.
3. Ibid., pp. 77–78.
4. Quoted in Rifa'at El-Sa'id, "Al-Fikr al-Ishtiraki al-Misri fi Matla' al-Qarn al-'Ishrin," *Al-Tali'ah* 4, no. 10 (October 1968): 60.
5. Salama Musa, *Al-Ishtirakiyah* (Cairo: Al-Misriyah al-Ahliyah Press, 1913), p. 2.
6. Ibid., p. 14.
7. *Tarbiat Salama Musa* (Cairo: Mu'asasat al-Khanji, 1958), p. 269.
8. The article, entitled "Al-Iqtisad al-Siyasi," was presented without the author's name. See *Muntakhabat al-Mu'ayyad li 'Am 1890* (Cairo: Al-Mu'yyad Press, 1891). This article is perhaps the first publication of Marxist thought.
9. Ibid., p. 292.
10. Ibid., pp. 292–93.
11. Mustafa Hassanain al-Mansuri, *Tarikh al-Mathahib al-Ishtirakiyah* (Cairo: N.p., 1915), pp. 49, 67.
12. Ibid., pp. 4, 5, 8, 11–13.
13. Ibid., p. 10.
14. Ibid., p. 94.
15. Ibid., p. 111.
16. Ibid., pp. 110–17. See Appendix A.
17. Amin 'Iz al-Din, *Al-Mansuri: Sirat Muthaqaf Thawri* (Cairo: Dar al-Ghad al-'Arabi, 1984), pp. 17, 19–20.
18. Ibid., pp. 16–20.
19. Ibid., p. 40.
20. Ibid., p. 61.
21. Haddad's early writings reflected a very conservative political orientation. In his introduction to the translation of David Watson Ronnie's book, Haddad observed, "no matter how powerful democracy becomes, aristocracy must exist . . . to safeguard it" (*Tarikh 'Asaas al-Shari' al-Engliziyah* [Cairo: Al-Miktaba al-Sharqiyah, 1906].

22. Reprinted in *Al-Hilal* (Cairo), December 1, 1967, p. 41.
23. Nicola Haddad, *Al-Ishtirakiyah* (Cairo: Dar al-Hilal, 1920), pp. 5–6, 126.
24. Ibid., pp. 58–61.
25. Ibid., pp. 77–80.

2. THE FIRST MOVEMENT, 1920–1928

1. *Al-Hilal* 2, no. 15 (1894), as quoted in 'Abd al-Wahad Bakr, *Adhwa' 'ala al-Nashat al-Shuyo'ie fi Misr* (Cairo: Dar al-Ma'rif, 1983), p. 18.
2. "Report of the General Governor of the Canal on the Disturbance by the Greek Dock Workers from October 1, 1894, to October 15, 1894, in the Canal Company," File 105, Domestic-Foreign, National Archives Office, Cairo.
3. Interview with 'Abd al-Fatah al-Qadhi (who was assigned in 1941 by the Egyptian Movement for National Liberation to write a history of Egyptian socialism) by Rifa'at El-Sa'id, Cairo, September 21, 1968.
4. Letter from the Office of the khedive to the Prime Minister dated 8 Jamadi the Second, 1300 h., File 81, Domestic-Foreign, National Archives Office, Cairo.
5. Rifa'at El-Sa'id, *Al-Asas al-Ijtima'ie lil Thawrah al-'Urabiyah* (Cairo: Madbouli, 1966), p. 198.
6. *LePhare d, Alexandrie,* May 13, 1901.
7. *Al-Ahram* (Cairo), January 19, 1907.
8. *Al-Moa'yyad* (Cairo), January 21, 22, 1907.
9. *Al-Ahram* (Cairo), January 24, 1907; *al-Moa'yyad* (Cairo), February 12, 1907.
10. Great Britain, Foreign Office, FO 141/779.
11. Archives of the Egyptian Ministry of the Interior, Office of General Security, September 28, 1921.
12. *Al-Ahram* (Cairo), March 7, 1924.
13. Dossier No. 31, *Malaf Kadhiyat al-Shuyo'iyah al-'Ula 1924,* Court Archives, Cairo, al-Mathaf al-Qadhi.
14. Alexandria Police Report (August 10, 1921) in letter (August 29, 1921) from the director general of public security to the Chancery of the British Residence; also Alexandria City Police reports, September 11 and 19, 1921, by the director of special section, Public Security Department, War Office, Cairo, FO 141/779, No. 9065.
15. FO 371/533327, File 6951.
16. *Al-Ahram* (Cairo), March 7, 1924.
17. Gamal al-Sharqawi, "Al-Nash'a wa al-Tatwor," in *Qadhia Fikriyah,* Book 5 (May 1987), p. 14.
18. 'Abd al-'Adhim Mohammed Ramadhan, *Tatawor al-Harakah al-Wataniyah fi Misr Min Sanat 1918 ila Sanat 1936,* 2d ed. (Cairo: Madbouli, 1983), p. 539.
19. Published under the title *Al-Harakah al-Ishtirakiyah* (Cairo: al-Matb'ah al-'Asriyah, ca. 1920).
20. *Al-Ahram* (Cairo), August 17, 1921.
21. Ibid.
22. Ibid., July 12, 13, 1922.
23. Ibid., March 11, 1924.
24. Ibid., December 14, 1921.
25. *Labour Monthly* 2 (March 1922): 267–69; *Communist Review* 2 (April 1922): 464–65.

26. *Al-Ahram* (Cairo), October 20, 1922.

27. Ibid., July 29, 1922, October 18, 1921.

28. Amin 'Iz al-Din, *Tarikh al-Tabaqah al-'Amilah al-Misriyah, 1919–1929* (Cairo: Dar al-Sha'ab, 1970), p. 127.

29. Labour Conciliation Board, Seventh Report (July 21 – March 1922), Submitted to His Excellency the Prime Minister, FO 141/779, File 9321/105.

30. *Al-Ahram* (Cairo), August 3, 4, 1922.

31. Ibid., August 3, 9, 1922.

32. Ibid., October 20, 1922, January 3, 1923.

33. *International Press Correspondence* (Moscow), 3, no. 2 (January 5, 1923): 21.

34. *International Press Correspondence* announced on January 5, 1923, the acceptance of all conditions by the central committee of the Egyptian Socialist party.

35. As quoted in Ramadhan, *Tatawor al-Harakah al-Wataniyah fi Misr,* p. 536.

36. Walter Lacqueur, *Communism and Nationalism in the Middle East* (New York: Praeger, 1957), pp. 34–35. See also FO 371/8968/6287 for the British report on these developments.

37. *Al-Ahram* (Cairo), February 22, 1924.

38. Amin 'Iz al-Din, *Tarikh al-Tabaqah al-'Amilah al-Misriyah,* pp. 134–35.

39. See FO 371/5005/511, FO 371/3719/130134, FO 371/6304/9985.

40. *Al-Ahram* (Cairo), August 3, 1922.

41. Mohummed Anis, *Dirasat fi Wathieq Thawrat 1919,* Vol. 1 (Cairo: Anglo-Egyptian Bookshop, 1963), p. 21.

42. FO 141/779. See also Hanna Batatu, *The Old Social Classes and the Revolutionary Movements of Iraq* (Princeton: Princeton University Press, 1978), p. 378.

43. *Al-Liwa'* (Cairo), September 5, 1921.

44. *Fatwa* issued by the Fatwa Office of Egypt, July 2, 1919. See complete text in Appendix B.

45. FO 141/779, No. 9065.

46. Memorandum from the Office of the Civil Commissioner, Baghdad, to the Secretary to the Government of India and the High Commissioner, Cairo, October 17, 1919, PRO/FO 141/779 No. 9065/28; Letter from Chelmsford to Lord Allenby, October 28, 1919, PRO/FO 141/779 No. 9065/30.

47. Informant's Report, Cairo, August 26, 1919, FO 141/779, File 9065.

48. *Al-Ahram* (Cairo), August 24, 1921.

49. A flyer widely circulated in Cairo following the *fatwa,* entitled *I'taniqu al-Balshafiyah Ayuha al-Misriyun: al-Balshafiyah wa al-Islam wa al-Sheikh Bakheit,* signed by al-Lajnah al-Musta'jalah. For the complete text see FO 141/779, File 9065.

50. Hussein Nameq, *Khulasat al-Iqtisad wa Nubtha Min al-Tarikh al-Iqtisadi* (Cairo: N.p., 1921), p. 102.

51. *Al-Ahram* (Cairo), September 10, 1921.

52. Ibid., September 14, 1921.

53. As described in an internal memorandum in the British High Commission, April 18, 1924, FO 141/779, File 9065/160.

54. Rogers to Furness, Ministry of the Interior, European Department, Office of Director General, February 28, 1924, FO 141/779, File 9065/152.

55. The cost-of-living increases are examined in an internal British High Commission memorandum dated April 18, 1924, FO 141/779, File 9065/160.

56. ALT to Mullock, FO 141/779, File 9065/153.

57. See FO 141/779, File 9065; Kingsford to Allenby, March 28, 1924, FO 141/779, File 9065/154.

58. *Al-Ahram* (Cairo), March 5, 13, 1924.

59. Ibid., March 7, 1924.

60. *Al-'Umal* (Cairo), April 18, 1924.

61. General Report on the Situation in Egypt Presented by the Egyptian Communist Party to the Executive of the Communist International (in French, about September 1, 1924), copy of report with letter, Liddell to Murray, September 14, 1924, FO 141/779, File 9065.

62. See Ramadhan, *Tatawor al-Harakah al-Wataniyah fi Misr,* p. 550.

63. "The Communist Movement in Egypt," May 21, 1925, FO 141/779, File 9065/198.

64. "The Communist Movement in Egypt," June 22, 1925, FO 141/779, File 9065/201.

65. *Al-Ahram* (Cairo), June 3, 1925.

66. Batatu, *Old Social Classes,* p. 381.

3. THE SECOND MOVEMENT, 1930–1950

1. *Kol Shei wa al-Duniya* (Cairo), May 17, 1926.

2. *Al-Ahram* (Cairo), August 9, 1924.

3. "Al-Maniah al-Yoom, Adolf Hitler," *Al-Fallah al-Iktisadi* (Cairo) 5, 12 (September–October 1938): xvi.

4. Personal letter from Marcel Israel to Rifa'at El-Sa'id, in the files of El-Sa'id.

5. Interview with Henri Curiel by Rifa'at El-Sa'id, Paris, February 25, 1970.

6. Ahmed Sadiq Sa'ad, *Safahat min al-Yasar al-Misri fi a'qab al-Harb al-'Alamiyah al-Thaniyah, 1945–1946* (Cairo: Madbouli Press, 1976), p. 43.

7. Ibid., p. 45.

8. Interview with Raymond Agion by Rifa'at El-Sa'id, Paris, April 4, 1973.

9. Marcel Israel, "A Report on the Beginning of the Workers' Movement in Egypt to the Italian Communist Party," 1952 (unpublished), from the files of Ismael and El-Sa'id.

10. Sa'ad, *Safahat min al-Yasar al-Misri fi a'qab al-Harb al-'Alamiyah al-Thaniyah,* pp. 47–49.

11. Interview with Sadiq Sa'ad by Tareq Y. Ismael, Cairo, December 27, 1986.

12. Interviews with Paul Jacquot-Descombes by Rifa'at El-Sa'id and Tareq Y. Ismael, Paris, November 1, December 18, 1968.

13. Sa'ad, *Al-Sahafah al-Yasariyah fi Misr* (Beirut: Dar al-Tali'ah, 1974), pp. 114–15.

14. Najiwah Hussein Ahmed Khalil, "Al-Quadhiyah al-Ijtima'iah fi al-Sahafah al-Misriyah: Munthu Intiha' al-Harb al-'Alimiyah al-Thaniyah Hatta Qiam Thawrat Yolyo 1952" (Ph.D. dissertation, College of Communications, Cairo University, 1986), pp. 379–89.

15. *Al-Fajr al-Jadeed* (Cairo), January 11, 19, 30, February 27, April 17, 1946.

16. Sadiq Sa'ad, *Mushkilat al-Fallah* (Cairo: Dar al-Qarn al-'Ashreen, 1945), pp. 4, 27–61.

17. Tariq al-Bushri, *Al-Harakah al-Siyasiyah fi Misr, 1945–1952* (Cairo: Al-Hai'ah al-Misriyah al-'Amah lil Kitab, 1972), p. 78.

18. Ibid., pp. 77–78.

19. *Al-Dhamir* (Cairo), November 11, 1945.

20. *Al-Katib* (Cairo) 12, no. 133 (April 1972): 146.

21. Sa'ad, *Safahat min al-Yasar al-Misrik fi a'qab al-Harb al-'Alamiyah al-Thaniyah,* p. 54.

22. Interview with Abu Seif Youssef by Tareq Y. Ismael, Cairo, October 8, 1986.

23. Interview with Sadiq Sa'ad by Tareq Y. Ismael, Cairo, December 24, 1986.

24. Ibid.

25. Interview with Abu Seif Youssef by Tareq Y. Ismael, Cairo, November 18, 1986.

26. Interview with Helmi Yassin by Tareq Y. Ismael, Cairo, November 22, 1986.

27. Interview with Mohammed Sayyid Ahmed by Tareq Y. Ismael, Cairo, December 18, 1984.

28. Interview with Sa'ad Zahran by Tareq Y. Ismael, Cairo, December 20, 1984.

29. Shuhdi 'Atiyah al-Shafi'e and Mohammed 'Abd al-Ma'boud al-Gibayli, *Ahdafuna al-Wataniyah* (Cairo: Al-Risalah Press, 1945), preface.

30. Ibid., pp. 8–10.

31. Ibid., p. 13.

32. Ibid., pp. 41–43.

33. Ibid., pp. 46–48.

34. Ibid., pp. 49–52.

35. Ibid., pp. 55–58.

36. Ibid., pp. 59–76.

37. *Al-Jamahir* (Cairo), April 7, 1947.

38. Ibid., April 21, 1947.

39. Ibid., April 28, 1947.

40. Interview with Henri Curiel by Rifa'at El-Sa'id, Paris, November 1–7, 1968.

41. Interview with Henri Curiel by Rifa'at El-Sa'id, Paris, January 24, 1970.

42. Ibid.

43. Gilles Perrault, *A Man Apart: The Life of Henri Curiel,* trans. Bob Cummings (London: Zed, 1987), p. 94.

44. Interview with Henri Curiel by Tareq Y. Ismael, Paris, December 18, 1969.

45. Interview with Sayyid Sulaiman Refae'i by Rifa'at El-Sa'id, Cairo, January 12, 1976.

46. Ibid.

47. After leaving prison in 1927, Husni al-'Arabi advocated the withdrawal of the Egyptian Communist party from the Comintern and its development as a legal political party operating in the open political forum. The party expelled him for this rejection of revolutionary principles, and he was not active again in political organizing until he joined Itihad Sho'ub wadi al-Nil.

48. Interview with 'Abd al-Fatah al-Sharqawi by Rifa'at El-Sa'id, Cairo, November 13, 1975.

49. Quoted in al-Bushri, *al-Harakah al-Siyasiyah fi Misr, 1945–1952,* p. 84.

50. Ibid., pp. 88–89.

51. Ibid., p. 100.

52. Sa'ad Zahran, *Fi Usul al-Siyasah al-Misriyah* (Cairo: Dar al-Mustaqbal al-'Arabi, 1985), pp. 128–29.

53. Shuhdi 'Atiyah al-Shafi'e, *Tatawor al-Harakah al-Wataniyah al-Misriyah, 1882–1956* (Cairo: Al-Dar al-Misriyah, 1957), p. 104.

54. Ibid., p. 108.

55. Interview with Sayyid Sulaiman Rifa'ie by Rifa'at El-Sa'id, Cairo, January 12, 1976.

56. Interview with Hussein Kamal al-Din, by Rifa'at El-Sa'id, Alexandria, February 12, 1976.

57. Ibid.; interviews with Rifa'ie and Mohammed Shatta, Cairo, February 4, 1976, and Mohammed Youssef al-Gindi, Cairo, February 4, 1976; both by Rifa'at El-Sa'id.

58. *Al-Jamahir* (Cairo), July 7, 1947.

59. Ibid., September 21, 1947.

60. Interview with Henri Curiel by Rifaʻat El-Saʻid, Paris, April 2, 1973.

61. Interview with Mohammed Sayyid Ahmed by Rifaʻat El-Saʻid, Cairo, June 16, 1976.

62. Interview with Saʻad Zahran by Tareq Y. Ismael, Cairo, December 28, 1984.

63. Interview with Mohammed Sayyid Ahmed by Rifaʻat El-Saʻid, Cairo, June 16, 1976.

64. Interview with Tareq Y. Ismael, Cairo, December 30, 1984.

65. Circular, October 14, 1948, in the files of Rifaʻat El-Saʻid.

66. Interview with Fuad ʻAbd al-Halim by Rifaʻat El-Saʻid, Cairo, December 27, 1975.

67. Interview with Mohammed Youssef al-Gundi by Rifaʻat El-Saʻid, Cairo, February 4, 1976.

68. Interview with Michele Kamil by Rifaʻat El-Saʻid, Beirut, May 26, 1975.

69. Ibid.

70. Interview with Ahmed Nabil al-Hilali by Rifaʻat El-Saʻid, Cairo, June 3, 1975.

71. *Al-Munadahmah al-Shuyoʻiyah al-Misriyah*, no. 16, undated, in the files of Rifaʻat El-Saʻid.

72. Interview with Mohammed Sayyid Ahmed by Rifaʻat El-Saʻid, Cairo, June 16, 1976.

73. Interview with Michele Kamil by Rifaʻat El-Saʻid, Beirut, May 26, 1975.

74. Interview with Nicola Ghazis by Rifaʻat El-Saʻid, Athens, March 10, 1976.

75. *Al-Tandhim*, October 22, 1949, in the files of Rifaʻat El-Saʻid.

76. Ibid., no. 3, December 5, 1949, in the files of Rifaʻat El-Saʻid.

77. *Al-Kader al-Shuyoʻie*, no. 12, January 20, 1950, in the files of Rifaʻat El-Saʻid.

78. Ibid., no. 11, January 11, 1950.

4. CHANGES IN THE 1950s

1. Walter Lacqueur, *Communism and Nationalism in the Middle East* (New York: Praeger, 1956), p. 46.

2. *Al-Bashir*, June 17, 1950.

3. *Al-Malayeen*, October 14, 1951.

4. Tariq al-Bushri, *Al-Harakah al-Siyasiyah fi Misr, 1945–1952* (Cairo: Al-Haiʼah al-Misriyah alʻAmah lil Kitab, 1972), pp. 423–24.

5. *Al-Ahram*, August 10, 1952.

6. *Al-Wagib*, January 1, 1953.

7. Ibid.

8. Ahmed Hamroosh, *Qisat Thawrat 23 Yolyo*, Vol. 4, *Shuhod Thawrat Yolyo* (Beirut: Al-Muʼasasah al-ʻArabiyah lil Dirasat wa al-Nashir, 1977), pp. 51–55, 471–83, 144–61, 167–72, 270–73.

9. Interview with Khalid Muhiyi al-Din, by Rifaʻat al-Saʻid, Cairo, March 23, 1980.

10. Interview with Henri Curiel by Rifaʻat al-Saʻid, Paris, February 25, 1970.

11. *Al-Malayeen*, June 10, 1951.

12. Ibid., June 17, 24, 1951.

13. File of the Case 264 High Military Court, 1954 (Cairo), p. 707.

14. *A Call for Students*, leaflet signed by Haditu-Alexandria, copy in possession of Rifaʻat El-Saʻid.

15. Interview with Mubarak 'Abdu Fadhil by Rifa'at El-Sa'id, Cairo, January 22, 1982.

16. Military Court case 80, 1954, al-Darb al-Ahmar, No. 264, p. 64, and *al-Tali'ah* 10, no. 9 (June 23, 1954).

17. Announcement in the files of Rifa'at El-Sa'id.

18. Interview with Farouk 'Abu Issa by Tareq Y. Ismael, Cairo, December 18, 1986.

19. *Al-Kader,* no. 5, November 1953, in the files of Rifa'at El-Sa'id.

20. *al-Tali'ah,* July 7, 1954.

21. Letter from Ahmed 'Ali Khadhir to Rifa'at El-Sa'id, September 26, 1979, in the files of Rifa'at El-Sa'id.

22. *Barnamij al-Hizb al-Shuyo'ie al-Misri Mukdam Min Nawat al-Hizb,* pamphlet in the files of Rifa'at El-Sa'id.

23. Leaflet in file case 724, High Military Court, 1952, p. 6.

24. File of case 50, High Military Court, 1954, p. 166.

25. The outline of the program in the files of Rifa'at El-Sa'id.

26. M. S. Agwani, *Communism in the Arab East* (London: Asia Publishing House, 1969), p. 79.

27. Leaflet of the Central Committee of the Unified Communist Party, November 1955, in the files of Rifa'at El-Sa'id.

28. Statement to the Egyptian People, April 1956, leaflet in the files of Rifa'at El-Sa'id.

29. Ahmed al-Rifa'i and 'Abd al-Mon'eim Shatlah, *Ayam al-Intisar* (Cairo: Dar al-Demoqratiyah al-Jadihda, 1957), p. 34.

30. Interview with Sadiq Sa'ad by Tareq Y. Ismael, Cairo, December 23, 1986.

31. *"Al-Taktik,"* summarized in File Case 1091, Military High Court, 1954, p. 293.

32. *Al-Tariq,* July 24, 1950, ibid., p., 279.

33. Interview with Helmi Yassin by Rifa'at El-Sa'id, Cairo, January 1, 1983.

34. Pamphlet of the Workers' Vanguard, original copy in the possession of Rifa'at El-Sa'id.

35. *Al-Muqawamah al-Sha'biyah,* published by the Workers' Vanguard, December 1, 1953, File Case 1091, 1954, High Military Court, p. 179.

36. Leaflet, *Ila al-Sha'ab al-Misri al-Basil,* August 5, 1956, in the files of Rifa'at El-Sa'id.

37. "Barnamij al-Hizb al-Shuyo'ie al-Misri," in *Rose al-Yussef* (Cairo), April 17, 1951. The program as published was subject to deletions to meet censorship regulations.

38. Interview with Fuad Morsi by Tareq Y. Ismael, Cairo, December 18, 1984.

39. *Rayat al-Sha'ab* (Cairo) no. 1, September 4, 1950.

40. No. 22, July 1952, File Case 348, 1952, High Military Court, p. 639.

41. *Al-Fashiyah 'Isabah wa Tadhlil Rakhis* (Cairo: Al-Hizb al-Shuyo'ie al-Misri, 1952), p. 38, a party pamphlet in the files of Rifa'at El-Sa'id.

42. No. 144, File Case 150, 1956, High Military Court.

5. THE COMMUNIST MOVEMENT AND NASSERISM

1. *Al-Fajr al-Jadeed,* May 16, 1945.

2. Ibid., September 16, 1945.

3. Ibid., October 1, 1945.

4. Shuhdi 'Atiyah al-Shafi'e and Mohammed 'Abd al-Ma'boud al-Gibayli, *Ahdafuna al-Wataniyah* (Cairo: Al-Risalah Press, 1945), pp. 29, 106.

5. Ibid., pp. 35–36.

6. Ibid., pp. 32–34.

7. Ibid., pp. 39–40.

8. *Al-Malayeen*, July 1, 1951.

9. *Al-Hisab*, April 10, 1925.

10. *Al-Fajr al-Jadeed*, November 1, 1945.

11. Ibid., vol. 13 (n.d.).

12. Ibid., February 20, 1946.

13. *Al-Dhamir*, November 17, 1945.

14. 'Abdel 'Azim Ramadhan, *Al-Fikr al-Thawri fi Misr Qabl Thawrat 23 Yulyu* (Cairo: Madbouli Library, 1981), p. 134.

15. Ibid., p. 149.

16. Ibid., pp. 150–51.

17. *Al-Dhamir*, October 17, 1945.

18. Ibid., October 24, 1945.

19. Al-Shafi'e and al-Gibayli, *Ahdafuna al-Wataniyah*, pp. 36–38.

20. 'Abdel Kader Yassin, "Al-Rabitah, al-Israeliyah li Mukafahat al-Sihyoniyah," *Shu'un Falastinia* 36 (August 1974): 105–21.

21. *Al-Jamahir*, May 5, 1947.

22. *Sawt al-Umma*, October 16, 1946, p. 3.

23. *Al-Jamahir*, May 5, 1947.

24. *Bayan al-Rabitah al-Israeliyah li Mukafahat al-Sihyoniyah* (Cairo: Al-Shabaksky Printing, 1947), p. 10.

25. Ibid., p. 12.

26. Ibid., pp. 9–11.

27. Ibid., p. 14.

28. The Makkabi was a Jewish organization of athletic teams and literary and artistic groups.

29. *Al-Jamahir*, April 18, 1947.

30. *Sawt al-Umma*, April 20, 1947.

31. Ibid., April 26, 1947.

32. Ibid., April 28, 1947.

33. *Al-Jamahir*, April 28, 1948, in Tariq al-Bushri, *Al-Harakah al-Siyasiyah fi Misr, 1945–1952* (Cairo: Al-Hai'ah al-Misriyah al-'Amah lil Kitab, 1972), p. 261.

34. *Al-Jamahir*, May 5, 1947.

35. Ibid., May 12, 1947.

36. Ibid., June 2, 1947.

37. Ibid., May 19, 1947.

38. Ibid., May 5, 1947.

39. Ibid., May 26, 1947.

40. Ibid., October 19, 1947.

41. Ibid., November 22, 1947.

42. Ibid., December 7, 1947.

43. Ibid., December 21, 1947.

44. *Al-Malayeen*, June 24, 1951.

45. Ibid., date not available.

46. *Al-Misri*, March 2, 1948.

47. Ibid., April 1, 1948.

48. *Al-Ahram*, March 5, 1947.

6. DISSOLUTION OF THE EGYPTIAN COMMUNIST MOVEMENT

1. Interview with Sa'ad Rahmi by Rifa'at El-Sa'id, Cairo, November 19, 1983.
2. Mubarak 'Abdu, handwritten manuscript, "History of the Egyptian Communist Movement," in the files of Rifa'at El-Sa'id.
3. Interview with Fakhri Labib by Rifa'at El-Sa'id, Cairo, April 1, 1983.
4. V. A. Lutskevich, *Nasser ma Ma'rakat al-Istiklal al-Iqtisadi,* trans. Selwa Abu Si'dah and Mohammed Wassil Bahr (Beirut: Dar al-Kalima, 1980), p. 86.
5. Minutes of the meeting of the Tripartite Coordination Committee, published by the Unified party, January 1957.
6. Ibid.
7. Ibid.
8. *ONITA* (Rome), May 14, 1957.
9. A leaflet entitled *Bayan ila al-Sha'ab,* dated February 1957, in the files of Rifa'at El-Sa'id.
10. Interview with Ahmed al-Rifa'i by Rifa'at El-Sa'id, Aden, April 22, 1983.
11. Interview with Sa'ad Rahmi by Rifa'at El-Sa'id, Cairo, November 19, 1983.
12. Interview with Anwar Ibrahim by Rifa'at El-Sa'id, Cairo, January 15, 1985.
13. In the files of Rifa'at El-Sa'id.
14. Interview with Ahmed al-Rifa'i by Rifa'at El-Sa'id, Cairo, April 22, 1983.
15. Interview with Sa'ad Rahmi by Rifa'at El-Sa'id, Cairo, November 19, 1983.
16. Interview with Mohammed 'Ali 'Amir, by Rifa'at El-Sa'id, Cairo, May 2, 1983.
17. *Hayat al-Hizb,* no. 1, March 22, 1958.
18. Interview with Fakhri Labib by Rifa'at El-Sa'id, Cairo, April 1, 1983.
19. Interview with Helmi Yassin by Rifa'at El-Sa'id, Cairo, February 8, 1986.
20. Interview with Fawzi Habashi by Rifa'at El-Sa'id, Cairo, May 17, 1983.
21. In the files of Rifa'at El-Sa'id.
22. Ibid.
23. Interview with Shahata al-Nashar by Rifa'at El-Sa'id, Cairo, June 9, 1983.
24. Interview with Gamal al-Sharqawi by Rifa'at El-Sa'id, Cairo, January 16, 1985.
25. *Haqieq al-Azzima alati Ta'radha Laha Hizbuna,* in the files of Rifa'at El-Sa'id.
26. Interview with Ahmed al-Rifa'i by Rifa'at El-Sa'id, Cairo, April 22, 1983.
27. Interview with Fakhri Labib by Rifa'at El-Sa'id, Cairo, April 1, 1983.
28. Ahmed Hamroosh, *Mujtama' Gamal 'Abd al-Nasser* (Beirut: al-Mu'asasah al-'Arabiyah lil Dirasat wa al-Nashir, 1978), p. 240.
29. Interview with Ahmed al-Rifa'i by Rifa'at El-Sa'id, Cairo, April 22, 1983.
30. See Hamroosh, *Mujtama' Gamal 'Abd al-Nasser,* p. 245.
31. Interview with Salih Mudrik by Rifa'at El-Sa'id, Alexandria, January 27, 1985.
32. Copy of the telegram in the files of Rifa'at El-Sa'id.
33. Interview with Fakhri Labib by Rifa'at El-Sa'id, Cairo, April 1, 1983.
34. Interview with Sa'ad Rahmi by Rifa'at El-Sa'id, Cairo, November 19, 1982.
35. Interview with Fuad Morsi by Tareq Y. Ismael, Cairo, December 18, 1984.

7. THE THIRD MOVEMENT, 1975–1988

1. Interview with Sha'rawi Jum'a by Tareq Y. Ismael, Cairo, May 18, 1987; also see Gamal Salim, *Al-Tandhimat al-Siriyah li Thawrat 23 Yolyo fi 'Ahd Gamal 'Abd al-Nasser* (Cairo: Madbouli, 1982), pp. 82–87.

2. Sha'rawi Jum'a tells the details of the story of Nasser's secret party, *Al-Mawqif al-'Arabi* 9, no. 65 (September 1985): 56–57.

3. Interview with Abu Sayf Youssef by Tareq Y. Ismael, Cairo, December 18, 1985.

4. Siton *'Aman Min Nidhal al-Shuyo'ieen al-Misrieen* (Beirut: Egyptian Communist Party, 1980), p. 49.

5. Ibid., pp. 35–36.

6. *Al-Wa'ie,* no. 11, May 1979 (internal party bulletin, circulated to party members only).

7. See Appendix C for the full text of report.

8. *Al-Intisar,* no. 10, January 1975.

9. Ibid.

10. Ibid., no. 13, June 1975.

11. Ibid., no. 10, January 1975.

12. Siton *'Aman Min Nidhal al-Shuyo'ieen al-Misrieen,* pp. 73–75.

13. Ibid., pp. 68–69.

14. Ibid., p. 71.

15. Ibid., pp. 89–115.

16. Ibid., p. 111.

17. *Al-Safir* (Beirut), November 17, 1980.

18. *Barnamij al-Hizb al-Shou'ie al-Misri: Min Wathieq al-Mu'tamar al-A'wal* (Beirut: Dar Ibn Khaldun, 1981), pp. 6–8.

19. Ibid., pp. 7–9.

20. *Barnamij al-Hizb al-Shou'ie al-Misri,* pp. 209–26.

21. Ibid., pp. 227–65.

22. Ibid., pp. 240–41.

23. Ibid., p. 281.

24. *Al-Yasar al-'Arabi* (Paris), no. 55, June 1983.

25. *Information Bulletin,* No. 13, 1983 (published in Toronto).

26. *World Marxist Review* 30 (February 1987): 95–96.

27. *Nashrah Ikhbariyah* 14, no. 98 (1987): 54–64.

28. *Taqrir 'an Intikhabat al-Naqabat al-'Umaliyah* (Cairo: Central Bureau of Egyptian Workers' Unions, Egyptian Communist Party, 1988).

29. Politbureau of the Egyptian Communist Party, *Al-Awdha' al-Rahina wa Mahamuna* (Cairo: 1988), p. 1.

30. Ibid., pp. 1–2.

31. Ibid., pp. 5–7.

32. Ibid., p. 8.

33. Ibid., p. 19.

34. This party has no affiliation with the party of the same name in 1957.

35. *Al-Shuyo'ie al-Misri,* September 1975, pp. 4–5.

36. Ibid.

INDEX

THE COMMUNIST MOVEMENT IN EGYPT

was composed in 10 on 12 Times Roman on a Linotron 202,
with display type set in Helvetica Bold,
by Partners Composition;
printed by sheet-fed offset on 50-pound, acid-free Glatfelter Natural Hi-Bulk,
Smythe-sewn and bound over binder's boards in Holliston Roxite B,
with dust jackets printed in two colors and laminated
by Braun-Brumfield, Inc.;
designed by Shawn Lewis,
and published by

SYRACUSE UNIVERSITY PRESS
SYRACUSE, NEW YORK 13244-5160